KITEWORKS

Explorations in Kite Building & Flying

KITEWORKS
Explorations in Kite Building & Flying

MAXWELL EDEN

 Sterling Publishing Co., Inc.   New York

Edited by Laurel Ornitz
Black-and-white and color illustrations by Alan Radom
Endpapers by Joe Muti
Photographs in "Construction" chapter by Alyce Parseghian

Library of Congress Cataloging-in-Publication Data

Eden, Maxwell.
    Kiteworks : explorations in kite building & flying / Maxwell Eden.
        p.   cm.
    Includes index.
    ISBN 0-8069-6712-9
    1. Kites. I. Title.
  TL759.E34 1989
  629.133′32—dc20   89-11372
                                            CIP

10 9 8 7 6 5 4

First paperback edition published in 1991 by
Sterling Publishing Company, Inc.
387 Park Avenue South, New York, N.Y. 10016
© 1989 by Maxwell Eden
Distributed in Canada by Sterling Publishing
℅ Canadian Manda Group, P.O. Box 920, Station U
Toronto, Ontario, Canada M8Z 5P9
Distributed in Great Britain and Europe by Cassell PLC
Villiers House, 41/47 Strand, London WC2N 5JE, England
Distributed in Australia by Capricorn Ltd.
P.O. Box 665, Lane Cove, NSW 2066
Manufactured in the United States of America
All rights reserved

Sterling ISBN 0-8069-6712-9   Trade
               0-8069-6713-7   Paper

Contents

APPENDICES   *275–287*

Color sections following pages 32, 96, and 192

For my mother, Adele, who taught me
that the sky's the limit.

Preface

How and why an event happens has always intrigued me as much as the event itself, if not more. So, here's how I came to write this book.

It was a dismal grey northeastern day in late November, and not particularly inviting weather for flying kites. Nevertheless, I packed my pinstripe delta that morning and drove several miles to a wooded park that had a large field. When I arrived at the upwind edge of the field, all was strangely quiet. The touch football games that usually monopolized the park this time of year were conspicuously absent. No doubt the combination of the cold weather and the preparations for the imminent annual turkey fete were keeping people at home that day. I began unrolling the kite, which was as drab as the day I had chosen to fly it.

A week earlier, when I was eager to build this kite, the yards of colored ripstop nylon I had ordered for the sail were delayed in the mail, so I decided extreme measures were necessary. I went to my dresser drawer and removed four new Brooks Brothers white cotton button-down shirts with grey pinstripes. I laid them out on a worktable near the sewing machine and sacrificed them. I had no remorse. I had my sail material.

The subject of kites had entered my life the previous July, at a surprise party for my thirtieth birthday. A friend had given me a long tube containing a kite. At the time I thought: What an odd gift for an adult. I put the kite away and forgot about it until one Sunday morning several weeks later when I had an itch to be outdoors but nothing special to do until I remembered the kite. So, with the cardboard tube slung over my shoulder like a quiver, I rode my bike to a nearby vacant parking lot.

A wind from the north blew steadily. I opened the tube, removed the kite, and put it together. In an instant, the kite caught me off-guard. It leapt from my hand, tugging and pulling until it wrestled free. As I stood there holding the line and watching the kite soar upwards, a totally unanticipated euphoria overcame me. I was elated and puzzled. I felt in balance, simultaneously grounded and elevated. Enthralled with what I had thought was merely a child's toy, I lost all track of time and flew the kite till sunset. I pedalled home that evening, feeling weightless, harmoniously sandwiched between *yin* and *yang*, knowing there was more to kite flying than met the casual eye.

I flew this kite whenever I could. I kept it in the trunk of my car and brought it to work with me. I took long lunch breaks alone. Who would understand my aerial trysts?

Now it was nearly Thanksgiving. It didn't matter that the skies remained grey and the field empty. I was occupied with assembling my pinstripe delta. With a gentle breeze at my back, I released the kite to its fate. I had never liked those shirts and wished them well in their new incarnation. The kite pulled away from me, taking line from my reel in fluid motion. Eventually, my delta found a smooth and steady airstream about 1,000 feet up and fixed itself at a high angle of flight. Occasionally fluttering but mostly still, my handiwork seemed painted on an expansive overcast canvas.

After a while, my white triangle in the sky began to shimmer like a mirage in the desert. At first I thought the sun was trying to break through the cloud cover, but it wasn't. When the shimmering ceased, the kite appeared up close, as if I were peering at it through powerful binoculars. Instead of the solid object it had been a moment ago, my erstwhile shirts had become what I can only describe as a transparent triangular window.

I rubbed my eyes. It was still there. A three-dimensional hole, like the side of a pyramid, had opened up in the sky. Beyond the window, I saw a landscape of geometric shapes and forms, familiar yet curiously unidentifiable. My kite had become a lens—an acute focal point balanced or caught be-

Illus. 1. The page in Fuller's Synergetics *that inspired me to write this book—I'm pointing to a tetrahedron.*

tween realities. Was I looking in or out? Was there anyone looking back? The possibilities were staggering.

The window in the sky remained, and the geometric objects beyond, whatever they were, spun about in slow motion. I stood there for a long time until it began to make sense.

The sky had become a blank envelope waiting for both an address and sufficient postage. My kite became a surreal stamp—the kind minted only in dreams—and a realm beyond the frontier became the address. As if this were not enough, the kite itself seemed to breathe in cadence with my own breath.

Just as the background shapes and forms began to take on definition, the shimmering effect returned and the scene dissolved as in a dream. I squinted but the magic window that had appeared at arm's length was now far away at the end of my kite line and had turned back into ordinary Oxford cloth. After several minutes, I accepted that the phenomenon had ended. I packed up my kite and rode off across the field. A wide gap broke in the clouds and a full moon lit the way home.

Although I enjoyed flying kites during the rest of that year, nothing extraordinary happened. I forgot about kites and left for California to seek new challenges.

San Francisco, ten years later: I was sitting in the living room of an apartment in the Fillmore district when, for no apparent reason, someone handed me a hefty-sized book called *Synergetics: Explorations in the Geometry of Thinking*[1] by R. Buckminster Fuller. I had heard Fuller's name intermittently over the years in conjunction with his architectural invention of the geodesic dome. As I held the book, it occurred

to me that the last time I had seen his name in print was in the obituary column.

I flipped open to a page randomly and there, staring back at me, were shapes and forms—familiar geometric patterns—I had nearly made out in a vision years ago. I thumbed through more pages. There were triangles, tetrahedrons, and elongated diamonds, as well as combinations of forms ranging from simple to complex. I yelled: *This guy's drawings are kites!*

The scope of Fuller's thought was astounding. He was a transcendentalist, sorcerer, inventor, philosopher, poet, and mathematician. The essence of *Synergetics*, to paraphrase Fuller, is this: There's no way of predicting the purpose or behavior of the whole by examining its parts individually.

In turn, by examining the separate elements of a kite, there's no way to predict one of its collective effects—the pleasure it can bring to a kite flier. That's synergy.

Fuller says that the four-sided polyhedron, the tetrahedron, is the basic structural unit of the physical universe. It occurs conceptually, independent of events and independent of relative size—the great pyramids of Giza and my triangular pinstripe delta kite.

I finally had a theory, if not the explanation, of my strange experience in the park years ago. Although I didn't know why it happened, I did know that my kite had become a triangular window into the structure of reality. I was inspired, and decided to write this book.

[1]Published by Macmillan Publishing Co., Inc., 1979.

Introduction

This book is about the experience of building and flying kites. I wrote it for all kite fliers; whether or not they have ever flown a kite is unimportant.

The book includes instructions for making a collection of kites acquired from kite builders around the world. There are inexpensive, simple-to-make projects—such as origami flying-bug and McDonald's coffee-cup kites—as well as more challenging, award-winning, architecturally dazzling flying sculptures. My idea was to present an array of exciting kites that would compel readers to then investigate and discover the magic of kiting for themselves.

It's been said that if you truly comprehend the nature of a single object, you have discovered the universe. It turns out that kites can be a glorious means of coming to that understanding.

Though much of the material in the book came directly from experts, I assumed nothing worked as well as touted until I tried it myself. I selected this kite collection mainly according to the following criteria: simplicity, ingenuity, and craftsmanship. All the kites featured here are reliable fliers, all the tips work, all the accessories are worth looking into, and all the construction ideas have been tested.

In addition to the specific instructions for making each kite and the general information on materials and construction, there are kite lore and kite gossip as well as stories about inventors, expanding the subject of kites into the realms of history, science, and philosophy.

* * *

Having totally immersed myself within this book during its conception, research, and writing, I began to feel that it was my sanctuary, my house. Now that it's complete, I invite you inside. This house has many different windows and every kite tells a story.

Illus. 2. World's largest kite. (Photo by Valerie Govig.)

BEFORE YOU BEGIN

1
Anatomy of a Kite

A kite is a heavier-than-air tethered aircraft kept aloft in a perpetual stall by the wind.

A kite possesses three essential characteristics:

- a structure designed to gain lift from the wind,
- a flying line (tether) that keeps the kite from blowing away, and
- a bridle to direct the face of the kite at the proper angle to the wind for lift.

A bridle consists of a series of two or more lines attached directly to the kite. The bridle lines are connected to each other and then to the tether. The primary advantage of a bridle system is that the tow point can easily be adjusted for prevailing wind conditions. Some kite designs do away with bridles altogether by having a single-line tether connected directly to a fixed fulcrum along the mast or on a keel.

Illus. 3 shows the basic generic kite types. In Illus. 4–6 you can see how the design of a kite has influenced its nomenclature.

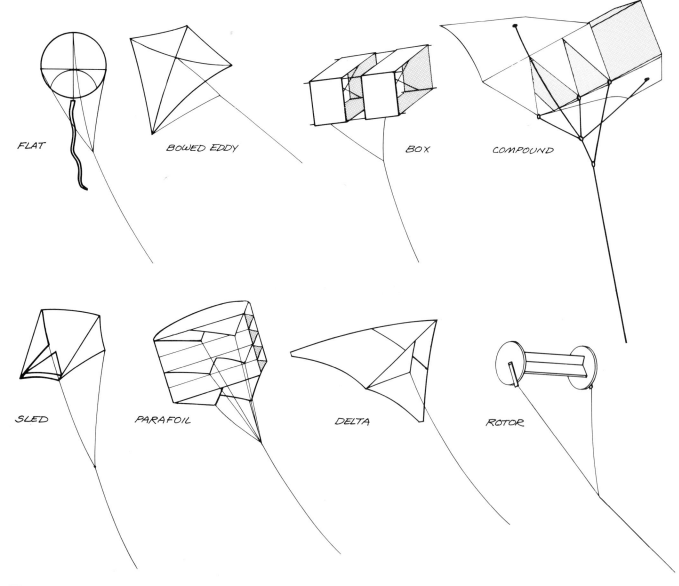

FLAT   BOWED EDDY   BOX   COMPOUND

SLED   PARAFOIL   DELTA   ROTOR

Illus. 3. Generic kite types.

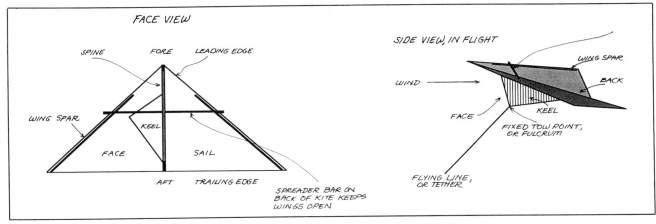

Illus. 4. The delta.

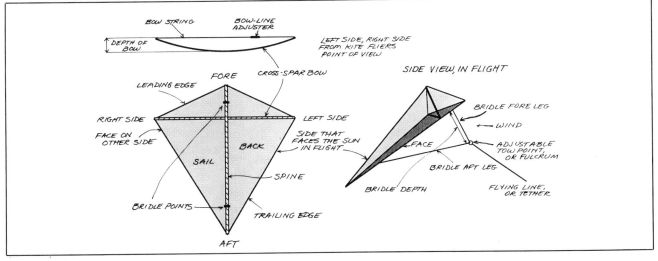

Illus. 5. The Eddy.

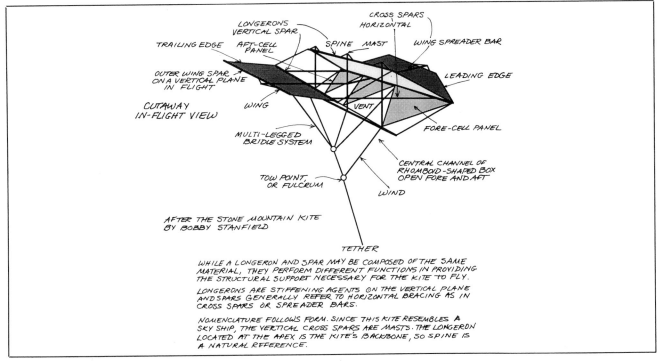

Illus. 6. The compound.

2
Kite Flying Basics

Real Kiters Don't Run Upwind

Take the time now to understand the basics of flying kites so that you can enjoy kite flying later.

The idea of running with a kite has for years been romanticized in books, movies, and other media. Unless you want the exercise, running is not the way to launch a kite. Remember to wear gloves with all hard-pulling kites and to fly in open areas.

1. Beginners may opt for a high start launch for two reasons: It's easier—and while the air may be still on the ground, steady winds capable of flying a kite may be just 100 feet up. Have a friend stand about 100 feet downwind with the kite. Your assistant should be facing you while gently holding the kite. Place some tension on the flying line. With a steady breeze behind you, begin tugging on the flying line and the kite will rise upwards (Illus. 7). You may also self-launch the kite by letting it fly from your hand as it takes line out (Illus. 8).

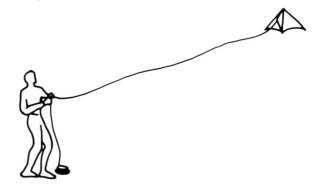

Illus. 8

2. If your kite goes into a power dive, don't panic or pull on the line. Don't drop the reel as it may spin and travel out of control and cause injury. Simply allowing the flying line to go slack will usually right the kite in midair (Illus. 9).

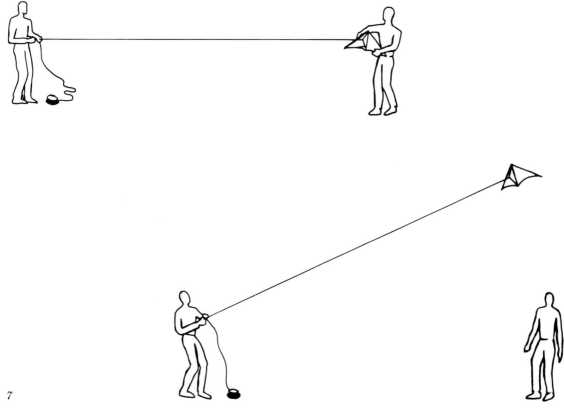

Illus. 7

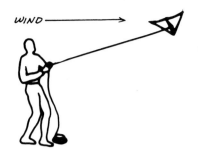

WIND ⟶

Illus. 9

3. To pull in a hard-pulling kite, have a friend at your back taking up the slack line. Walk the stubborn flier down by pulling in the flying line, hand over hand (Illus. 10). Wear gloves.

5. When two kite lines cross, pulling causes friction that will often cut one or both lines (Illus. 12). Good-bye kites.

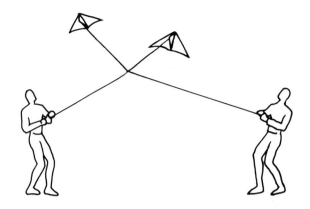

Illus. 12

6. Instead of pulling, both kite fliers should walk towards one another until their lines uncross as they pass each other (Illus. 13). This is also a good way to make new friends.

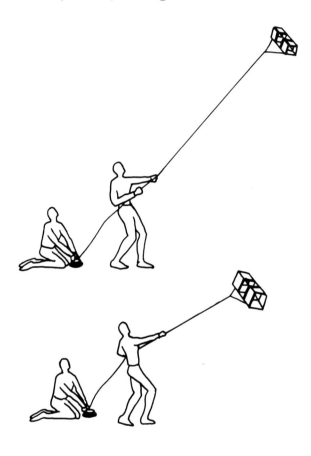

Illus. 10

4. Use a pull-down reel to bring down a hard-pulling kite. Place the pulley over the flying line and walk the kite down. Have a friend reel in the flying line under some tension (Illus. 11).

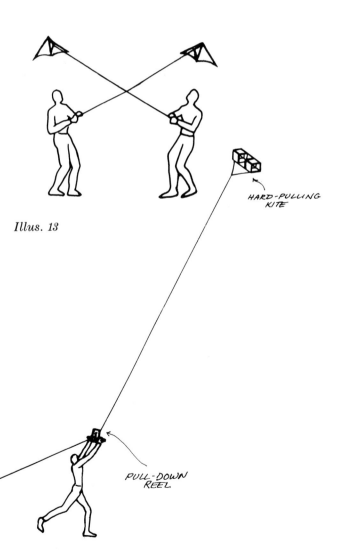

Illus. 13

HARD-PULLING KITE

PULL-DOWN REEL

Illus. 11

3

Aerodynamics

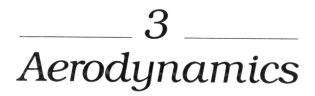

Kites are heavier-than-air flying structures controlled by three main forces: *lift*, *gravity*, and *drag*.

In addition to lifting the weight of the kite upwards, the force of the wind must overcome the resistance of the air to the forward motion of the kite. This is what is known as drag. The efficiency of a kite is rated by its L/D (lift to drag) ratio. A low L/D ratio results in a kite flying low on the horizon. Conversely, a kite with a high L/D ratio will fly well above the horizon. Delta kites as a rule have high L/D ratios. It is not uncommon for one to rise directly overhead at a 90° angle to the kite flier.

As shown in Illus. 14, (A) lift, (B) gravity, and (C) drag converge to form (D) the center of pressure. The kite's (E) angle of attack—the amount of sail area exposed to the wind—is regulated at the tow point, which should be adjusted to line up with the center of pressure. The precise tow point is the kite's balance point, or fulcrum.

The flying line maintains constant pressure against the sail, which causes lift. (See Illus. 15.) The center

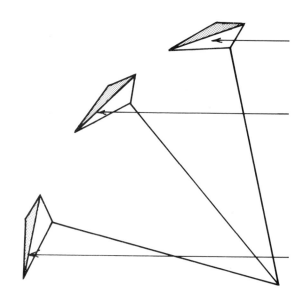

Illus. 15

of pressure shifts forward as the kite levels out in flight.

Up high in a steady airstream, a kite moves neither forward nor backward, seemingly indifferent and unaffected by gravity. How can this be? In simplest terms, this is possible because the *lifting force of the wind* overcomes the downwards pull of *gravity*. There is, however, more to this airworthy tale. Lift has a cast of supporting players, namely *Newton's third law of motion*, *Bernoulli's Principle*, and the rising-air twins—*thermal* and *updraft*.

The Lost Case of the Past Catching Up with the Future

London, 1809[1]. The study of the masterfully deductive sleuth, Sherlock Holmes. With him is his friend and associate, Dr. John H. Watson.

"I say, this is exciting news," Dr. Watson says, reading the *London Times*.

Holmes is busy tuning his violin.

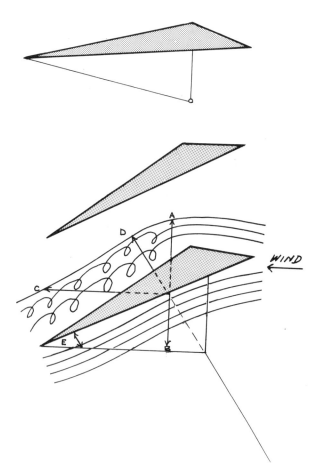

Illus. 14

"The article says Sir George has discovered . . ."

"Sir George?" Holmes tries to place the name.

"Quite, yes. Sir George Cayley, the inventor chap. You know."

Holmes plucks a string and smiles, indicating that his violin is now in tune. "Yes, of course, my dear fellow."

"It appears Sir George has finally discovered the scientific principle that allows a kite to fly."

Holmes continues to fiddle around.

"Shall I go on?" Watson inquires.

Holmes nods.

"Ah, let me see," Watson says, as he scans the story. "Here it is. It seems the wind pressure on the inclined surface of a kite actually enables it to lift weight."

Holmes has taken a bow to the violin strings and tries a few notes before saying, "Hardly front page news in 1809. I would call it a case of the past catching up with the future."

Watson is puzzled by Holmes's paradoxical statement.

"Not front page news, you say. Past catching up with the future? Confound it, Holmes, what do you mean?"

Holmes puts the violin down and thoughtfully lights his pipe. "The principle in question was previously available and common knowledge among the scientific community."

Watson places the newspaper aside and walks over to the liquor cabinet to pour two glasses of sherry. He offers a refreshment to Holmes, who is more concerned with his train of thought.

"No thank you, my dear fellow. The facts are that the explanation for why a kite can fly had been discovered centuries ago. The seventeenth century to be precise."

"Hmmm. That long ago," Watson mutters to himself before adding, "I believe that era was called the Age of Reason, a time of great scientific inquiry throughout Europe."

"Correct, Watson." Holmes continues, "The one who is credited was the most influential scientist of the time."

"An Englishman, I'll wager," Watson adds.

"Correct again. In the year 1687, Sir Isaac Newton formally introduced his third law of motion, 'to every action there is an equal and opposite reaction.' "

To illustrate this law, Holmes takes a big puff on his pipe and blows the smoke straight ahead. "The smoke is repelled in the opposite direction and in direct proportion to how hard I can blow it out." To show how the wind is deflected off a surface, Holmes blows a steady stream of smoke against his palm.

"As usual, Holmes, you are the keen observer. Newton's law predated and explained Sir George's conclusion that kites fly because of the principal lift generated by the downwards deflection of the wind from the sail."

"Well put, Watson. So, you see, the news is hardly new." Holmes picks up his violin bow. "In fact, I have been considering a theory of my own. I have reason to believe that if the straight cross spar of today's common diamond-shaped kites were bowed, not unlike the bow in my hand, the result would add increased buoyancy and preclude the need for those confounded tails."

"Astonishing, Holmes. How do you do it?"

"Elementary, my dear Watson."

If Holmes could have seen further into the future, he would have, no doubt, included Swiss physicist Daniel Bernoulli in his case of the past catching up to the future. In 1738, Bernoulli published a remarkable work on fluid (air and water) motion called *Hydrodynamica* that included a scientific observation now known as *Bernoulli's Principle*. This principle laid the groundwork for the future study of aerodynamics by anticipating the efficiency of a cambered wing—the key to manned flight, which Sir George Cayley[2] undertook a century later and the Wright brothers made practical in 1903.

A Wind Tunnel

Anyone who has playfully fingered the wind outside the window of a moving car has felt the fundamental forces of aerodynamics. The airstream created by the moving car divides and flows around the stationary hand. With fingers pointed into the wind and the palm of the hand held horizontal, there is minimum lift and drag. Elevate the palm slightly above the horizontal and the deflected wind lifts the hand upwards. Further increasing the angle of the palm induces turbulence and additional drag, thereby limiting lift as the hand falls back nearly vertical towards the horizon. Though this is a rudimentary example of aerodynamics, a kite fixed in the sky above the horizon is subject to the same forces as the hand out the window.

A Breathtaking Experience

Try this simple experiment. With your thumbs positioned on top, hold an $8\frac{1}{2} \times 11''$ piece of paper along the ends on the short side. Place the edge near your lips and blow hard and steady along the top portion. If done properly, the airstream over the top will have created a vacuum of sufficient pressure to cause the paper to rise upwards.

You have just demonstrated *Bernoulli's Principle*—that the pressure of a moving gas decreases as its velocity increases. This law of aerodynamics explains why airplanes fly and sailboats sail. A cambered airplane wing is a more efficient airfoil than your paper sheet, or a kite for that matter, because the airflow is forced to move faster and farther over the top of the curved surface than across the flat bottom section. The greater the pressure exerted upwards the better form of lift. In the same fashion that gives lift to the airplane wing, a sailboat is pulled—not pushed—across the water as it tacks diagonally into the wind.

Most kites fly at an inefficient high angle of attack in a permanent stall. This is poor aerodynamic design for an airplane but essential for a kite that wants to stay put. The exception is the parafoil kite (see Chapter 38).

Illus. 16 shows an airfoil and a parafoil. The parafoil is modelled after a cambered airplane wing. Its effi-

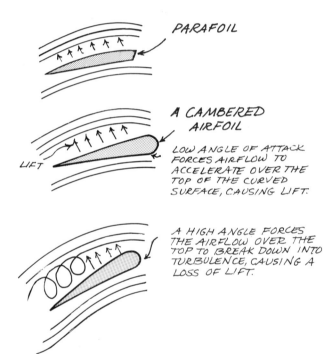

Illus. 16

cient low angle of attack utilizes Bernoulli's Principle in attaining a high L/D ratio and considerable lift with minimal drag. Most kites, however, are pushed more than they are pulled upwards, as with a cambered airfoil or the paper sheet example. Admittedly, Bernoulli's Principle plays a minor role with them, though it does contribute some lift to kites designed to adopt a low angle of attack.

More Hot Air

Kites also gain altitude by means of conditions called *updrafts* and *thermals*. Updrafts are created by the wind rushing upwards along the edges of mountains

and cliffs. Thermals are rising bubbles of hot air, often spanning miles, frequently found over large flat areas on hot days; the open desert and empty asphalt parking lots are natural breeding grounds for thermals. Hang gliders, sailplanes, soaring birds, and kites—especially deltas—can float high overhead for hours by taking advantage of these forms of air support.

The Ocean of Air

The air is an ocean complete with currents, turbulence, and resistance to objects in its path; the hand outside the car window proved this. But getting a kite airborne is just the first step. Since the kite operates in a three-dimensional space, it can rotate freely on three separate axes: the longitudinal roll, the lateral pitch, and the vertical yaw (see Illus. 17). All three must be controlled to maintain a kite's stability and prevent it from crashing.

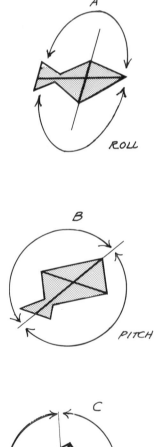

Illus. 17

Kites and Sailboats

Although kite flying is not precisely the same as sailing, both have conceptual similarities; thus, sailing can be compared with kite flying to illustrate how various kite forms maintain directional stability.

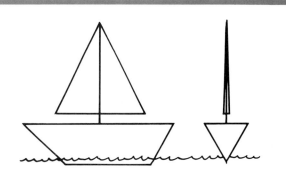

This sailboat utilizes a bow design for self-regulating buoyancy. The bow also acts as a knife cutting through the water.

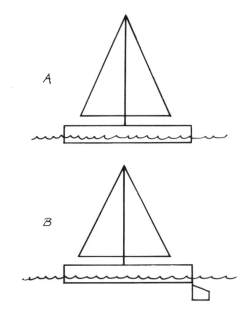

Here, A shows a raft with just a sail—and no directional stability upon the water; B shows the same raft with both a sail and rudder—and directional stability achieved.

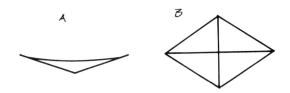

Here are two types of kites with a bowed design: (A) an Eddy and (B) a box kite. The dihedral angle automatically compensates for directional instability.

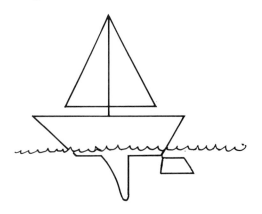

Here you can see a sailboat utilizing the stabilizing elements of bow, keel, and rudder to maintain its heading.

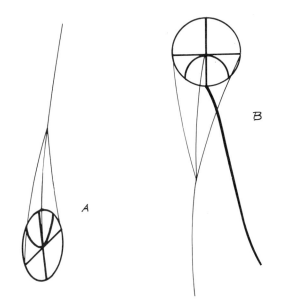

Likewise, A shows a flat- or plane-surface kite without a stabilizing tail skimming erratically on the wind; B shows the same kite with a tail balanced on the wind.

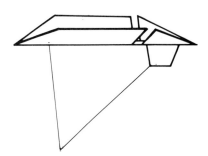

The roller kite with a rudder, shown here, is a fixed dihedral design.

How High Is My Kite?

Here's a fair method for determining your kite's approximate altitude.

Choose a day with steady winds. Begin your calculations once the kite is flying in a fixed position with minimal movement. Careful measurements will result in a more precise reading. You'll need a friend to assist you.

The following steps are shown in the diagram.

1. Fix the kite's flying line to a stationary object.
2. Sight your kite using the clinometer (A to B). Have your friend read the angle indicated by the plumb line on the protractor.
3. Have your friend stand directly underneath the flying kite. Measure the distance between you (A) and your friend (C). Measure the length of your friend's normal stride; then multiply that number by the number of steps to the kite.
4. Multiply the tangent of the angle read in step 2 by the distance AC.
5. Add your height to the number determined in step 4 for the altitude of your kite.

Trigonometry 101

Note: A missing dimension of a right triangle (one angle being 90°) may be determined if two other parts are known. In this case, the angle A and the distance AC are known to calculate the unknown altitude CB.

Note: If using a range-finder instrument, keep in mind that it provides a more accurate reading of the distance AB, not the altitude. Insert the range-finder figure to complete the calculation as given.

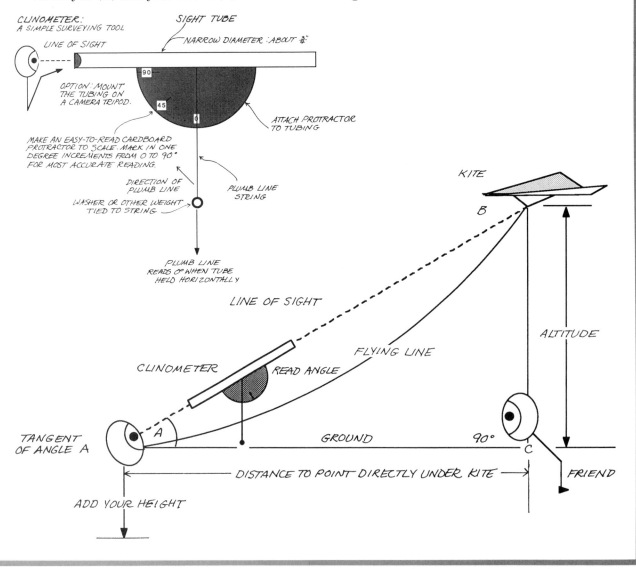

CLINOMETER:
A SIMPLE SURVEYING TOOL

LINE OF SIGHT

SIGHT TUBE

NARROW DIAMETER : ABOUT ⅜"

OPTION : MOUNT THE TUBING ON A CAMERA TRIPOD.

ATTACH PROTRACTOR TO TUBING

MAKE AN EASY-TO-READ CARDBOARD PROTRACTOR TO SCALE. MARK IN ONE DEGREE INCREMENTS FROM 0 TO 90° FOR MOST ACCURATE READING.

DIRECTION OF PLUMB LINE

PLUMB LINE STRING

WASHER OR OTHER WEIGHT TIED TO STRING

PLUMB LINE READS 0° WHEN TUBE HELD HORIZONTALLY

LINE OF SIGHT

KITE

B

ALTITUDE

CLINOMETER

READ ANGLE

FLYING LINE

TANGENT OF ANGLE A

A

GROUND

90°

C

FRIEND

DISTANCE TO POINT DIRECTLY UNDER KITE

ADD YOUR HEIGHT

Wind Speed Chart at a Glance

Beaufort's Scale

In 1806, British Navy Rear Admiral Sir Francis Beaufort developed a convenient maritime wind scale based on observing natural phenomena to aid sailors in gauging wind conditions at sea. Steady winds of 3 to 18 mph suit most kites. Stunt kites are most responsive in moderate-to-strong winds of 15 to 25 mph. Oriental tissue fighters can streak though the sky in virtually no wind at all. Learn under what conditions a particular kite flies best. Gathering micro-meteorological data is a rewarding experience. Beaufort's full nautical scale ranges from dead calm at zero to hurricane-force-12 winds. In the next column is a modified landlubber's version with ratings from zero to 6 for the kite flier.

A heavy-pulling kite caught in strong winds can be a hazardous affair. Do not attempt to fly in winds that conflict with common sense. Heavy-pulling kites can be brought down safely with the proper equipment. A pull-down reel is a useful tool (see Chapter 10).

Beaufort's #	Conditions	MPH	Land Effects
0	dead calm	0	smoke rises vertically
1	light air	1–3	smoke drifts indicating wind direction
2	light breeze	4–7	wind felt on face, leaves rustle, weather vanes spin
3	gentle breeze	8–12	leaves and small twigs in constant motion, light flags extended
4	moderate breezes	13–18	dust and loose paper blown about, small branches sway
5	fresh breeze	19–24	small trees sway, marginal-strength kite lines break
6	strong breeze	25–31	large branches move, flying is risky, experienced stunt kite fliers only

[1]To dramatize a point, I have taken some licence as the Sherlock Holmes mysteries took place in the late 1800s.
[2]In addition to introducing a fundamental principle of flight in 1809, father-of-aeronautics Cayley is also credited with the first-recorded manned glider flight. But actually Cayley only designed the craft; it was his coachman who made the historic glide in 1818.

4
The Kite Doctor

Regardless of how light and structurally symmetrical you've built your kite, you must connect your flying line to the precise spot upon which the kite balances itself against the wind. As illustrated in the section on aerodynamics, this crucial spot is the kite's tether point, or fulcrum.

Given that the kite design is sound and there is sufficient wind, the majority of flight-performance ills can be traced to an improperly positioned tether point. Additional lateral balance is gained by adjusting the depth of the bow (increasing or decreasing the dihedral angle) on bowed kites, such as the Eddy or the *rokkaku*. Excluding the small, flat maneuverable fighter kites, a proper-length tail on plane-surface kites is necessary for stability.

As the amount of wind striking the kite's face is predominately responsible for lift, placing the tow point high for high winds and lower for low winds allows the kite to make the best of the prevailing conditions. Should you wish to test the ultimate balance of your kite, fly it in heavier-than-usual winds at the end of short line. The increased airflow will either verify the symmetry of your kite or exaggerate any imbalance. A well-balanced kite trimmed for high winds, however, will fly right even in minimal wind conditions.

A visual check of the angle of flight between you and the airborne kite is a reliable indicator of its L/D ratio (see page 18 in "Aerodynamics") or relative efficiency. All kites, whether high or low L/D ratio designs, adopt varying degrees of flight (angle of attack) with respect to the horizon. On the average, the flying line holds a correctly tethered kite against the wind along a ±45° diagonal path.

Tether points are located approximately one-third down from the top of the kite's mast and extend outward for about one-half the length of the mast at ±90°, or a right angle.

Single-line tethers connect directly to a point along the kite's mast, or on the ventral keel tip in the case of a delta kite. As no adjustments are possible with this type of configuration, the fulcrum must be correct to begin with.

Bridles connect to the kite in two or more places and offer flexibility since the tether point can be adjusted both fore and aft.

Before committing your untested kite to the air, check for balance or imbalance at the tether point. With your back to the wind, hold the tow point and feel how the kite flies. If it rises slowly and steadily, then you have found the fulcrum, the tether point. If the kite won't rise, or if it rushes upwards too quickly and swoops about in tight circles, check the chart below for a likely prescription.

Kite Prescription Chart at a Glance

Symptom	Rx
Kite won't rise.	If the tether is too low, adjust upwards in ½″ increments and launch until the kite wants to climb. If there's too much drag, reduce the tail length since the kite may be too heavy for prevailing winds.
Kite rushes upwards and swoops in tight circles before crashing.	If the tether is too high, adjust downwards in ½″ increments until the kite stabilizes. On bowed kites, lessen tension on bow line.
Kite oscillates from side to side.	There may be a lateral stability problem, especially on high aspect-ratio (considerably wider on the horizontal than vertical) designs. Multiple bridle lines should be of even tension and length; try adding a drogue or tail. On deltas, moving the wing spreader bar forward in ½″ increments towards the nose shifts the center of gravity, allowing the wings to self-adjust.
Kite leans to one side.	Inspect multiple bridles for even tension and length. Replace uneven length or warped wooden wing spar on deltas. Sometimes reversing wing spars does the trick. Check fabric for grain imbalance on bias-sensitive kites (see "Making a Full-Size Kite Pattern").
Unstable behavior.	Try a longer bridle. Sled kites, for example, require a bridle length at least 3 times the height of the kite.

5
Kite Safety

As with any sport, the potential hazards of kite flying should not be taken lightly. Always remember that irresponsible flying may cause injury and that the kite flier is totally accountable for flying safely.

Here are some important guidelines.

I will never fly a kite:

- in wet or stormy weather (Illus. 18), or use wet flying line.

Illus. 18

- near electric power lines, transmission towers, or antennas (Illus. 19). (If your kite gets hung up on one, have the discipline to walk away without trying to retrieve it. Your next kite will be a better one *because you will still be alive to fly it.* If you must get it back, contact the utility company.)

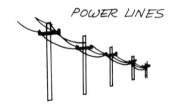

Illus. 19

- with wire for a flying line, or metal as part of the structure. (An exception is the nearly insignificant amount of aluminum or brass used as ferrules or scuff plates on certain kite designs in this book.)
- over public streets, areas congested with people, or highways.
- in fields or other open spaces strewn with rocks and other obstacles than can trip me up.
- over kite-eating trees (Illus. 20). (If your kite is

Illus. 20

attacked by a tree, sometimes giving the line slack allows the wind to work it free.)
- while walking blindly backwards (Illus. 21).

Illus. 21

- using unfamiliar equipment. (Reels spinning out of control are dangerous, and Kevlar flying line used in dual-line stunt kiting is capable of cutting and causing serious injury to anyone caught in its flight path.)
- over 500 feet in altitude near airports (Illus. 22). (Better yet, avoid air-traffic patterns altogether. The Federal Aviation Administration [FAA] has a single regulation governing kites under 5 pounds in weight: No person may operate a kite in a manner that creates a hazard to persons, property, or other aircraft.)

Illus. 22

I will:

- wear protective gloves when flying hard-pulling kites.
- use the correct (lb. test) flying line for the kite.
- protect my eyes from the sun's ultraviolet rays.
- wear a suitably rated sun screen for my skin type since overexposure to the sun's rays may cause skin cancer.
- know the limitations of my kites and equipment.
- know my own limitations, especially when flying high-speed stunt kites.
- fly large kites *only* with the proper preparation and supervision.

6
Tools and Materials

All the tools, construction materials, and techniques shown and described in this section were used to construct the kites in this book. On one end of the spectrum the tools and materials can be as elementary as scissors, glues, paper, tape, and string; the other end includes more sophisticated means.

Tip: After choosing a kite, assemble *all* the required tools and construction materials *before* beginning the project.

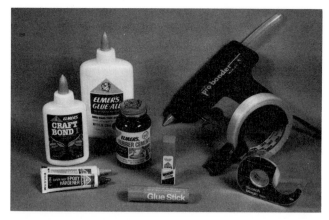

Illus. 23. Select the right glue for the job. Glue guns are convenient and super-glues work fast.

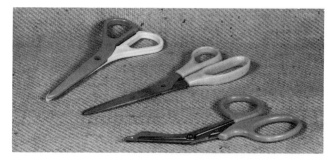

Illus. 24. From left to right: children's safety scissors for paper or fabric—not fingers—standard scissors, and angled shears for cutting heavy cardboard templates.

Illus. 25. A grommet tool maker (front) and metal shears for cutting out aluminum (flat-stock .020) templates. A seam ripper (right) for opening seams.

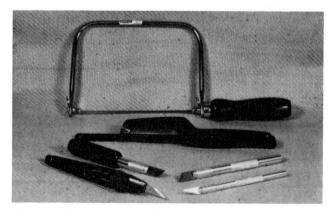

Illus. 26. Hobby saws and knives are a useful part of the kite builder's tool kit.

Illus. 27. T-squares are essential for making true straight lines.

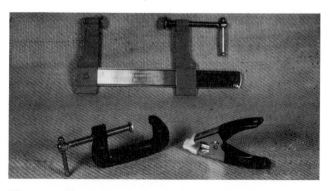

Illus. 28. Clamps come in all sizes and are especially helpful when joining woods. For an example of using clamps to build a laminated bow, see Liddell's Keeled Diamond Eddy Kite (Chapter 28).

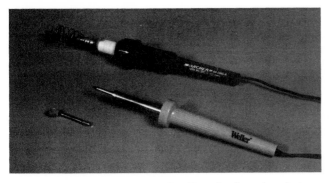

Illus. 29. Top: A professional sail maker's tool, a hot tacker with a release spring can be used for temporarily tacking together pieces of synthetics, such as ripstop nylon, to make sewing quicker and easier. Middle: A soldering iron with a conical tip along with a Teflon wheel guide can be used for cutting ripstop. Bottom: The smoothing-tip accessory is used for heat-sealing plastic.

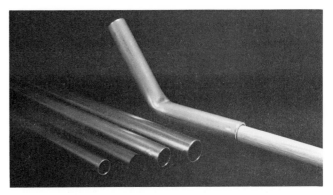

Illus. 30. Use only high-grade 6061-T aluminum, or better, for fixed dihedral connectors. The aluminum must be strong enough to accept a bend without weakening in flight.

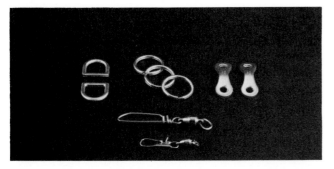

Illus. 31. From left to right: d-rings, split key rings, guy-line adjusters (sliders) for bow lines, and fishing swivel hooks.

Illus. 32. Wooden beads with holes are useful for tension-line systems. The vinyl end caps fit over the spar tips and prevent wear on sail pockets.

Illus. 33. Filament-wound epoxy tubing is stiff, nearly indestructible, and relatively light for its strength.

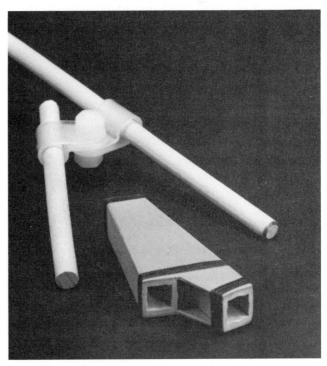

Illus. 34. Middle: a custom-fabricated ABS plastic di-hedral connector for the Stone Mountain Kite (see Chapter 37). Two nylon cable clamps serve the same purpose.

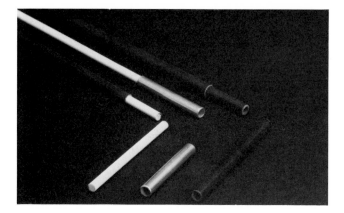

Illus. 35. The right connection for spar material. I.D. (inside diameter) and O.D. (outside diameter) of spar tubing generally indicates the type of ferrule. Basic joint configurations include: (left) internal fibreglass-rod ferrule, (middle) external aluminum ferrule over fibreglass rod, and (right) internal epoxy-tubing ferrule connecting epoxy tubing. Usually half of the ferrule is glued in position and the other half left free to accept a spar. This method makes breaking down long spars for transport an easy affair.

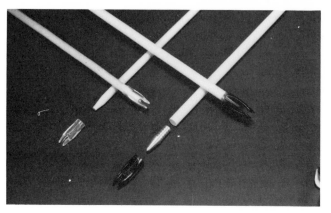

Illus. 36. Arrow nocks are a convenient means of connecting spars to the sail. Round the ends of hardwood dowels for a secure fit. Glue the metal insert in the hollow epoxy tubing; then glue the arrow nock over the insert.

Illus. 38. A Chesapeake II reel with a body bar brace for moderate-to-strong-wind kites, by Vincent Gerardi. The black knob controls a built-in braking system.

Illus. 37. Two pull-down reels, by "Wild Bill" Isenhart of Ohio. These accessories are not fully appreciated until a heavy-pulling kite refuses to come down. The pulley is placed over the flying line and the kite is literally walked down.

Illus. 39. Braided Dacron is a good overall flying line. It is strong and abrasion-resistant, in 500 to 3,000' lengths, and in 20 to 500 lb. test.

Illus. 40. Stunt-kite line must be light and have minimal stretch for best control. Spectra line, shown here, is ten times stronger than steel and 75 percent stronger than Kevlar. Knots in Spectra are OK; but for added security, use Dacron sleeving or a knotless system. Kevlar is five times stronger than steel but has limited resistance. A knot in Kevlar will cut through itself.

Illus. 41. A wind-speed indicator (left) and a range finder for determining a kite's altitude are useful accessories.

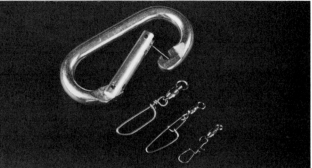

Illus. 42. A carabineer (left) is a sturdy spring-loaded clamp suitable for heavyweight bridle-line tow points (mountain climbers use them routinely) or for attaching flying line to a dog stake or ground anchor. For light-to-medium pulling kites, use fishing swivels (right) to connect flying line to the kite's tow point. Ball-bearing swivels are the most durable.

Illus. 43. Arrow nocks with inserts to fit hollow epoxy tubing.

Illus. 44. Certain kite designs call for strong spars that flex evenly without warping. Fibreglass rod fits the bill and comes in various diameters and lengths.

Illus. 45. When your kite is several thousand feet out, a two-speed cordless drill and winder attachment take the drudgery out of hauling in all that flying line. (Deep-sky reel by Bill Sonntag.)

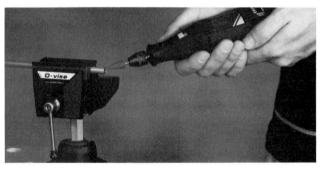

Illus. 46. A Dremel Moto-Tool with a deburring bit smooths edges of freshly cut metal tubing for use as ferrules or dihedral connectors.

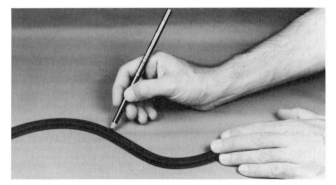

Illus. 47. A Flexicurve strip for drawing freehand curves on templates or directly onto the kite material.

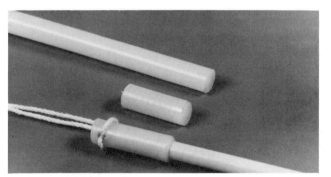

Illus. 48. Nylon rod cut to size and bored to make spar end caps, as for the Stone Mountain Kite.

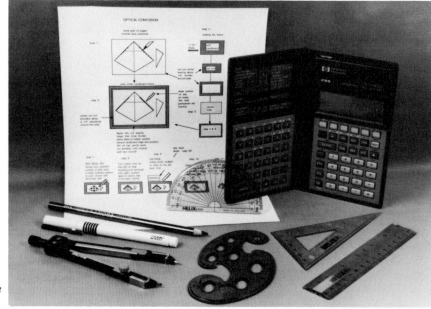

Illus. 49. Applying mathematical principles in designing kites brings abstract formulas down to earth and makes learning fun. A scientific calculator simplifies the process of computing angles and places the world of algebra, trigonometry, and calculus in the palm of your hand. A compass, protractor, french curve, ruler, and right triangle are also tools of the trade for the would-be designer.

7

Construction

While no one plans to fail, a thoughtful person never fails to plan.

This section deals with basic framing materials and how to use them, as well as specific arrangements for connecting the sail to the finished structure.

Most kites require a supportive structure to maintain the shape of the sail. (The exception is the parafoil kite, which assumes an airfoil exclusively by the force of the wind.) Constructing a reliable framework suitable for a given design requires knowledge of materials in addition to a straightforward building strategy.

Basic Spar Materials— Wood, Fibreglass Rod, and Epoxy Tubing

Tip: Before cutting fibreglass rod, epoxy tubing, or other synthetic spar material to size, create a pro-

totype set of spars of less-expensive hardwood dowel to establish an exact fit. After you have successfully flown the kite with the dimensionally correct surrogate spars, cut synthetic rod or tubing using dowel measurements.

Invest in a good-quality fine-tooth hobby saw to cut wood, fibreglass rod, and epoxy tubing. Cutting synthetics requires safety precautions, so wear protective eye covering as well as a suitably rated filter mask to keep from inhaling glass particles (Illus. 50).

For fibreglass and epoxy ferrules, sanding all rough edges prevents splintering and ensures a proper fit. To keep fibreglass or epoxy dust from contaminating the air and entering your lungs, use an extra-fine-grade sandpaper, such as 3M's Wetordry (use wet), specifically made for synthetics.

Prevent stress on sail pockets by rounding the edges on wooden spars. Add vinyl end caps on the tips of fibreglass rod and epoxy tubing. (Fibreglass-rod tips may also be rounded off, though vinyl end caps are a quicker fix.)

See Illus. 51 for typical arrangements of synthetic spars and Illus. 52 for typical arrangements of wood spars.

Aluminum Tubing

Although metal spars for kites are out because of potential electric shock hazards, high-grade aluminum (6061-T) and arrow-shaft-grade aluminum have their place (see Spar Material Chart at a Glance on pages 40–41).

Typical uses:

- As fixed dihedral connectors (for stabilizing bows). The aluminum must be strong enough to retain a bend without weakening under in-flight stress. Three methods for making a fixed dihedral connector are shown in Illus. 53.
- As sleeve reinforcements over spar joints—where two spars join to make one length. See Illus. 54.
- As scuff protectors to prevent spar wear through contact with other surfaces (Illus. 54).

Cutting Aluminum and Brass Tubing

Unlike epoxy tubing that maintains its wall integrity when cut, the inner wall, or inside diameter (I.D.), of

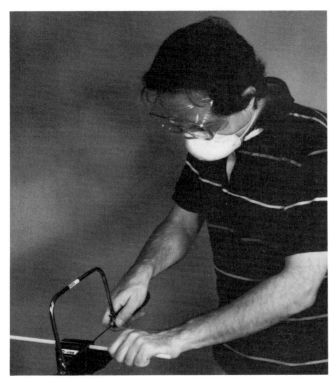

Illus. 50. Wearing protective eye covering and a filter mask are important safety precautions when you are cutting synthetics.

aluminum arrow-shaft-grade or brass tubing collapses or crimps as the saw cuts through. This crimp may cause problems when adapting the tubing as an external ferrule for a snug fit.

For example, fitting a .253 I.D. aluminum arrow shaft over a .250 O.D. epoxy tubing or fitting a .265 I.D. aluminum shaft over .261 epoxy tubing could be impaired by crimping. Another consideration to explore is tolerance. Metal tubing specifications of the same I.D. may vary, so it's a good idea to measure tubing with calipers. External and internal ferrules should fit as tightly as possible for strongest joints. In some cases, the only option may be to use a drill to bore existing tubing to your requirements.

Here are three ways to overcome the crimp factor:

- Use a fine-tooth hobby saw to cut the tubing slightly larger than required. Sand the ends flat until the crimp is gone.
- Another technique to prevent the inner walls from turning inward is to mount the tubing on a lathe. Place a hobby saw against the metal and let the lathe cut the tubing; the spinning action barely affects the tube's I.D.
- Try a tube cutter designed to cut with a minimum of crimping.

As a final touch, carefully file and smooth the inside, outside, and face of the tubing end. A Dremel Moto-Tool drill with a deburring stone bit will give you professional results.

Polypropylene or Vinyl Tubing

Polypropylene or vinyl tubing comes in a variety of I.D.'s and grades: clear, soft, semirigid, and nylon reinforced. You can straight-cut, mitre-cut, or drill the tubing to form many spar joints and connections. Hint: A bit of talcum powder eases tubing over tight spars. Illus. 55 shows typical uses of polypropylene tubing in frame construction.

Nylon Cable Clamps

Nylon cable clamps, used to secure wire cables, are conveniently held together with nylon screws and nuts. Available in many sizes, cable clamps are easily combined to form a variety of secure spar-connection joints. (See the Stone Mountain kite.) Illus. 56 shows typical uses of nylon cable clamps in frame construction.

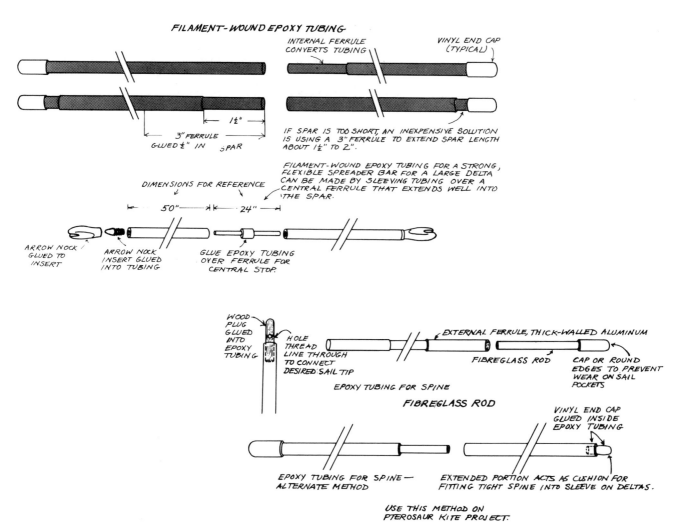

FILAMENT-WOUND EPOXY TUBING

INTERNAL FERRULE CONVERTS TUBING

VINYL END CAP (TYPICAL)

1½"

3" FERRULE GLUED ½" IN SPAR

IF SPAR IS TOO SHORT, AN INEXPENSIVE SOLUTION IS USING A 3" FERRULE TO EXTEND SPAR LENGTH ABOUT 1½" TO 2".

FILAMENT-WOUND EPOXY TUBING FOR A STRONG, FLEXIBLE SPREADER BAR FOR A LARGE DELTA CAN BE MADE BY SLEEVING TUBING OVER A CENTRAL FERRULE THAT EXTENDS WELL INTO THE SPAR.

DIMENSIONS FOR REFERENCE

50"   24"

ARROW NOCK GLUED TO INSERT

ARROW NOCK INSERT GLUED INTO TUBING

GLUE EPOXY TUBING OVER FERRULE FOR CENTRAL STOP.

WOOD PLUG GLUED INTO EPOXY TUBING

HOLE THREAD LINE THROUGH TO CONNECT DESIRED SAIL TIP

EXTERNAL FERRULE, THICK-WALLED ALUMINUM

FIBREGLASS ROD

CAP OR ROUND EDGES TO PREVENT WEAR ON SAIL POCKETS

EPOXY TUBING FOR SPINE

FIBREGLASS ROD

VINYL END CAP GLUED INSIDE EPOXY TUBING

EPOXY TUBING FOR SPINE — ALTERNATE METHOD

EXTENDED PORTION ACTS AS CUSHION FOR FITTING TIGHT SPINE INTO SLEEVE ON DELTAS.

USE THIS METHOD ON PTEROSAUR KITE PROJECT.

Illus. 51. Synthetic spars—typical arrangements.

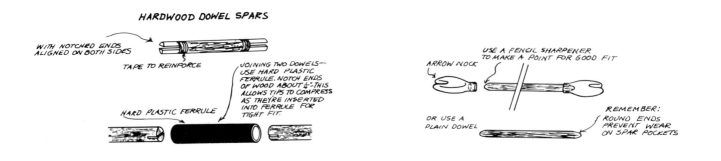

HARDWOOD DOWEL SPARS

WITH NOTCHED ENDS ALIGNED ON BOTH SIDES

TAPE TO REINFORCE

JOINING TWO DOWELS— USE HARD PLASTIC FERRULE. NOTCH ENDS OF WOOD ABOUT ½". THIS ALLOWS TIPS TO COMPRESS AS THEY'RE INSERTED INTO FERRULE FOR TIGHT FIT.

HARD PLASTIC FERRULE

ARROW NOCK

USE A PENCIL SHARPENER TO MAKE A POINT FOR GOOD FIT

OR USE A PLAIN DOWEL

REMEMBER: ROUND ENDS PREVENT WEAR ON SPAR POCKETS

Illus. 52. Hardwood dowel spars—typical arrangements.

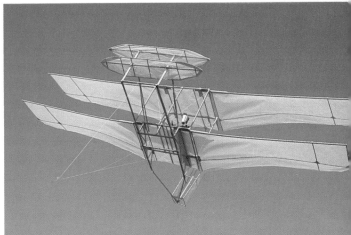

Left: birds flying in a train (kites and photo by Joel Scholz). Below: a Wright Flyer Kite of balsa and Silkspan from Squadron Kites (photo courtesy of Stratton Air Engineering).

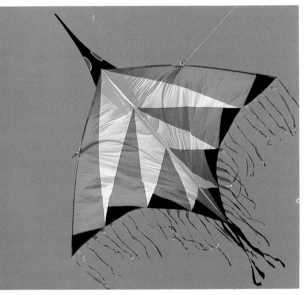

Above: a good-luck crane (photo by Pete Hubbell). Left: detail of the Pterosaur Kite by George Peters (pages 251–261).

A

Counterclockwise: a Trefoil Delta Kite in butterfly motif by Helen Bushell (pages 243–246), the Dragonfly Kite by Adrian Conn—a Hewitt Flexkite variation (pages 166–169), and the Seventh Wonder Delta Kite (photo by Pete Hubbell).

B

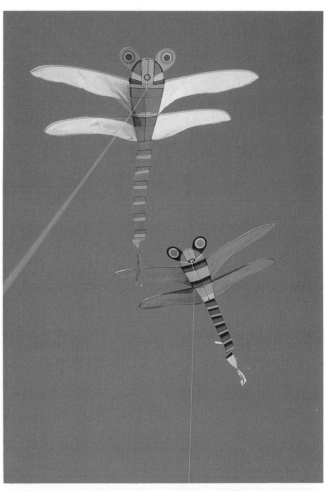

Clockwise: a Japanese o-dako kite (photo by Pete Hubbell), majestic Dragonflies—8 ft. × 9 ft. of ripstop nylon and fibreglass rod (kites and photo by George Peters), and Groucho on rokkaku (kite and photo by John Karel).

From top to bottom: Star Trek's U.S.S. Enterprise Kite by Joel Scholz (photo by Richard Robertson); detail of Scott Spencer's Pentagon Facet Kite (the Kaleidekite is a facet kite), showing how gradations of colored ripstop nylon can create a stunning effect; and the Hawaiian Team Stunt Kite (from Top of the Lines Kites).

D

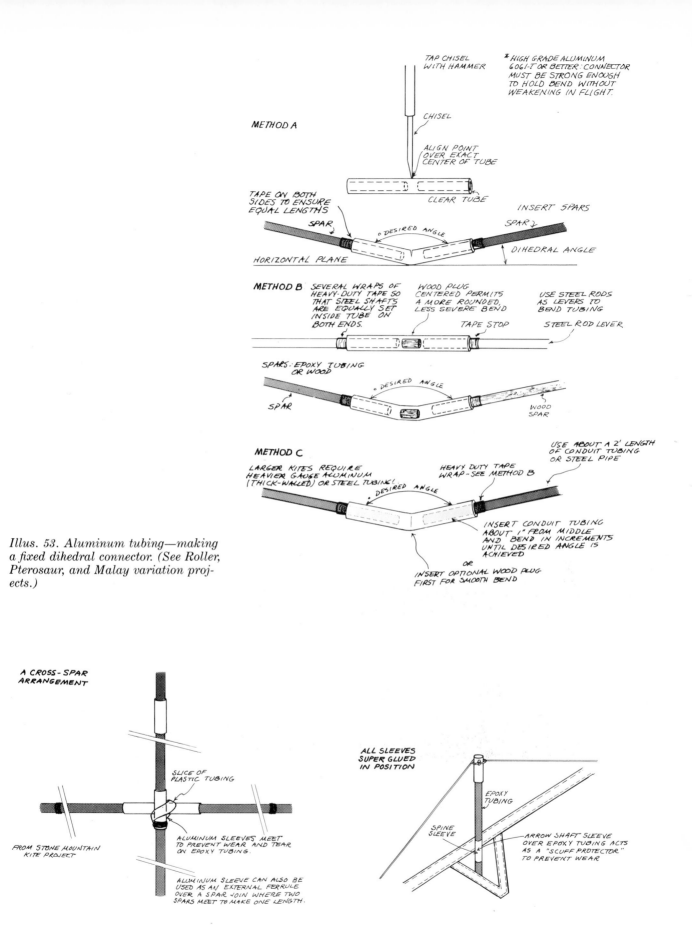

TAP CHISEL
WITH HAMMER

* HIGH GRADE ALUMINUM
6061-T OR BETTER. CONNECTOR
MUST BE STRONG ENOUGH
TO HOLD BEND WITHOUT
WEAKENING IN FLIGHT.

METHOD A

CHISEL

ALIGN POINT
OVER EXACT
CENTER OF TUBE

TAPE ON BOTH
SIDES TO ENSURE
EQUAL LENGTHS

CLEAR TUBE

INSERT SPARS

SPAR

SPAR

DESIRED ANGLE

DIHEDRAL ANGLE

HORIZONTAL PLANE

METHOD B   SEVERAL WRAPS OF
HEAVY-DUTY TAPE SO
THAT STEEL SHAFTS
ARE EQUALLY SET
INSIDE TUBE ON
BOTH ENDS.

WOOD PLUG
CENTERED PERMITS
A MORE ROUNDED,
LESS SEVERE BEND

USE STEEL RODS
AS LEVERS TO
BEND TUBING

TAPE STOP

STEEL ROD LEVER

SPARS - EPOXY TUBING
OR WOOD

DESIRED ANGLE

SPAR

WOOD
SPAR

METHOD C

LARGER KITES REQUIRE
HEAVIER GAUGE ALUMINUM
(THICK-WALLED) OR STEEL TUBING!

HEAVY DUTY TAPE
WRAP - SEE METHOD B

USE ABOUT A 2' LENGTH
OF CONDUIT TUBING
OR STEEL PIPE

DESIRED ANGLE

INSERT CONDUIT TUBING
ABOUT 1" FROM MIDDLE
AND BEND IN INCREMENTS
UNTIL DESIRED ANGLE IS
ACHIEVED
OR
INSERT OPTIONAL WOOD PLUG
FIRST FOR SMOOTH BEND

Illus. 53. Aluminum tubing—making a fixed dihedral connector. (See Roller, Pterosaur, and Malay variation projects.)

A CROSS-SPAR
ARRANGEMENT

SLICE OF
PLASTIC TUBING

ALL SLEEVES
SUPER GLUED
IN POSITION

EPOXY
TUBING

SPINE
SLEEVE

ARROW SHAFT SLEEVE
OVER EPOXY TUBING ACTS
AS A "SCUFF PROTECTOR"
TO PREVENT WEAR

FROM STONE MOUNTAIN
KITE PROJECT

ALUMINUM SLEEVES MEET
TO PREVENT WEAR AND TEAR
ON EPOXY TUBING.

ALUMINUM SLEEVE CAN ALSO BE
USED AS AN EXTERNAL FERRULE
OVER A SPAR JOIN WHERE TWO
SPARS MEET TO MAKE ONE LENGTH.

Illus. 54. Arrow shaft grade aluminum tubing—typical uses.

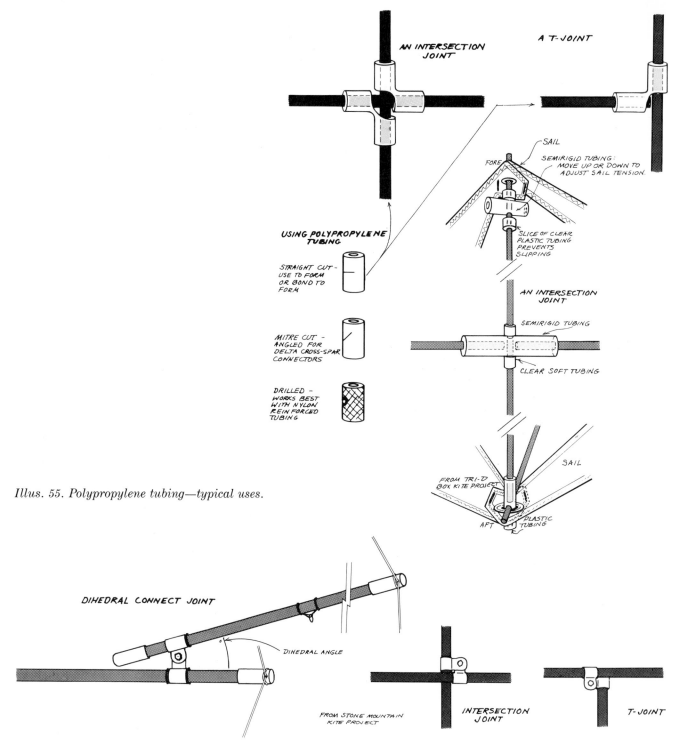

AN INTERSECTION JOINT

A T-JOINT

SAIL

SEMIRIGID TUBING: MOVE UP OR DOWN TO ADJUST SAIL TENSION.

FORE

SLICE OF CLEAR PLASTIC TUBING PREVENTS SLIPPING

USING POLYPROPYLENE TUBING

STRAIGHT CUT - USE TO FORM OR BOND TO FORM

AN INTERSECTION JOINT

SEMIRIGID TUBING

MITRE CUT - ANGLED FOR DELTA CROSS-SPAR CONNECTORS

CLEAR SOFT TUBING

DRILLED - WORKS BEST WITH NYLON REINFORCED TUBING

FROM TRI-D BOX KITE PROJECT

SAIL

AFT

PLASTIC TUBING

Illus. 55. Polypropylene tubing—typical uses.

DIHEDRAL CONNECT JOINT

DIHEDRAL ANGLE

FROM STONE MOUNTAIN KITE PROJECT

INTERSECTION JOINT

T-JOINT

Illus. 56. Nylon cable clamps—typical uses.

Sail-Tension Options

The objective is to fasten the sail to the kite frame without having the tension on the spars tear out the pockets during flight. The solution is to distribute the stress load evenly over the kite.

A method of quickly adjusting sail tension is also useful. Facet kites (see the Kaleidakite project) and other designs employ some form of sail-tension adjustment as a means of assembly, as well as a convenient means of fine-tuning the sail tension for the prevailing winds. (Liddell's Keeled Diamond Eddy

Kite uses a tension system to regulate the sail for the prevailing wind conditions. The *rokkaku* combines an adjustable bow and spine to achieve just the right sail tension.) See Illus. 57 for sail-tension options.

See Illus. 58 for typical arrangements of spar pockets and tape loops. Spar-tension options: beads and an arrow nock or a notched spar with a knotted-line loop and a dowel-bead system.

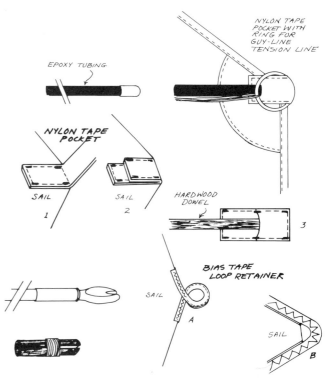

Illus. 58. Spar pockets and tape loops—typical arrangements.

stress of larger deltas. Because of its pliable nature, clear plastic tubing works well to hold fore and aft spreaders on high-stress stunt kites. After a time, connect systems usually end up as a matter of personal preference. See Illus. 59 for Delta spreader-bar options.

Spar Shock-Cord System

The tent industry has been using this system for years to keep struts from getting lost and to facilitate setup time. But it's also a useful assembly option for kite makers. A $\frac{3}{32}''$ elastic cord running the length of the epoxy tubing serves two purposes: The sections are conveniently held together, and the spars easily break down into small, transportable packages. The spar shock-cord system is shown in Illus. 60.

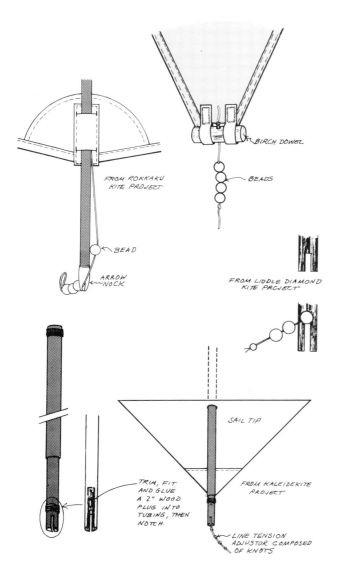

Illus. 57. Sail-tension options.

Delta Spreader-Bar Options

Size and delta type are factors to consider in choosing a spreader-bar connect system. While reinforced pockets are suitable for deltas under 7½', a D- or nylon ring fitted as shown in Illus. 59 endures the

Glues

A super (Cyanoacrylate adhesive) glue, such as Elmer's Wonder Bond Plus, is good to use for bonding synthetic ferrules, arrow nocks, plastic tubing, and vinyl end caps in place. Use carpenter's yellow glue or a white glue for porous materials—for instance, Elmer's Glue-All for wood and polystyrene foam. Epoxy adhesive, such as Hobby Poxy II, bonds both synthetics and woods. Quick-setting (5- or 10-

minute) epoxy speeds up construction time and is convenient for field repairs. Rubber cement is a good choice for tissue paper kites, like the Szilagi Fighter. For more specific glue suggestions, see spar and sail material charts at a glance in the next chapter. Prior to using any adhesive, be sure to read the instructions.

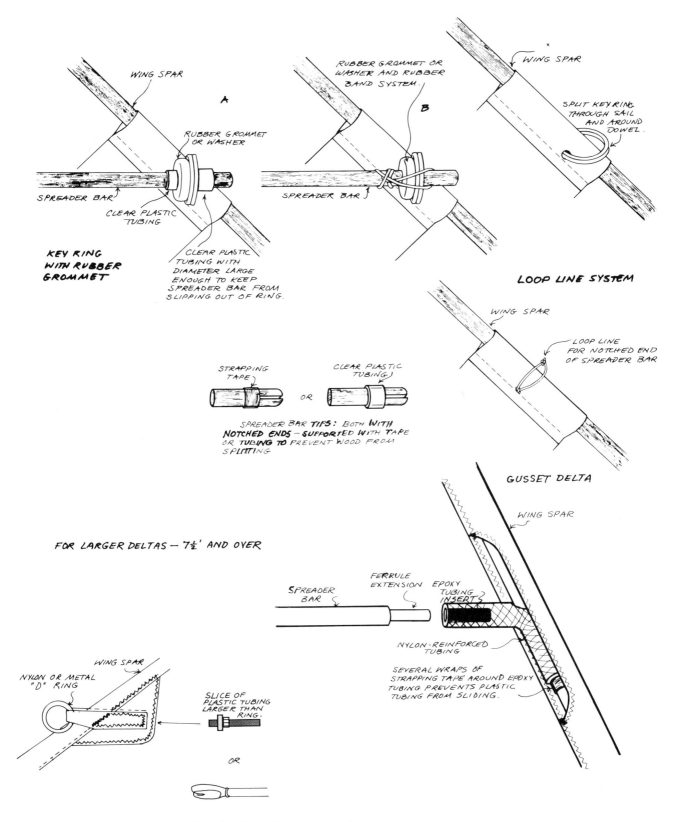

Illus. 59. Delta spreader-bar options (continued on next page).

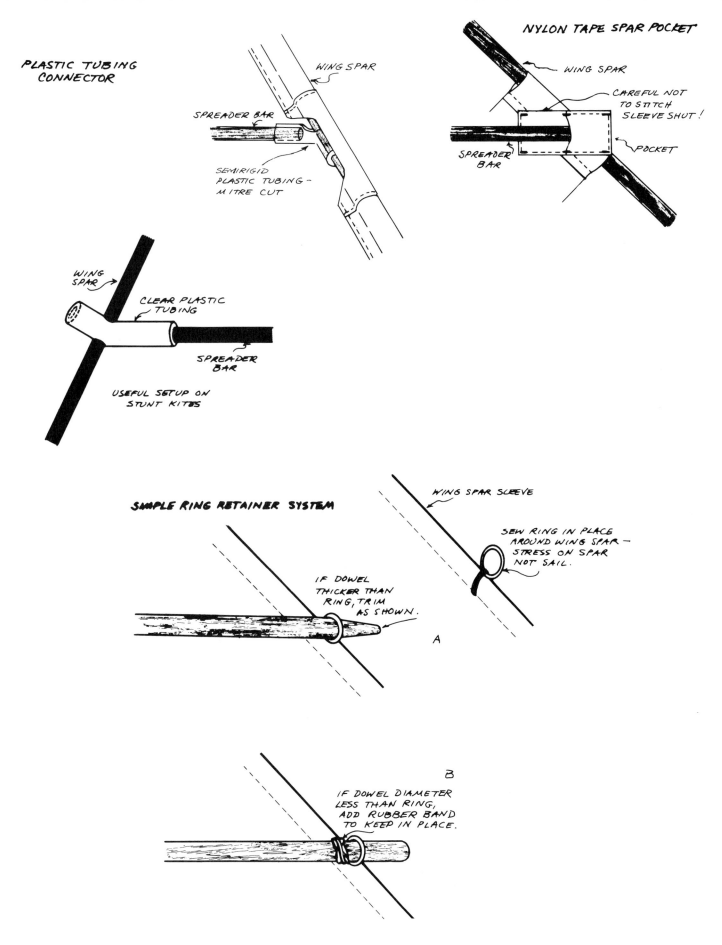

PLASTIC TUBING
CONNECTOR

WING SPAR

SPREADER BAR

SEMIRIGID
PLASTIC TUBING —
MITRE CUT

NYLON TAPE SPAR POCKET

WING SPAR

CAREFUL NOT
TO STITCH
SLEEVE SHUT!

SPREADER
BAR

POCKET

WING
SPAR

CLEAR PLASTIC
TUBING

SPREADER
BAR

USEFUL SETUP ON
STUNT KITES

SIMPLE RING RETAINER SYSTEM

WING SPAR SLEEVE

SEW RING IN PLACE
AROUND WING SPAR —
STRESS ON SPAR
NOT SAIL.

IF DOWEL
THICKER THAN
RING, TRIM
AS SHOWN.

A

B

IF DOWEL DIAMETER
LESS THAN RING,
ADD RUBBER BAND
TO KEEP IN PLACE.

37

SHOCK CORD
GOES THROUGH
HOLLOW FERRULE

FINAL PRODUCT: A SPAR
WITH SECTIONS CONVENIENTLY
HELD TOGETHER THAT BREAKS
DOWN FOR EASY TRANSPORT.

NOTE: DO NOT MAKE CORD TENSION
TOO TIGHT - THE IDEA IS FOR THE
SPAR TO SNAP TOGETHER UNDER
SLIGHT TENSION AND FOLD EASILY
WITHOUT STRESS ON CORD.

$\frac{3}{32}$" ELASTIC CORD
RUNS THROUGH
SPAR LENGTH

ALUMINUM
INSERT

TIE OFF
BOTH ENDS

TYPICAL SETUP

Illus. 60. Spar shock-chord system.

8
Sail and Spar Materials

The wide array of lightweight, durable, and accessible kite-building material currently available offers every kite builder the opportunity to construct a rich variety of kites. While there is no ideal sail or spar material, there are ideally suited materials for specific types of kites.

Technology is not always better. For instance, despite the availability of more modern materials, the traditional Indian fighter and the Japanese Nagasaki *hata* kites—both ancient Eastern light-wind kites—remain perfectly suited to paper-and-bamboo construction. However, certain kites—box, compound, and delta, for example—are well-suited to synthetic materials, such as ripstop nylon and epoxy tubing.

When selecting materials, the idea is to combine them to achieve the strongest and lightest kite for the wind conditions under which it is designed to fly. Let's say you wish to design a strong-wind box kite. Ripstop nylon would be the natural choice for the sail. If, however, you want to decorate (other than appliqué) the sail material, you would have to com-

promise some sail strength and go with an alternative like Tyvek or cotton.

In choosing sail material, you also need to consider bonding techniques. To continue with the previous example, let's say you narrowed the materials down to Tyvek or cotton, but you don't have access to a sewing machine or you haven't tried your hand at sewing yet. Fortunately with Tyvek you don't need to worry because you can use white glue to hem it and get excellent results.

Spars cannot be taken for granted—as mere sticks that support the sail. They are as crucial as the sail and thus warrant equal consideration. Though fibreglass rod and epoxy tubing are stronger and stiffer than wood, they are generally heavier and cannot replace the organic suppleness of woods and bamboo that is necessary for certain applications.

See the following sail and spar material charts at a glance for an overview of applications and general characteristics.

Sail Material Chart at a Glance

Sail[1]	Material	TRF[2]	Notes	Bonding	Weights & Grades	Decorating	Typical Uses
ripstop	urethane-coated nylon	10	best all-around kite fabric; lightweight, strong, tear-resistant	sew; observe grain when cutting & piecing	.5 oz., .6 oz., .75 oz., 1.5 oz.; standard width: 41"; 1.5 oz. available in 60" width	many colors; piecing, appliqué, silk-screen	most kites
laminates	2 & 3-ply combinations plus scrim; Dacron, Spectra, Kevlar, Mylar[3]	10	by weight, strongest and most stable sail material available	sew; observe grain when cutting & piecing; reinforce stitching with 2.2 Dacron-strip tape with adhesive backing	.95 oz. and up, 54" widths	red, white, blue; piecing	stunt kites, high-wind kites
taffeta	nylon	7–8	high-count (quality) strong, washable; lower cost than ripstop	sew; observe grain when cutting & piecing	± 1.2 oz.; width: 45"	many colors; piecing & appliqué	dragon kites, windsocks, small deltas, streamers & tails
Tyvek	spunbonded olefin	6–7	tear-resistant, like paper yet much stronger, relatively inexpensive	sew; Elmer's White Glue-All	1025D & 1058D are stiff and like paper; 1443R is soft, like fabric; 60" widths	white only, most mediums that work on paper, weld colored trashbag plastic to surface	most kites, holds up well, ideal material for experimentation prior to committing to more expensive fabrics
plastic trash bag	polyethylene	5–7	readily available, inexpensive, lightweight	heat-welding, glue stick, Scotch Magic or strapping tape	.5 mil to 1.5 mil	most markers, heat-welding, different plastic colors	small to medium kites
Mylar	polyester film	3–7	lightweight high-tensile strength until torn, attracts static charge in thin film grades	Scotch Magic or strapping tape	.06 mil to 3 mil	transparent, variety of colors, permanent ink markers	miniature kites, small fighters, dragon & box kites, Rogallo's Flexikite
poplin	cotton	6–8	lightweight, fine weave; porosity increases wind range of kite	sew; observe grain when cutting & piecing	various close weaves	dyes, batik, silk-screen, paints, pigment markers	most kites
paper	wood, plant fibres	2–5	readily available, most grades inexpensive; lightweight	glues: stick, rubber cement, white; tapes: Scotch Magic & strapping	art or Madras tissue, construction grade, shopping-bag grade	most media	light-to-gentle-wind kites, small fighters

(Continued on next page.)

Sail Material Chart at a Glance *(continued)*

Sail[1]	Material	TRF[2]	Notes	Bonding	Weights & Grades	Decorating	Typical Uses
silkspan	water-insoluble paper	2–5	inexpensive; lightweight; porous; once glued onto frame, spraying with water tightens silkspan drum tight	White Glue-All; Elmer's Craft Bond 1	3 weights: OO, GM, SGM	dyes, some heavy markers	small box-kite designs

[1]Ultraviolet (U.V.) light degrades most materials, including sail fabric. Avoid unnecessary exposure when not flying kite.

[2]Tear-resistance factor, where 10 is strongest.

[3]Laminates—2-ply: densely woven Dacron, Kevlar, or Spectra with Mylar; 3-ply: Dacron, Kevlar, or Spectra scrim (loosely woven grid) sandwiched between Mylar.

Spar Material Chart at a Glance

Consider the purpose, size, and projected total weight of your kite as well as your budget when choosing spar material. In general, woods are acceptable for low-to-medium-wind kites; synthetics and high-wind kites are made for each other.

Material	Advantage	Disadvantage	O.D./Inches	Lengths/In.	Typical Uses
fibreglass rod	virtually unbreakable, uniform construction for balance	heavier in oz./ft. than other materials	³⁄₃₂ to ⁹⁄₃₂″	48 to 72″	stunt kites, small fighters, high-wind kites in general
hardwood dowel	lightweight, inexpensive, easy to work with	prone to warping after extended use, especially under humid conditions; least resilient and subject to breaking	⅛ to ⅜″	48″	most kites, good for determining spar dimensions and test flights
Sitka spruce (rectangular)	lightweight aircraft quality; stable, won't twist like dowel	less resilient than synthetics	⅛ sq ″ to ½ × 1″	36 to 48″	classic Eddy kite, any design where torque and twist would hinder performance, kites requiring built-up framework
filament-wound epoxy tubing	lightweight, stiff, as uniform as fibreglass rod at a fraction of the weight	higher cost	.250 to .610	32½ to 54½″	most kites benefit from this material, especially stunt and other high-wind kites
aluminum-carbon (arrowshaft) tubing	stiff, uniform; by weight, the strongest spar material currently available	higher cost	.261 to .297	32½″	when keeping weight down is critical

(Continued on opposite page.)

Material	Advantage	Disadvantage	O.D./Inches	Lengths/In.	Typical Uses
graphite (arrowshaft) tubing	lightweight, extremely stiff	higher cost	.220, .230, .240	32½"	when low weight and maximum strength are critical, stunt kites
bamboo	lightweight, stiff, resilient; a classic material	takes time to master bamboo, but well worth it!	cut to size	cut to size	giant to miniature kites, large Oriental kites, critical as bow and spine for small fighter kites
boron	strongest known material by weight; uniform, stiff	brittle, easily broken; can splinter, so take precautions (see "Miniature Kites")	0.004	cut to size	miniature kites
brush bristles (nylon monofilament)	strong, flexible, inexpensive substitute for bamboo	n/a	.012; .020; .026; .032; .06	10 to 12½"	miniature kites

Spar Comparison Chart at a Glance

The following spar materials, weights, and stiffness factors (where .1 is most flexible) have been selected to illustrate typical uses and to serve as a guide for future projects.

Type	O.D./Inches	Weight/Oz./ft.	Stiffness Factor	Typical Uses
fibreglass rod	³⁄₃₂"	.112	.1	small fighter kites
fibreglass rod	⅛"	.176	.2	small dragon kites
ramin dowel	³⁄₁₆"	.128	.4	small deltas & sleds
fibreglass rod	³⁄₁₆"	.352	.7	medium dragon kites
ramin dowel	¼"	.240	1.0	medium deltas & sleds
epoxy tubing	.261	.206	1.5	medium deltas & sleds
aluminum-carbon tubing	.234	.231	6.0	medium deltas & box kites
graphite tubing	.220	.207	5.0	medium deltas & stunt kites
fibreglass rod	¼"	.656	2.0	8' deltas & box kites
ramin dowel	⁵⁄₁₆"	.416	2.3	6' delta spreader bar
epoxy tubing	.298	.273	2.6	medium deltas & box kites
epoxy tubing	.317	.346	3.0	10' deltas
epoxy tubing	.350	.338	4.0	8 to 10' delta spreader bar
ramin dowel	⅜"	.723	5.0	10' delta spreader bar
epoxy tubing	.370	.537	6.0	6' box & compound kites
epoxy tubing	.414	.584	13.0	large kites
epoxy tubing	.505	.846	20.0	large kites
epoxy tubing	.610	1.0	25.0	large kites

9
Flying Line

The Big One That Got Away

Kiting aficionado, author, and master of public relations Will Yolen had commissioned me to design and build a large red, white, and blue kite for an Olympic Kite promotional tour. A sunny day one month later, the 22′ × 10′ Olympic Delta was ready for its maiden voyage.

Yolen, myself, and a friend brought the untested kite to a large empty field. As we assembled the kite, the ripstop and Dacron sail billowed and crackled in the steady 8-mph breeze. When we were ready to launch, I handed Yolen a spool of 500-lb. test leech line. He shrugged, patted his tuna fishing reel, and assured me his 180-lb. test line would do. "Will," I said, "this kite's going to pull like an elephant not a tuna." But he insisted on using his line, so we assumed our lift-off positions.

The kite flew up like a giant patriotic moth. Yolen leaned back to counter the kite's forward pull. Yanked several feet towards the kite, he yelled out that he couldn't believe the incredible pull in such a light wind. Several seconds later, his line snapped as if it were mere sewing thread. Yolen landed flat on his derrière and looked up in disbelief. The kite bucked overhead for an instant before nosing downwards. The Olympic hopeful began its descent by gliding forward; its target was the man with the tuna reel.

Yolen dropped his fishing rod and began running. The kite looked like a fantastic bird of prey—its shadow following poor Yolen as he scrambled for his life across the grass. The kite had a high-L/D ratio and it seemed to glide forever. Several hundred feet later, the kite swooped down and, barely missing Yolen, dug its nose into the ground on impact. I ran over to Yolen, who was only out of breath. I told him that maybe he should be in the Olympics anyway—as a sprinter.

Though the passing of time and the fact that no one was hurt makes this story amusing now, the possibility of injury and the necessity of selecting the right flying line should not be taken lightly.

Choosing the Right Flying Line

The earliest kite-flying lines were organic—meaning they were made from things that grow naturally from the earth. In ancient China, kite fliers used pure-silk line. Cotton and hemp are other fibres that have served well for centuries. To this day, the Japanese continue the labor-intensive tradition of making their own flying line from various plants. It is synthetics, however, developed during the last 40 years, that offer the greatest variety and improvements in flying line (see the Flying Line Chart at a Glance on the opposite page).

Basic Flying-Line Practice

All too often flying line is a mere afterthought—a knotting, twisting, gnarling, kinking, fraying, breaking, but necessary element in kite flying. However, while these annoyances and possible hazards may occur, they need never plague the prepared safety-conscious kite flier.

These rules are guidelines, not commandments. Conservative judgment is your best authority for the salvation of your flying line, your kite, yourself, and the innocent bystander.

- To avoid line burn, develop the habit of *always wearing gloves* (open-finger variety) when flying medium-to-hard-pulling kites. Light-wind kites, such as Indian fighters, are exceptions, though fast-moving cotton line has been known to cut skin. Waxed-linen line reduces the risk of line burn when flying small fighter kites.
- Flying line should have a tensile strength (average breaking load) of about three times the kite's total area in square feet. For example, use a minimum 30 lb.–test line on a kite with a surface sail area of 10 sq. ft. Use the following formula for a more accurate reading: Line strength = ⅕ × surface area (square feet) × maximum wind velocity (mph). Tak-

ing this example at 20 mph: $\frac{1}{5} \times$ 10 sq. ft. $\times$ 20 mph = 40 lb.–test line.

Note: Dual-line stunt kites are an exception because they are flown under high stress. The line strength is typically eight to ten times the kite's sail area in square feet.

- Wind speed and line condition also directly affect the line's breaking point. A strong, sudden gust can break a weakened line or one that minimally respects the recommended tensile strength. Variations of 6–14 percent in stated line strengths are typical.

- Do not exceed the line's recommended working load. Better yet, allow for a 20 percent safety margin in tensile strength.
- Avoid using and replace flying line that shows signs of wear in the fibre.
- Synthetic fibres—such as nylon, Dacron (polyester), Spectra line (polyethylene), and Kevlar—are weakened by the sun's ultraviolet rays; so avoid unnecessary exposure to direct sunlight.
- Avoid line abrasions and kinks. Read worn and twisted line as a warning to replace it.
- Store your line in a clean, dry place.

Flying Line Chart at a Glance

Ultraviolet light degrades most line material, especially synthetics; so avoid unnecessary exposure.

Line	Fibre	Advantage	Notes	Lengths/Ft.	Lb.-Test	Typical Uses
braided Dacron	polyester	strong, abrasion-resistant	stretch	1,000', 3,000'	20 to 500	most kites
twisted Dacron	polyester	inexpensive	stretch	1,000'	20 to 50	light-wind kites
braided nylon	nylon	stable, inexpensive	stretch	1,000', 3,000'	20 to 250	most kites
braided, waxed Kevlar	Kevlar	5 $\times$ stronger than steel; low stretch	limited abrasion resistance; knots in Kevlar will cut through itself; a knotless or Dacron-sleeve-system required	300', 1500'	50 to 900	stunt kites
Spectra	polyethylene	10 $\times$ stronger than steel; 75% stronger than Kevlar; low stretch; UV-resistant	low melt point; easily cut by other type lines; knots OK; knotless or Dacron sleeve optional	300', 1500'	75, 135, 200, 300, 450	stunt kites
waxed linen	flax	prevents line burn; easy to handle, won't twist	not as responsive as cotton line	1,000'	12	small fighter kites
low-stretch cotton	cotton	inexpensive	can twist and curl up; line burn possible	500'	8	small fighter kites

10
A Line-Retrieval System

Reels, Spools, Hoops, and Bobbins

In addition to choosing the appropriate flying line for your kite, you also need to select the right line-retrieval system. Though usually categorized generically as "reels," line winders fall into four distinct categories: reels, spools, hoops, and bobbins.

Determining which line winder is best for you often comes with experience, though there are a few considerations to keep in mind based solely on practicality rather than personal preference. For example, control over an Indian fighter kite demands rapid hand movements. Consequently, a side-winder-type system, such as a spool or a hoop, that allows the line to slip off freely and quickly is required. Conversely, a hand-held deep-sky reel that releases and retrieves line directly from its rotating center, though inappropriate for the Indian fighter, is a good choice for soaring kites, such as deltas or rollers (Illus. 61). The Korean fighter is an exception. This kite is traditionally and deftly maneuvered with a hand-held spoke type of rotating reel (Illus. 62).

Illus. 61. A deep-sky reel for deltas, rollers, and other light-wind kites (left). Two bobbins, with and without handles, for light-to-medium-wind kites (right).

Illus. 62. Korean el-lai *reel.*

Dual-line stunt kites are a category unto themselves, as they require hand-control grips for flight as well as a winder to keep both lines organized when putting the kite away (Illus. 63).

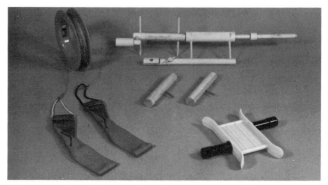

Illus. 63. Duel-line reel options for stunt kites.

Transferring Flying Line

Line usually comes on a cardboard or plastic spool or tube—but don't assume the end of the line is attached to it. If you have bought a winder with line already on it, again don't assume that the line is tied to it, or your kite may end up in novel territory, as in *Gone with the Wind.*

Transferring flying line to a reel is a simple matter, providing you plan your moves in advance. My preferred method: Choose a day when wind conditions are adequate to lift your kite; however, don't try this in brisk winds that will subject the line to heavy stress. Begin by flying your kite using the line's original spool, or whatever it came on. After playing out all but about 8 feet of line, wrap the line several times around a stationary object, like a dog stake or your foot (wear substantial shoes). With the kite flying off the stake or shoe, your hands are free to secure the end of the line to the reel. Having a friend to assist you simplifies the process.

Once the line is tied to a winder:

- Remove the line from the stationary object. Then reel or haul in the line under enough tension so that it wraps smoothly onto the winder.
- When using a deep-sky reel, let the line alternate from side to side as you crank the winder, usually in a clockwise motion.
- On handle-type bobbins, such as the Japanese *itomaki* in Illus. 64, use a figure-eight winding mo-

Illus. 64. Japanese itomaki *bobbin-type reel—used for kite flying and fishing.*

tion. This method of line handling incorporates a natural antitwisting action that has been used by sailors for centuries when storing rope.

Making sure that the line goes on and off in the same direction will prevent the dreaded kinks, gnarling, and aggravation associated with line twisting. Stunt kite fliers often use a simple hoop or a winder specifically designed to retrieve dual lines. If one line can get twisted, two means double-trouble. Instead of winding the line onto the hoop, turn the hoop so that the line winds onto the core to prevent twisting.

Additional Precautions

A reel feeding out line too fast with its external knobs spinning out of control can break fingers. Though kite flying is often perceived as a relaxing pastoral pastime—which it can be—it usually demands attention. Be alert and don't let things fly off the handle.

It is good practice to keep at least 200 feet of reserve line on your reel. Should your kite get caught in a power dive, letting out the reserve allows the kite to right itself before crashing. As a visual alert, use a permanent red soft-tip marker and color your line for about 10 feet in front of your reserve length. You can also mark your line (measure footage from the center outward) with different colors to indicate how much line has been fed out.

The pressure on a reel core can be crushing. Don't wind heavy-pulling kites directly onto the winder without creating some slack first; use a pull-down reel, or walk the kite down by pulling the line in hand over hand, to lessen tension as you move towards the kite. Better yet, haul the line in hand over hand with a friend at your back reeling the line onto the winder.

It's a good idea to label your reels with line strength and length. A piece of masking tape for a label is useful because you can remove it should you change flying lines. Also, inscribe your name and address directly onto the winder in case it gets lost.

Take care of your reels as you would any piece of valuable equipment. Ultraviolet light is destructive to plastic and woods. When it's not in use, avoid leaving your winder exposed to the sun and store it in a dry place.

Instructions for making two types of pull-down reels are shown in Illus. 65.

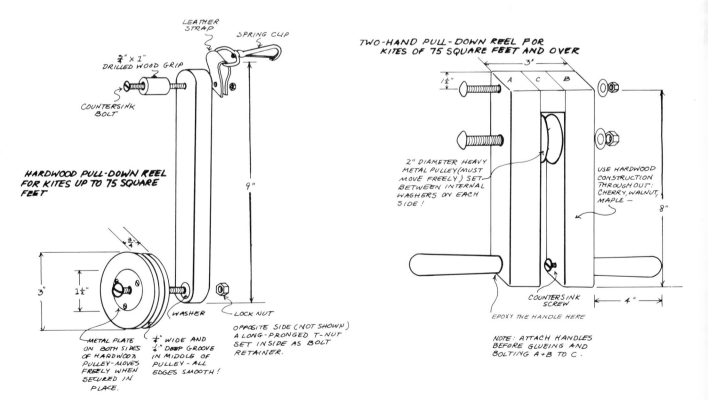

Illus. 65. Instructions for making two kinds of pull-down reels.

11
Getting To Know the Ropes

Knots, Hitches, and Loops

Rope literature shows that there are some 4,000 different types of knots. What if your life depended on tying the right one? Would you survive? A lot hangs on the proper knot. Your kite's fate depends on it.

Once you've chosen the correct flying line for your kite, learning a few basic reliable knots could mean the difference between enjoying your well-built kite or watching weeks, perhaps months, of work drift off at the end of a poorly tied tether point.

First, let's define our terms. A *knot* generally refers to the place where the end of a line is passed through a loop in itself, or to any purposeful lump in the line. A *bend* is a knot joining two lines. A *hitch* is a knot joining a line to something else, like a ring or a spar. A *loop* is a knot joining a line to itself.

"Knots," although necessary, represent a weakness in the line since they tend to cut into themselves under stress.

The following knots are useful for the kite flier. Keep in mind that reliable knots are pulled tightly and evenly. Practise them until you can make them at will.

- **Bowline** (Illus. 66.) A secure and reliable knot that locks with little chance of slipping. The greater the strain placed on it, the tighter it holds. The bowline may not be as reliable with synthetic lines, so securing the ends with an extra half-hitch is recommended.
- **Fisherman's knot** (Illus. 67.) Two overhand knots forced up against one another. Use this knot to join lines of equal diameter.
- **Daisy-chain loop** (Illus. 68.) Convenient for storing long multiple bridle lines. A simple tug on the lowest loop unravels the chain neatly.
- **Overhand loop** (Illus. 69.) A simple way to attach swivels; used in conjunction with a lark's head knot that becomes a hitch when secured to the swivel. Also used in forming the fulcrum loop on the bridle of a fighter kite; used with a slip knot on the flying-line end.
- **RED connection loop** (Illus. 70.) Named after Red Braswell, designer of the Rotor Kite project. Useful as a running line for connecting kite trains and as means of securing an adjustable flying line to stunt kite bridles (see the Turbo Stunt Kite proj-

ect). Note: Stopper knots have many uses. In kiting, a stopper prevents the end of the line from coming out of the knot or checks a loop's movement along the line. The simplest type of stopper knot is the overhand, shown here.
- **Lark's head hitch** (Illus. 71.) A knot converted to a hitch when fixed to a split key ring. Easily adjustable, though prone to slipping if not pulled tight.
- **Round turn and two half hitches** (Illus. 72.) An all-around knot that will securely support heavy loads. Good for attaching a flying line to a spar or ring.
- **Toggle hitch** (Illus. 73.) Works best under tension as its curved lines tend to come easily undone. Good for securing secondary lines in kite train formations.

Illus. 66. Bowline.

Illus. 67. Fisherman's knot.

A SIMPLE TUG UNRAVELS THE CHAIN NEATLY.

Illus. 68. Daisy chain loop.

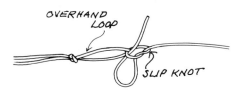

Illus. 69. Slip knot (with overhand loop).

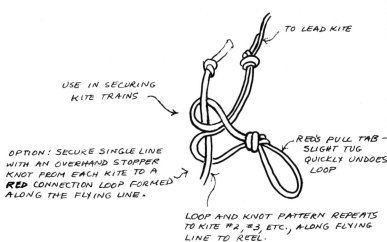

TO LEAD KITE

USE IN SECURING
KITE TRAINS

OPTION: SECURE SINGLE LINE
WITH AN OVERHAND STOPPER
KNOT FROM EACH KITE TO A
RED CONNECTION LOOP FORMED
ALONG THE FLYING LINE.

RED'S PULL TAB—
SLIGHT TUG
QUICKLY UNDOES
LOOP

LOOP AND KNOT PATTERN REPEATS
TO KITE #2, #3, ETC., ALONG FLYING
LINE TO REEL.

Illus. 70. RED connection loop.

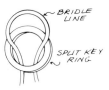

BRIDLE
LINE

SPLIT KEY
RING

Illus. 71. Lark's head hitch.

EASILY
SECURED AND
ADJUSTED
ALONG THE
BRIDLE

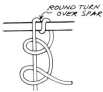

ROUND TURN
OVER SPAR

*Illus. 72. Round turn and two half
hitches.*

Illus. 73. Toggle hitch.

A Knotless System[1] for Stunt Kite Flying

Stunt kite flying demands strong line with minimal stretch, such as synthetic Kevlar or Spectra. Unfortunately, a knot in Kevlar will eventually cut through itself. A knotless system, however, provides a secure loop that won't weaken the line. While knots in Spectra line are acceptable, it's a good idea to either sleeve the ends or take the time to use a knotless loop.

Making a Knotless Loop

You will need a knotless tool or a small latch hook found in knitting supply shops (Illus. 74). Use heavy-

LATCH IN OPEN POSITION

Illus. 74: Top: small latch-hook tool. Bottom: wire-sleeving tool.

pound (200) test braided-Dacron line for sleeving material. For a smooth, knotless loop (Illus. 75), ma-

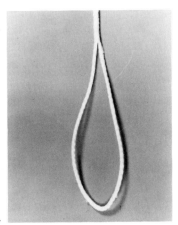

Illus. 75. A knotless loop.

nipulate the line as required with a light touch (pulling and pushing gently). Practise the following steps until it all comes together.

1. (See Illus. 76.) Beginning about 3″ from the end, compress the line to open the weave.
2. (Illus. 77.) With the point of the latch hook open, insert the tool into the hollow center of the line. Carefully *push* the line onto the tool; the tip of the tool must remain within the center of the weave as you do this step. Have the tool point exit about 2″ from where it entered.

3. Close the latch on the tool point around a loop of the line.

4. Pull the tool back through the center of the line, pulling the loop through.

5. (Illus. 78.) Hold the formed loop with one hand. Use your other hand to gently slide the sleeve over all the way in the opposite direction from the loop. The sliding action turns the sleeve inside out. The free end of the line will now be away from the loop.

6. (Illus. 79.) Insert the tool tip (latch open) about 4″ from the sleeved section and *push* the line onto the tool. Exit the line about 1″ from the sleeved section.

7. Close the tool around the free end of the line. Pull the tool back out as you bring the free end through the center of the line. You may have to compress the 4″ section slightly to get the tool and line through.

8. (Illus. 80.) Trim the excess ends and smooth out the closed splice for a finished knotless loop. In the process, you may have to gently pull and push on the loop and sleeve until the line comes together as one smooth piece.

9. A knotless loop is required at both ends. The dual lines must be equal in length for proper control of your stunt kite.

10. To make equal-length flying lines:
    a. Make a knotless loop on one end of each flying line.
    b. Secure both loops to a stationary object and unwind both flying lines under equal tension.
    c. Trim the unlooped ends, at an angle, to equal lengths.
    d. Mark each line about 8″ from the trimmed end.
    e. Make a knotless loop in each line with the mark at the tip, or middle, of the loop.

Once you've made your knotless loops, you'll have to protect the portion that is attached to the clips and handles—or directly to the bridle line itself (see the no-metal bridle configuration option illustrated with the Turbo Stunt Kite project).

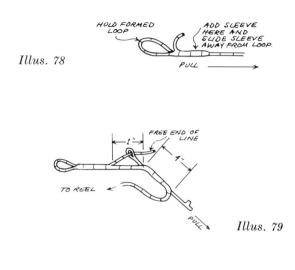

Illus. 78

Illus. 79

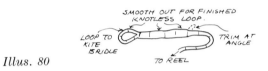

Illus. 80

Clip Attachment

1. Cut a 1″ piece of sleeving material. Heat-seal the ends to prevent fraying without melting the openings closed.

2. Insert the knotless tool through the middle of the sleeve.

3. Use the tool to pull the loop through the sleeve.

4. Bend the loop back over itself until the tip is over the sleeving material.

5. Pinch the loop and sleeving material together, and pull the knotless loop over itself until the tip is at the center of the sleeving material. Pinch the tip of the loop and the sleeving material together and pull on the trailing edge of the line to form a padded loop. Make sure the loop tightens around the sleeving material and not on itself. (See Illus. 81.)

6. Attach your clips (the Cross-Lok type that opens at both ends) so that the loops lock on the padded area only! (See Illus. 82.)

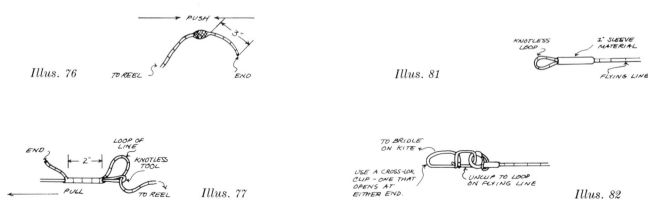

Illus. 76

Illus. 77

Illus. 81

Illus. 82

Handle Attachment

1. Cut about a 24″ piece of sleeving material; heat-seal the ends and fold in half.
2. (See Illus. 83.) Insert the loop of your flying line through the loop of the sleeving material.
3. (Illus. 84.) Bring the ends of the sleeving material through the loop in the flying line and pull tight.
4. Be sure the flying line loop does not pull on itself.
5. (Illus. 85.) Attach the ends of the sleeving material to your handles.

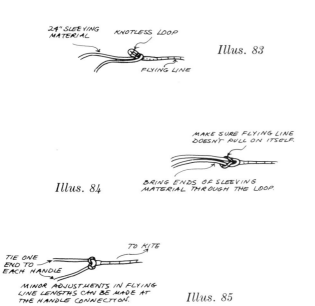

Illus. 83

Illus. 84

Illus. 85

Splicing Lines

1. Compress the line to loosen the weave, as shown with the knotless loop.
2. (See Illus. 86.) Insert the tool tip (latch open) in line A about 6″ from the end. *Push* the line onto the tool for about 2″ and exit the line.
3. Use the tool to pick up line B and pull it back through line A.
4. (Illus. 87.) Next, insert the tool into line B about 4″ down from where it enters line A. Exit line B about 1″ from where it enters line A.
5. (Illus. 88.) Pick up line A and pull it back through line B.
6. (Illus. 89.) Trim both ends and smooth out the completed splice.

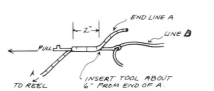

Illus. 86

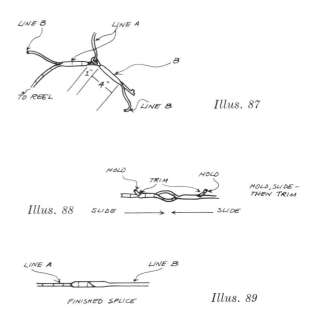

Illus. 87

Illus. 88

Illus. 89

Sleeving Line—an Alternative to the Knotless System

A quick alternative to the knotless system is to simply sleeve the flying line and make an overhand loop on both ends. A wire-loop sleeving tool is required.

1. Cut a length of Dacron sleeving 12″ long and heat-seal the ends to prevent fraying.
2. (See Illus. 90.) Insert the tool through the sleeve and pick up the flying line.
3. Pull the line back through the Dacron sleeve.
4. (Illus. 91.) Tie an overhand loop in the sleeved line.
5. (Illus. 92.) Attach your clip or handle to the sleeved loop.

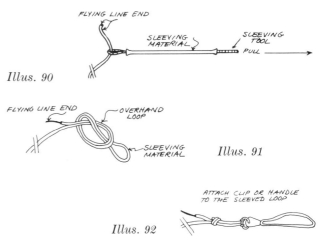

Illus. 90

Illus. 91

Illus. 92

[1]Knotless system, instruction and tips, courtesy Fran Gramkowski, High Fly Kite Company.

12
Working with Ripstop Nylon

It is perhaps no accident that the best all-around kite fabric was originally developed as an inexpensive synthetic replacement for silk in the production of parachutes during World War II. Ripstop nylon is commonly used today for spinnakers on sail boats and for wind-breaker jackets. Available in a kaleidoscope of colors, ripstop has all the properties of a nearly ideal kite fabric: low weight, high tear strength, and almost no porosity.

The word *ripstop* was coined from the way the fabric is woven. Within the tight nylon weave, a larger-diameter thread runs crisscross, forming a checkerboard of small squares. This interwoven grid gives the material *rip-stopping* properties. Should the fabric get punctured, the hole will not spread but remain contained within the interlocking network of small squares—an especially important characteristic for parachutes.

Coated with urethane (which holds up better than ripstop coated with acrylic), ripstop is virtually wind- and waterproof. The urethane coating makes the fabric look slick and shiny. Inspect the material carefully; sometimes there is more coating on one side than the other. When you are making a kite, you want the slicker side facing the wind.

Ripstop is available in weights per square yard. For example, .75-oz.-grade ripstop, popular among kite builders, is its weight per square yard. (See the Sail Material Chart at a Glance on pages 39–40.) Dif-fering-weight horizontal strips of ripstop can be combined on a kite without offsetting kite balance (see Illus. 93).

Marking

Before you begin marking,[1] use masking tape, lead bars, or heavy magnets to keep the fabric taut and stationary on your cutting table. Employing magnets of different weights and sizes on a metal work surface covered with ¼" tempered plate glass is an especially good way of securing fabric. Plan the layout of the kite by arranging the templates until you get maximum use out of the material. You also need to consider the bias, or the diagonal, in the material. Because even ripstop has a tendency to stretch along the bias, you will have to plan how the kite parts will be cut to maintain an even bias on both sides of the kite. An uneven bias arrangement in horizontally sensitive kites, such as deltas, will cause the kite to lean to one side. Although box kites and parafoils, for example, are less prone to imbalance due to grain orientation, an uneven bias will eventually diminish performance.

Ripstop, as with all woven cloth, is strongest on the straight part of the weave. To combat fabric fatigue and stretch, the preferred method of cutting ripstop is to follow the sail maker's rule: The grain (the straight of the weave) should follow the unsup-

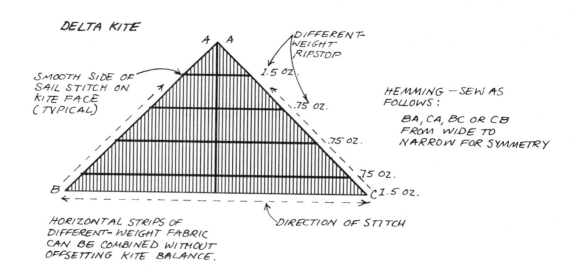

Illus. 93. A delta kite made of differing-weight ripstop.

ported edges of the sail. Because ripstop isn't always cut and wound straight onto the roll at the factory, lay the edges of your pattern along the *straight of the grain* as a guide for a perfect cut. See Illus. 94–97, as well as Illus. 104 (page 57).

Transfer the shape of the template onto the fabric (see Chapter 14). Be sure to allow enough material for hems and spar sleeves. A black lead pencil is my favorite marker.

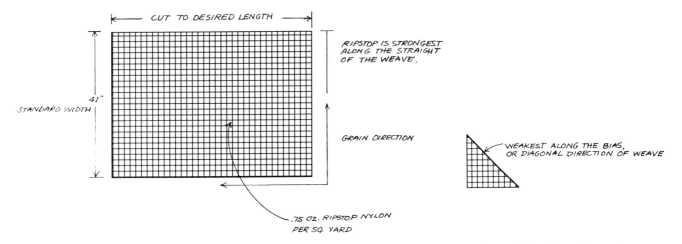

Illus. 94. Cut ripstop along the straight of the weave, where it's strongest. Paper, plastic, and Tyvek can be cut in any fashion because they have no grain direction.

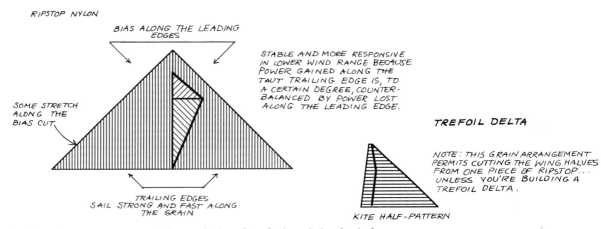

Illus. 95. Good grain arrangement for deltas designed to fly in minimal wind.

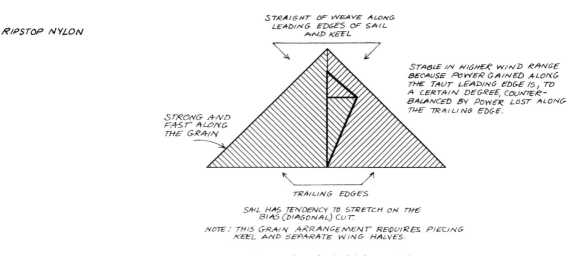

Illus. 96. Good grain arrangement for deltas designed to fly in higher wind.

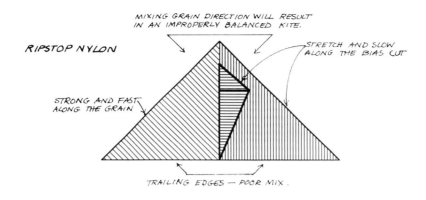

MIXING GRAIN DIRECTION WILL RESULT IN AN IMPROPERLY BALANCED KITE.

RIPSTOP NYLON

STRETCH AND SLOW ALONG THE BIAS CUT

STRONG AND FAST ALONG THE GRAIN

TRAILING EDGES — POOR MIX.

Illus. 97. Wrong grain arrangement for any delta kite.

Cutting

Your options for cutting include a scissors, hobby knife, or hot cutter. Scissors are your best option if you don't have a suitable cutting surface. With the fabric held taut, barely open the *sharp* scissor blades and begin cutting by moving the scissors through the material. Practise on scraps first. (Scissors work particularly well when you are cutting trash-bag-grade plastic.)

The surface that facilitates the fastest cutting and the one that will last indefinitely is ¼″ tempered plate glass. Alternative cutting surfaces include Formica and tempered Masonite board. Use a Formica surface you no longer need since a hobby knife will scratch it and the heat of a hot cutter will alter its color. You can use the smooth side of ¼″ tempered Masonite board, although it dulls blades quickly and, when you're hot-cutting, ripstop sticks to it. Glass is so superior to any other cutting surface that I recommend its use for best results. Companies specializing in replacing commercial windows, often listed in the phone book yellow pages, are a good source of inexpensive ¼″ tempered plate glass. They will often have salvageable remnants from a broken store window that can be cut to your specifications. You can usually strike a bargain. Remember to have them smooth all the edges.

In terms of straightedges, yardsticks, strips of wood, Formica, and Masonite are all workable options. While a metal straightedge is alright for use with a hobby knife, metal will absorb heat from a low-watt hot-cutter tip and reduce cutting efficiency. Tempered Masonite is a better choice for a straightedge since it is unaffected by high temperatures and draws virtually no heat from a hot cutter. An inexpensive and efficient way to go is to have a lumber yard cut a number of ¼″ tempered Masonite board strips to various lengths: 2″ × 24″, 2″ × 36″, 2″ × 48″, and so on. Make sure the edges are smooth so that your hot-cutter tip won't stick and get caught up on snags during cutting. Any ripstop sticking to the Masonite edge after cutting can be easily peeled away.

Hot-cutting is my preferred method for cutting ripstop nylon because in one economical action, it cuts clean, seals the edge, and prevents fraying. Although it's not necessary if you're hemming or tape-binding the edges, I still prefer hot-cutting ripstop as a matter of practice. The lower temperatures are suited to slower hand speeds—the higher temperatures to faster hand speeds. Practise on scraps until you find a hand speed and temperature that suits you.

Although a hot cutter fitted with a flat spade or pencil tip will cut ripstop adequately, a cone-shaped tip used with a Teflon guide wheel is an excellent system for both cutting and adding hem widths. For even heat distribution, don't let fabric residue build up on the tip. Keep it clean with a fine wire brush. *Note: When hot-cutting ripstop, ventilate your work area to minimize inhaling potentially irritating fumes.*

Sewing

When sewing you will need to keep the ripstop seams and edges aligned. With patience and skill you can hold separate pieces of fabric together by hand as you sew, though this is a tedious process. A more convenient method, as mentioned throughout this book, is hot-cutting two layered pieces of ripstop; this fuses the layers for a baste strong enough to keep the edges together until sewn.

You can also baste with masking tape or glue sticks. Although glue sticks are convenient, residue will quickly build up on your needle unless you spread the adhesive outside the stitch line. In general, for those areas difficult to hold in place by hot-cutting, such as a double-fold hem, my preference is to spot-weld with a hot tacker and sew (see Illus. 98).

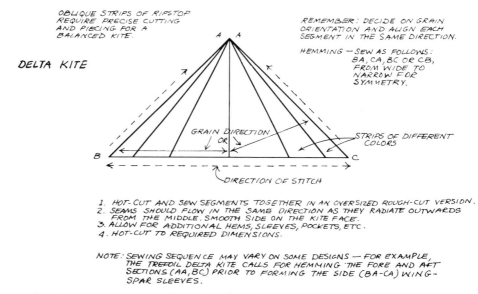

OBLIQUE STRIPS OF RIPSTOP REQUIRE PRECISE CUTTING AND PIECING FOR A BALANCED KITE.

DELTA KITE

REMEMBER: DECIDE ON GRAIN ORIENTATION AND ALIGN EACH SEGMENT IN THE SAME DIRECTION.

HEMMING — SEW AS FOLLOWS: BA, CA, BC OR CB, FROM WIDE TO NARROW FOR SYMMETRY.

GRAIN DIRECTION OR

STRIPS OF DIFFERENT COLORS

DIRECTION OF STITCH

1. HOT-CUT AND SEW SEGMENTS TOGETHER IN AN OVERSIZED ROUGH-CUT VERSION.
2. SEAMS SHOULD FLOW IN THE SAME DIRECTION AS THEY RADIATE OUTWARDS FROM THE MIDDLE. SMOOTH SIDE ON THE KITE FACE.
3. ALLOW FOR ADDITIONAL HEMS, SLEEVES, POCKETS, ETC.
4. HOT-CUT TO REQUIRED DIMENSIONS.

NOTE: SEWING SEQUENCE MAY VARY ON SOME DESIGNS — FOR EXAMPLE, THE TREFOIL DELTA KITE CALLS FOR HEMMING THE FORE AND AFT SECTIONS (AA, BC) PRIOR TO FORMING THE SIDE (BA-CA) WING-SPAR SLEEVES.

Illus. 98. Piecing and sewing sequence must always be planned in advance.

Edge Binding

Although hems can be used (Illus. 99), there are other ways of binding edges. Single- or double-fold polyester/cotton bias tape works well when binding

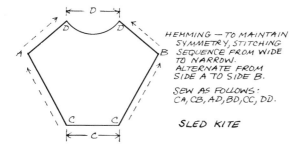

HEMMING — TO MAINTAIN SYMMETRY, STITCHING SEQUENCE FROM WIDE TO NARROW. ALTERNATE FROM SIDE A TO SIDE B.

SEW AS FOLLOWS: CA, CB, AD, BD, CC, DD.

SLED KITE

Illus. 99. Calculate the kite's total dimensions based on how you want to finish the edges. Extra fabric is necessary for hems. For a simple sled kite, hot-cut ripstop, which won't fray, and dispense with a hem. For a neat touch, add single-fold bias tape over the hot-cut edges.

around curves. For a strong, lightweight, ¼", single-fold, homemade edge binding, hot-cut 1" strips of .75 oz. or 1.5 oz. ripstop and fold ¼" of each side inward towards the middle. Cut these ripstop strips on the bias to accommodate curves, otherwise cut with the straight of the grain. When every ounce counts, as it does with the Stone Mountain Kite, using ripstop strips for edge binding as well as for longeron sleeves shaves fractions of ounces off the total weight.

Sometimes the edge binding has to serve as both hem and spar sleeve. Double-fold bias tape, available in polyester/cotton blends, can often serve this dual purpose, though the color range is limited and larger sizes may be difficult to obtain at your local store. Taffeta, on the other hand, is available in many colors and can be cut on the bias to form strips of any size. Piece the taffeta strips together by joining each sec-

tion along a diagonal cut. By making a zigzag stitch using the same color thread, you can create a nearly invisible seam when the strips are folded and stitched onto the kite. This taffeta technique is put to good use in making the elliptical curved wing of the Hewitt Flexkite project. The technique is shown in Illus. 100.

Needle and Thread

A regular sharp needle used with cotton-covered polyester thread is fine for most kites. High-tension kites, such as parafoils, require a stronger polyester or a nylon-bonded thread. Don't buy cheap bargain thread. You don't want your kite falling apart under stress. Adjust your sewing machine to eight stitches per inch for a basic straight stitch. More stitches per inch may weaken the ripstop and cause tearing at the seams. A zigzag stitch can be set to 15 or 16 stitches per inch.

Repairs

Crack-and-peel ripstop nylon repair tape is an adhesive-backed fabric available in 2" rolls and a variety of colors. Cut a piece to overlap your tear by 1½" to 2". Peel off the protective backing, position the tape over the tear, and paste it down. Next, burnish the area completely with a spoon or other tool. This forces the glue to spread out evenly onto the ripstop. For added strength, go over the repaired area with a warm iron. Don't try to remove the patch at this time. To permanently repair your tear, let the patch set for two days and then remove it.

---

[1]Tips for working with ripstop nylon courtesy of Bill Tyrrell, The Fabric Lady.

ALTHOUGH BIAS-TAPE BINDING
IS COMMERCIALLY AVAILABLE,
SOMETIMES A FINISH REQUIRES
CUSTOMIZATION FOR VARIOUS
REASONS. SIZE, COLOR, WEIGHT,
AND PURPOSE MAY BE FACTORS.

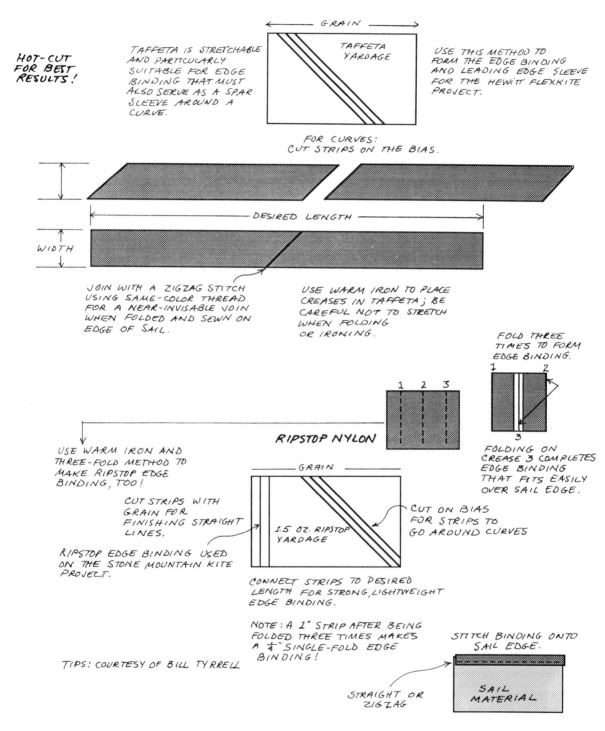

TAFFETA OR RIPSTOP

HOT-CUT
FOR BEST
RESULTS!

GRAIN

TAFFETA
YARDAGE

TAFFETA IS STRETCHABLE
AND PARTICULARLY
SUITABLE FOR EDGE
BINDING THAT MUST
ALSO SERVE AS A SPAR
SLEEVE AROUND A
CURVE.

USE THIS METHOD TO
FORM THE EDGE BINDING
AND LEADING EDGE SLEEVE
FOR THE HEWITT FLEXKITE
PROJECT.

FOR CURVES:
CUT STRIPS ON THE BIAS.

DESIRED LENGTH

WIDTH

JOIN WITH A ZIGZAG STITCH
USING SAME-COLOR THREAD
FOR A NEAR-INVISABLE JOIN
WHEN FOLDED AND SEWN ON
EDGE OF SAIL.

USE WARM IRON TO PLACE
CREASES IN TAFFETA; BE
CAREFUL NOT TO STRETCH
WHEN FOLDING
OR IRONING.

FOLD THREE
TIMES TO FORM
EDGE BINDING.

1   2

3

FOLDING ON
CREASE 3 COMPLETES
EDGE BINDING
THAT FITS EASILY
OVER SAIL EDGE.

1   2   3

USE WARM IRON AND
THREE-FOLD METHOD TO
MAKE RIPSTOP EDGE
BINDING, TOO!

RIPSTOP NYLON

CUT STRIPS WITH
GRAIN FOR
FINISHING STRAIGHT
LINES.

RIPSTOP EDGE BINDING USED
ON THE STONE MOUNTAIN KITE
PROJECT.

GRAIN

1.5 OZ. RIPSTOP
YARDAGE

CUT ON BIAS
FOR STRIPS TO
GO AROUND CURVES

CONNECT STRIPS TO DESIRED
LENGTH FOR STRONG, LIGHTWEIGHT
EDGE BINDING.

NOTE: A 1" STRIP AFTER BEING
FOLDED THREE TIMES MAKES
A ¼" SINGLE-FOLD EDGE
BINDING!

TIPS! COURTESY OF BILL TYRRELL

STITCH BINDING ONTO
SAIL EDGE.

STRAIGHT OR
ZIGZAG

SAIL
MATERIAL

Illus. 100. Making your own edge binding.

13
Making a Full-Size Kite Pattern

Unless you already have a full-size pattern for your kite, you will need a technique to enlarge your small design to a working template.

Kite patterns composed of angles—essentially straight lines arranged in squares, triangles, and rectangles—are sized up by simply measuring the stated lengths and connecting lines to form a shape. Delta, Eddy, and box kites are in this group.

While designs containing curves, radius cuts, or scallops can be sized up through precise measurements, this method is somewhat difficult and time-consuming. Instead, consider the following four techniques to make a full-size template of your pattern.

- **Opaque projector** (Illus. 101.)   Most libraries and schools have one. They can enlarge your designs to any size you choose by projecting your small drawing onto sheets of paper or cardboard. Trace the projected image for a full-size template.
- **Pantograph** (Illus. 102.)   A relatively inexpensive tool that can be adjusted to enlarge your drawing. As you trace the smaller design, the opposite end of the tool sketches the full-size pattern onto paper or another suitable surface.
- **Square to Square** (Illus. 103.)   Begin by drawing a graph of equally spaced squares over a copy of your design. Next, draw a larger grid of an equal number of squares on your template material. With the smaller-design grid for reference, use a pencil to make dots where the design outline touches lines on the larger graph. By focusing on where a particular line passes through a square (⅓, ½, or ¾ up), you can quickly connect the dots. Sketch in the pattern square by square until a rough pattern is completed. Now, go back and smooth out all the lines with a soft-tip marker, and you've got your full-size template.

    Hint: Establishing a whole-number scale (no fractions or inches) expedites drawing a relationship between the smaller and larger grid. Let's say your full-size kite is 6 feet tall. If each square on the smaller grid represents one square inch, draw 72 real inch squares on your full-size grid to create the pattern.
- **Computer-generated pattern**   A highly efficient method for both designing kites and producing patterns. See Illus. 128–130 on pages 72–73 in "Kite Design by Computer."

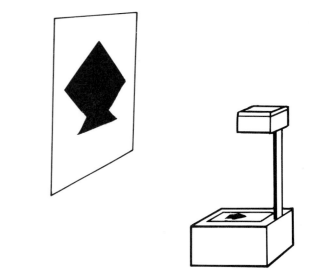

Illus. 101. Opaque projector.

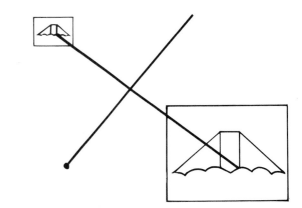

Illus. 102. Pantograph.

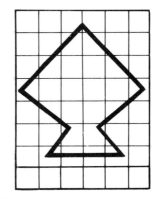

Illus. 103. Square to square.

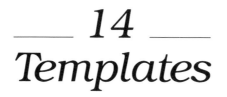

14
Templates

A template is a full-size pattern that is used as a guide in marking and cutting material. You have two options when cutting a kite sail: You can either measure and mark dimension lines directly onto the material or make a template of the pattern with the required dimensions for each kite part. The latter method, however, is a recommended step in the kite-making process that repays the builder with more evenly cut and better-flying kites.

Directly marking the material works best for kites composed of interconnecting straight lines, such as delta, Eddy, and box kites. Simply connect the points and use a straightedge when cutting. Curves are more difficult to cut without a template.

Margaret Greger, author of *Kites for Everyone*, takes an approach to kite making that reflects the clothing end of sewing. She recommends using a dressmaker's tracing wheel and large sheets of tracing paper in dark and light colors to transfer the pattern onto the fabric. "If you are cutting two pieces or two sides at once," she says in her book, "tracing paper under the fabric, facing up, and on top of the fabric, facing down, will enable you to mark both ends at once."

Template Materials

Which template material you choose depends largely on your requirements. Plain paper is adequate for one-time use. However, a more durable template made of tagboard or cardboard is a must in a classroom situation when you're cutting many designs for eager would-be kite builders.

Heavier-weight kraft paper is sufficiently stiff to last through marking and cutting several kites. Kraft paper is also easily cut, so it's a good choice when making numerous intricate appliqué templates of different shapes. White kraft paper, commonly called white butcher's paper, works well, too.

In addition to various paper stocks, more permanent template materials include:

- .020″-grade aluminum-sheet stock—thin and easily cut with metal shears. Flatten with a rubber mallet; smooth the edges with sandpaper. (See the Sting Ray Kite project.)
- ³⁄₁₆″ foam board—lightweight, rigid, strong. Made of polystyrene foam laminated between two paper board facings. Cut with a razor or hobby knife.
- ⅛″ plywood or tempered masonite sheet—stiff, per-

manent, and often used in classrooms for the durable half-template for the ubiquitous sled kite. Teachers can enlist the aid of shop classes to saw these templates.

Tips

1. One way to ensure precise stitching lines is to make the template the same size as the finished kite. Once the shape is traced onto the material, the outline then becomes the exact fold line for stitching. Prior to cutting, remember to add allowances to the outline for seams, spar sleeves, hot-cutting-trim overlap, and so forth.
2. Whenever possible, use half-pattern templates to ensure symmetry. For precise cutting, place the template over material that is held absolutely flat on the work surface. Templates are also helpful in aligning edges with the grain as well as getting the most economical cut from the fabric with kites made from several pieces. (See Illus. 104.)
3. When hot-cutting, plain paper templates often stick to the fabric. Should this happen, carefully separate the template from the fabric with a hobby knife or thin letter opener.

The Teflon Cutting Wheel Solution[1]

Problem: When hot-cutting sail material using cardboard templates and other paper products, the intense heat of the hot-cutter tip burns and destroys the template edges in the process.

Solution: A Teflon cutting wheel permits the use of inexpensive cardboard templates and cuts smoothly while preventing wear along the template edge. Teflon has a high tolerance to heat and will not deteriorate during the cutting process.

Problem: Once you have cut a template to the finished dimensions of the kite as recommended in Tip #1, it is difficult to trace one or more uniform parallel hem lines, especially around curves, from the template edge.

Solution: A Teflon wheel makes a convenient guide in marking the additional hem allowance. A set of Teflon wheels in sizes of ¼″, ⅜″, ½″, and so on, makes tracing the required hem width a simple matter.

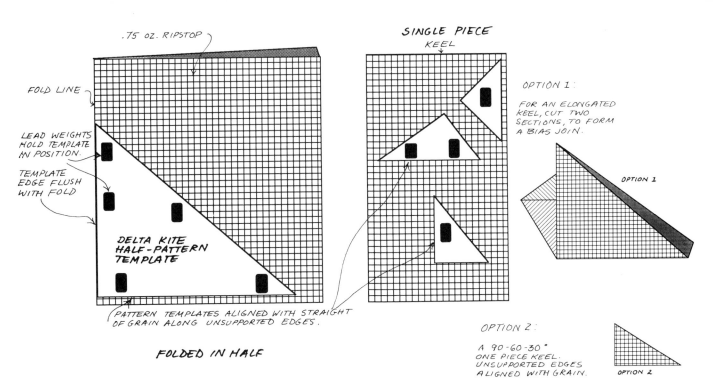

.75 OZ. RIPSTOP

FOLD LINE

LEAD WEIGHTS
HOLD TEMPLATE
IN POSITION.

TEMPLATE
EDGE FLUSH
WITH FOLD

DELTA KITE
HALF-PATTERN
TEMPLATE

PATTERN TEMPLATES ALIGNED WITH STRAIGHT
OF GRAIN ALONG UNSUPPORTED EDGES.

FOLDED IN HALF

SINGLE PIECE
KEEL

OPTION 1:

FOR AN ELONGATED
KEEL, CUT TWO
SECTIONS, TO FORM
A BIAS JOIN.

OPTION 1

OPTION 2:

A 90-60-30°
ONE PIECE KEEL.
UNSUPPORTED EDGES
ALIGNED WITH GRAIN.

OPTION 2

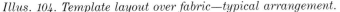

Illus. 104. Template layout over fabric—typical arrangement.

How to Make a Teflon Cutting Wheel

The cutting wheel is made from a ¼″ sheet of Teflon. The idea is to construct a wheel with a funnel-shaped hole in the middle and a flanged edge that slips under the template. A conical-shaped hot-cutting tip inserted into the hole easily guides the wheel.

Illus. 105 shows a Teflon cutting wheel. In the cutaway view:

- A is the countersunk hole for the conical-shaped hot-cutting tip.
- B is the tapered flange that slips under the template edge.
- C is the vertical wall that rolls against the template edge.
- D is the diameter, or twice the hem width.
- R is the radius, which determines the hem width and represents the distance between the hot-cut line and the edge of the template.

To construct a Teflon cutting wheel, follow these steps:

1. After deciding on finished-wheel size, saw an oversized disk from the Teflon sheet.
2. Locate the precise center of the roughly hewn circle and mount it on a hobby lathe machine.
3. Use a chisel to cut and smooth the wheel to your desired overall diameter, twice the radius, or hem width, as shown in Illus. 105. Work slowly and gauge your progress frequently. You can always

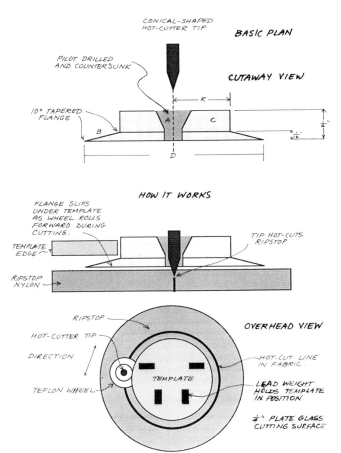

CONICAL-SHAPED
HOT-CUTTER TIP

BASIC PLAN

CUTAWAY VIEW

PILOT DRILLED
AND COUNTERSUNK

10° TAPERED
FLANGE

HOW IT WORKS

FLANGE SLIPS
UNDER TEMPLATE
AS WHEEL ROLLS
FORWARD DURING
CUTTING.

TEMPLATE
EDGE

RIPSTOP
NYLON

TIP HOT-CUTS
RIPSTOP.

OVERHEAD VIEW

RIPSTOP

HOT-CUTTER TIP

DIRECTION

TEFLON WHEEL

TEMPLATE

HOT-CUT LINE
IN FABRIC

LEAD WEIGHT
HOLDS TEMPLATE
IN POSITION

¾″ PLATE GLASS
CUTTING SURFACE

Illus. 105. Teflon cutting wheel.

shave away excess, but you can't add to the Teflon. Use an angled chisel to form a 1⁄16″ tapered flange to ±10°. Round off any burrs on the sharp edge of the flange to prevent it from catching on the pattern.

4. Mount the wheel on a drill press. First drill a pilot hole and then countersink to form the tunnel-shaped opening that allows freedom of movement for the conical-shaped hot-cutter tip.

5. Place a pencil inside the hole and run it along a template to verify that the radius, or hem width, is correct.

[1]Concept used with permission of Curtis Marshall. His article on the subject, "A New Nylon Cutting Technique," first appeared in *Kite Lines*, Summer 1979, page 19.

15
Reaping What You Sew

Sewing is not difficult—it simply requires a positive state of mind. Make a detour around frustration: Don't sew when you're tired and prone to making errors. A steady pace makes for even stitches, which is more important than speed. Familiarize yourself with your sewing machine and try out all its features. You can only learn to sew by sewing.

Different fabrics have individual sewing characteristics. Because of its slippery texture, ripstop nylon needs constant attention. For better control in

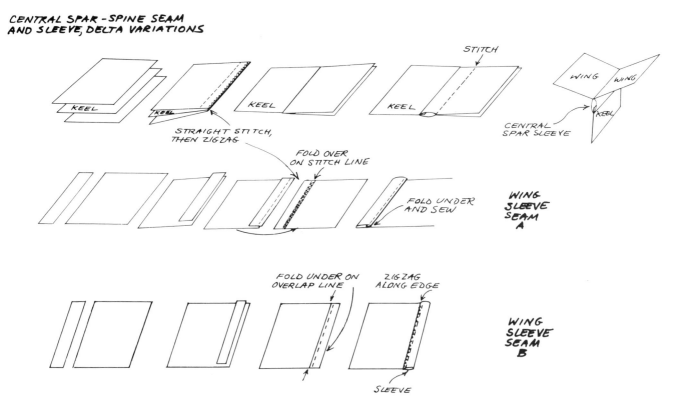

Illus. 106. Wing-sleeve seam (A and B) and central spar sleeve.

guiding ripstop through your machine, use Tacky Fingers or a similar product—or simply wet your fingers on a damp sponge. Tyvek and cotton have a coarser texture and are less likely to shift about as you sew.

Before beginning work on the actual kite sail, practise on scraps until you get a feel for the sewing machine and how the fabric responds. As a rule, you act as a guide while the machine pulls the fabric through as it stitches. Experiment with different stitches and at different speeds. Soon, you will discover a natural flow taking place between you and your sewing machine. Careful work, sometimes inching your way across a seam, is the hallmark of patience and a well-crafted kite.

The seams and stitching combinations in Illus. 106–113 are useful in kite making.

Illus. 107. Double-fold edge seam.

Illus. 108. Bias-tape seam.

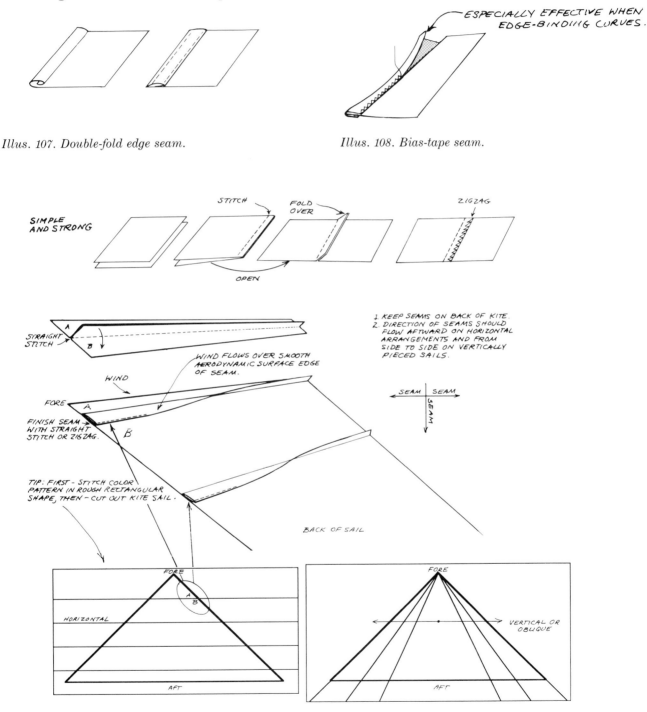

Illus. 109. Sail seam.

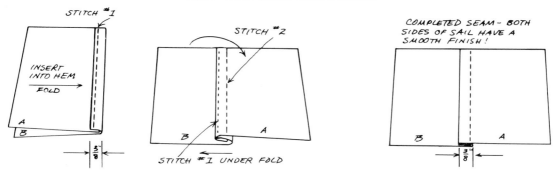

A STRONG AERODYNAMIC SEAM – NO DRAG
FROM LOOSE EDGES ALONG HEMS!

STITCH #1

INSERT INTO HEM
FOLD

A
B

3/8"

STITCH #2

STITCH #1 UNDER FOLD

B
A

COMPLETED SEAM – BOTH
SIDES OF SAIL HAVE A
SMOOTH FINISH!

B
A

3/8"

Illus. 110. Flat fell seam.

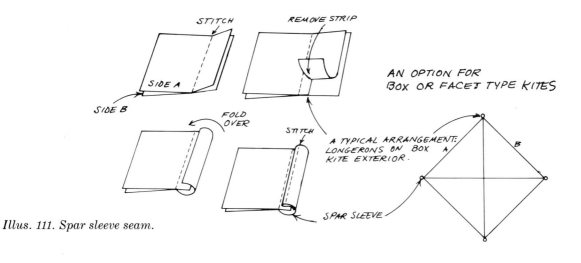

STITCH

SIDE A

SIDE B

REMOVE STRIP

FOLD OVER

STITCH

SPAR SLEEVE

AN OPTION FOR
BOX OR FACET TYPE KITES

A TYPICAL ARRANGEMENT:
LONGERONS ON BOX
KITE EXTERIOR.

B
A

Illus. 111. Spar sleeve seam.

STITCHES

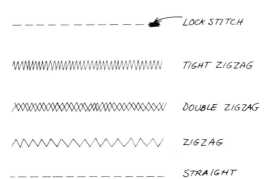

LOCK STITCH

TIGHT ZIGZAG

DOUBLE ZIGZAG

ZIGZAG

STRAIGHT

Illus. 112. Useful stitches.

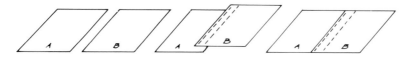

A   B   A B   A   B

Illus. 113. Lapped-join seam.

16
Heat Sealing

Taping and gluing are two ways to build polyethylene (plastic) and Tyvek kites, though these bonds eventually deteriorate. Another method worth exploring is a more permanent technique called heat sealing. Manufacturers of plastic kites have been using a form of heat sealing for many years.

Although soldering irons and hot cutters have been used to heat-seal plastic, results have been inconsistent because even the lowest-wattage unit produced too much heat. Without the proper temperature setting, heat sealing was a hit-or-miss proposition.

The key to the problem was to somehow regulate the heat. While sophisticated, electronically controlled temperature soldering guns are available, there is a less expensive solution. The soldering iron, or gun, is plugged into a dimmer switch that is, in turn, plugged into an outlet. See Illus. 114. Wattage of the soldering unit is not critical because the tem-

perature is controlled by adjusting the dimmer switch.

Use Illus. 114 for reference in setting up a heat-sealing session. For straightedges, use strips of Formica or tempered masonite; these materials are poor conductors of heat and won't reduce the effective working temperature of the smoothing tip. The plastic on the bottom won't stick to the ¼" plate-glass surface.

Begin with simple joins. Experiment with dimmer settings and how fast you move the tip over the seam. The combination of heat and speed makes for a solid, uniform seal along the plastic seam. Wax paper keeps the hot tip from sticking to the plastic. Replace the wax paper as necessary since it deteriorates quickly with each pass of the smoothing tip.

Once sealed, let the plastic seam cool for a few minutes. Inspect the bond for uniformity and holding

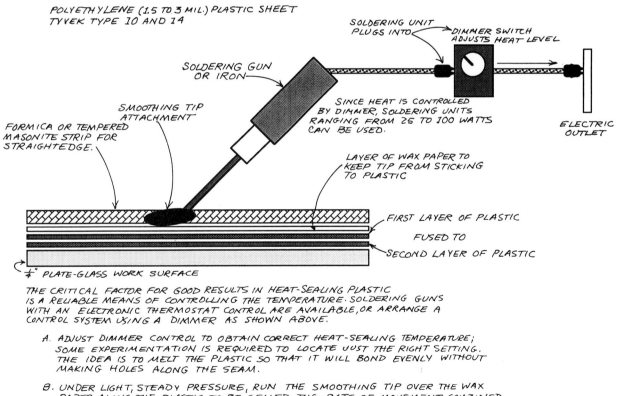

THE BASIC CONCEPT

POLYETHYLENE (1.5 TO 3 MIL.) PLASTIC SHEET
TYVEK TYPE 10 AND 14

SOLDERING UNIT PLUGS INTO

DIMMER SWITCH ADJUSTS HEAT LEVEL

SOLDERING GUN OR IRON

SMOOTHING TIP ATTACHMENT

SINCE HEAT IS CONTROLLED BY DIMMER, SOLDERING UNITS RANGING FROM 25 TO 100 WATTS CAN BE USED.

FORMICA OR TEMPERED MASONITE STRIP FOR STRAIGHTEDGE.

ELECTRIC OUTLET

LAYER OF WAX PAPER TO KEEP TIP FROM STICKING TO PLASTIC

FIRST LAYER OF PLASTIC

FUSED TO

SECOND LAYER OF PLASTIC

¼" PLATE-GLASS WORK SURFACE

THE CRITICAL FACTOR FOR GOOD RESULTS IN HEAT-SEALING PLASTIC IS A RELIABLE MEANS OF CONTROLLING THE TEMPERATURE. SOLDERING GUNS WITH AN ELECTRONIC THERMOSTAT CONTROL ARE AVAILABLE, OR ARRANGE A CONTROL SYSTEM USING A DIMMER AS SHOWN ABOVE.

A. ADJUST DIMMER CONTROL TO OBTAIN CORRECT HEAT-SEALING TEMPERATURE; SOME EXPERIMENTATION IS REQUIRED TO LOCATE JUST THE RIGHT SETTING. THE IDEA IS TO MELT THE PLASTIC SO THAT IT WILL BOND EVENLY WITHOUT MAKING HOLES ALONG THE SEAM.

B. UNDER LIGHT, STEADY PRESSURE, RUN THE SMOOTHING TIP OVER THE WAX PAPER ALONG THE PLASTIC TO BE SEALED. THE RATE OF MOVEMENT COMBINED WITH THE TEMPERATURE OF THE TIP WORK TOGETHER FOR A SOLID, EVEN JOIN.

Illus. 114. Heat sealing.

power along the seam. Test the bond by tugging at it. A strong bond will hold. If the seam comes apart, more heat is required, so try again.

Note: Bonding polyethylene to polyethylene and Tyvek to polyethylene works, though Tyvek to Tyvek *does not*. While it is possible to fuse Tyvek to itself using only heat, strong seals are not possible because melting the material destroys its fibre structure.

Some application ideas:

• Fuse small sheets of different-colored plastic together to create your own design.

• Decorate Tyvek kites (sewn or glued) by fusing (appliqué style) colored plastic onto the sail area.
• Fuse Tyvek on stress areas of plastic kites; use Tyvek to form spar pockets and sleeves.
• Fuse a Tyvek keel to a plastic delta, as shown in Illus. 115. The advantage of Tyvek over a plastic keel is that it won't deform under stress in higher winds.

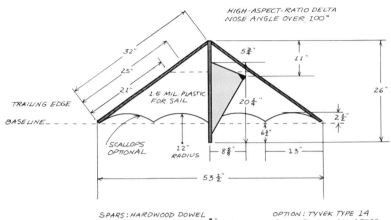

Illus. 115. A heat-sealing project.

17

Kite Graphics—Piecing and Appliqué

Colors: vibrant, subdued, stimulating, eye-pleasing! Designs: provoking abstractions or stark realism! Whether simply combining strips of fabric or piecing together an intricate appliqué, colors and designs can elevate an ordinary kite to heights of artistic expression.

Ripstop nylon is a strong, lightweight, durable, and highly translucent fabric that resists conventional means of decorating, such as drawing with soft-tip markers or painting. This seeming drawback, however, presents an opportunity: By connect-

ing strips of different-colored ripstop or doing elegant appliqué work, all kinds of dramatic designs are possible. Since you can draw or paint on other kite-sail materials—like paper, Tyvek, and plastic—the focus here will be on ripstop nylon, though the principles of piecing and appliqué can be applied to other fabrics—like taffeta and cotton poplin. (For information on decorating other materials, see the Sail Material Chart at a Glance on pages 39–40.)

When thinking of graphics in general, consider that your kite will be seen from a distance of at least

62

several hundred feet. Simple patterns in bold, contrasting solid colors show up best. Refer to the kites in this book for ideas. Before committing your ripstop to the hot cutter, try out your color combinations first. One method is to sketch your kite on white paper and then make photocopies of your drawing. Use colored soft-tip markers to create several designs in different colors; then hold them up to a light source and select the scheme that looks best. You can also create different-colored designs on a computer. Because shapes and colors can be changed and combined instantly with a computer paint program, the effort turns into play. (See "Kite Design by Computer.")

Once you're pleased with your design, hang swatches of ripstop in your color combinations against a sunny window for a true reading of how your kite will appear in flight. While you're there, see what colors are possible by layering. Generally, two layers of the same color intensify the original color while three layers create a dark, almost opaque effect. By using multiple layers of different colors, you can create subtle gradations of tone and shading.

A dark color framing a lighter color enhances both the appearance and size of the kite. If you've decided to use only one color for your kite, offsetting the kite perimeter with black or a contrasting edge binding will make a definitive aerial statement.

Appliqué

Appliquéing means laying pieces of fabric on top of each other for an ornamental effect. While it's true that precise detail work on a kite is often lost at a distance, the overall look of appliqué is visually striking, whether viewed indoors on a wall or outdoors overhead. See Illus. 116 and 117 for examples of appliqué work from Kevin Shannon's Warrior Rokkaku kite. It's best to use larger (at least 6 feet), stable kite forms as a canvas for appliqué. To provide a dimensionally stable sail for your appliqué work, use one oversized underlying piece of fabric in the basic shape of the kite for the background. This is important if there are many small pieces to be applied or if you will be cutting away large pieces from the background.

Dark and light backgrounds create different looks. Dark backgrounds provide a stained-glass effect; that is, after you cut away the fabric to let the sun shine through. Light backgrounds, white in particular, are best for appliquéd kites having many shapes and colors. A white background often intensifies the appliquéd colors, and you don't have to cut any of it away; since ripstop is lightweight, this material will not significantly affect the kite's flight performance.

After you've cut all your individual appliqué

Illus. 116. Appliquéd Warrior Rokkaku kite.

pieces, it's a good idea to position them on your background material to see how your design looks close up and from a distance. Small strips of Scotch double-stick tape work well for this. In the excitement of laying out your kite design, don't forget to make allowances for hems, sleeves, keels, pockets, and any other structural elements that might interrupt the flow of your graphics.

Illus. 117. Appliqué detail.

The Pattern

White ripstop can serve as both the pattern and the background material if you don't mind the tracing lines showing on the back of the kite. Using the wrong side of the sail material, draw the full-size design directly onto the white ripstop. Use a lead pencil or, for a coordinated look, a soft-tip marker the same color as the appliqué piece to fit in that space. Not confident about your freehand style? Use different-size straightedges and plates as guides.

Once the outline of the design is complete, place

colored pieces of ripstop, which will become the appliqué sections, over the pattern. The outline of the design on the white background will show through the colors. Trace the outline of each individual section of the design onto each piece of colored ripstop. Hint: When you are tracing patterns onto a *dark* sail background, use a light table or similar device to shine light through the pattern.

Now, carefully cut out the ripstop sections along the marked borders. Hot-cutting each appliqué section will prevent fraying.

If you don't want tracing marks on your sail material, you can draw the design on kraft paper, poster board, or other suitable template material, and then cut out the individual sections to be used as templates. (For more information on templates, turn to Chapter 14.) Depending on how close you have come to the edge when hot-cutting around the templates, each piece of ripstop will have a slight overlap. This extra material can be used in manipulating each piece to fit (overlap or butt as necessary) in the final design.

Keeping the Pieces in Place

You will have to use some technique to keep the individual pieces of ripstop in place while sewing. Although pinning, basting, fusible bonding, and using glue sticks will work, my choice is using either a hot tacker (a sail maker's tool designed for this purpose) or 3M's Photo Mount Spray Adhesive. Each has its own merits.

Position the appliqué pieces on the *face* of the sail. As a rule, dark colors should overlap light colors. If you are using different-weight ripstop, the heavier should be on the bottom.

Hot-Tacking

Even though you could hot-tack each color section from the face side, try this method instead. Because colors will show through a white sail, try hot-tacking from the back, or wrong side, of the kite towards the front. As it spot-welds both pieces of fabric, the fine point of the hot tacker will make a smaller, less noticeable hole coming from the back to the face side of the kite. (See Illus. 118.) Hot-tack around each piece at 1″ to 2″ intervals. Then stitch over all tack marks for an impeccable look.

Spray Adhesive

This method works well if you follow these rules:

- Make sure your work area is ventilated to avoid inhaling potentially irritating fumes.
- Practise on scraps first.

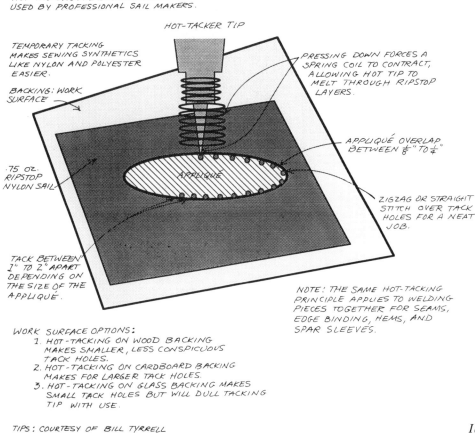

HOT TACKERS ARE BASTING TOOLS USED BY PROFESSIONAL SAIL MAKERS.

HOT-TACKER TIP

TEMPORARY TACKING MAKES SEWING SYNTHETICS LIKE NYLON AND POLYESTER EASIER.

BACKING: WORK SURFACE

PRESSING DOWN FORCES A SPRING COIL TO CONTRACT, ALLOWING HOT TIP TO MELT THROUGH RIPSTOP LAYERS.

APPLIQUÉ OVERLAP, BETWEEN ⅛″ TO ¼″

APPLIQUÉ

.75 OZ. RIPSTOP NYLON SAIL

ZIGZAG OR STRAIGHT STITCH OVER TACK HOLES FOR A NEAT JOB.

TACK BETWEEN 1″ TO 2″ APART DEPENDING ON THE SIZE OF THE APPLIQUÉ.

NOTE: THE SAME HOT-TACKING PRINCIPLE APPLIES TO WELDING PIECES TOGETHER FOR SEAMS, EDGE BINDING, HEMS, AND SPAR SLEEVES.

WORK SURFACE OPTIONS:
1. HOT-TACKING ON WOOD BACKING MAKES SMALLER, LESS CONSPICUOUS TACK HOLES.
2. HOT-TACKING ON CARDBOARD BACKING MAKES FOR LARGER TACK HOLES.
3. HOT-TACKING ON GLASS BACKING MAKES SMALL TACK HOLES BUT WILL DULL TACKING TIP WITH USE.

TIPS: COURTESY OF BILL TYRRELL

Illus. 118. Hot tacking.

- Spray the back of the smaller piece to be applied to the larger background fabric.
- Use plenty of newspaper or other protective covering in your work area.
- Use the absolute minimum of spray to hold the ripstop in place. Wait 5 minutes for some drying to take place, and then apply the piece to the background fabric. Hint: Rubber-cement thinner will remove spray adhesive from ripstop.
- Too much spray will gum up your sewing needle and make your kite sail permanently tacky, and who wants a tacky kite that picks up sand, dust, and other debris?

Hint: When placing individual appliqué pieces onto a blank background, select a major reference point and build your design out from there. Whenever possible, working from the middle outward makes for better symmetry. If your design has a sizeable open gap where the background sail shows through, cut a scrap in this exact shape and temporarily position it on the sail. Use the scrap as your reference in placing the other design segments around it. Remove the scrap when done. Use rubber-cement thinner to dissolve any adhesive residue left on the sail.

Sewing

Sew one piece at a time. A straight stitch is the best all around. However, zigzag stitches are particularly good for going around curves, and can be used as a design element as well. Keep the sail as flat as possible while you work. Using edge binding along the kite's perimeter will help to stabilize the completed kite sail.

Hint: Use adhesive-backed 2-oz. Dacron for small appliqué pieces with curves that may be difficult to stitch. Available in colors, this material is used by sail makers to create permanent insignias on sails.

To Cut Away the Background or Not?

You have two options:

- Leave the background as is. This is perfectly acceptable and often preferable when the background enhances the colors.
- Cut away portions of the background to create a desired effect or to remove an unwanted effect.

If you choose to cut away background material, facing the back of the kite, separate the layers of fabric with a pin and carefully cut the back layer off with sharp scissors. You can cut as close to ⅛″ inch to the stitching without compromising the strength of the seam. The excess material can also be hot-cut. Use scissors to rough-out the back, leaving a 1″ edge. Next, put a curved metal edge under the fabric to ensure that your hot cutter won't do a worst-case scenario of burning a hole in the kite. A Dritz EZY Hem Gauge makes a good metal shield.

Finally, inspect the appliquéd sail against the sun to make sure everything checks out to your liking before completing the kite with hems, sleeves, and pockets.

[1]Thanks also to Jon Burkhardt for tips used in this chapter.

18

Tails and Drogues

The innovation of the self-correcting and buoyant bowed kite has given rise to a variety of tailless wonders. Nevertheless, the concept of the tail has not been abandoned. Though no longer strictly necessary, tails have continued to adorn and evolve with all kite forms. In some cases, the additional drag of adding a tail to a tailless kite increases the maximum wind range of the kite. Adding a tail, however, can change the kite's center of gravity; when this happens, adjust the fulcrum, or tow point, as necessary.

Tails existed on kites for thousands of years without any radical departure in design until Sir George Nares of England invented the wind cup during the nineteenth century. Nares's wind cup, or drogue, was a marked improvement over conventional tails in stabilizing flat and bowed kites. While both tails and drogues provide drag, or controlled resistance, as a means of stabilizing a kite, each operates on a different principle.

Tails cause drag by adding surface area to the

trailing edge of the kite. Pennants, banners, ladders, streamers, fringes, tassels, and pony tails (streamers flowing off a lead line) fall into the tail category. However, long serpent-type kites are simply flat, extended kites.

Drogues are short conical-shaped wind socks that are attached to the kite with a lead line. Open at both ends, drogues are self-regulated because they act like air buckets in tow—the greater the wind, the greater the resistance. In moderate winds, air channels through the tapered funnel uneventfully, with the kite flying straight and true despite the appendage. But when air compression through the opening increases in heavier winds, the overflow spills out, creating additional drag; this action forces the drogue to pull even harder, causing the kite to rely on the drogue for maintaining its horizontal equilibrium. Since the drogue works on the principle of leverage, longer lead lines are recommended for heavier-pulling kites; multiple drogues can be flown by connecting a series of lead lines.

While a tail seven to eight times the length of the kite's spine can be used as a guideline, the only way to tell if the tail isn't too short or too long is to fly the kite. The quintessential tail allows the kite to fly in the widest wind range by automatically compensating for any imbalances.

Here are a few tail and drogue variations.

- **Pennants and banners** (Illus. 119.) A pennant is simply a fully tapered tail; a banner is a parallel tail with an optional slight taper.
- **Ladders** (Illus. 120.) Built on the ladder concept, these tails resemble narrow paper-and-bamboo roll-up shades. They are supported by battens, so they are stiffer, offering considerable drag for hard-pulling kites. They provide excellent stability for flat kites, especially the serpent variety.
- **Drogues** (Illus. 121 and 122.) This no-nonsense basic wind cup can be made to rotate, adding glamour to its stodgy image.
- **Tubes** (Illus. 123.) These lantern-type tails combine elements of traditional banner tails and drogues. The ends of the inflatable tails may be left open or closed (open on Pterosaur Kite project, closed on Sting Ray Kite project).
- **Spinners** (Illus. 124 and 125.) These parachutelike creations are swirling drogues in drag, and can lend a kinetic charm to any kite. Spinners can also be flown off the flying line for decoration or in a series, as with standard drogues.

Banner and pennant tails work best with flat kites. Use streamers with bowed kites. High-aspect-ratio designs with excessive lift often fare best with drogues. Pony tails work best with parafoils.

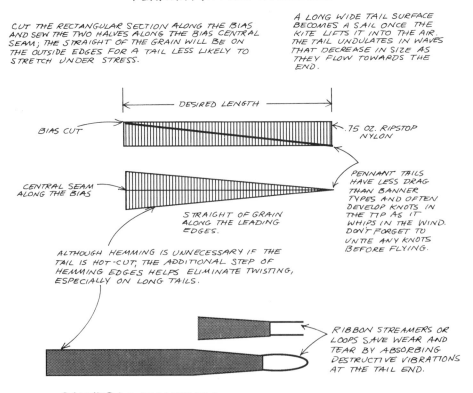

Illus. 119. Pennant and banner.

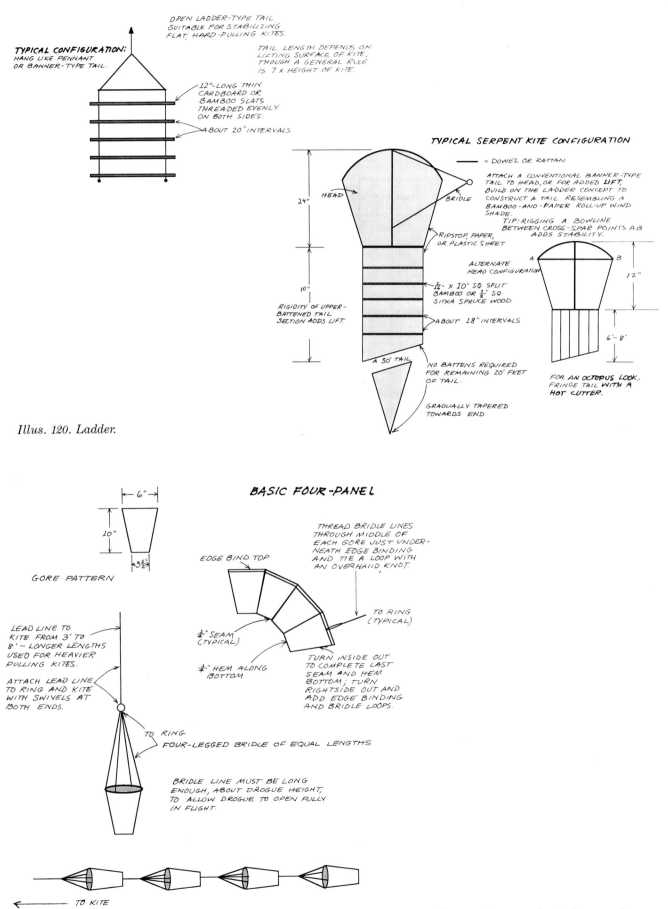

OPEN LADDER-TYPE TAIL
SUITABLE FOR STABILIZING
FLAT, HARD-PULLING KITES.

TYPICAL CONFIGURATION:
HANG LIKE PENNANT
OR BANNER-TYPE TAIL.

TAIL LENGTH DEPENDS ON
LIFTING SURFACE OF KITE,
THOUGH A GENERAL RULE
IS 7 X HEIGHT OF KITE.

12"-LONG THIN
CARDBOARD OR
BAMBOO SLATS
THREADED EVENLY
ON BOTH SIDES.

ABOUT 20" INTERVALS

TYPICAL SERPENT KITE CONFIGURATION

—— = DOWEL OR RATTAN

HEAD

24"

BRIDLE

ATTACH A CONVENTIONAL BANNER-TYPE
TAIL TO HEAD, OR FOR ADDED LIFT,
BUILD ON THE LADDER CONCEPT TO
CONSTRUCT A TAIL RESEMBLING A
BAMBOO-AND-PAPER ROLL-UP WIND
SHADE.
TIP: RIGGING A BOWLINE
BETWEEN CROSS-SPAR POINTS A B
ADDS STABILITY.

RIPSTOP, PAPER,
OR PLASTIC SHEET

ALTERNATE
HEAD CONFIGURATION

A   B

12"

10"

RIGIDITY OF UPPER-
BATTENED TAIL
SECTION ADDS LIFT.

1½" X 10" SQ. SPLIT
BAMBOO OR ⅛" SQ.
SITKA SPRUCE WOOD

ABOUT 18" INTERVALS

6'-8'

A 30' TAIL

NO BATTENS REQUIRED
FOR REMAINING 20' FEET
OF TAIL.

FOR AN OCTOPUS LOOK,
FRINGE TAIL WITH A
HOT CUTTER.

GRADUALLY TAPERED
TOWARDS END

Illus. 120. Ladder.

BASIC FOUR-PANEL

6"

10"

3½"

GORE PATTERN

EDGE BIND TOP

THREAD BRIDLE LINES
THROUGH MIDDLE OF
EACH GORE JUST UNDER-
NEATH EDGE BINDING
AND TIE A LOOP WITH
AN OVERHAND KNOT.

LEAD LINE TO
KITE FROM 3' TO
8'—LONGER LENGTHS
USED FOR HEAVIER
PULLING KITES.

ATTACH LEAD LINE
TO RING AND KITE
WITH SWIVELS AT
BOTH ENDS.

¼" SEAM
(TYPICAL)

¼" HEM ALONG
BOTTOM

TO RING
(TYPICAL)

TURN INSIDE OUT
TO COMPLETE LAST
SEAM AND HEM
BOTTOM; TURN
RIGHTSIDE OUT AND
ADD EDGE BINDING
AND BRIDLE LOOPS.

TO RING
FOUR-LEGGED BRIDLE OF EQUAL LENGTHS

BRIDLE LINE MUST BE LONG
ENOUGH, ABOUT DROGUE HEIGHT,
TO ALLOW DROGUE TO OPEN FULLY
IN FLIGHT.

TO KITE

DROGUES FLOWN IN SERIES

Illus. 121. Drogue—basic four-panel.

BASIC FOUR-PANEL WITH INTERNAL HELICAL FINS

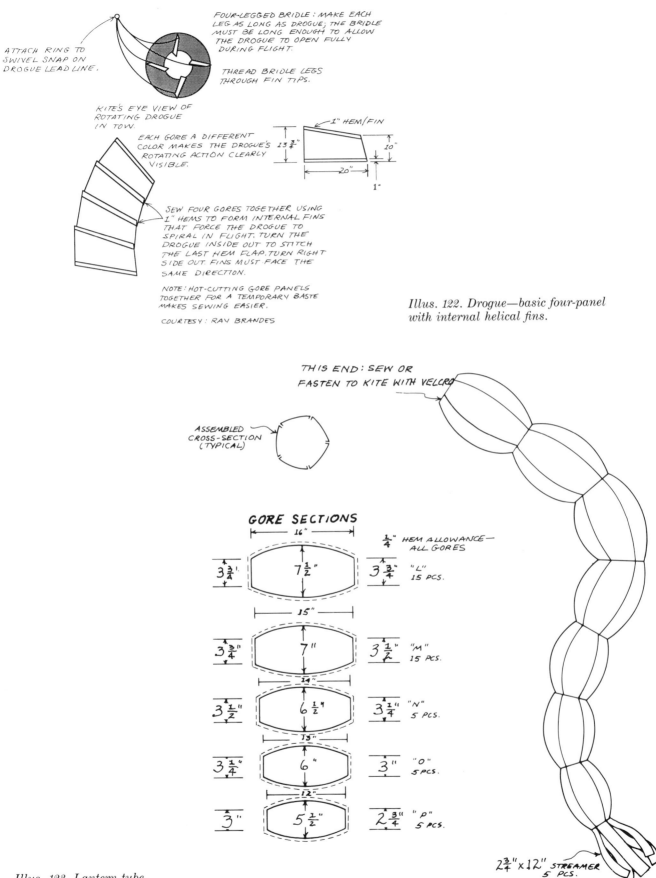

ATTACH RING TO SWIVEL SNAP ON DROGUE LEAD LINE.

FOUR-LEGGED BRIDLE: MAKE EACH LEG AS LONG AS DROGUE; THE BRIDLE MUST BE LONG ENOUGH TO ALLOW THE DROGUE TO OPEN FULLY DURING FLIGHT.

THREAD BRIDLE LEGS THROUGH FIN TIPS.

KITE'S EYE VIEW OF ROTATING DROGUE IN TOW.

EACH GORE A DIFFERENT COLOR MAKES THE DROGUE'S ROTATING ACTION CLEARLY VISIBLE.

1" HEM/FIN

13¾"

10"

20"

1"

SEW FOUR GORES TOGETHER USING 1" HEMS TO FORM INTERNAL FINS THAT FORCE THE DROGUE TO SPIRAL IN FLIGHT. TURN THE DROGUE INSIDE OUT TO STITCH THE LAST HEM FLAP. TURN RIGHT SIDE OUT. FINS MUST FACE THE SAME DIRECTION.

NOTE: HOT-CUTTING GORE PANELS TOGETHER FOR A TEMPORARY BASTE MAKES SEWING EASIER.

COURTESY: RAY BRANDES

Illus. 122. Drogue—basic four-panel with internal helical fins.

THIS END: SEW OR FASTEN TO KITE WITH VELCRO

ASSEMBLED CROSS-SECTION (TYPICAL)

GORE SECTIONS

16"

¼" HEM ALLOWANCE— ALL GORES

3¾" 7½" 3¾" "L" 15 PCS.

15"

3¾" 7" 3½" "M" 15 PCS.

14"

3½" 6½" 3¼" "N" 5 PCS.

13"

3¼" 6" 3" "O" 5 PCS.

12"

3" 5½" 2¾" "P" 5 PCS.

2¾" × 12" STREAMER 5 PCS.

Illus. 123. Lantern tube.

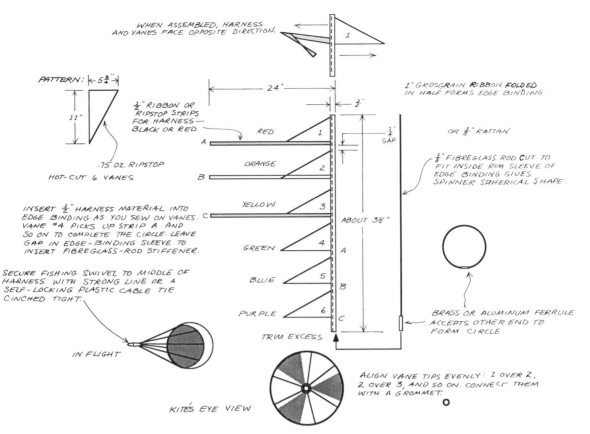

WHEN ASSEMBLED, HARNESS AND VANES FACE OPPOSITE DIRECTION.

PATTERN: ├─ 5¾" ─┤

11"

.75 OZ. RIPSTOP

HOT-CUT 6 VANES

½" RIBBON OR RIPSTOP STRIPS FOR HARNESS— BLACK OR RED

├──── 24" ────┤ ½"

A ─ RED 1

B ─ ORANGE 2

C ─ YELLOW 3

GREEN 4 A

BLUE 5 B

PURPLE 6 C

TRIM EXCESS

INSERT ½" HARNESS MATERIAL INTO EDGE BINDING AS YOU SEW ON VANES. VANE #4 PICKS UP STRIP A AND SO ON TO COMPLETE THE CIRCLE. LEAVE GAP IN EDGE-BINDING SLEEVE TO INSERT FIBREGLASS-ROD STIFFENER.

SECURE FISHING SWIVEL TO MIDDLE OF HARNESS WITH STRONG LINE OR A SELF-LOCKING PLASTIC CABLE TIE CINCHED TIGHT.

IN FLIGHT

KITE'S EYE VIEW

1" GROSGRAIN RIBBON FOLDED IN HALF FORMS EDGE BINDING.

OR ⅜" RATTAN

¼" GAP

ABOUT 38"

⅛" FIBREGLASS ROD CUT TO FIT INSIDE RIM SLEEVE OF EDGE BINDING GIVES SPINNER SPHERICAL SHAPE.

BRASS OR ALUMINUM FERRULE ACCEPTS OTHER END TO FORM CIRCLE.

ALIGN VANE TIPS EVENLY: 1 OVER 2, 2 OVER 3, AND SO ON. CONNECT THEM WITH A GROMMET.

Illus. 124. Rainbow windspinner.

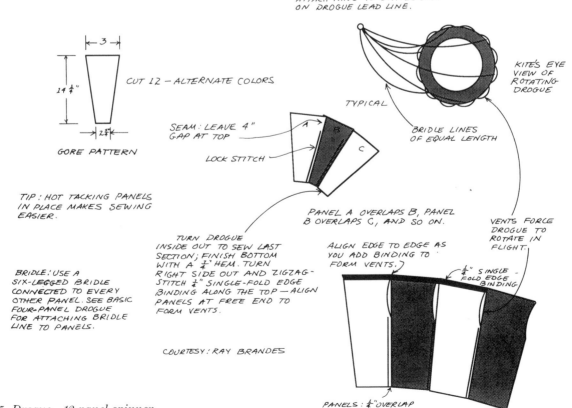

ATTACH RING TO SWIVEL SNAP ON DROGUE LEAD LINE.

├─ 3 ─┤

14 ¼"

├ 2¼" ┤

GORE PATTERN

CUT 12 — ALTERNATE COLORS

SEAM: LEAVE 4" GAP AT TOP

LOCK STITCH

A B C

TYPICAL

KITE'S EYE VIEW OF ROTATING DROGUE

BRIDLE LINES OF EQUAL LENGTH

PANEL A OVERLAPS B, PANEL B OVERLAPS C, AND SO ON.

TIP: HOT TACKING PANELS IN PLACE MAKES SEWING EASIER.

TURN DROGUE INSIDE OUT TO SEW LAST SECTION; FINISH BOTTOM WITH A ¼" HEM. TURN RIGHT SIDE OUT AND ZIGZAG-STITCH ¼" SINGLE-FOLD EDGE BINDING ALONG THE TOP — ALIGN PANELS AT FREE END TO FORM VENTS.

BRIDLE: USE A SIX-LEGGED BRIDLE CONNECTED TO EVERY OTHER PANEL. SEE BASIC FOUR-PANEL DROGUE FOR ATTACHING BRIDLE LINE TO PANELS.

ALIGN EDGE TO EDGE AS YOU ADD BINDING TO FORM VENTS.

VENTS FORCE DROGUE TO ROTATE IN FLIGHT.

¼" SINGLE-FOLD EDGE BINDING

COURTESY: RAY BRANDES

PANELS: ¼" OVERLAP

Illus. 125. Drogue—12-panel spinner.

Making a Tapered Lantern Tube Tail

Designed after Adrian Conn's Dragonfly

Construction

Use .75-oz. ripstop nylon, and follow these steps.

1. Make gore templates and cut out, as shown in Illus. 123 . Add a ¼″ hem allowance.
2. Sew the five sections of each lantern together with the right sides facing one another. The tail will be turned right-side out later. *Leave one seam open.*
3. Align and stitch the ends of all the lantern sections together. Hem the open end of the *first* lantern; then add streamers to the end lantern.
4. Run a stitch along the length of the open seam to close the tube. Turn the lantern inside out.
5. Velcro strips are convenient for connecting the tail to the kite, or use your own fastening method.

19

Kite Design by Computer

Computer-savvy readers will readily grasp the benefits of a drafting or computer aided design (CAD) program for kite design. For those unfamiliar with personal computers, kite design can be a great way to discover how working on a computer encourages exploration.

Just as word processing has all but made the conventional typewriter obsolete, CAD programs are replacing traditional methods of drafting and designing.[1] While you must still direct the CAD program, the net result is like having a team of architects and graphic artists at your disposal.

Although using pencil and paper or a computer to work on a kite design is a personal choice, a common reaction after using a CAD program goes like the old saw: *I've been rich and I've been poor, and believe me, rich is better*—rich, in this case, is using the computer.

A well-engineered CAD program, such as MacDraft for the Macintosh computer, provides an environment in which you can intuitively express your ideas without having to deal with the tedious aspects of the design process. The major advantage of CAD programs is that you can draw and manipulate life-size objects on your computer screen. A drawing scale set at ¾″ = 1′, for example, covers most drawing requirements for a kite designer. Overall, computerizing kite designs provides an inherently effi-

cient drawing system. And existing work can be saved in a file for retrieval and editing at a later time.

Operations

Begin by utilizing your CAD program to illustrate an existing kite design. After that, the sky is the limit in designing your own kite.

1. What will my kite look like if I match this color with that color? You can take out your colored pencils and begin filling in the empty spaces on paper, or take part in some software magic made possible by a computer paint program. With just slight movements of the mouse—the device for manipulating on-screen information, especially useful in drawing—you can manipulate an electronic palette of colors. (My preference is the Turbo mouse from Kensington.) You can instantly combine colors and instantly change them, until you arrive at a color scheme for your kite sail that pleases you.

Design

2. Drawing to scale manually is a laborious task that is compounded in difficulty if the design calls for precise curves and radius cuts. But with a CAD program, such as MacDraft, the process is greatly simplified.

Illus. 126 shows a computer screen, labelled "My Kite," from a Macintosh with MacDraft's tool box palette. All functions are visually oriented and ac-

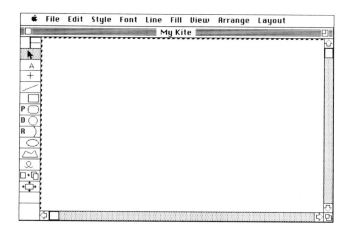

Illus. 126. Macintosh computer screen with MacDraft's tool-box palette (courtesy of Innovative Data Design, Inc.).

tivated by a mouse that is also used to draw objects on the screen. By selecting a tool from the vertical box on the left or choosing a feature from the horizontal options menu above the screen, you can easily set scale, and draw perfect lines and curves as well as geometric shapes to form objects. The compound kite shown in Illus. 127 is an example of a three-dimensional object drawn on the computer.

Here are a few operations to give you an idea of how the MacDraft tool box palette works. Activating the oval shape draws ovals; the D box draws

circles; and the R box creates a desired radius, as shown in the double-scalloped delta kite example in Illus. 128. By selecting *View* from the menu, you can zoom in for detail work or zoom out to see entire drawings; by selecting *Arrange*, objects can be rotated in one-degree increments. Select *Fill* from the menu for a variety of ink-and-fill patterns. Creating grid backgrounds to simulate the weave in ripstop nylon is especially helpful in determining grain orientation and template layout; adding various percentages of tone gives depth to perspective drawings, as with the compound kite in Illus. 127. Activating the next-to-last tool box from the bottom instantly duplicates your drawing.

3. Once the design dimensions and color combinations have been worked out, MacDraft will compute how much fabric of each color is required by automatically calculating areas of the desired object.

4. How to get the most out of your fabric is especially important when you are cutting with the grain. On-screen manipulation of templates over a grid determines, for example, the most economical use of ripstop nylon. See Illus. 129, as well as Illus. 104 on page 57.

Patterns:

5. No matter how you cut it, making a full-size pattern is time-consuming. But when the kite plan is stored on your computer, you can adjust your scale drawing to full-size and print the design. (See Illus. 130.) Once you have your full-size pattern, you can make a permanent template by pasting the printout over a sheet of ¼″ tempered Masonite board. Cut out each section as required.

Illus. 127. Macintosh computer and keyboard.

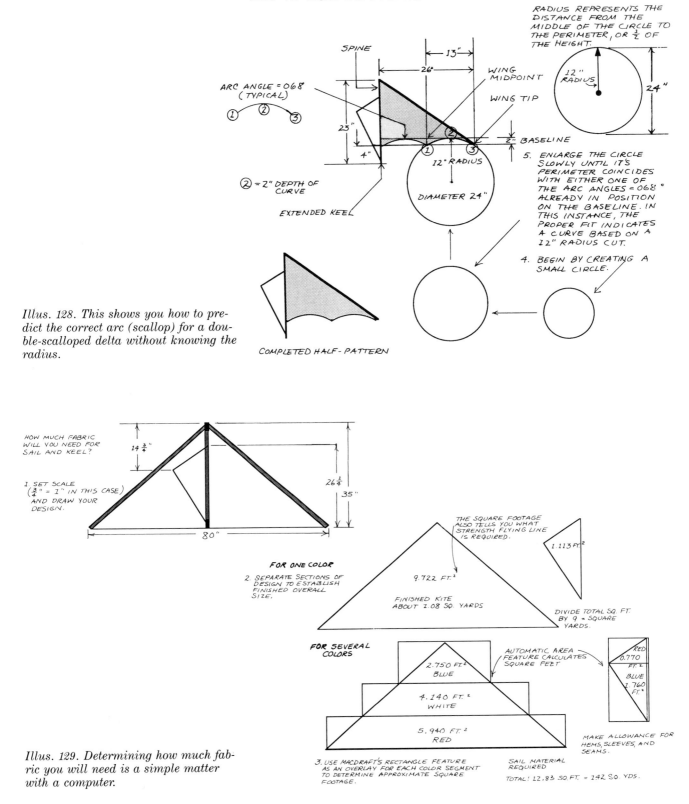

NOTE: DIMENSIONS ARE AUTOMATICALLY DISPLAYED ON COMPUTER SCREEN AS YOU WORK.

1. SET SCALE: ($\frac{3}{4}$" = 1' IN THIS CASE) AND DRAW.

2. LOCATE THE WING HALF MIDPOINT AND MARK THE POSITION.

3. ACTIVATE MACDRAFT'S 3-POINT RADIUS FEATURE TO FORM THE ARC. CONNECT THE THREE KNOWN POINTS 1-2-3 AND MANIPULATE THE ARC UNTIL IT CONFORMS TO THE REQUIRED 2" HEIGHT — FITTING BETWEEN THE SPINE AND MIDWING AND FORMING AN ARC ANGLE = 068. WITH THE DUPLICATE FEATURE, MAKE COPY OF THE ARC AND POSITION IT BETWEEN THE WING MIDPOINT AND WING TIP ALONG THE BASELINE.

RADIUS REPRESENTS THE DISTANCE FROM THE MIDDLE OF THE CIRCLE TO THE PERIMETER, OR $\frac{1}{2}$ OF THE HEIGHT.

SPINE

13"

26"

WING MIDPOINT

WING TIP

12" RADIUS

24"

ARC ANGLE = 068 (TYPICAL)

① ② ③

23"

② 3

①

2" BASELINE

4"

12" RADIUS

DIAMETER 24"

② = 2" DEPTH OF CURVE

EXTENDED KEEL

5. ENLARGE THE CIRCLE SLOWLY UNTIL IT'S PERIMETER COINCIDES WITH EITHER ONE OF THE ARC ANGLES = 068° ALREADY IN POSITION ON THE BASELINE. IN THIS INSTANCE, THE PROPER FIT INDICATES A CURVE BASED ON A 12" RADIUS CUT.

4. BEGIN BY CREATING A SMALL CIRCLE.

COMPLETED HALF-PATTERN

Illus. 128. This shows you how to predict the correct arc (scallop) for a double-scalloped delta without knowing the radius.

HOW MUCH FABRIC WILL YOU NEED FOR SAIL AND KEEL?

14 $\frac{3}{4}$"

26 $\frac{1}{4}$"

35"

1. SET SCALE ($\frac{3}{4}$" = 1" IN THIS CASE) AND DRAW YOUR DESIGN.

80"

FOR ONE COLOR

2. SEPARATE SECTIONS OF DESIGN TO ESTABLISH FINISHED OVERALL SIZE.

THE SQUARE FOOTAGE ALSO TELLS YOU WHAT STRENGTH FLYING LINE IS REQUIRED.

1.113 FT.²

9.722 FT.²

FINISHED KITE ABOUT 1.08 SQ. YARDS

DIVIDE TOTAL SQ. FT. BY 9 = SQUARE YARDS.

FOR SEVERAL COLORS

AUTOMATIC AREA FEATURE CALCULATES SQUARE FEET

2.750 FT.² BLUE

4.140 FT.² WHITE

5.940 FT.² RED

RED 0.770 FT.²

BLUE 1.760 FT.²

MAKE ALLOWANCE FOR HEMS, SLEEVES, AND SEAMS.

Illus. 129. Determining how much fabric you will need is a simple matter with a computer.

3. USE MACDRAFT'S RECTANGLE FEATURE AS AN OVERLAY FOR EACH COLOR SEGMENT TO DETERMINE APPROXIMATE SQUARE FOOTAGE.

SAIL MATERIAL REQUIRED

TOTAL: 12.83 SQ. FT. = 1.42 SQ. YDS.

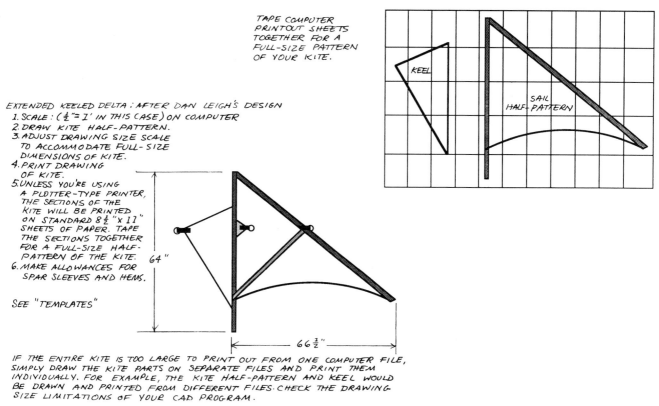

TAPE COMPUTER PRINTOUT SHEETS TOGETHER FOR A FULL-SIZE PATTERN OF YOUR KITE.

KEEL

SAIL HALF-PATTERN

EXTENDED KEELED DELTA : AFTER DAN LEIGH'S DESIGN
1. SCALE : (½" = 1' IN THIS CASE) ON COMPUTER
2. DRAW KITE HALF-PATTERN.
3. ADJUST DRAWING SIZE SCALE TO ACCOMMODATE FULL-SIZE DIMENSIONS OF KITE.
4. PRINT DRAWING OF KITE.
5. UNLESS YOU'RE USING A PLOTTER-TYPE PRINTER, THE SECTIONS OF THE KITE WILL BE PRINTED ON STANDARD 8½" X 11" SHEETS OF PAPER. TAPE THE SECTIONS TOGETHER FOR A FULL-SIZE HALF-PATTERN OF THE KITE.
6. MAKE ALLOWANCES FOR SPAR SLEEVES AND HEMS.

SEE "TEMPLATES"

64"

66½"

IF THE ENTIRE KITE IS TOO LARGE TO PRINT OUT FROM ONE COMPUTER FILE, SIMPLY DRAW THE KITE PARTS ON SEPARATE FILES AND PRINT THEM INDIVIDUALLY. FOR EXAMPLE, THE KITE HALF-PATTERN AND KEEL WOULD BE DRAWN AND PRINTED FROM DIFFERENT FILES. CHECK THE DRAWING SIZE LIMITATIONS OF YOUR CAD PROGRAM.

Illus. 130. Making a full-size pattern by computer.

[1]Computer-generated line art can be found throughout this book.

20

Maneuverable Kites—Eastern Fighters and Western Stunt Kites

There are two kinds of maneuverable kites: the single-line fighter originally from the Far East and the dual-line steerable stunt kite of the West. Though their number of lines distinguishes one from the other by definition, they are also world's apart in terms of design, custom, and operation.

How these two types of maneuverable kites fly is representative of their different characters. The magic of a paper-and-bamboo fighter is its agile responsiveness in a mere whisper of wind. In contrast,

a steady 15–20-mph-plus wind harnesses the raw pulling power of a high-tech stunt kite made of epoxy tubing and ripstop nylon. (See Illus. 131 and 132 for an example of both types of kites.)

As different as these kites are, East does meet West in one harmonious respect: Maneuverable kites as a group are simultaneously the most physically demanding and the most relaxing kites to fly. If you view relaxation as a state of mind clearly focused, then this statement isn't as contradictory as it may

Fighter Kites

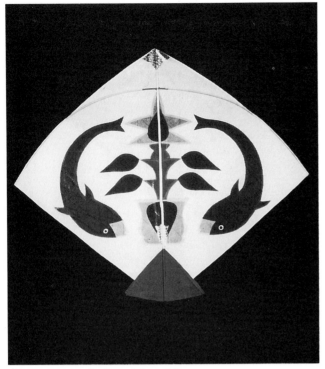

Illus. 131. An Indian fighter kite.

seem. Controlling a maneuverable kite calls upon the body and the mind to work together in discipline and concentration. By focusing on a single intention, a meditative by-product is achieved. A little practice on the flying field quickly verifies this paradoxical relaxed state. As you become adept at directing the kite overhead, extraneous thoughts dissolve. Rhythmic and coordinated eye-hand movements offer an almost hypnotically direct connection between you and the kite. Soon, the kite becomes an extension of yourself; nothing else exists. Your mind is set free to experience a retreat of the moment, secured at the end of the flying line.

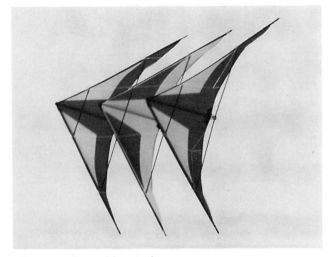

Illus. 132. Stunt kite stack.

Fighter kites spread outward over the centuries from ancient China as a result of imperialistic land grabbing, Mongol invasions, and European trade. By about 1200 A.D., the people of India, Korea, and Siam had incorporated the small, swift fighter kite into their arts, sports, and religion. Buddhist monks in the Far East found fighter kites particularly enlightening and carried them along on their pilgrimages. This is not surprising since Buddhism teaches the practice of meditation. With time, countries in the Far East developed a rich heritage surrounding the fighter kite. Construction, flying techniques, and rules became traditions—some held as family secrets that have been handed down by word of mouth through generations. The sport of flying fighter kites was inexpensive and served as a release for the people who lived a harsh rural life. The game varied from country to country but basically had the same combative nature throughout the Far East.

Europeans knew little about the East until the peripatetic Venetian explorer, Marco Polo, began snooping around the area in the thirteenth century. A keen observer, Polo noted the uses of kites in his journal as he trekked across China, India, and Southeast Asia.

Kite sculptor Tal Streeter provides an overview of fighter kites in his book *The Art of the Japanese Kite*[1]: ". . . generally, small, highly maneuverable kites were attached to strings partly coated with powdered glass (when it was available), sharp sand, or ground pottery, and sometimes scythelike knife blades. A kite fighter tried to bring another kite down out of the sky by skillful maneuvering. By crossing an opponent's line with his own and moving back and forth, he could wear away or cut the other flying line. At this point, the loser's kite floated away free, while the victor proclaimed his invincibility and challenged all bystanders."

The gossamer fighter kite of India, the quintessential fighter to many, is inseparable from the romanticism of the culture. Tales of gods and goddesses indulging in kite fighting are found in the ancient religious writings of the *Vedas* and in the classical Sanskrit epic of India, the *Ramayana*. During the Muslim reign in the fourteenth century, queens and princesses were kept in seclusion within palace walls; they were virtual prisoners in paradise, where their favorite pastime was kite fighting. Kites were also used as trusted go-betweens. For instance, a popular theme in Indian art shows a young lover skillfully landing his kite, containing a love note, into the hands of a maiden isolated in a tower.

Folk tales, like kite festivals, abound in India.

There is a legend of the fabulously wealthy, though spiritually bankrupt, King Gupta, who longed for *something more*. Hearing of the king's plight, a wise doctor arrived at the palace with a kite under his arm and challenged the king to a *pench*, or kite-fighting contest. Although the king lost the match, he had actually won because he found what he was seeking: He had recaptured his vigor for living through the simple pleasure of watching his kite in the sky. After a long happy life, the king left his people this message written above his palace gate:

> *My kite is like the morning star*
> *an early candle in the sun*
> *my kite is beauty*
> *on the back of a rolling wind.*

This King Gupta legend and the poem appear in master Indian kite-flier Dinesh Bahadur's book *Come Fly a Kite*.[2]

The largest kite festival in India, the *Utran*, coincides with the beginning of the winter solstice. The celebration takes place in the state-capital city of Ahmedabad each year on January 14, the day the winds shift from the land to the Arabian Sea. Business as usual comes to a halt as millions of people converge upon the city to participate in the spectacle. From sunrise to sunset, kites nearly block out the sun as battles are orchestrated from crowded flat roofs. With the overwhelming number of people taking part, it is usually impossible to identify opponents.

In a typical year, Indian kite fliers go through millions of kites. These kites are professionally crafted by families who have been making kites for centuries. Prior to distribution, they store the kites in air-tight containers, where they contract and expand many times until seasoned during the year-long process. The Indian passion for kites is reflected in their native language of Hindi, in which there are more than 100 words for kite.

Kite flying has always been common in Thailand (formerly Siam). In the kite-fighting competitions in ancient Siam, the kites were imbued with gender identity and were handled by teams. These battles continue today—usually in March, in the public area adjacent to Bangkok's Grand Palace.

There is the male *chula* (Illus. 133) and the female *pakpao* (Illus. 134). Both are made from materials dictated by tradition. For example, the bamboo must be of the *sisuk* variety from Thailand's jungles; line is made from fibres combed from the bark of the *ban* tree. Construction is labor-intensive and must be carried out in the time-honored fashion. The process is slow and painstaking.

Ron Spaulding, founder of the Thai Kite Heritage Group in Bangkok, provides a fascinating look inside the culture. In the minds of the Thais, he says, the *chula* is a precision combat machine. Months are spent fine-tuning the kites for the annual competition, which lasts approximately 30 days. An incredible 20 to 30 years of kite-making experience is required to master the art of creating a truly

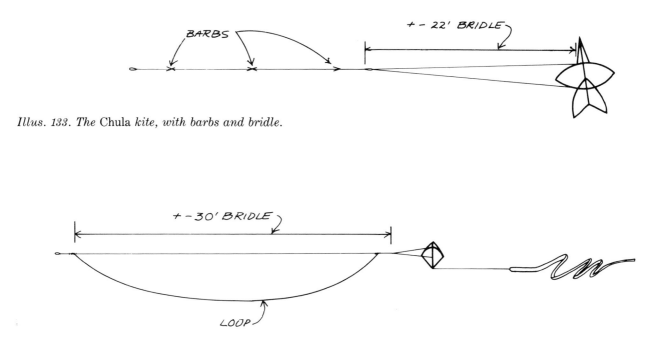

Illus. 133. The Chula *kite, with barbs and bridle.*

Illus. 134. The Pakpao *kite, with loop, bridle, and tail.*

maneuverable *chula* kite. There are perhaps fewer than 10 people out of the entire Thai population of 10 million who can make a true *chula* kite. Given these statistics, keeping the tradition alive in its pure form remains a challenge for Spaulding's Heritage Group.

The *chula* is a strong, over-7-feet-tall, five-pointed-star-shaped kite with barbs attached to its line for snagging the female. A team of at least 20 people is required to launch, maneuver, and retrieve a *chula*.

The *pakpao* is a petite, about-3-feet-tall, highly maneuverable and flirty diamond-shaped kite. It can ensnare its victim with either one of two feminine wiles: Its long tail can strangle the male, or it can trap him with the long loop hanging beneath its flying line.

The subtlety of the sport is that neither tries to destroy the other. The objective is not to cut but to engage. He attempts to abduct her; she attempts to capture him. Therein lies the game, which, by the way, is overseen by referees. As everyone recognizes the universal role of the players, spectators become as excited over the match as the handlers. Orchestras traditionally accompany a competition. If a *chula* abducts a *pakpao*, the music sadly laments her fate. If she captures him, the orchestra happily teases the male. Spectators can follow the action with their eyes closed.

Although Buddhism landed on the shores of Japan around the sixth century, Japan did not get wind of the small, agile fighter kite until early in the seventeenth century. Concerned that Christianity would undermine native customs and the political power of the shogun at the time, Japan remained for many years essentially an isolationist country. It was in the port city of Nagasaki that the formidable fighter kite called *hata* finally came into being. The word *hata* means flag in Japanese and suggests the route the kite took to reach the port of Nagasaki. Nearly identical in structure to the Indian fighter kite, the *hata* features the same red, white, and deep-blue color scheme of the Dutch flag. Because the tradition of flying *hata* fighter kites is found only in Nagasaki, it is accepted that the inspiration for the *hata* came from India by way of Dutch traders.

In *The Art of the Japanese Kite*, Streeter quotes Tadao Saito from his book *High Fliers: Colorful Kites from Japan*: "The strictest rule governing these hata kite fights is that the loser must bear no grudge. Ill feelings must not linger until the following day; instead, the battle must create between the combatants a link that should develop into friendship. This attitude of bloodthirsty battle contrasted by a sense of tranquility is typical of the southern part of Japan."

In the early 1960s, Surendra Bahadur introduced Indian fighter kites to New York City. Charismatic and friendly, Bahadur loved flying his kites in Central Park every Sunday, where he attracted crowds eager to try this new form of kite flying. He later opened the Go Fly A Kite shop on the upper East Side of Manhattan. His nephew and kite-fighting champion Dinesh Bahadur (author of *Come Fly a Kite*) had a flare for publicity and has successfully promoted the sport throughout the United States.

Stunt Kites

Modern dual-line stunt kites originated in the military. In 1942, Commander Paul Edward Garber designed an inexpensive moving-target kite for the U.S. Navy to use in gunnery practice (Illus. 135). Before then, according to Garber, gunnery practice primarily consisted of shooting at clouds.

Illus. 135. Paul Garber holding his invention, the U.S. Navy Target Kite Mark I, used for gunnery practice.

* * *

I first saw stunt kites in 1980, when I was living in Venice, California, a colorful beach community just south of Santa Monica. Along the wide expanse of beach, I would often see small, triangular rainbow stunt kites, in stacks numbering as many as fifty, tearing through the air. At the time, stunt kites were an oddity, even among kite fliers.

One day I was walking along the sand and heard a distinctive roar. I looked up and saw a chevron configuration about 6 feet wide swoop sharply overhead.

The unusual kite looked like a high-aspect-ratio hang glider in tow as it maneuvered downwind towards the water.

A bearded man wearing a baseball cap was the pilot. He seemed to be having a great time, so I approached him to find out more. The kite tacked horizontally along the beach, hovered, and landed in one smooth motion. The man told me he had designed the kite and was manufacturing it down in San Diego. As we spoke, people came up to him, as I had, and ended up buying a kite. The bearded man was Don Tabor, now president of Top of the Line Kites.

Since that encounter on Venice Beach nearly 10 years ago, Tabor has continued to demonstrate the merits of stunt kiting around the world. Today, stunt kites—with their dynamic action, precision control, and speed—have exploded onto the international kite scene. Flying stunt kites (power flying) has become a physically demanding and challenging new sport, and competition is in the wind for those who relish testing their own limits.

Stunt Kite Flying Basics[3]

Because stunt kites are designed to perform best under high stress, they require special handling and equipment—as well as a tenacious adherence to safety rules. Stunt kites operate on a simple principle: Pull right to go right and left to go left. Practise basic control over the kite first; style will come later.

Stunt kites are light (about one pound) and capable of speeds in excess of 70 mph; a Flexifoil was clocked at over a hundred! *At these speeds, irresponsible flying can cause injury and property damage. The axiom is this: Stunt kites are not dangerous, unless you are.*

Unlike conventional kites, dual-line stunt kites will not go up automatically and remain airborne; instead they must be properly launched and constantly steered to remain in the air.

Preflight Checklist

- Select a kite with sufficient room at the front and sides; stunt kites can fly ±90° to either side of the wind.
- Check wind speed and direction.
- Connect one end of the flight lines to the kite bridle, left to left and right to right.
- Unroll the flying lines completely, walking upwind until you reach the handles. The angle of the kite should be less than 30° to the wind direction so that the kite won't take off accidentally.
- Make sure both flying lines are exactly the same length and not crossed.
- Although a stunt kite can be self-launched, beginners would do well to have a friend prop the kite

against the wind in a ready position.
- Make sure the flight path is clear.

Flying Basics

- Begin with your hands side by side about chest high.
- In light winds, stepping back will add wind speed and ease launching; in stronger winds, the kite will rise from your friend's hands at your command.
- Don't forget that you are in control at all times. Don't oversteer as the kite rises. You must steer the kite upwards when launched. Keeping the kite straight the first few seconds is critical.
- Going straight: If you maintain equal tension on both flying lines with your hands even, the kite will move in a straight line in whatever direction it is pointed or already travelling in.
- Turning: Bring one hand towards your body. This will cause that side (wing) of the kite to stall and lose speed; the other wing will fly around the stalled one.
- If you pull harder on the left handle, the kite will turn left. It will continue turning left as long as you keep pulling harder with the left hand. Pulling harder on the right hand reverses the process.
- The arc (turn) of flight is maintained as long as your hands don't move (remain unequal).
- As the difference between the pulling of your hands increases, the turns get sharper. A slight pull produces a wide turn and a hard pull makes a sharp turn.
- Unwinding: A 360° turn, or loop, puts a twist in the flying line. You can still control the kite since the lines slide through the twists during maneuvers. Depending on what type of line is used, about 15 to 20 twists can be made before control is seriously hampered. Remove twists by looping in the opposite direction.

Landing

- Fly your kite to the edge of the wind until it hovers in one place. Hovering can be done at any height.
- When your kite is about one foot off the ground, quickly walk towards the kite and it will gracefully settle down.

Do's

- Think when you fly and stay alert for the unexpected.
- Maintain all equipment in good condition.
- Know your limitations; don't fly in winds that defy your ability to control the kite.
- Know your kite's operating limits.
- *In a dangerous situation, throw the handles down.*
- If you use loops or straps, make sure you can get out of them easily.
- Be courteous; take turns and yield to other fliers.

Your actions are important to the general public's image of the sport.

- Your flying area should be free of obstacles—such as trees and power lines, as well as pedestrians and vehicles. Stay away from congested areas in general.
- Make sure you have clearance behind you, as well, for maneuvering room.
- Be sure the potential flight path of your kite is clear of people. *Kevlar line can cut and injure.*

Don't's

- Don't underestimate the power and pull of the kite in strong winds, especially during dives.
- Don't lose track of where you are flying and wander into another's flight space.
- Don't leave your kite unattended; someone may trip over your flying line or, worse yet, launch your kite and become a danger to anyone in the area. A lone kite is an easy target for theft.
- Don't fly within 3 miles of an airport (federal law).
- Don't fly near power lines or in stormy weather.

Stunt Kite Maneuvers

Some common stunt kite maneuvers are shown in Illus. 136. *B* stands for basic, *I* for intermediate, and *E* for experienced.

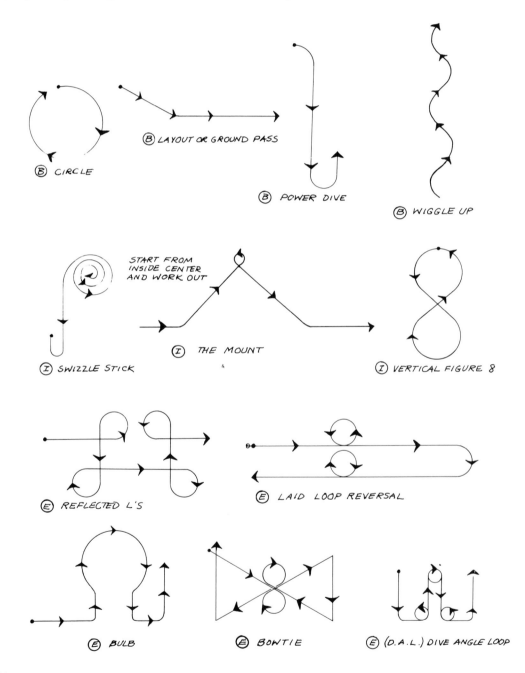

Illus. 136. Stunt kite maneuvers.

Turn to Chapter 49 for the Sanjo Rokkaku, Szilagi, and Nagasaki Hata fighter kite projects; turn to Chapter 55 for the Turbo Stunt Kite project.

The Flexifoil

The Flexifoil is a maneuverable kite capable of hurtling through the air in excess of 100 mph.

To the casual eye, the Flexifoil appears to be a modified Jalbert parafoil (see Chapter 38). Both kites are soft and have cells that inflate with air entering the leading edge. A closer look, however, reveals significant design differences. The parafoil is essentially an inflated fabric wing with a flat bottom, curved canopy, ventral fins, and shroud lines, and flies at a fixed angle of attack. Tethered only from its leading edge with two control lines, the teardrop-wing Flexifoil self-adjusts (shape of arc) in flight to wind speeds ranging from 8 to as much as 50 mph. The variable angle of attack is made possible by a *flexible* fibreglass-rod spar fitted along the leading edge of the *airfoil*, hence the name, *Flexifoil*.

Coinventors of the Flexifoil Ray Merry and Andrew (Wilf) Jones met in 1971 as first-year industrial design students at Newcastle-upon-Tyne Polytechnic College, situated 200 miles north of London in Northumberland. As part of a class assignment, they collaborated on sculptural forms of inflatable polyethylene. Though they quickly arrived at the basic idea for a wind-inflated airfoil, the production model Flexifoil took them several years to develop.

Ironically, Merry and Jones had no conscious intention of developing a kite, let alone a ma-neuverable one that could fly so fast. The idea was to create an air-lifting system that could raise sculptures into the sky. As for the parafoil, Merry didn't learn about Dom Jalbert's wind-inflated design until 1975. At first, Merry and Jones were disappointed upon seeing the parafoil, but then decided, apart from the inflation similarity, that they were developing something quite different. The Flexifoil came about independently through trial and error. Had Merry and Jones seen the parafoil earlier, they probably would have scrapped the entire project.

Merry summarized the development of the Flexifoil. He said that their approach in working with soft air-filled organic shapes was totally intuitive. They began working with polyethylene tubes, some 100 feet long. After trying various forms, they settled on bag shapes and soon graduated to more aerodynamic wing configurations in an attempt to make them fill up with air and fly. Adding the rigid cross stick along the leading edge of their kinetic-type sculptures came early on in their experiments. Flights were erratic. One day, however, everything fell into place. After flipping over on its back, the wing took off and adopted an improved high angle of flight. This was a purely accidental discovery.

The following rare photographs illustrate the evolution of the Flexifoil. (Unless otherwise noted, the photos are courtesy of Ray Merry.)

A 50' × 1.5' white poly-ethylene tube filled with wind, illustrating airflow currents.

79

Left: two bags on elastic rope for exploring turbulence. In front of college building, Newcastle-upon-Tyne, England, 1972. Bottom: Ray Merry flying a 3' × 8' clear polyethylene tube bag with a small opening on elastic rope over the frigid North Sea at Tyne-Mouth, England, in 1972.

Merry with an experimental 3' polyethylene wind-inflated aerofoil kite. Note: Early polyethylene models were heat-sealed with a soldering iron.

Bag and 2' Flexifoil of clear polyethylene sheet "flown" on elastic line (1972).

A 6' clear polyethylene Flexifoil with full-width flowing sheeting demonstrates the wing's ability to showcase aerial art forms (1973).

Top: an early polyethylene 6′ Flexifoil making a horizontal low-level pass. Note that the arc deepens as the wind speed increases. Left: Reminiscent of the Wright brothers' encampment at Kitty Hawk, North Carolina, in 1900, here are Merry and Jones with their experimental Flexifoils at their shelter and storage area, christened "Limpet," in 1974.

*Top: Jones holding their first fabric 16'
Flexifoil. Note the separate air intakes
for each cell. The leading edge spar is
a combination of bamboo and fibreglass rod. Right: one of four prototype
20' wingspan Flexifoils made for sailing experiments. The wing is clearly
teardrop shaped (1975). Incidentally, in
1982, British racing sailor Ian Day
achieved a world speed record of 25.03
knots (nearly 29 mph) in his Flexifoil-
powered catamaran, Jacob's Ladder.*

Top: Jones on board a land rig for a Flexifoil propulsion system. A stack of Flexifoils managed to drag the land vehicle sideways in a light wind. Note the dual-line heavy-duty winch. Right: a stack of 22 6-foot Flexifoils flying in Sea Isle, New Jersey. In sufficient wind, this stack could easily tow a land-based vehicle or a catamaran across water (photo by author).

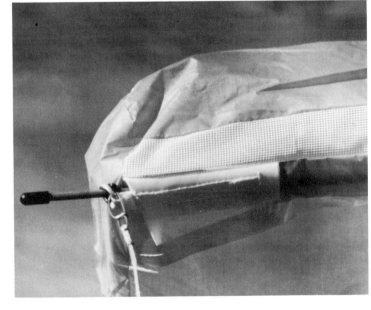

Top: inventor Ray Merry with a production ripstop Flexifoil at the 1988 East Coast Stunt Kite Championships III, in Wildwood, New Jersey (photo by Pete Hubbell). Left: left leading-edge detail of a Flexifoil—fibreglass-rod spar and nylon mesh covering an air intake vent (photo by author).

The Windbag Ultralight: a Flexifoil wing fixed to a canard-type radio-controlled model airplane. The propeller is on the rear of the plane.

An airborne Windbag flying from right to left.

Wind Curtain in the Grand Canyon supported by a Flexifoil—art installation concept by Ray Merry.

21

Benjamin Franklin—and How a Kite Won the American Revolution[1]

The New Prometheus

June, 1752: By flying a kite during a thunderstorm, Benjamin Franklin proved that lightning was not a

Illus. 137. The national memorial to Benjamin Franklin.

supernatural power but a natural phenomenon called electricity.[2] Up until Franklin's enlightening experiment, lightning had mystical meaning that struck terror in people's souls; the deadly bolts from heaven had been generally perceived as the wrath of the gods.

If electricity could be drawn to a kite in a storm,

Franklin reasoned, lightning could be safely absorbed by a grounded iron rod attached to a house. While there was some skepticism at first, lightning rods began rising over buildings in Philadelphia, Boston, and New York City. Soon, Europe began putting up rods and eventually Franklin's invention proved itself successful.

Franklin had not only brought fire from heaven, but now showed others how to control it. He was the toast of the colonies and, more importantly, Europe, as well.

The era between 1683 through 1789 was called the Age of Reason in Europe. Studying the universe and laws of nature was at an all time high and scholars were the superstars of the age. It was on this learned stage that Franklin's kite experiment gained him worldwide respect and admiration as a scientist, equal in importance to any European scholar. He was elected a member of the Royal Society of London (for improving natural knowledge) and praise followed him everywhere. Immanuel Kant, the German philosopher, proclaimed Franklin "the new Prometheus," a fitting title for one who reached up into heaven and brought man an incredible new form of fire.

The Dawn of Independence

September, 1776: In their struggle for freedom, American patriots endured misery and deprivation. Shortages of guns and gunpowder were chronic and food rations were often nonexistent. The trickle of ammunition that had been smuggled into the colonies from France was barely enough.

With General George Washington's Continental Army suffering the hardships at Valley Forge, Benjamin Franklin was chosen to persuade the French aristocracy to aid the American cause. Franklin's reputation preceded him as he had already been elected to the French Academy of Sciences several

87

years earlier. Dressed in plain garb like a Quaker, the kite flier from the colonies arrived in France on December 21, 1776, to a hero's welcome.

Why should France help a bunch of colonists seeking liberty from another monarchy? Rebellion against a sovereign could set an unfavorable precedent for France, where the people had no freedom. In addition, France's royal treasury was in terrible shape from the country's own wars and privileged extravagances. But France and England were old enemies and revenge often outweighs caution. And ironically the French nobility were taken with the unassuming scientist, and soon became intent on helping Franklin.

February, 1778: While Washington's army lay in near ruin at Valley Forge, the French signed an open alliance with the United States. For France, that meant renewed hostilities with Great Britain. The Revolutionary War went on for years, putting a tremendous strain on French resources. It was, however, Franklin's continued pleas for arms and supplies throughout the war that fueled the Continental Army.

October 17, 1781: English General Charles Cornwallis surrendered to an army of French and American soldiers at Yorktown, Virginia. The Americans had won. The Treaty of Peace with England was signed on September 8, 1783, in Versailles, France.

Benjamin Franklin flew a kite and snatched the power of lightning from the sky, galvanizing the forces of destiny to win a revolution.

[1]The substance of this historic episode was gleaned from Isaac Asimov's book *The Kite that Won the Revolution* (Boston: Houghton Mifflin Company, 1963).

[2]Flying a kite in stormy weather should not be taken lightly. Soon after Franklin's success, George William Richman, a Swedish professor working in St. Petersburg, Russia, repeated the kite experiment. A spark jumped from an iron rod to his head, killing him instantly.

22
Hargrave's Kites

Lawrence Hargrave— Inventor and Humanitarian

Anyone interested in aviation and kites will eventually cross paths with Lawrence Hargrave, who developed the box, or cellular, kite (Illus. 140), one of the eight generic kite forms. From the moment I ran into Hargrave on the printed page, I sensed that here was a man of character, a man worth knowing.

Lawrence Hargrave was born in Middlesex, England, on January 29, 1850. When he was fifteen, he and his mother moved to New South Wales, Australia, where his father and brother had emigrated nine years earlier. By this time, his father had become Judge in the Supreme Court of Australia and Solicitor General of New South Wales.

Though Judge Hargrave wished his son to follow in his footsteps, it soon became clear that Lawrence had no interest in law. Instead, at seventeen, he went to work for the Australian Steam and Navigation Company, where he spent five years gaining practical experience in engineering. Soon after, the young

Hargrave jumped at the chance to join a wily Italian naturalist, Luigi d'Albertis, in exploring the Fly River in the wilds of New Guinea. Despite being warned that all he could expect was slavishly hard work, Hargrave was drawn by his desire to be among the first outsiders to explore the mysterious interior of this uncharted land. This desire outweighed any fears he might have had; he endured the hazards of the jungle as well as fevers and hostile natives.

After he returned from New Guinea, he settled in Sydney, the capital of New South Wales. In 1878 he married Margaret Johnston and took a position as extra observer at the Sydney Observatory. He decided that his future lay in scientific inquiry and soon became interested in artificial flight, or aerial navigation as it was then called. A quiet, bearded man, Hargrave must have been quite a sight as he carried out his kite experiments near his estate at Stanwell Park Beach.

In one episode in 1894, he was lifted above the beach, shown in Illus. 138, by four of his box kites. Spectators watched on as the kites carried him out over the sea, dumping him near a shipwreck. These experiments at Stanwell Park ultimately led to air travel, though Hargrave received little credit for his contributions.

Illus. 138. History recreated: a train of Hargrave replicas in 1988 rising above Stanwell Park Beach. The kites in this photo were built by Civil and Mining Engineering students at the University of Wollongong, New South Wales.

Many people thought that Hargrave was eccentric or mad when he talked of such an improbable notion as a flying machine. Though he was sensitive about the reactions of others, he had the inner resolve to shut out negativity and criticism in order to continue with his work.

It was Hargrave's intense commitment to developing an inherently stable lifting surface that eventually led to his invention of the box kite—though he had intended to invent an airplane, not a kite. The box kite, an entirely new class of kite, was a by-product of his labors.

Hargrave was a private, almost reclusive person. Adverse to blowing his own horn, he was at the same time magnanimous and warm towards his fellow man. Instead of obtaining patents for his inventions, he shared them freely for the benefit of all.

By 1897, the box kite had become popular in the United States. E. T. Horsman, who also marketed William Eddy's bowed tailless kite, was selling a *patented* modified box kite, called the Blue Hill Box Kite. The inventor was listed as H. H. Clayton, chief observer at the Blue Hill Observatory in Massachusetts. Hargrave's name was conspicuously absent since he hadn't obtained a patent.

Hargrave spent more than thirty years in aeronautical research, during which time he invented the radial rotary engine and anticipated both the turbine and jet engine. He maintained a correspondence with a cluster of men who made up the world aviation community. Hargrave's letters and news clippings of the time reveal an intense competition among these men. Many were blinded by the limelight and gave in to self-promotion. Hargrave, however, throughout his career, managed to remain above the patent wars, misrepresentation, and claims to discredit others that seemed to permeate the aviation community.

Although best known for his scientific achievements, he was also a humanitarian who envisioned a future made brighter by aviation. The issues that concerned him are still relevant today: the need for curbing overpopulation, better treatment of native races, open sharing of information to accelerate technological development, and world peace.

Beginning in 1906, Hargrave began to search for a permanent home for nearly 200 priceless models of kites and flying machines that chronicled his achievements and failures. When the collection was turned down by New South Wales, he offered it to the English, French, and American governments—but was rejected. Finally, in 1910, his collection was eagerly accepted by the Deutsches Technological Museum in Munich.

However, during the Second World War, a world struggle decided by *air power*, most of Hargrave's models were destroyed when the Allies bombed Munich. Though a handful of models survived, the episode marked an ironic end for a collection of kites and flying machines that contributed much to making aviation a reality.

The Development of the Box Kite

Illus. 139 shows the major steps leading towards the development of Hargrave's box kite. He constructed the kites from a range of materials, including thin aluminum and tin sheeting, timber spars, and tissue paper. Hargrave's experiments included work with dihedral-based configurations (1 in Illus. 139) to cylindrical shapes, and finally to rectangular open-cell types that led to the perfected box kite (Illus. 140).

Hargrave's box kite could be folded easily for transport. Its spars were streamlined to minimize drag and resistance. And its vertical cords in the middle could be adjusted for maximum vertical and horizontal tension of the surfaces.

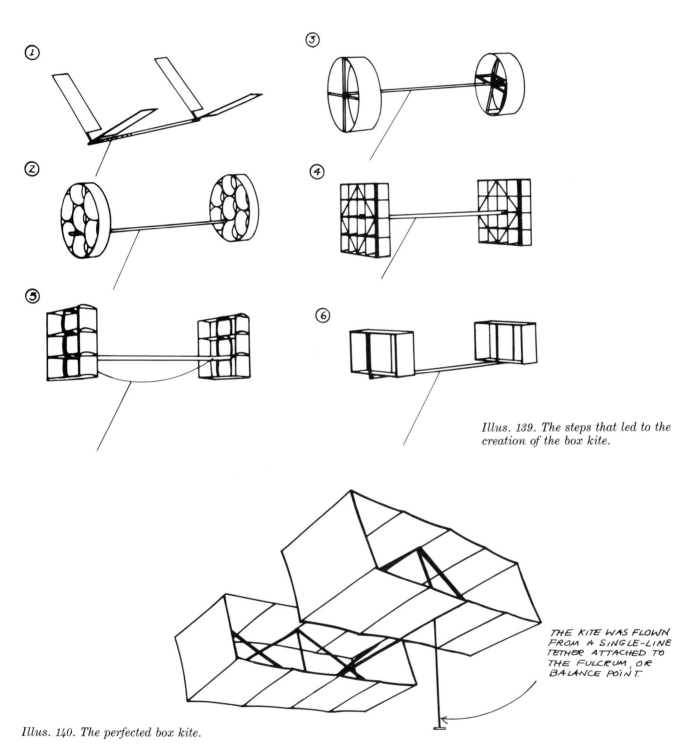

Illus. 139. The steps that led to the creation of the box kite.

THE KITE WAS FLOWN FROM A SINGLE-LINE TETHER ATTACHED TO THE FULCRUM, OR BALANCE POINT.

Illus. 140. The perfected box kite.

Hargrave's Soaring Machines

For his soaring machines, Hargrave looked to nature for clues—from measuring the wing membrane of a flying squirrel to examining the wing tips of an albatross, known for its incredible soaring abilities. (See one of Hargrave's soaring machines in Illus. 141.) The significance of Hargrave's pioneering work with soaring machines was seen later when the Wright brothers incorporated his ideas to improve the performance of their gliders after 1899.

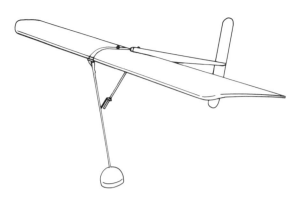

Illus. 141. A soaring machine.

23
Kites and Myths

Myths are instruction for the spirit, says wise teacher of mythology Joseph Campbell. Typically, myths draw on a timeless past where gods and heroes engage in mystical experiences about birth, death, creation, resurrection, revelation, fertility, and initiation. Myths are subtle inventions that exist on two levels of consciousness: universal and local. Universal myths connect us to the natural world; these myths address the planetary citizen. Local myths (most religions fall into this class) connect people to a particular society; these myths focus on the group as the center of life.

Myths do not come into existence full-blown. They are born of dreams that awake the dream in others. A myth usually begins as an allegory with an underlying theme accepted as a truth; then with time and embellishments, the allegory takes on the status of a myth.

Austrian psychiatrist and founder of psychoanalysis Sigmund Freud said myths from the unconscious are released in dreams. Carl Jung, Freud's contemporary, took the concept further by saying that all people share the same mythic symbols as part of what he called the *collective unconscious.*

Although folklore and legends in the Far East, most notably China and Japan, are particularly rich in kite tales, it is in the Pacific island cultures of Indonesia, Micronesia, Melanesia, and Polynesia that kites take on a clear mythological meaning. Kites in the tropics sustained physical as well as spiritual needs. With frameworks made from leaves, bark, and sticks, these kites were used for hundreds of years as aerial fishing rods. Traditional tales speak of kites as divine instruments used in matters of justice and as a means of protection from evil. Polynesians, in particular, associated kites with deities, the soul, and as a means of making contact with the gods in heaven. Most of their kites were shaped like birds, and were often seen soaring upwards in the steady trade winds. Tribal chiefs used special kite forms in rituals, as knights used heraldry, to identify themselves to the tribe and gods.

In the central Pacific, kite-god dramas abound in the local lore of the Hawaiian Islands. Kites were perceived as manifestations of the gods, as well as celestial objects flown by the gods in struggles among themselves and the elements. Since kite flying was a way of communing with heaven, flying high was a common practice. Kites were also employed to establish land ownership. A kite would be released and a claim would be made to the area where it fell. Ownership of land essentially rested on the unbiased divinity of a god in the form of a kite.

Personal experiences can also take on mythical dimensions. For instance, a kite flying *up* in relation to the flier *below* can be a reminder to the flier of the duality of nature—which is life and death. Just as we see and hear to make sense of our physical environment, seeing and hearing *symbolically* can lead us into an awareness of the spirit.

24

The Mystique of the Eddy Kite

Among the general population of the West, the elongated-diamond shape of the tailless Eddy kite (shown in Chapter 27) is essentially synonymous with kite-shaped. This observation has been made by others and is hardly startling news, though it does raise the intriguing question as to why a diamond shape and not another. What is there about a diamond-shaped kite that has caused the collective psyche to grip it with such permanence?

Haunted by this cultural curiosity, I searched for references concerning the possible symbolism of the elongated-diamond-shaped kite in Western culture. But my research failed to uncover any clues, and my quandary escalated. The absence of a documented theory of some kind seemed to me a gaping hole in kite lore.

Then, quite unexpectedly, I came across an explanation in an environment totally removed from my kite research; the discovery was as unorthodox as it was enlightening. Before relating my experience, a brief look backward at the facts I did uncover is in order for perspective.

Although tailless kites had been common in the East for centuries, the innovative leap from tail to tailless kites didn't take place in the West until 1893 when William Eddy developed his tailless diamond-shaped kite in America. That same year, however, Lawrence Hargrave invented his tailless box, or cellular, kite in Australia. Hargrave's box kite was a byproduct of his efforts to develop a lifting structure capable of manned power flight.

Now, my original inquiry was compounded by another demanding question: Why was it that the box kite didn't etch itself into Western consciousness as the preeminent kite form instead of the diamond-shaped Eddy?

Though trains of Eddy kites were being used to raise meteorological instruments to record heights, the superior stability and lifting power of Hargrave's box-kite design soon became the kite of choice for researchers at the U.S. Weather Bureau and the Blue Hill Observatory near Harvard College in Massachusetts. Furthermore, the box kite directly influenced the Wright brothers and their experiments that culminated in the first successful powered manned flight in 1903.

However, while Eddy ardently sought publicity for his kites and experiments, Hargrave shunned the limelight. So, was it simply a matter of Eddy being a media darling of his time? Not likely, when you consider the exploits of Samuel Franklin Cody, another kite flier of the era. A flamboyant cowboy, showman, and kite enthusiast, Cody gained international attention for his awesome, ever-increasing-in-size, winged batlike modified box kites. I labored over the facts again and again. Why, I wondered, didn't the spectacular Cody kite have the enduring quality of the Eddy?

I had been plodding on without turning up a shred of evidence when I received an invitation to a festive ceremony. On a bright Sunday morning I found myself sitting in the first pew of a small town church listening to the young pastor at the pulpit. Diffused light from the stained-glass windows bathed the small congregation.

When the pastor stepped off to one side to make a point during his sermon, the large simple cross that hung on the wall directly behind the pulpit lit up from the sunlight. At that moment, I was struck with a realization that chilled my core.

The whole thing made perfect sense now. I closed my eyes to invoke the Eddy kite image in my mind's eye. Yes, the framework of the kite was nearly identical in proportion to what is perhaps the most recognizable religious icon in Western mythology. I took a deep breath and sat back.

To confirm the theory, one need only fly an Eddy kite and look up. With the magnificent illuminating power of the sun, the structure of the cross becomes a silhouette etched upon the surface of the sail.

25
World Kiting Records

These are world kiting records[1]–not claims. Records are verifiable through photographs, witnesses, notarization, and documentation. Claims, on the other hand, assert something as a fact without necessarily having third-party proof.

Altitude (highest single kite): 12,471 feet (3,801 metres)

On February 28, 1898, in Milton, Massachusetts, near the Blue Hill Observatory outside of Boston, a modified Hargrave box kite with about 86 sq. ft. of sail area rose more than 2 miles over the earth's surface. The kite's flying line was piano wire with a breaking strength of 330 lbs. The flight was conducted by meteorologists Henry Helm Clayton and A. E. Sweetland under the supervision of Abbot Lawrence Rotch, director of the privately operated observatory.

Altitude (highest kite train): 31,955 feet (9,740 metres)

This as-yet-unbroken record was achieved with eight kites over Lindenburg (now East Germany) on August 1, 1919.

Distance (traction on land): 113 miles (182 kilometres)

In the 1820s, George Pocock sped about (at ±25 mph) the English countryside in his *Char-volant*, a four-wheeled carriage towed by controllable kites. Though precise distances are unknown, estimates range up to 113 miles for a trip made in 1827. Pocock did make one documented journey of 60 miles as the crow flies from Southampton to London.

Duration (outdoors): 180 hours and 17 minutes

Under the direction of Harry Osborne, the Edmonds Community College kite team at Long Beach, Washington, kept a J-25 parafoil aloft from August 21 to 29 in 1982.

Fastest kite (measured speed): 108 mph (174 kph)

On May 16, 1987, Troy Vickstrom piloted a speeding 10-ft. Flexifoil across the beach in Lincoln City, Oregon. Documentation of the record came from the local police. Vickstrom was issued a traffic citation for exceeding maximum speed in an area with a posted speed limit of 20 mph.

First aerial photograph by a kite-borne camera: June 20, 1888

Arthur Batut took the first aerial photograph from a kite-lifted camera in Labruguiere, France, on June 20, 1888 (Illus. 142). William A. Eddy (see "The Eddy Kite") of Bayonne, New Jersey, took the first kite aerial photographs in the United States on May 30, 1895.

Illus. 142. This is one of Arthur Batut's aerial photographs taken in 1888.

First kite patent granted in the United States: January 2, 1866

Patent #51,860 was issued to William Perrins for a hexagon-shaped flat kite with two inwardly bent (curved) masts. Since 1866, a total of 575 kite patents have been issued by the U.S. Patent Office. In addition, there are 101 patents that are cross-referenced into kite subclasses from a nonkite classification. Ironically, some of these cross-referenced patents are more important to kiting than those classed by the examiner as kite patents. For example, the parafoil is classed as a parachute and Rogallo's Corner kite as a radar reflector. There are also 20 kite design patents and five reissued patents, for a grand total of 701 patents related to kites as of December 1, 1987.[2]

Largest kite: 5,952 sq. feet (553 sq. metres)

The record was set on August 8, 1981, by a Dutch team on the beach at Scheveningen, The Netherlands, with a 506-lb. inflatable airfoil type of kite (Illus. 143).

Unofficially, since no claims were made, the largest

kite ever built was the Budweiser parafoil, which measured 115' × 124', or 14,260 sq. ft., nearly three times the area of the Dutch kite. Built under the supervision of Harry Osborne, the giant required 10 men just to move it. Flown by a team of 22 people at the Washington State International Kite Festival at Long Beach in 1983, the kite was anchored to two dumpsters fully loaded with sand. As the kite began to rise, it amazed onlookers by dragging both dumpsters sideways nearly 4 feet across the loose sand. Soon after, people reported hearing what sounded like the loudest lightning they had ever heard. The 2″-thick nylon flying line with its ±25,000-lb. work load had snapped under the intense pulling power.

Largest delta: 1,406 sq. feet. (131 sq. metres)

Californians Tony Cyphert and Gene Carey joined forces to build a giant delta that measured 37½ ft. high with a wingspan of 75 ft. The kite's maiden voyage took place in San Diego on September 4, 1982, and lasted for 25 minutes.

Largest Peter Lynn Tri-D Box: 1,136 sq. feet (105 sq. metres)

In 1982, Bill Tyrrell and Bob Sessions built an awesome Tri-D Box that measured 40′ × 35′. The spars were aluminum tubing and ripstop nylon was used for the sail material. The kite was flown successfully on several occasions.

Longest Thai cobra kite: 2,313 feet (705 metres)

On November 15, 1987, Michel Trouillet, Pierre Agniel, and Philippe Bertron of the Kite Club of Montpelier, France, led a crew of 16 kite fliers in a successful launch of a 128-lb. fabric serpent. The 7-minute flight took place at the airfield in Nimes-Courbessac, France, in front of an estimated crowd of 3,000, including photographers and reporters. The

triumphant trio estimates that the project, from drawing board to lift-off, required 2,000 hours at a cost of 45,000 francs (8,000 dollars).

The French team had broken the record of 2,133 feet (650 metres) set by Herman van den Broek and Jan Pieter Kuil of The Netherlands on August 11, 1984.

Most consecutive days of individual kite flying: 366 days

C. W. (Bill) Mosely of Converse, Texas, flew one or more kites every day from October 25, 1983, to October 24, 1984 (a leap year), for a total of 366 days. That's some perseverance!

Most kites on one line: 2,233

Under the direction of Kinji Tsuda, the Hiroshima Kite Club set the record recognized by the Japanese Kite Association. The 13″ × 13″ (34cm × 34cm) Diamond Eddy–shaped kites were made of bamboo spars with plastic sail material.

Most dual-line kites stunted in train: 179

Ken Frederick of San Diego flew and maneuvered the centipedelike record-setting stack of modified Hyperkites at Long Beach, Washington, on August 23, 1986.

Most kite books written by one author: 20

More books on kiting have been written by the Japanese than by any other nationality. The most prolific of these authors is Kazuo Niisak, who wrote about 20 kite books between 1969 and 1987.

[1]Some items have been reprinted from *The Bearly-Made-It List of Little-Known World Kiteflying Records* with permission from Dirt Cheap Press, 1988.

[2]Kite patent information courtesy of Ed Grauel. Every kite-related patent issued in the United States with a brief description, including number, names, and dates, may be purchased directly from Grauel—at 500 Elmwood Terrace, Rochester, New York 14620.

Illus. 143. Largest kite.
(Photo by Valerie Govig.)

KITE PROJECTS

Trefoil Dragon (pages 247–250).

E

Sting Ray (pages 169–181).

Left: the Totem Kite—a Hewitt Flexkite variation (pages 166–169). Bottom: Pterosaur (pages 251–261).

G

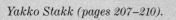

Yakko Stakk (pages 207–210).

Kaleidekite (pages 143–148).

H

Stone Mountain (pages 152–161).

Turbo Stunt Kite (pages 261–265).

J

Counterclockwise from top: Bullet (pages 116–118), Barn Door (pages 203–206), and Hornbeam Sled (pages 111–114).

Winged Box (pages 132–134).

26
Some Overall Tips

The projects in this book are basically arranged in an increasing order of complexity. Most have an introduction, followed by diagrams and instructions. Remember: There is no *one way* to build a kite— there are only *ways that work*.

Certain kite-building techniques are common to many of the projects, and are discussed in general terms in the first part of the book. Should any questions arise that are not covered in a project, refer to the chapter dealing with the topic. Also, the charts at a glance provide a quick, comprehensive overview of many techniques and materials.

In most cases, symmetry, crucial for a balanced kite (an asymmetrical kite will fly if properly counterbalanced), is assured when the kite sail is measured and cut from the centerline outward. Making the sail usually calls for such processes as hemming, reinforcing stress points, forming spar sleeves, and adding pockets.

So, you've gone by the book, but your kite still has turned out dimensionally different than stated. No matter how precisely you work, slight differences may creep in. Cutting, piecing, and sewing often conspire to promote discrepancies. However, flight performance will not suffer if marginal variations are distributed evenly. But it is important to be diligent about conforming to specified degrees for angles on wings, noses, and dihedrals.

If instructions for a delta kite, for example, call for a 60″ wingspan (30″ each wing half) and your kite comes out with a wingspan of 62″ (31″ each wing half), your delta will still be symmetrical and will fly well. Another example: A dimension given for a spar length may not fit your finished kite. Since your work is always the yardstick when fitting spars, make it a rule to cut spars based on the measurements of your kite.

Here is a useful checklist before beginning a kite project.

1. First, review the basics of kite building and flying. Look over the various kites and then choose a kite that interests you. Simple kites are great, too; there is nothing inherently superior about a complex kite.
2. Decide what materials you'll need and then obtain them. The list should include tools, flying line, and some form of line-management system—such as a reel or hoop. Don't forget gloves to protect your hands if you're making a hard-pulling kite.
3. Choose an appropriate work area and create an environment that's right for you.
4. Use caution with glues and all tools, especially the power variety.
5. Children must *always* be supervised. Also, keep animals away from the work area for their own safety.
6. Get a clear idea of how the kite is assembled, taking note of any building options. It's a good practice to construct the kite in your mind before you begin.

Although the exhilaration of seeing your kite in the sky is probably your ultimate goal, enjoy the process and craft of getting up there. Don't rush, work precisely, and take pride in your creation.

If you have any questions regarding resources for tools and materials, write to me care of Sterling Publishing Company for a comprehensive list of mail-order outlets.

27

The Eddy Kite

An Eddy Kite by Any Other Name—How About a Woglom?

On August 1, 1898, William Abner Eddy of Bayonne, New Jersey, filed an application to patent his now famous Eddy kite. Twenty months later, on March 27, 1900, Eddy's U.S. patent no. 646375 was approved. However, several years earlier, another gentleman by the name of William Totten Woglom, who lived just across the Hudson River from Eddy in New York City, filed a patent application for his Parakite. On May 1, 1900 (about five weeks after Eddy had received his patent), Woglom's U.S. patent no. 648544 was finally granted after nearly four and a half years—an inordinate amount of time to wait in those days. It was clear that both men had drawn inspiration from the two-stick bowed Malay kite

flown for centuries in the Far East (shown in Illus. 144), since the Eddy and the Parakite were nearly identical.

Was the Eddy kite a modified Parakite or was it the other way around? Both kites were diamond-shaped and had no tail. Both required a baggy-fitting sail wider than its frame, but Woglom's Parakite had an extra touch—a fashionable set of pleats in the center.

Whether Eddy and Woglom developed their improved Malay kites independently of one another is unknown. Some insight regarding the affair may be gleaned, however, from a closer look at the chain of events from the point of view of amateur kite sleuth David Lockley of London.

In a paper investigating the genuine Eddy kite[1], Lockley suggests that the question is not why Woglom's application was delayed and not granted until after Eddy's patent was approved, but, rather,

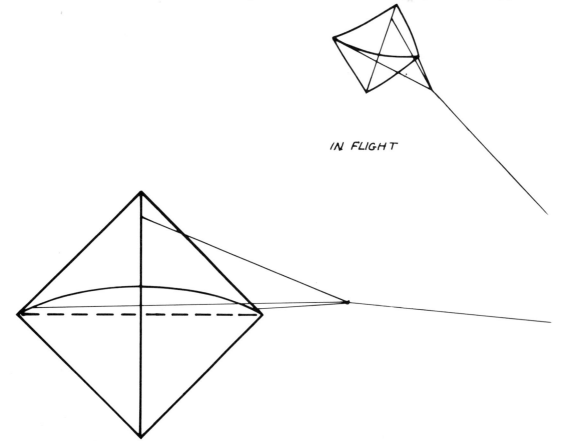

IN FLIGHT

Illus. 144. The Javanese bowed kite, known in the West as the Malay kite.

why did Eddy, who had essentially developed his tailless bowed kite as early as 1893, waited five years to apply for a patent.

According to Lockley, one possible scenario might go as follows: Though Eddy had completed his basic design by 1893, he continued to improve the kite in collaboration with others—namely, meteorologists at the Blue Hill Observatory in Massachusetts and a Charles Flanders of New York, who had previously made and flown a Malay kite in Cape Town, South Africa. Flanders suggested double-bowing the cross spar at an angle similar to a bird's wing that has completed its upwards stroke. Consequently, Eddy's original kite had a cross spar that was bent downwards and backward, which made it resemble the bow of an Indian fighter or Nagasaki *hata* kite in the deflected position during flight. Another consideration could have been that many details of Eddy's invention had been previously published in various scientific journals and had therefore become common knowledge.

Conceivably, Eddy delayed in filing as a matter of conscience. With a public roster of outside influences contributing to the design and prior public disclosures, he probably wrestled with the dilemma of deciding what to patent under his name. Eddy's application may have moved through the official machinery as quickly as it did because the patent office was already aware of Eddy's pioneering work with kites.

Though conjecture is stimulating, the real answers to why Eddy delayed in filing and why the patent examiners lingered over Woglom's claim are still open to speculation.

Reconstructing a Genuine Eddy Kite

For years, kite builders have reported varying degrees of success with the Eddy kite design. Some disgruntled fliers have gone so far as to insist that the kite needs a tail—clearly a heretical conclusion. But the problem in reconstructing a genuine Eddy kite actually stems from design inaccuracies perpetuated over the years.

In the main, kite books written since 1896 have often altered the original Eddy design. The simple reason these kites won't perform in a wide range as touted is that the essential details that made Eddy's tailless kite a stable flier have been virtually omitted.

Construction

Lockley performed many geometric calculations to arrive at the precise dimensions for reconstructing an authentic Eddy kite.

The following information is based on his calculations. You may wish to round off fractional numbers to the nearest ½ inch for convenience—for example, a 68.4″ cross spar to 68½″, or a 70.89 sail width to 71″.

As you note the following points, refer to Illus. 145 and 146.

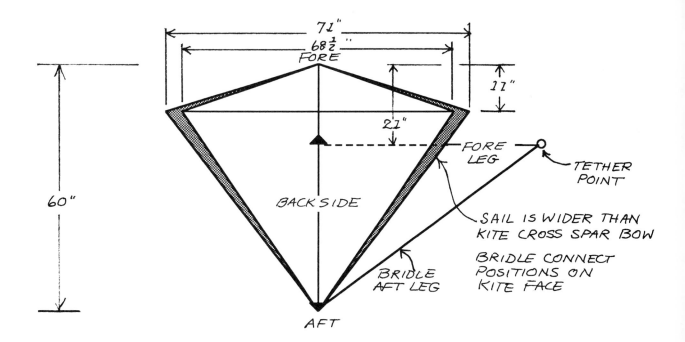

Illus. 145. A genuine Eddy Kite—sail and bridle positions.

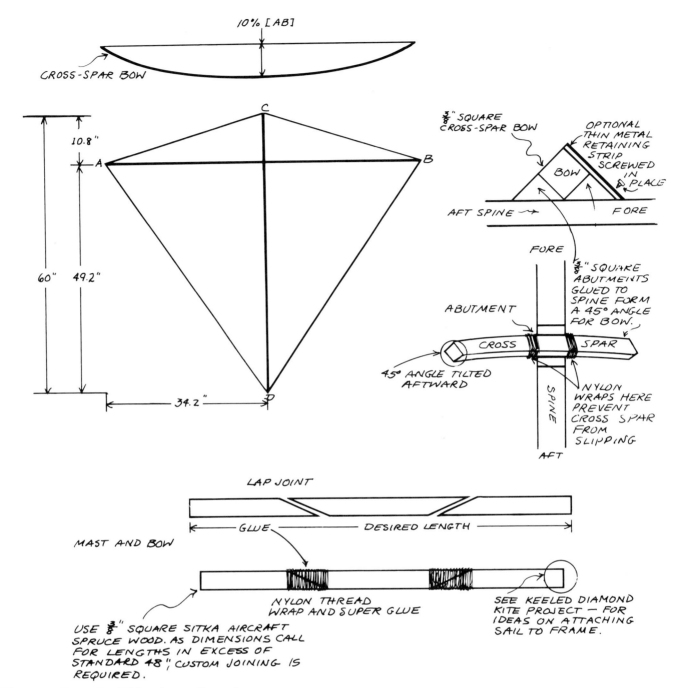

10% [AB]

CROSS-SPAR BOW

⅜" SQUARE
CROSS-SPAR BOW

OPTIONAL
THIN METAL
RETAINING
STRIP
SCREWED
IN
PLACE

BOW

AFT SPINE →

FORE

FORE

⅜" SQUARE
ABUTMENTS
GLUED TO
SPINE FORM
A 45° ANGLE
FOR BOW.

ABUTMENT

CROSS   SPAR

45° ANGLE TILTED
AFTWARD

SPINE

NYLON
WRAPS HERE
PREVENT
CROSS SPAR
FROM
SLIPPING

AFT

C

A   B

10.8"

60"   49.2"

34.2"   D

LAP JOINT

GLUE   DESIRED LENGTH

MAST AND BOW

NYLON THREAD
WRAP AND SUPER GLUE

SEE KEELED DIAMOND
KITE PROJECT — FOR
IDEAS ON ATTACHING
SAIL TO FRAME.

USE ⅜" SQUARE SITKA AIRCRAFT
SPRUCE WOOD. AS DIMENSIONS CALL
FOR LENGTHS IN EXCESS OF
STANDARD 48", CUSTOM JOINING IS
REQUIRED.

Illus. 146. A genuine Eddy—frame dimensions.

- The 68.4″ cross spar is bowed 10 percent (of AB) and tilted 45° towards the bottom.
- The cross spar should be square (⅜″), not rectangular.
- The spine is 60″ long; the cross spar intersects the spine at 10.8″ (or 18 percent of CD) from the fore end.
- The center of gravity, or fulcrum position, is located 35 percent of CD down from the fore end. This is the top leg of the bridle position; secure the lower leg to the aft end.
- Sail dimensions (allow for hemming) should be

about 3⅝ percent wider than the cross spar—in this case, 70.89″ wide and 60″ high. Stability of the Eddy is assured because of the dihedral effect of the bowed cross spar that is enhanced by a slightly loose sail billowing out evenly along the trailing edge.

Original sail-material recommendations were thin manila paper for light winds and fabric (varnished to minimize porosity) for high winds. For your replica, try a ripstop sail for light winds and cotton poplin (unvarnished) for breezier days.

- Continuous framing cords are not required; in fact,

they may cause stability problems along the trailing edges.
- The trailing edges should not be under tension as this prevents the correct reflex-inverted (billowing out) airfoil section from developing.
- No tail is required.

Flight Data: Wind range: 5–25 mph
Line: 100 lb. test

AE: ±65°
Wear gloves

The Flat Malay Variation

This kite is similar to the Eddy Kite, without the extra-wide fabric (see Illus. 147). An optional stabilizing fin for the kite is shown in Illus. 148.

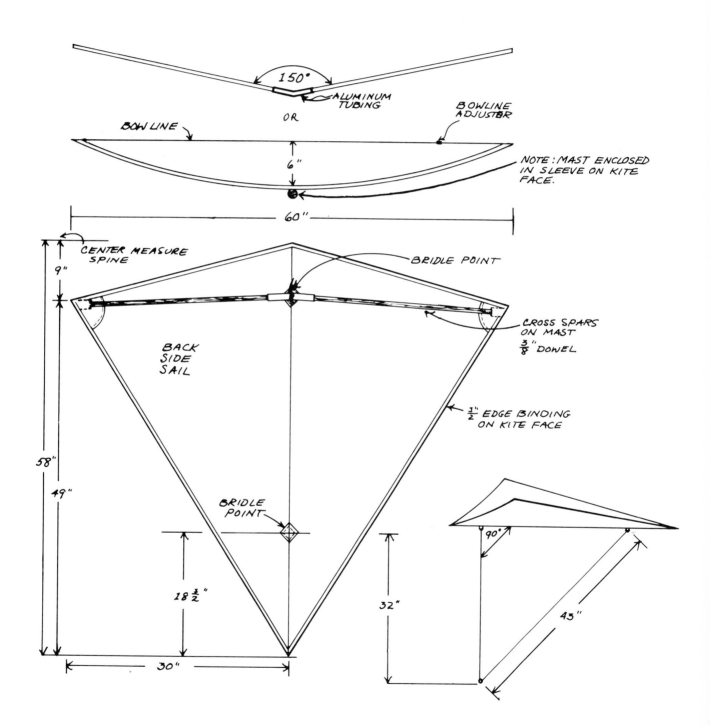

Illus. 147. Malay variation.

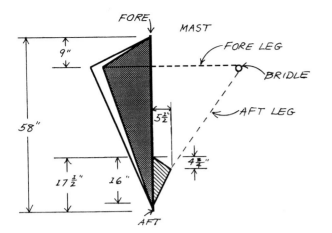

FORE

MAST

FORE LEG

BRIDLE

AFT LEG

9"

5½"

58"

17½"   16"

4¾"

AFT

ADDING FIN PREVENTS WOBBLE
IN RIPSTOP VERSION OF FLAT
MALAY.

CONCEPT: COURTESY OF DAN LEIGH

Illus. 148. Optional stabilizing fin for the flat Malay variation.

[1]Lockley, David, "Will The Real Eddy Stand Up Please: The Geometry of the Eddy Kite," London, 1987.

28

The Keeled Diamond Eddy Kite

Design: Courtesy of Jack Liddell

Please Take a Bow

The Keeled Diamond Eddy Kite is Jack Liddell's updated version of the classic Eddy Kite. (See Liddell's Diamond Eddy in Illus. 149, and in color on the cover.) Liddell chose straight-grained rectangular Sitka aircraft spruce to produce lightweight torque-resistant spars. Although the kite looks simple, cutting, ripping, planing, sanding, gluing, clamping, sanding again, and laminating woods are all required to make its airworthy framework.

Precision scarf-joint fittings (Illus. 150) allow you to break down the kite for easy transportation. To adjust the sail tension for the prevailing wind conditions, Liddell devised a simple, yet effective, bead-tension system. The stabilizing keel eliminates wobble altogether for a kite that flies straight and true each time. The star, indeed the heart, of this stable flier is the strong, flexible laminated cross-spar bow—which can take a *bow* for its performance.

Materials

To make this kite you need:
• 2.5 yards of .75 oz. ripstop nylon,
• four pieces of ⅛″ × ¼″ × 3″ aircraft plywood,
• two pieces of ⅛″ × 1¹⁄₃₂″ × 5⅛″ aircraft plywood,
• two pieces of ⅛″ × 1¹⁄₃₂″ × 6⅛″ aircraft plywood,
• two pieces of ⅛″ × ¹⁵⁄₁₆″ × 3″ aircraft plywood,
• two pieces of ⅛″ × ⅜″ × 3″ aircraft plywood,
• one piece of ⅜″ × ⅝″ × 44½″ Sitka aircraft spruce,
• one piece of ⅜″ × ⅝″ × 30¼″ Sitka aircraft spruce,
• one piece of ¼″ × ¾″ × 25″ Sitka aircraft spruce,
• one piece of ⅛″ × ¾″ × 20″ Sitka aircraft spruce,
• one piece of ⅛″ × ¾″ × 18″ Sitka aircraft spruce,
• one piece of ⅛″ × ¾″ × 16″ Sitka aircraft spruce,

- two pieces of ¼″ × ¾″ × 22¼″ Sitka aircraft spruce,
- two pieces of ¼″ × ⅜″ × 1″ hard maple blocks,
- one 6–32 × 1½″ bolt,
- one 6–32 blind nut,
- four ½″ × 2″ birch dowels,
- sixteen (small with hole) wooden beads,
- 7′ 75 lb.–test braided-Dacron line,
- three ¼″ I.D. brass grommets,
- eight strips of ¾″ × 4″ nylon webbing,
- 24″ of 150 lb.–test braided-Dacron line,
- one 3″ × 7″ 4 oz. Dacron reinforcement, and
- one bow-line adjuster.

Details

Except as otherwise noted, the following details are shown in Illus. 151.

- (Detail 1.) Outer-bow spar: bow-line secure point. Typical end: wooden beads fit in a slot. Moving in either direction adjusts the tautness of the sail.
- (Detail 2 in Illus. 152.) Outer cross spar, side view: ½″ × 2″ birch dowel, wood beads, 150 lb. braided Dacron, ¾″ × 4″ nylon webbing, 75 lb.-test braided-Dacron bow line, and hard maple block for bow line.
- (Detail 3 in Illus. 153.) Sail tip, aft end. Birch dowel is drilled through the middle for the adjustment beads and Dacron line; nylon webbing stitched to the sail forms loops for the dowel; .75 oz. ripstop sail; ½″ hem.
- (Detail 4.) Frame—Sitka aircraft spruce, 3⁄16″ width × ½″ depth, notched ends (typical).
  Top spine (⅜″ × ⅝″ × 44½″), lower spine (⅜″ × ⅝″ × 30¼″), laminated-bow spar (¾″ × ⅝″ × 28¼″), outer-bow spars (¼″ × ¾″ × 22¼″), and 6–32 blind nut.
- (Detail 5.) Scarf joints. ⅛″ aircraft plywood—bevelled, nylon-wrapped, and glued. Step 24.
- (Detail 6.) Retainer joint. Step 26. (Also, see Illus. 159.)
- (Detail 7.) Bow line—7′ of 75 lb. braided Dacron, bow-line adjuster, hard maple block (¼″ × ⅜″ × 1″), 6–32 × 1½″ bolt, laminated bow, and spine.

Flight Data: Wind range: 5–25 mph
Line: 100 lb. test
AE: ±65°
Wear gloves

Construction

As you go through these steps, refer to Illus. 154 or other illustrations that are specifically noted.

1. Measure and cut two sets of panels A and B as well as single-keel panels C and D from .75 oz.

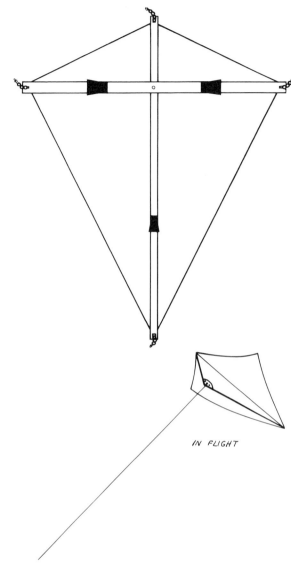

Illus. 149. The Keeled Diamond Eddy.

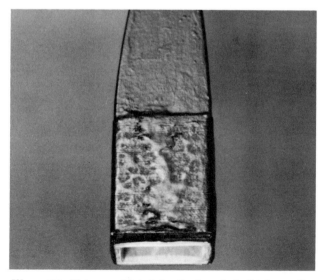

Illus. 150. This scarf joint for the bow is built from ⅛″ aircraft plywood.

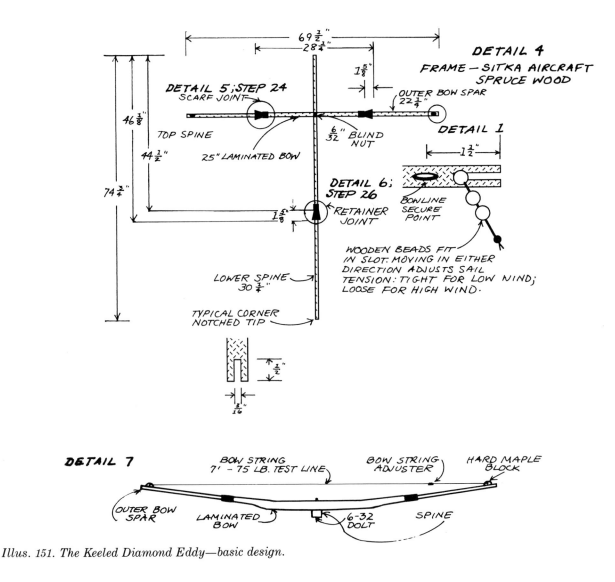

DETAIL 4
FRAME — SITKA AIRCRAFT
SPRUCE WOOD

69½"
28¼"

1⅝"

46⅛"

DETAIL 5; STEP 24
SCARF JOINT

OUTER BOW SPAR

TOP SPINE

OUTER BOW SPAR
22¼"

DETAIL 1

1½"

44½"

25" LAMINATED BOW

6/32" BLIND NUT

BOWLINE
SECURE
POINT

DETAIL 6;
STEP 26

74¾"

RETAINER
JOINT

WOODEN BEADS FIT
IN SLOT: MOVING IN EITHER
DIRECTION ADJUSTS SAIL
TENSION: TIGHT FOR LOW WIND;
LOOSE FOR HIGH WIND.

1⅝"

LOWER SPINE
30¼"

TYPICAL CORNER
NOTCHED TIP

½"

3/16"

DETAIL 7

BOW STRING
7' — 75 LB. TEST LINE

BOW STRING
ADJUSTER

HARD MAPLE
BLOCK

OUTER BOW
SPAR

LAMINATED
BOW

6-32
DOLT

SPINE

Illus. 151. The Keeled Diamond Eddy—basic design.

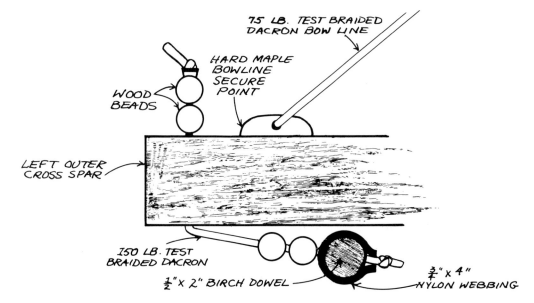

75 LB. TEST BRAIDED
DACRON BOW LINE

HARD MAPLE
BOWLINE
SECURE
POINT

WOOD
BEADS

LEFT OUTER
CROSS SPAR

150 LB. TEST
BRAIDED DACRON

½" X 2" BIRCH DOWEL

¾" X 4"
NYLON WEBBING

Illus. 152. Detail 2—outer cross spar, side view.

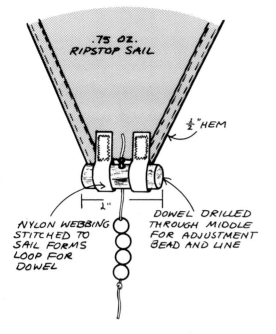

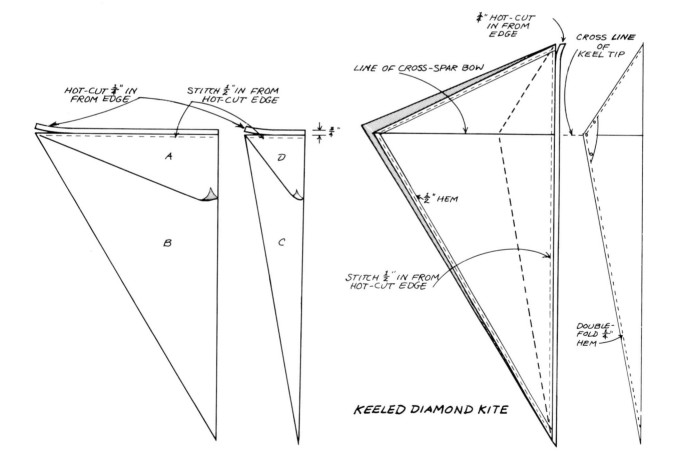

ripstop. Add a ½″ seam allowance on all outside edges and a ¾″ allowance for all inside sail seams for a ¼″ hot-cut trim waste. The keel is slightly shorter than the main sail to accommodate the tension bead system on fore and aft positions of the spine. See the hemmed dimensions. Note: The direction of the grain is aligned along the leading edges. (Also, see Illus. 155.)

2. With the glossier side (face) of panels A and B facing each other, hot-cut ¼″ from the edge and weld together. Similarly, weld panels C and D at the seam line, as shown.

3. Hot-cut a 4 oz. Dacron reinforcement for the keel tip.

Sewing:

4. With panels A and B still in position, stitch ½″ in from the hot-cut edge. Next, unfold the panels. With the ½″ hem—A towards B—sew again along the edge to form a sail seam. Repeat for the second set. Double-stitch ½″ perimeter hems.

5. Join keel panels C and D with a sail seam. The hem should fold downwards from D to C. Cut a 4 oz. Dacron reinforcement and stitch it onto the

Illus. 153. Detail 3—sail tip, aft end.

Illus. 154. Cutting, piecing, and sewing.

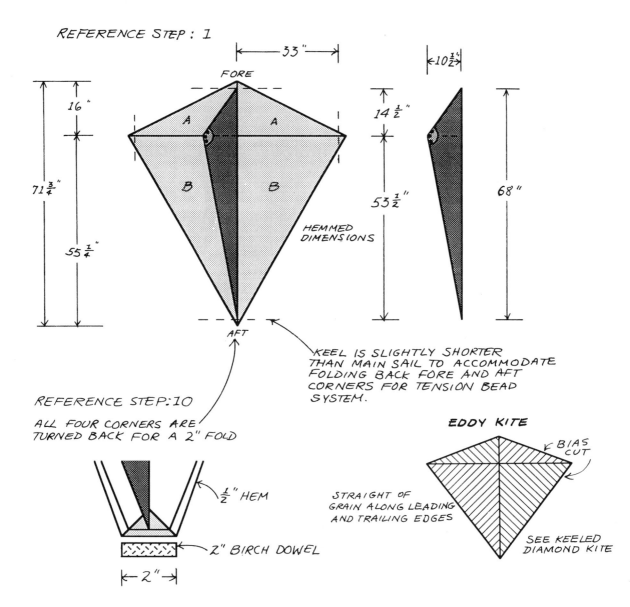

REFERENCE STEP : 1

33"

FORE

16"

71¾"

55¼"

A   A

B   B

HEMMED
DIMENSIONS

AFT

10½"

14½"

53½"

68"

KEEL IS SLIGHTLY SHORTER
THAN MAIN SAIL TO ACCOMMODATE
FOLDING BACK FORE AND AFT
CORNERS FOR TENSION BEAD
SYSTEM.

REFERENCE STEP: 10

ALL FOUR CORNERS ARE
TURNED BACK FOR A 2" FOLD

½" HEM

2" BIRCH DOWEL

2"

EDDY KITE

BIAS CUT

STRAIGHT OF
GRAIN ALONG LEADING
AND TRAILING EDGES

SEE KEELED
DIAMOND KITE

Illus. 155. Steps 1 and 10.

keel tip. Finish the outside edges with a double-fold ¼" hem.

Hot-cutting:

6. Sandwich the keel between the kite halves, with the glossier sides facing inward. The cross line of the keel tip must line up with the cross-spar bow. Weld all three pieces together with ¼" hot-cutter trim.

Sewing:

7. With the keel held in place between the kite halves, stitch ½" in from the edge. Fold the hem to one side and stitch along the edge to complete the sail seam.

Hot-cutting:

8. Cut eight ¾" × 4" nylon-webbing strips.
9. Cut four 6" lengths of 150 lb.–test Dacron.
10. Square off the corners of the kite sail by hot-cutting or fold back until the corner measures 2"

to match the 2" sail-tension system. (See Step 10 in Illus. 155, as well as Detail 3 in Illus. 153.)

Hobby saw:

11. Cut four ½" × 2" birch dowels and drill ⅛" holes in the centers.

Sewing:

12. Tightly wrap 4" nylon-webbing strips around the birch dowel. Mark the position and stitch to form loops for the birch dowel.
13. Stitch two nylon-webbing loops at each corner.

Assembly:

14. Position the birch dowels inside the nylon-webbing loops and insert the wooden bead line through the hole. Melt the line edges.
15. Insert three ¼" I.D. grommets in the keel tip.

Making the Frame

Hobby saw:

The spine and bow are constructed from Sitka

aircraft spruce. Cutting actually means ripping each section with a band saw, planing smooth all rough edges, and finally cutting to size. Refer to the dimensions specified in Detail 3 (Illus. 153).

16. The spine: Cut the Sitka spruce to the correct lengths. A retainer joint built up from ⅛" aircraft plywood is added to the lower end of the top part of the spine. (See Illus. 151.)

17. The cross-spar bow: Begin by first cutting the outer-spar sections to the dimensions shown in Illus. 156.

18. The fore and aft tips of the spine and the outer sections of the bow are notched by first drilling a ³⁄₁₆″ hole ½″ in from the edge as shown in Illus. 156. (Drilling starter holes first prevents wood from splitting.) Finish by cutting a slot up to the

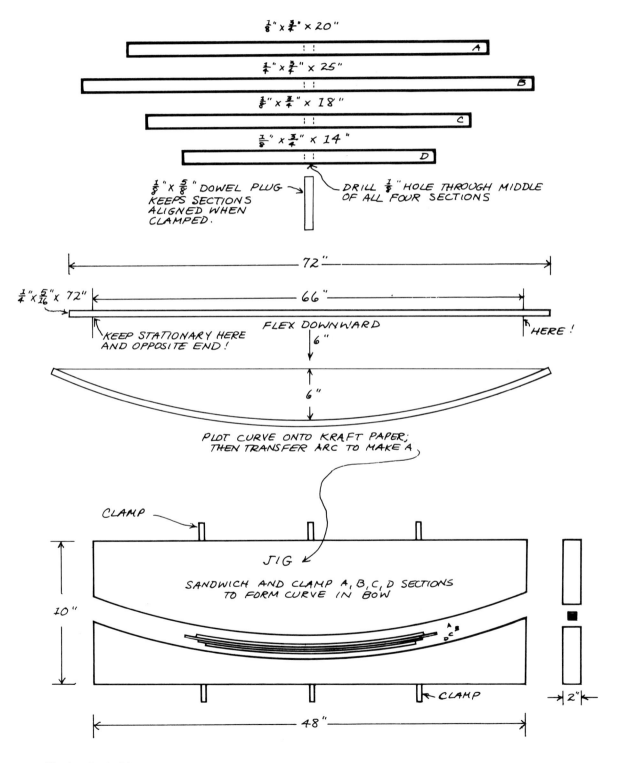

Illus. 156. The laminated bow.

hole with a band saw. Maple blocks are epoxied in position below the notches on the outer section of the bow.

Making the Laminated Bow

19. After ripping and planing, the wood is sandwiched as shown in Illus. 156.

    Drill a ⅛″ hole through the middle of all four sections. This hole serves a twofold purpose: A dowel is inserted during the jig stage; later, it's used for a bolt that locks the bow and spine together.
20. Construct a jig from a wood-block section, measuring 2″ × 10″ × 48″, with clamps positioned as shown in Illus. 156.
21. The curve in the jig is plotted, using a spruce strip measuring ¼″ × ⁵⁄₁₆″ × 72″. With the wood held stationary 3″ in at both ends, flex the strip of wood 6″ downwards. Do this on top of kraft paper and trace the curve with a pencil. Transfer the arc line onto the wood block to make the laminated bow jig. (See Illus. 156.)
22. Coat the inside edges with Hobbypoxy Formula 2 epoxy glue (working time is about 45 minutes), sandwich the sections together, and insert a ⅛″ wooden dowel plug in the hole.
23. Remove the completed bow section from the jig. Prepare both ends for scarf joints by bevel-sanding the two ⅛″ laminated sections for 1″ as indicated in Illus. 157.

Making Scarf Joints

24. ⅛″ aircraft plywood is bevel-sanded 1″ to match the bevel on the bow. Glue in place with super glue.
25. Wind the nylon thread tightly, just short of breaking it. Saturate the thread with super glue. (See Illus. 158.)
26. Make the retainer joint for the spine to the dimensions shown in Illus. 159. Note: Seal the wood on all spar pieces with a coat of Sig Nitrate Clear Dope reduced with Sig Dope Thinner for good brushing.
27. Paint the joints with flat black paint.
28. Lastly, position the sail so that it rests perfectly centered on the frame.

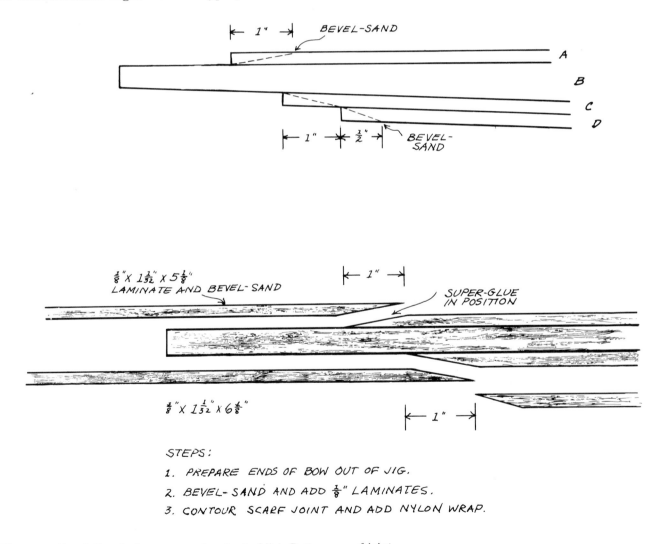

Illus. 157. Top: left end of cross-spar bow (out of jig). Bottom: scarf joint.

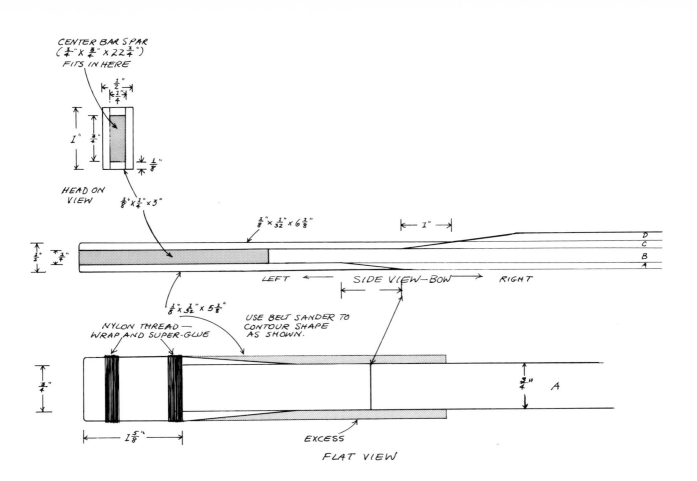

Illus. 158. Step 3—scarf joint.

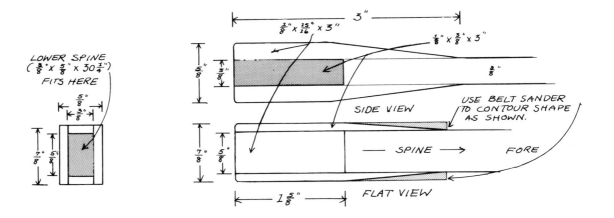

Illus. 159. Step 26—spine retainer joint.

29

Sled Kite Variations—the Scott Sled, Hornbeam Mark I, American Sportsman, and Twin-Trapezoid Vented Sled

The Allison Polymorphic Kite, or The Sled Scott Decision

The sled is one of eight generic kite types. It has been generally assumed that the name, sled, was chosen because the kite resembles a sled in flight. A little digging into kite history, however, reveals a different explanation.

Unlike the ancient flat or more contemporary keeled delta whose moment of creation remains undocumented, the birth of the sled can be traced back to its inventor, William M. Allison.

When he was a young boy, Canadian-born Allison moved during the late 1920s or early '30s to Dayton, Ohio (home of the Wright brothers, at the turn of the century). As an adult, Allison enjoyed helping kids fly their kites, and eventually began experimenting on designs of his own. Around 1950, in a flash of insight, he developed a flexible kite, which he referred to as polymorphic (see Illus. 160). At the time, Al-

lison didn't realize that his semirigid kite was destined for unparalleled popularity. Although he applied for a patent soon after its invention, he had to wait until 1956 for approval.

Allison's flexible kite remained relatively obscure until 1961 or '62 when Frank H. Scott, another Ohio resident, saw a simple advertisement for it in a model airplane publication. According to Scott[1], with only a rudimentary sketch of the kite in the ad to go on, he was inspired to develop a similar design of his own. The early Scott Sleds, as they were called, featured an inverted triangular vent in the lower half with parallel sides, instead of tapered ones towards the trailing edge as illustrated in the ad.

Scott's modified flexible kite flew well enough—and the whole matter could have ended there, except that Frank's father, Walter Scott, who "built sleds by the bushel," sent them as gifts to friends all over the world, including Bob Ingraham, founder of *Kite Tales: The Kiteflier's Magazine*, forerunner to *Kite Lines Magazine*. After a brief write-up by Ingraham in 1964, the Scott Sled, in all its variations, took off.

As for Scott's decision to call his kite a sled, his thinking was in tune with Allison's: The kite was polymorphic, or flexible, and it flew, making it a Flexible Flyer, a brand name for a sled, known to most children in snowbound states. It had never occurred to Scott to call his kite a sled because of its airborne shape.

The Sled Kite—General Tips and Information

While many variations on the sled kite exist, these adaptations are proven performers: the Hornbeam Sled Kite Mark I, the Scott Sled, Ed Grauel's Twin-Trapezoid Vented Sled, and the American Sportsman Keeled Sled by Harry Sauls. Instructions for building each of these kites appear on the following pages.

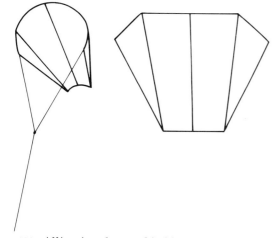

Illus. 160. Allison's polymorphic kite.

A thermal soarer, the sled fares best in light steady winds. Its lack of lateral stiffeners is a mixed aerodynamic blessing. While its flexible canopy adopts a negative dihedral curve providing lift in light winds, the kite collapses easily in crosswinds and flutters earthwards with little chance of recovery from its doomed trajectory.

The sled flies best at the end of a long bridle—typically three times the height of the kite for each leg of the bridle. The long shroudlike lines allow the canopy to open up completely by taking full advantage of available wind as with a descending parachute.

As you begin a project, remember to adhere to the indicated measurements for best results. Dimensions represent the *completed* kite. Construction text is kept to a minimum, though tips pertaining exclusively to a particular design are provided. Building plastic versions (1.5 to 3 mil.) is fairly straightforward. After some experience with tape and plastic, try heat-sealing for a neat, strong plastic bond (see Chapter 16). A tip on cutting plastic: Lightly dampen the side facing the work surface to keep the plastic uniformly flat.

When assembling and sewing ripstop, cotton, or Tyvek-type-14 sleds, remember to make allowances for hems, pockets, and reinforcements at stress areas. Refer to the Brandes Flare Kite project in the next chapter for construction ideas that you can apply to the fabric design.

A bridling tip: Before attaching line to the kite, determine the required bridle length, fold it in half, and tie an overhand 2″ loop in the middle. Measure both legs to precisely the same dimensions and mark the positions. Tie the bridle ends to the keel tips using the marks for reference.

The Scott Sled

After Frank Scott's Design

Construction

As you go through these tips, refer to Illus. 161 for dimensions.

1. Make a kite half-pattern template.
2. Cut out the kite.
3. Use Scotch transparent tape to hold the ³⁄₁₆″ longeron dowels in position prior to cutting the vent. Add strapping tape to prevent the dowels from tearing through fore and aft.
4. Cut out the vent; to prevent tearing at corners, add tape over the cuts or make the points of the triangle slightly rounded.
5. To strengthen the keel tips for the bridle line, use gummed loose-leaf reinforcements (one on either side of each tip) or simply add strips of strapping tape and punch a ⅛″ hole for the bridle.
6. Use 30 lb.–test for the bridle.

Flight Data: Wind range: 4–18 mph
Line: 30 lb. test
AE: ±55°

The Hornbeam Sled Kite Mark I—a Trash Bag Plastic Sled

After Guy D. Aydlett's Design

Hornbeams are reliably good fliers. Instead of holes or other perforations in the canopy to improve sta-

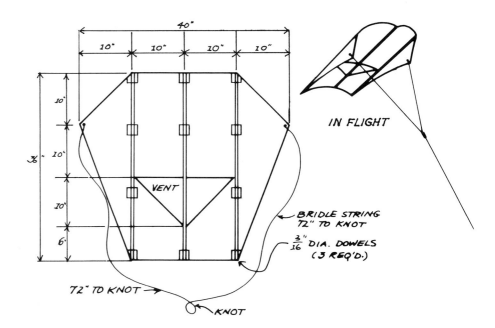

Illus. 161. The Scott Sled Kite.

bility, an arc, or crescent, along the midsection creates an equalizing airflow over the kite's leading edge (see Illus. 162, and page K for the kite in color). Do not diverge from the module relationships in the design.

Construction

1. First, scale the kite based on the design shown in Illus. 163. Establish your module unit by dividing the height by 4. For a 36″ kite: 36 ÷ 4 = 9; multiply each module by 9 for a 36″ version of the kite. For a 16″ kite, multiply modules by 4. A kite with 16″ or 24″ longerons makes efficient use of both standard 48″ dowels (a ⅛″ dowel for 24″ and smaller) and large-size trash bags.
2. Make the kite half-pattern template (Illus. 164).
3. Two 24″ kites may be cut from an unopened trash bag. Trim the sealed bottom end and the top as required to lay the trash bag completely flat. Align the straight sides of the templates along the bag's fold lines (Illus. 165).
4. Cut out a half-pattern for a complete kite (Illus. 166).

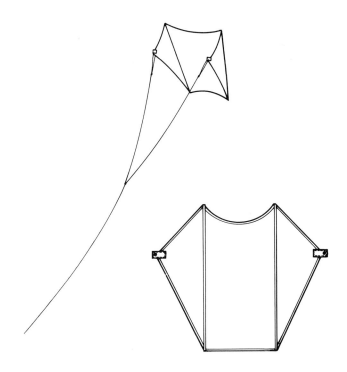

Illus. 162. The Hornbean Sled Kite Mark I.

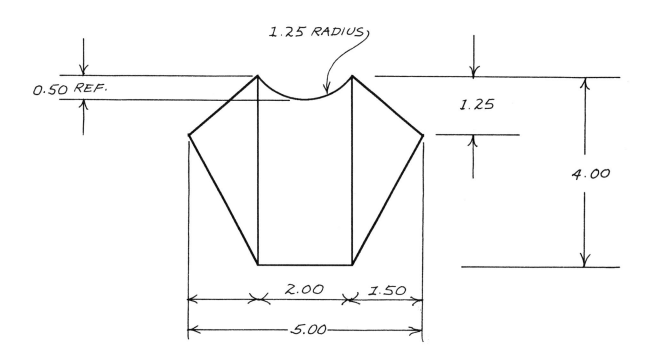

Illus. 163. Step 1.

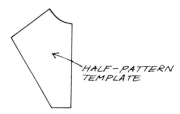

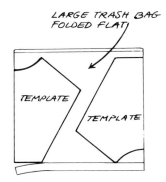

Illus. 164. Step 2.

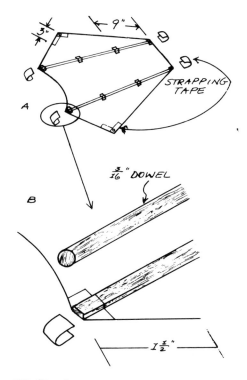

Illus. 167. Step 5.

LARGE TRASH BAG
FOLDED FLAT

TEMPLATE

TEMPLATE

Illus. 165. Step 3.

COMPLETED
KITE SAIL

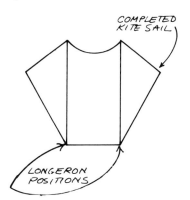

LONGERON
POSITIONS

Illus. 166. Step 4.

middle of the bridle and attach the flying line. (See Illus. 168.) Note: Adding crepe paper streamers to the aft tips of kites 24″ and under makes the kites more stable in higher winds.

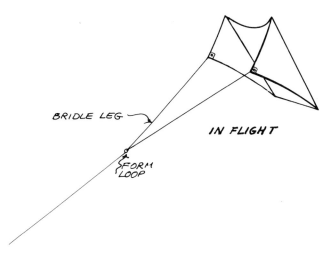

BRIDLE LEG

IN FLIGHT

FORM
LOOP

Illus. 168. Step 6.

5. Use 3″ strips of Scotch transparent tape to secure the longerons in position as shown in A of Illus. 167. Two strips of tape, fore and aft, are sufficient for 16″ kites that can be flown from heavy carpet thread for buttons. Larger kites need additional tape to keep the longerons in position.

The kite shown here illustrates taping (9′ apart) a 36″ kite with ¼″ dowels for longerons. Reinforce the bridle connect points with an overlapping section of strapping tape; punch holes in the keel tips for the bridle.

Optional detail: (See B of Illus. 167.) The tape will hold the longeron tips more securely if the dowel ends are sanded flat as shown. Add strapping tape to prevent the dowel from poking through the transparent tape.

6. The bridle should be three times the height of the kite. For a 36″ version, tie the ends of 18′ of 30 lb.–test line to the keel tips. Form a loop at the

7. Keel tip option: (See the steps in Illus. 169.) Use strapping tape to secure a ¾″ × ⅛″ dowel in place to absorb the stress of the bridle. Punch a ⅛″ hole for the bridle line.

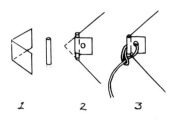

Illus. 169. Step 7.

A Tissue-Paper-and-Straw Sled

Follow the preceding construction steps for the Hornbeam Sled to make a tissue-paper-and-straw sled of smaller proportions (see Illus. 170). Use striped Madras or craft-quality tissue paper. For an 8″ kite, multiply modules by 2. For a 16″ kite, multiply by 4. Splice the straws to size using the method described for Coffee Cup Kites in Illus. 273 on page 184.

Use Scotch transparent tape, fore and aft, to hold the straw longerons in place. Add a strip of tape in the center, too. With a small strip of transparent tape, secure a bridle made of carpet thread for buttons to each keel tip. Another method is to glue gummed loose-leaf reinforcements on each keel tip, and tie the bridle ends through the holes. Tape a

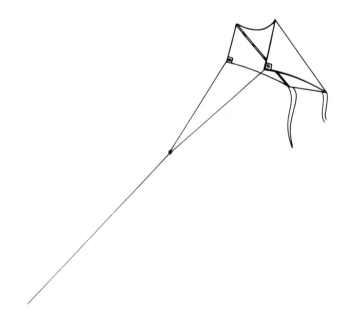

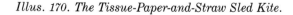

Illus. 170. The Tissue-Paper-and-Straw Sled Kite.

6′ × 1″ crepe-paper streamer tail in the middle or add one to each aft end for stability and color.

The American Sportsman Keeled Sled

Design: Courtesy of Harry Sauls

Harry Sauls's American Sportsman Keeled Sled is aptly named since it pulls like a game fish, especially when climbing upwards towards a high angle of elevation. This sled is steadier than the original and capable of maintaining lateral stability in crosswinds.

Several elements in the American Sportsman modification have contributed towards the improved design. First of all, a series of triangular vents balance the airflow through and over the kite sail; the vents also permit the kite to shed the potential hazards associated with high winds and unexpected gusts. A four-legged bridle helps counteract the main drawback of the original design—lateral instability. A central keel provides added stability—much as it does on a delta, though in reverse. Instead of forming a positive dihedral angle (wings swept upwards, as on a delta), the Sportsman forms a rounded elongated M-shape, or negative dihedral, along the canopy.

Construction

As you go through these tips, refer to Illus. 171.

1. Make pattern templates for the kite parts: the main canopy, side keels, and central keel.
2. Make the sail from .75 oz. ripstop; Tyvek type 14 is also a good choice. For a trash bag version, use heavier 3 mil. plastic and tape all stress points securely. Better yet, heat-weld the plastic seams and longeron sleeves for a stronger kite.
3. Longeron options: ⁵⁄₁₆″ dowel with aluminum-tubing connectors for plastic or Tyvek, and K75 epoxy tubing with ferrule connectors for ripstop.
4. Though not necessary, adding heavy-duty rubber bands to the bridle-line connect points on the keel allows the kite to alter its flight angle in gusts. Instead of a broken bridle or having the kite streak out of control, the kite merely sheds extra wind. (See the Roller Kite project for the bridle arrangement.)
5. Fix the bridle as shown in the illustration using 150 lb. test.

Flight Data: Wind range: 6–20 mph
Line: 150 lb. test
AE: ±60°
Wear gloves

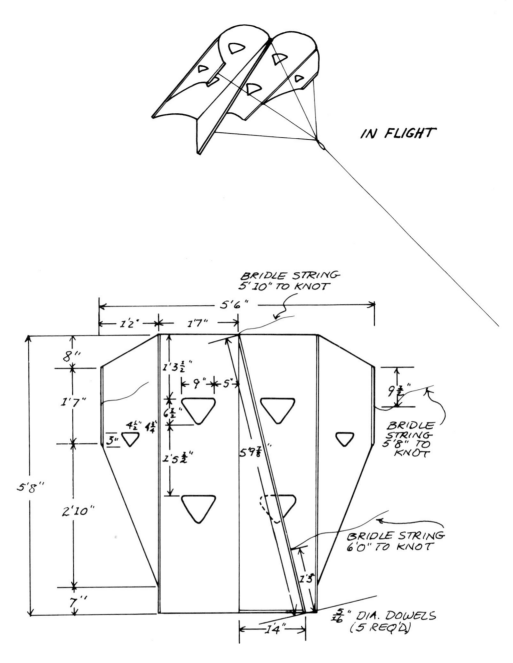

IN FLIGHT

BRIDLE STRING
5'10" TO KNOT

5'6"

1'2"   1'7"

8"

1'3½"

1'7"

9"   5"

6½"

9½"

4½" 1¼"

BRIDLE
STRING
5'8" TO
KNOT

3"

2'5½"

5'8"

5⅞"

2'10"

BRIDLE STRING
6'0" TO KNOT

1'5

7"

14"

5/16" DIA. DOWELS
(5 REQ'D)

Illus. 171. The American Sportsman Keeled Sled Kite.

Dimensions for a Smaller Version

For a smaller version of the American Sportsman, apply the overall construction concept, but use the following dimensions:

• length: 4'
• width: 3' 9½"
• width of panels: 9½" and 13¾"
• width of vents: 3½" and 6½"
• length of longerons: 13¾", 4', and 4¼"
• length of bridle lines: 4', 4', 4'2", and 4'4"
• depth of keel at rear: 11"
• bridle and flying line: 75 lb. test

The Twin-Trapezoid Vented Sled

Design: Courtesy of Ed Grauel

Construction

As you go through these tips, refer to Illus. 172.

1. Make the kite half-pattern template.
2. Cut out the kite and vents. Option: The vents can be left attached at the leading edge.

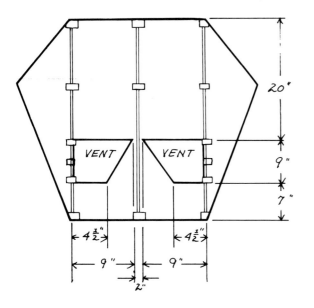

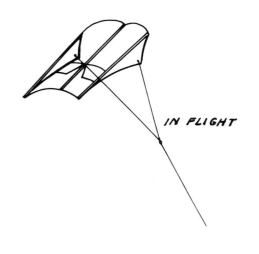

IN FLIGHT

Illus. 172. The Twin-Trapezoid Vented Sled Kite.

3. Refer to the construction tips for the Scott Sled Kite for taping longerons and reinforcing keel tips.
4. Longerons: ⅛″ for the middle dowel, and ³⁄₁₆″ for the side longerons. Option: ⅛″ × ³⁄₁₆″ rectangular Sitka spruce for all three longerons.
5. Make a 72″-long bridle from 30 lb.–test line.

Flight Data: Wind range: 4–20 mph
Line: 30 lb. test
AE: ±60°

[1]Frank Scott, "Correcting Kite History," *Kite Lines*, Winter-Spring 1981, pg. 8.

30

More Complex Sled Kites—the Bullet, Brandes Flare, and Fluted Sled

The Bullet Kite

Design: Courtesy of Ed Grauel

Two Scoops To Go

Ed Grauel's patented Bullet design is the result of his effort to eliminate the sled kite's tendency to wobble and yaw. Sometime around 1973, after trying various types of vents and keels without success, Grauel thought of placing a cover, or canopy, behind the central portion of the sled. The canopy was left open, fore and aft, allowing air to flow freely between the front and rear covers. (For another canopied variation, see the Fluted Sled.)

The canopy, however, didn't improve the kite's performance. As Grauel was about to dismantle the kite, he recalls, "A flash came out of the blue to sew the front and back covers together at the lateral center, forming two channels instead of one." After some sewing and test-flying, Grauel says: "For reasons I can't explain, making two air channels out of one not only eliminated the wobble, but produced a stable and well-flying kite with a high lift ratio." The kite's rapid climbing ability led Grauel to name it Bullet.

Compare the half-pattern for the Bullet's face (step 1 in Illus. 173) with Guy D. Aydlett's Hornbeam Mark I sled half-pattern (in Illus. 164 in the previous chapter). Notice that both kites incorporate the crescent shape along the leading edge to improve performance—but for different reasons. The double crescent along the Bullet face permits the canopy to effectively scoop and channel air towards the trailing edge, whereas the single crescent on the Hornbeam's face reverses the instability along the leading edge. (See the Bullet in color on page K.)

Materials

To make this kite you need:
- 1½ sq. yards of .75 oz. ripstop or type-14 Tyvek—for face, canopy, and optional drogue;
- three ³⁄₁₆″ × 26″ dowels—for longerons;
- ¼″ nylon tape—for drogue and bridle loops;
- ¼″ double-fold bias tape;
- 30 lb.–test line—for 12′ bridle; 5′ lead line—for drogue; and
- ¾″ split key ring—for tether connect point.

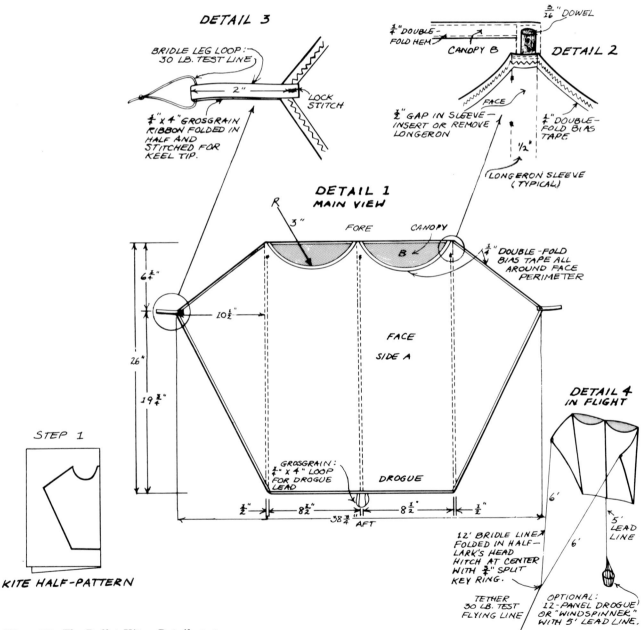

Illus. 173. The Bullet Kite—Details 1–4.

Details

See Illus. 173 for the following details.

- (Detail 1.) Main view—completed kite.
- (Detail 2.) Longeron sleeve.
- (Detail 3.) Keel tip and ¼″ × 4″ nylon-tape bridle leg loop; 30 lb.–test line.
- (Detail 4.) Kite in flight. 12′ bridle folded in half with larks' head hitch in middle on ¾″ split key ring; optional 12-panel drogue or windspinner with 5′ lead line; tether: 30 lb.–test flying line.

Flight Data: Wind range: 5–25 mph (drogue over 15)
Line: 30 lb. test
AE: ±55°

Construction

Hot-cutting:
1. Make a half-pattern template of the face based on the dimensions of the completed kite (Detail 1). Place the vertical edge of the template on the fold of the sail material and hot-cut. Open hot-cut edges carefully.
2. Fold another piece of sail material in half and cut a canopy to the dimensions shown in Illus. 174.

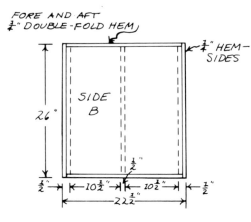

Illus. 174. The Bullet—Step 2.

Sewing:
3. Canopy: Edge-finish, fore and aft, with a ¼″ double-fold hem. Add a simple ¼″ hem on both sides. The completed canopy should measure 26″ × 22½″. (See Detail 2.)
4. Finish the face with ¼″ double-fold bias tape along the entire perimeter (Detail 2).

Hot-tacking:
5. Mark sleeve stitch lines on side "A" of the face to coincide with sleeve marks on side "B" of face.
6. Align the sleeve marks and tack the canopy to the face from the middle sleeve outward. See Illus. 175.

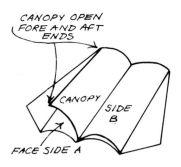

Illus. 175. The Bullet—Step 6.

Sewing:
7. Begin at the middle sleeve and stitch along the tack marks to form the longeron sleeves. Leave a ½″ gap in the stitching near the fore ends to insert or remove spars, as shown in Detail 2. Note: The leading and trailing edges of the canopy are left open, forming two air channels.
8. Stitch the drogue loop at the aft end of the face and bridle loops, as shown in Detail 3.

Hobby saw:
9. Cut three ³⁄₁₆″ × 26″ dowels; trim to fit in sleeves if necessary.

Assembly:
10. Add the 12′ bridle; locate the middle and make a lark's head hitch on the ¾″ split key ring. Add an optional drogue to stabilize the kite in winds over 15 mph. (To make a drogue, turn to Chapter 18.) Attach the tether to the ring—and fly.

The Brandes Flare

Design: Courtesy of Raymond V. Brandes

Glory Days—Made in the U.S.A.

During his drive from New Jersey to Washington, D.C., for the 1986 Smithsonian Kite Festival, Ray Brandes listened to fellow New Jerseyan Bruce Springsteen's "Born in the U.S.A." on his car stereo, and among the songs on the tape was the hit "Glory Days." Little did Brandes know that it would be *his* glory day—for, at the festival to come, with his version of the sled kite, he would win a blue ribbon for none other than "Best Patriotic Kite." (See the Brandes Flare in Illus. 176, and in color on page P.)

General Tips and Information

While many sled variations call for cutting vents in the sail to improve performance, the Brandes Flare has no holes. This kite is based on units of 10 inches, though any preferred dimensional unit would work.

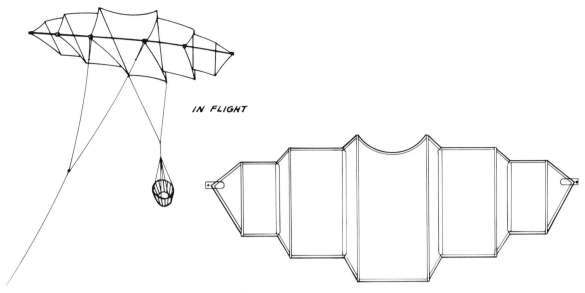

Illus. 176. The Brandes Flare Kite—in flight and back view.

Multiply each module by 10 to arrive at the kite's dimensions. For example, to arrive at the dimension for height, multiply the module 4 by 10 units to get 40 inches.

Constructing the central sled and fins from one color permits you to cut them from one piece of material. Remember to allow for 1″ of extra material for longeron sleeves, and to make a ½″ hem allowance wherever wing panels join.

For the more ambitious kite builder using a parallel color scheme, as with the Brandes Flare shown on page M, plan horizontal sail seams so that the edges end up stitched downwards on the backside. A flat sail seam permits air to flow freely over the kite. Seams facing the wrong direction hinder performance by creating resistance, turbulence, and drag.

When cutting multicolored kites in general, begin with material sewn together first and larger than your templates. For this kite, Brandes made 10 yards of stitched-together striped ripstop in red, white, and red again (basically creating a bolt of combined colors) and then placed the templates over the material. This is easier than trying to piece many sections together accurately. Don't be stingy with fabric; you'll always find use for remnants.

Materials

To make this kite you need:
- 5 yards × 41″ of .75 oz. ripstop or grade-14 Du Pont Tyvek,
- ½″ single-fold seam-binding tape,
- 4 oz. Dacron or crack-and-peel ripstop—for reinforcements,
- 100 lb.–test braided Dacron—for bridle,
- 30 lb.–test braided Dacron—for drogue bridle and line,
- eight ¼″ × 48″ pieces of hardwood dowel or a ³⁄₁₆″ × 48″ fibreglass rod for longerons,
- ¼″ grommets or twill tape for drogue bridle attachments,
- five ½″ O.D. × ¼″ slices of surgical tubing stoppers,
- epoxy tubing (two FL.370 × 48″) and fibreglass ferrule (FL.291 × 32½″)—for spreader bar,
- fishing swivel, and
- two ¾″ split key rings—for bridle and drogue connect points.

Details

See Illus. 177 for the following details.

- (Detail 1.) Left side: wing panels and keels positioned flat for sewing. Right side: wing panels and keels in flight attitude.
- (Detail 2.) 1″ extra material is folded in half to form vertical sleeves; leave a ¾″ gap in the sleeve to insert or remove the longerons.
- (Detail 3.) ½″ hem overlap; align and stitch the sail seam onto the corresponding keels.
- (Detail 4.) Two 48″ pieces of FL.370 epoxy tubing for the spreader bar; 32½″ FL.291 fibreglass ferrule connecting the spreader bar; ½″ FL.370 epoxy stopper glued in the center.
- (Detail 5.) The spreader bar passes through all keel tips and bridle loops; ½″ snug-fitting surgical tubing stoppers at each wing tip; for the two-legged bridle—60″ each leg to the key ring; lark's head hitch; two-legged drogue bridle—60″ each leg with six 60″ lines to the drogue.

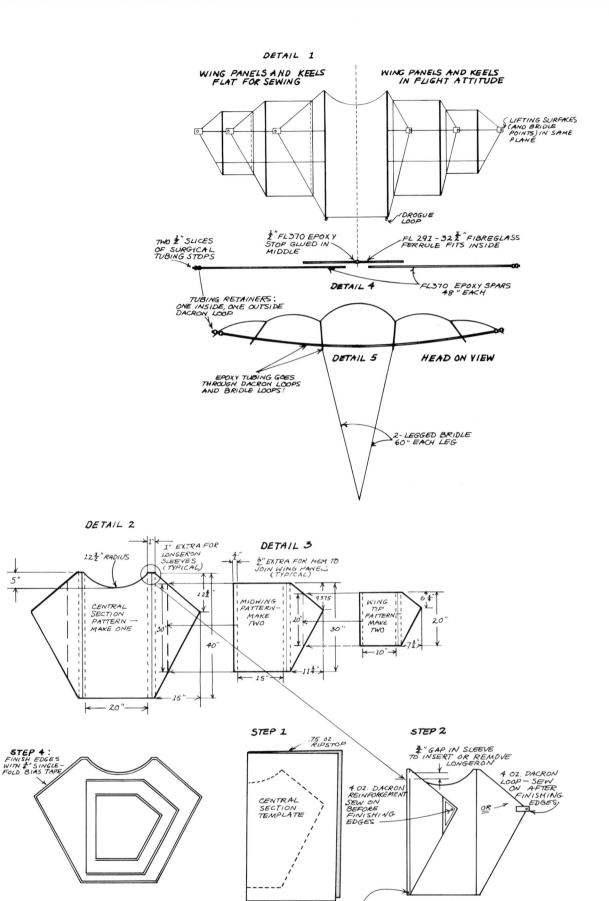

DETAIL 1

WING PANELS AND KEELS
FLAT FOR SEWING

WING PANELS AND KEELS
IN FLIGHT ATTITUDE

(LIFTING SURFACES
(AND BRIDLE
POINTS) IN SAME
PLANE

DROGUE
LOOP

TWO ½" SLICES
OF SURGICAL
TUBING STOPS

½" FL370 EPOXY
STOP GLUED IN
MIDDLE

FL 291 - 32½" FIBREGLASS
FERRULE FITS INSIDE

DETAIL 4

FL370 EPOXY SPARS
48" EACH

TUBING RETAINERS:
ONE INSIDE, ONE OUTSIDE
DACRON LOOP

DETAIL 5

HEAD ON VIEW

EPOXY TUBING GOES
THROUGH DACRON LOOPS
AND BRIDLE LOOPS!

2- LEGGED BRIDLE
60" EACH LEG

DETAIL 2

12½" RADIUS

5"

1"

1" EXTRA FOR
LONGERON
SLEEVES
(TYPICAL)

DETAIL 3

½"

½" EXTRA FOR HEM TO
JOIN WING PANELS
(TYPICAL)

CENTRAL
SECTION
PATTERN —
MAKE ONE

12½"

40"

30"

9.375

MIDWING
PATTERN —
MAKE TWO

20"

30"

WING
TIP
PATTERN
MAKE TWO

6¼"

20"

7½"

15"

20"

15"

11¼"

15"

10"

STEP 4:
FINISH EDGES
WITH ¼" SINGLE-
FOLD BIAS TAPE

STEP 1

.75 OZ.
RIPSTOP

CENTRAL
SECTION
TEMPLATE

STEP 2

¾" GAP IN SLEEVE
TO INSERT OR REMOVE
LONGERON

4 OZ. DACRON
REINFORCEMENT
SEW ON
BEFORE
FINISHING
EDGES

4 OZ. DACRON
LOOP - SEW
ON AFTER
FINISHING
EDGES

OR

EYELETS (GROMMETS) OR
LOOPS FOR DROGUE "BRIDLE"

Illus. 177. The Brandes Flare—details and steps.

Flight Data: Wind range: 4–18 mph
Line: 100 lb. test
AE: ±70°
Wear gloves

Construction

The following instructions are based on using one color for the sail. As you go through these steps, refer to Illus. 177.

Hot cutting:

1. Measure and hot-cut the central section and the accompanying wing panels to the dimensions indicated. (See Step 1 and Details 2 and 3.)
2. Hot-cut six 4 oz. Dacron reinforcements (or crack-and-peel ripstop) for the keel tips. (See Step 2.)
3. Note: The high-aspect ratio (the *span* is considerably greater than its width, or *cord*) of this kite generally results in higher aerodynamic efficiency compromised by lack of stability. A drogue or tail is required even in light winds.

   To make the drogue, hot-cut 12 sections of ripstop to the dimensions shown. (Refer to "Tails and Drogues" for construction details.) Add a six-legged bridle with each leg as long as the drogue.

   Option: Instead of using a drogue, cut six 10′ × 2″ tail strips of ripstop and affix them to the bottom of each longeron sleeve for a flowing aerial display.

Sewing:

4. Finish the edges with double-folded bias tape as shown in Step 4. Note: Sew on triangular Dacron reinforcements prior to finishing the edges. Then, after finishing them, sew on the Dacron loops.
5. Fold the 1″ extra material in half to form ½″ vertical pockets on the back of the central section; leave a ¾″ gap in the stitching for installation or removal of the longerons. Use the same method to form the longeron sleeves on the remaining wings, and connect them to the adjacent panels with a sail-seam stitch.

   Sew ¼″ twill tape loops for the drogue bridle at the bottom of both central longerons when forming the sleeves. Option: Substitute grommets for loops.

Hot cutting:

6. Use a conical-shaped tip on your hot cutter to melt holes in the Dacron reinforcement material large enough for the spreader bar to pass through.

Hobby saw:

7. Cut the spreader, ferrule, and pieces of surgical tubing to size.

Assembly:

8. Cut three sets of ¼″ dowel to size and insert them into the longerons pockets. Assemble as illustrated.

9. Make the bridle from 100 lb.-test braided Dacron. Thread the bridle loops through the Dacron reinforcements and secure them with a knot. Insert the spreader through the reinforcements and the bridle loops as shown. Attach the drogue to the loop with a fishing swivel.

The Fluted Sled

Design: Courtesy of
Helen Bushell

Music of the Wind

The flute is the music of the wind and the theme of this sled variation. Hovering overhead, the Fluted Sled has vents that catch the wind at just the right pitch and angle. The Fluted Sled is shown in flight in Detail 1 of Illus. 178; to see this sled in color, turn to page M.

General Tips and Information

On the technical end, the success of the Fluted Sled hinges on one critical dimension: 153° + 1° measured from the horizontal centerline with a protractor. Extending the lines outward to the side keel panels marks the fulcrum points.

Here's bad news and good news. First, the bad news: Since the dimensions for this kite call for widths in excess of the standard 41½″ for .75 oz. ripstop, you'll have to piece sections together. The good news is that this presents an opportunity to combine colors that please you.

A tip: Tyvek is available in 60″ widths, which means you can make the Fluted Sled from two whole pieces, if you don't mind an all-white kite. (Tyvek can be decorated with heavy-duty fabric markers.)

Materials

To make this kite you need:
- 6 yards of .75 ripstop, or 4½ yards of 60″-wide Tyvek;
- two pieces of ⅜″ × 48″ dowel or K75 epoxy tubing—for longerons, ferrules (fitting longerons: measure first, then cut);
- ⅜″ × 20″ dowel or K75 epoxy tubing—for space bar;
- 4 oz. Dacron reinforcement material—for fulcrum points;
- ¼″ single-fold bias tape;
- six vinyl end caps—for longeron tips and space bar;
- ⁵⁄₁₆″ I.D. polypropylene tubing—for space bar;
- ¾″ split key ring; and
- 12′ of 100 lb.–test braided Dacron—for bridle.

Details

- (Detail 1 in Illus. 178.) In flight. The space bar prevents the bridle from twisting; 56″ from the keel to the space bar; 18″ from the space bar to the two point; 12′ of bridle line.
- (Detail 2 in Illus. 178.) Space-bar tip. The line is glued between the vinyl end cap and the slice of polypropylene tubing.
- (Detail 3 in Illus. 178.) 12″ of bridle line: 56″ from the fulcrum point to the space bar, 16″ to the middle of the lark's head hitch on the key ring.
- (Detail 4 in Illus. 179.) The bridle connect point. Dacron-reinforce first; then add the grommet. Use ¼″ single-fold bias tape.
- (Detail 5a in Illus. 180.) Main view. 1″ sleeve; 2½″ gap in the sleeve stitching, for inserting or removing the longerons; ¼″ single-fold bias tape along the face and keel perimeter. Kite dimensions: 48″ height; 72″ width; 72″ rear fluted canopy stitched evenly onto the face section at 7″ increments; 3½″ vents on the kite face; stitch outside 1″ of the canopy to the keel for the longeron sleeve.
- (Detail 5b in Illus. 181.) Angular-keel option. The rounded fluttering keel can be eliminated by drawing connecting lines from the longeron ends to the bridle point. Trim the excess. Follow the instructions in Step 3.
- (Detail 6 in Illus. 182.) Ensure symmetry by hot-tacking the middle of the canopy to the bottom of

the face, from front to back. Work left or right to complete.

Flight Data: Wind range: 5–15 mph
Line: 100 lb. test
AE: ±65°
Wear gloves

Construction

As you go through these steps, refer to the various details.

Hot-cutting:
1. Measure and hot-cut the sail face and back canopy to the dimensions shown. See the pattern in Illus. 183 and a typical piecing arrangement in Illus. 184.

   With a straightedge and pencil, lay a grid over the face to fix the middle points for each vent. These are reference points from the left corner of the leading edge: The cross-hair middle of the vent is 6″ down and 3½″ in from the vertical side of the face; the panel segments are 7″ apart.
2. The curve of the side keels is a 24″ radius measured from a point along the horizontal centerline as shown. Tie a pencil to a 2′ length of string and fix the other end to the radius point. Hold the string out to the edge and mark the arc. Next, establish the fulcrum points by using a protractor to mark the 153° angle from the midpoint of the centerline.

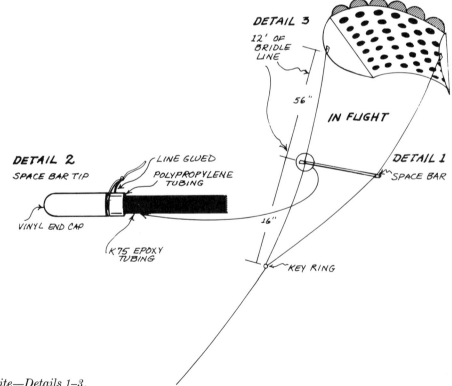

Illus. 178. The Fluted Sled Kite—Details 1–3.

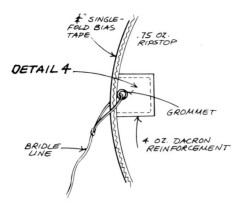

DETAIL 4

¼" SINGLE-FOLD BIAS TAPE

.75 OZ. RIPSTOP

GROMMET

BRIDLE LINE

4 OZ. DACRON REINFORCEMENT

Illus. 179. The Fluted Sled—Detail 4.

3. Fold the face in half and hot-cut the radius curve in both keels for symmetry. Open the face and hot-cut the vents using a 3½" template.

Sewing:

4. Reinforce the fulcrum points as illustrated. Finish the perimeter of the sail face and keels with ¼" single-fold bias tape. Insert grommets at the fulcrum ½" from the edge.

5. Use a ¼" hem along the entire canopy section. Mark the back along the vertical (the side facing the sun) into six 12" segments that correspond to six 7" panels on the face.

6. To ensure symmetry, always work from the middle outward. Begin by aligning the middle stitch guideline of the canopy and the face as shown.

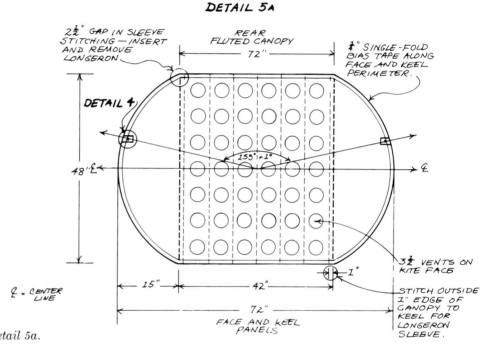

DETAIL 5A

2½" GAP IN SLEEVE STITCHING — INSERT AND REMOVE LONGERON

REAR FLUTED CANOPY
72"

¼" SINGLE-FOLD BIAS TAPE ALONG FACE AND KEEL PERIMETER.

DETAIL 4

48" ℄

155° ± 1°

℄

℄ = CENTER LINE

15"   42"

72"

FACE AND KEEL PANELS

3½ VENTS ON KITE FACE

1"

STITCH OUTSIDE 1" EDGE OF CANOPY TO KEEL FOR LONGERON SLEEVE.

Illus. 180. The Fluted Sled—Detail 5a.

DETAIL 5B

FORE

OPTION: FOR A STRONGER KEEL—CUT TWO SECTIONS TO FORM A BIAS JOIN WITH THE STRAIGHT GRAIN ALONG THE LEADING EDGES (SEE PAGE 57 FOR AN EXAMPLE OF A TWO-PIECE CAMBERED KEEL).

BRIDLE POINT (FULCRUM)

OPTION: ANGULAR KEEL

THE ROUNDED FLUTTERING KEEL CAN BE ELIMINATED BY DRAWING CONNECTING LINES FROM THE LONGERON ENDS TO THE BRIDLE POINT. TRIM EXCESS.

LONGERON

AFT

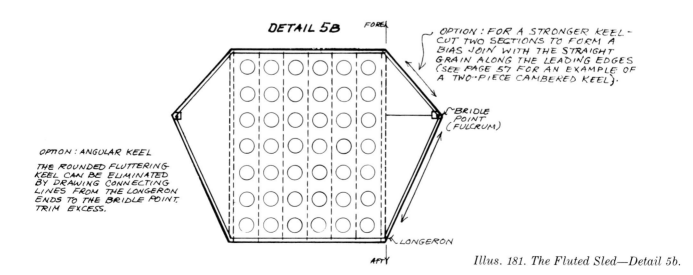

Illus. 181. The Fluted Sled—Detail 5b.

123

DETAIL 6

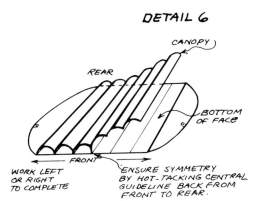

Illus. 182. The Fluted Sled—Detail 6.

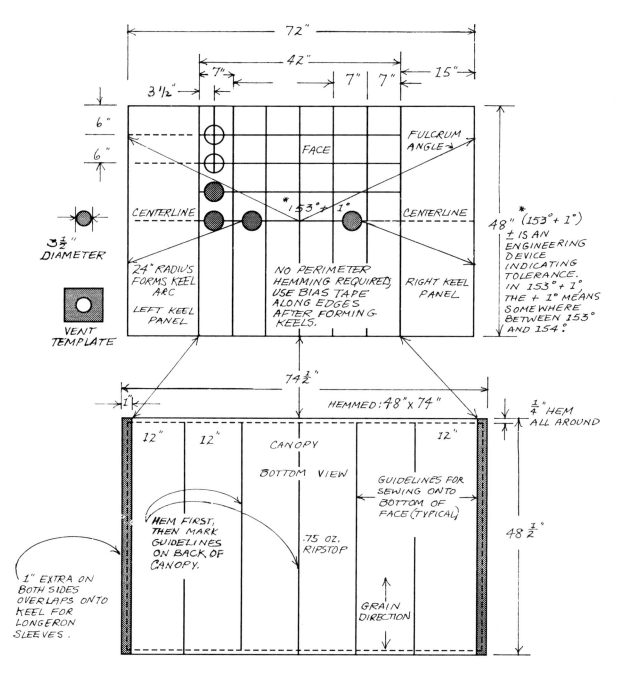

Illus. 183. The Fluted Sled—patterns.

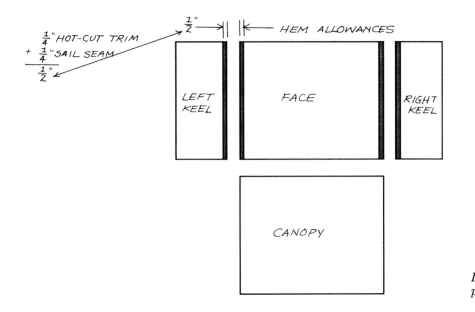

Illus. 184. The Fluted Sled—typical piecing arrangement.

Hot-tack the canopy onto the back of the face from the front to the rear.

7. Using the remaining stitch guidelines on the canopy, hot-tack in either direction until the canopy is completely secured to the bottom of the sail face. Stitch over the hot-tack tracks until all sections are sewn. Stitch the outside edge of the canopy to the keel on each side to form 1″ longeron sleeves.

Assembly:

8. Cut the longerons and the space bar to size. Fix the bridle as illustrated. Recommended bridle lengths for sled kites are typically 3 × the height (48″) = 12′.

31
The Rhomboid Box Kite

The Goose and the Box Kite—a Fable

It happened during the middle of the summer long ago. The hot sun was high and bright overhead. Barely a breeze blew across the meadow that stretched for miles towards the horizon. Not a tree was in sight. Purple and yellow wildflowers dotted the green carpet. A long piece of white line lay strewn, as if abandoned, for hundreds of feet along the grass. At the end of the line was a lone box kite.

The kite stood upright on its square base in the middle of the field, feeling useless and dejected because he couldn't fly. Where was the wind? he cried. Miles away, he saw several Indian fighter kites somehow flying effortlessly in and out of the clouds in the near-still air of the afternoon. The box kite felt sad; life had no purpose for him if he couldn't fly.

He looked up and prayed for wind. If only the wind picked up, he could achieve his ultimate purpose. But the air continued to move slowly around him. The kite looked downwards at the ground and sighed, thinking that his prayers would never be answered.

Suddenly, a shadow eclipsed the sun and a rush of air came up against one of the kite's flat sides, nearly tilting him over. He gazed upwards with hope in his heart. But no sooner had joy filled his sails then he realized that the breeze he felt was merely the stirring of a bird overhead.

"What's this, a goose? A silly goose?" he said.

The bird's enormous wings were completely spread open as he circled round and round. Finally, he made a precise two-legged landing near the kite.

"I saw you on the ground and felt you might need a hand," said the white-plumed bird.

The box kite couldn't hide his feelings.

"It can't be all that bad," said the bird. "Tell me about it."

In a whisper, the kite declared, "My creator has forsaken me. He became frustrated when I couldn't fly without more wind, and left me here on the ground."

The big white bird pecked at the ground, saying, "Go on, I'm listening."

"Well, that's it. I was made just yesterday, with hopes of high flying. I let my creator down and I'll remain here until the sun scorches my cotton sail to ashes or the rains destroy me."

"Black or white, is it? No in-between? What if the wind picks up? Surely you'll fulfill your birthright then?"

The box kite shrugged. There was no hope in his heart, and the bird felt the emptiness.

"The winds of fortune change for the brave and the patient," said the bird.

"Don't you understand? How would you? You're a goose. I am untethered. Should a wind come along, I would simply blow over without my line fastened to the earth."

The bird replied, "You are simply stuck in a thought. It's really a simple matter."

"You think so?"

"I know so. Yet, that is not the complete answer. You have an attitude problem. Take it from an expert."

The kite got riled, and said: "Attitude? What do you mean? I want to fly. I have prayed to fly. I have promised my soul to heaven for just one flight. I desire it more than anything." Worn out with explanations, the kite languished under the sun.

"I'm not sympathetic to despair," said the bird. "You take my meaning incorrectly."

"You said . . . attitude?"

The bird interrupted. "Yes, attitude. Flying requires the correct attitude."

"That's just what I . . ."

The bird began honking. "Listen. Attitude means how you face the wind. It has little to do with desire, more with posture, I'd say. You can't fly if you aren't facing the wind at the right angle."

"But I can't . . ."

"Just listen. If you want to be noticed, you must show more of yourself. In the case of the wind, you must change your attitude, your shape, and present more of what you are to the available fates and breezes."

"I am a square box kite. How can I change my shape? I'm not a genie, just a kite."

The bird stretched its neck as high as it could go. "Yes, it's true you are a square but only because you think you are."

"The power of thought. It seems I've heard that before, though I can't recall where," mused the kite.

"Change comes from inside. I'll show you. Look at me. A thought to my wings and look." The bird extended his enormous wings, easily catching the light air current. He had to balance himself on one leg and then the other to keep from lifting off the ground.

"Showing more gets attention. It works for me and it will work for you."

"I'm a box kite. Rigid sticks of equal length support this body. I can't change what I am."

"The idea is not to change what you are but to make the best of what you've got," said the bird, undulating his long neck. "Here, give me those rigid sticks that confine you to earth. And who said or where is it written that they have to be of equal length?"

The bird used its bill to pull out every stick that kept the kite rigid. The kite was now a mass of scattered sticks and loose fabric.

"You've destroyed me. I have nothing to hold me up. You call this help?"

The bird ignored the kite, though he did remark before flying off, "I'll return soon and you'll see I am your fowl weather friend."

For a long time, the box kite lay still under the unrelenting sun. Finally a familiar shadow circled over the field, and then the big white bird landed next to him. In his bill were sticks of two different lengths.

Placing the sticks near the kite, the bird said, "Here's your ticket to heaven, my friend." With that, the bird began positioning and fitting a new set of sticks within the cells of the hapless fabric. Within a few moments, the bird exclaimed, "Yes, that looks about right."

The kite was upright again. "Something feels different. It's subtle, but I definitely feel . . . bigger." But how is that possible, thought the kite. I'm a box kite. So much sail—no more, no less.

With the kite in a state of consternation, the bird picked up the end of the flying line, flew upwind and tied the line securely to a sturdy bush. By the time the bird returned, the kite had rediscovered himself.

"I'm wider than before. That's it, isn't it? I really don't understand how, but I feel lighter, too, somehow."

"Changing the size of your cross spars has made a new kite out of you." The bird opened its wings and cradled the kite between them. Turning the transformed kite towards the gentle breeze, he proclaimed: "You are not a square kite any longer but a rhombus kite with all the privileges due that form."

The mild breeze that had done little for the box kite before now lifted him off the earth for the first time in his short life. "I'm flying. I'm flying," called the kite.

Within moments, the flying line on the ground straightened, stretched, and became taut, as the rhombus rose higher and higher. The bird flew alongside. Nearly a thousand feet up now, the kite steadied and looked below. He felt that he was born to be at this elevation and his life's purpose was now fulfilled.

The bird circled the kite. "I knew you'd get the hang of it right off. You're on your own now."

Then a dreaded thought entered the kite's consciousness. "What if the wind stops, I'll sink like a stone," the kite yelled to the bird. "Don't leave me!"

The bird circled again, making sure that his wings didn't brush against the hysterical kite. "Look. Look down there."

As the kite peered down, joy exploded in his heart.

"Yes, it's my creator," said the kite.

"From now on, all will be well for you, my friend. Now I'm off on a journey to another tale."

"How can I repay you? What can I do?" asked the kite.

Swoosh went the bird as he dove and circled back again.

"Just pass what you've learned along. Someday you'll meet a kite with a problem. Consider it payment in full."

"Done," said the rhombus.

"One more thing . . ."

The rhombus looked apprehensive.

"I am a swan, not a goose!"

With that said, the swan flew off quickly, then dipped one wing and banked to the left for a last look back. A happy small boy had taken the flying line from the bush to fly his kite.

Aspect Ratio and the Rhomboid Box Kite

In basic terms, the aspect ratio of a surface answers the aerodynamic question: How great is its span compared to its average chord, or width. While this may seem esoteric to the lay person, aspect ratio is responsible for a kite's lifting efficiency.

A rhombus-shaped box kite has a higher aspect ratio than its square counterpart (see Illus. 185). This

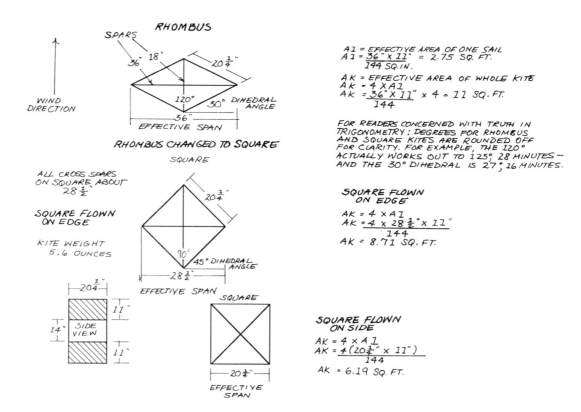

Illus. 185. Square kite changed to rhombus.

means that the rhombus presents more sail area to the wind, making it an efficient and superior light-wind box kite. While some high-aspect-ratio lifting surfaces, like delta shapes, often trade substantial lift ability for stability, a three-dimensional rhombus offers virtually all the benefits of a higher aspect configuration without giving up stability.

The box kite is an ideal example to illustrate aspect ratio since it can be changed to a rhombus by simply changing the size of its cross spars. The chart in Illus. 186 shows how performance in several categories varies by simply changing the aspect ratio, dihedral angle, and bridle configuration. While the formulas provided do not account for all aerodynamic variables, they do provide specific numbers for comparison.

Although you don't need to know about aspect ratio and other aerodynamic principles to enjoy kite flying, a basic understanding is helpful should you decide to design your own kite. The main considerations in kite design are aspect ratio, effective lifting area, sail loading (Illus. 187), and dihedral angle. An explanation of how these elements affect flight, as well as a formula to determine, in advance, the minimum wind speed necessary to lift your kite can be found in Illus. 186.

BOX KITE WEIGHT IN OZ. = 5.6	RHOMBUS	SQUARE ON EDGE	SQUARE FLAT
ASPECT RATIO	$\frac{56}{11} = 3.27$	$\frac{28.5}{11} = 2.59$	$\frac{20.25}{11} = 1.84$
EFFECTIVE LIFTING AREA IN SQ. FT.	11	8.71	6.19
SAIL LOADING $\frac{WT. \quad OZ.}{EFF. AREA FT.^2}$	$\frac{5.6}{11} = .51$	$\frac{5.6}{8.71} = .64$	$\frac{5.6}{6.19} = .90$
MINIMUM WIND SPEED REQUIRED MPH $= 7 \sqrt{\frac{W \quad OZ.}{A \quad ft.^2}}$	$7\sqrt{.51} = 5.0$	$7\sqrt{.64} = 5.6$	$7\sqrt{.90} = 6.7$

THE COEFFICIENT 7 IS USED FOR KITES REQUIRING MORE LIFT. USE 5 FOR LIGHT-WIND KITES LIKE DELTAS.

HERE'S ANOTHER METHOD OF DETERMINING THE EFFECTIVE LIFTING AREA OF KITES WITH SURFACES AT ANGLES TO THE HORIZONTAL WITHOUT KNOWING SPAR DIMENSIONS.

YOU WILL NEED TO KNOW:
  • TOTAL AREA OF THE SAIL SURFACE IN SQ. FT.,
  • THE DIHEDRAL ANGLE, AND
  • THE COSINE OF THE DIHEDRAL ANGLE.
THEN MULTIPLY THE AREA BY THE COSINE OF THE DIHEDRAL ANGLE FOR THE EFFECTIVE SPAN.

Illus. 186. Comparison chart.

EFFECTIVE AREA OF LIFT REFERS TO THE AMOUNT OF AREA YOU WOULD MEASURE IF YOU PROJECTED A SILHOUETTE OF THE KITE IN ITS FLIGHT ATTITUDE ON A SCREEN. SIDE PANELS THAT EXIST IN THE PLANE OF FLIGHT, SUCH AS KEELS ON DELTAS, PROVIDE NO VERTICAL LIFT AND ARE NOT INCLUDED AS A LIFTING SURFACE.

WHILE THESE CALCULATIONS DO NOT CONSIDER POCKETING, BRIDLE SETTING, AND OTHER FACTORS, THE FIGURES ARE USEFUL AS A UNIFIED BASIS FOR COMPARISON.

BOOKS ON TRIGONOMETRY FEATURE TABLES WITH ALL THE COSINES FROM 0 TO 90°; A SCIENTIFIC CALCULATOR OR A COMPUTER PROGRAM WITH A SCIENTIFIC CALCULATOR FUNCTION ARE ALSO CONVENIENT MEANS FOR DETERMINING THE COSINE VALUE OF THE DIHEDRAL ANGLE.

ONE OF FOUR PANELS OF A BOX KITE LIFTING SURFACE — HORIZONTAL PLANE — ° DIHEDRAL ANGLE

Illus. 187. It's true that the best laid plans often never get off the ground. . . . Yet Charlie Brown is right—sail loading is an essential consideration in determining the efficiency of a kite. (Courtesy of United Media.)

128

Materials

To make this kite you need:
- .75 oz. ripstop or 1½ yards × 41" of Tyvek Type 14—for cells,
- eight ¼" × 36" hardwood dowels,
- four ¼" × 18" hardwood dowels,
- 1" × 16" nylon webbing,
- ¼" (I.D.) × 36" semirigid plastic tubing,
- 6 feet of 50 lb.–test line—for bridle, and
- a ¾" split key ring.

Details

See Illus. 188 for the following details.
- (Detail 1.) Main view. The fore and aft cells, and the bridle connect points.
- (Detail 2.) Top view. The cross spar and longeron.
- (Detail 3.) In flight. The bridle fore leg is 30" to the loop; the aft leg is 39" to the loop.
- (Detail 4.) The lark's head hitch with a ¾" split key ring. Attach flying line to the ring.

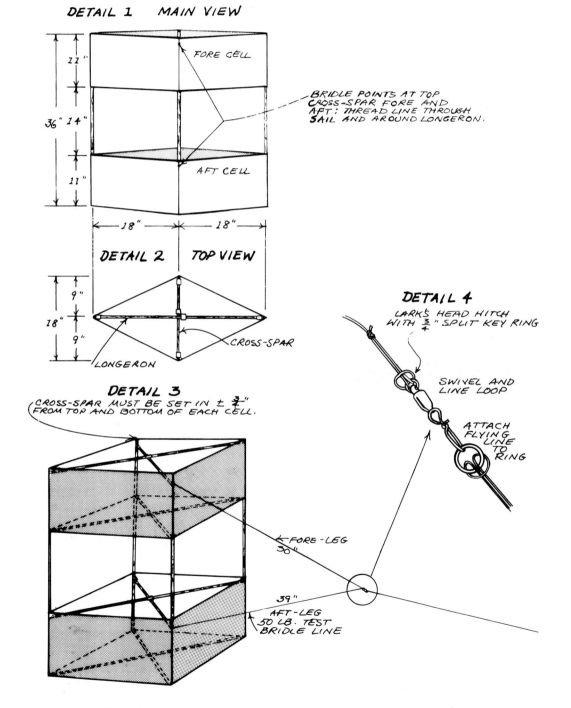

DETAIL 1   MAIN VIEW

22"

36" 14"

11"

FORE CELL

BRIDLE POINTS AT TOP
CROSS-SPAR FORE AND
AFT: THREAD LINE THROUGH
SAIL AND AROUND LONGERON.

AFT CELL

18"   18"

DETAIL 2   TOP VIEW

9"

18"

9"

CROSS-SPAR

LONGERON

DETAIL 3
CROSS-SPAR MUST BE SET IN ± ¾"
FROM TOP AND BOTTOM OF EACH CELL.

FORE-LEG
30"

39"

AFT-LEG
50 LB. TEST
BRIDLE LINE

DETAIL 4
LARK'S HEAD HITCH
WITH ¾" SPLIT KEY RING

SWIVEL AND
LINE LOOP

ATTACH
FLYING
LINE
TO
RING

Illus. 188. The Rhomboid Box Kite—details.

Flight Data: Wind range: 8–15 mph
Line: 50 lb. test
AE: ±60°
Wear gloves

Construction

Hot cutting:

1. Mark and hot-cut a standard roll of ripstop into four 12″ panels for the fore and aft cells (Illus. 189).

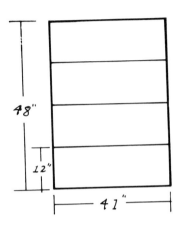

Illus. 189. Step 1.

Sewing:

2. Align panel one over two, and panel three over four. Mark centerlines and stitch edges ¼″ in from the edge as shown in Illus. 190.

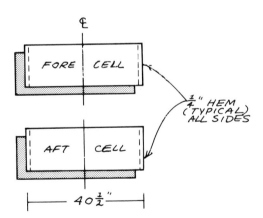

Illus. 190. Step 2.

3. The height of each cell should measure 11″ after you've made a ¼″ double-fold hem on both edges (Illus. 191).

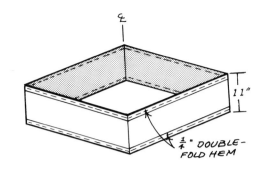

Illus. 191. Step 3.

Hot cutting:

4. Hot-cut 1″ nylon webbing into pockets and loops as shown in Illus 192.

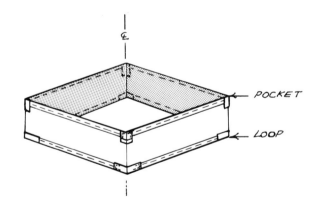

Illus. 192. Step 4.

Sewing:

5. Sew pockets on top half and loops on lower half of each corner of both cells. See Illus. 193, as well as Illus. 195.

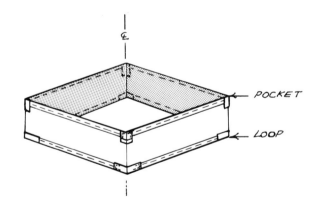

Illus. 193. Step 5.

Hobby saw:

6. To make longeron and cross-spar connectors, cut 18 sections from 1½″ × ¼″ I.D. semirigid plastic tubing; then slice each section halfway through at the center (Illus. 194).

7. Cut all spars—four longerons at ¼″ × 36″, four cross spars at ¼″ × 36″, and eight cross spars at ¼″ × 18″.

130

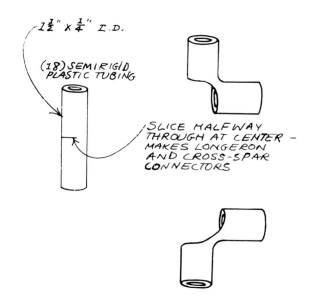

1½" × ¼" I.D.

(18) SEMIRIGID PLASTIC TUBING

SLICE HALFWAY THROUGH AT CENTER — MAKES LONGERON AND CROSS-SPAR CONNECTORS

Illus. 194. Step 6.

Assembly:

8. Turn the cells so that the pockets and loops are inside (Illus. 195). Position the plastic tubing connectors as shown in the Detail. Then insert the longerons through the loops and into the pockets.

9. Intersect 18″ and 36″ cross spars using a plastic tubing connector (Illus. 196). Make four sets.

10. Place the cross spars into the fore and aft cells. (See Detail 3 in Illus. 188 for reference.) Cells should be taut, but they shouldn't distort the sail. If adjustment is required, trim the 18″ cross spar slightly.

11. Thread the 50 lb.–test line bridle through the sail and around the longerons at the fore and aft top cross-spar points. (See Details 2 and 3 in Illus. 188.) The fore leg of the bridle is ±30″ to the lark's head hitch; the aft leg is ±39″.

12. Attach the tether split key ring and fly the kite on its edge!

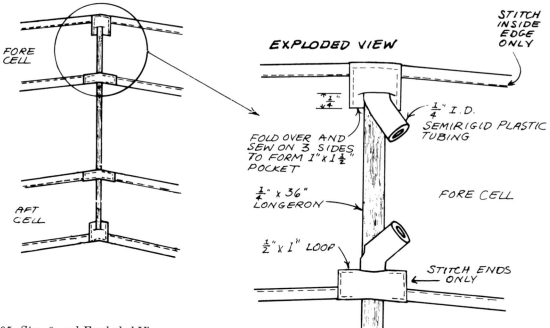

FORE CELL

AFT CELL

EXPLODED VIEW

STITCH INSIDE EDGE ONLY

FOLD OVER AND SEW ON 3 SIDES TO FORM 1″ × 1½″ POCKET

¼" I.D. SEMIRIGID PLASTIC TUBING

¼" × 36″ LONGERON

FORE CELL

½" × 1″ LOOP

STITCH ENDS ONLY

Illus. 195. Step 8 and Exploded View.

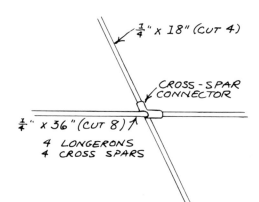

¼" × 18″ (CUT 4)

CROSS-SPAR CONNECTOR

¼" × 36″ (CUT 8)
4 LONGERONS
4 CROSS SPARS

Illus. 196. Step 9.

32
The Winged Box Kite

The Kite That Suspended a Talk Show

I had been asked to help promote a kite festival in Florida, which was why I was a guest several weeks later on a Jacksonville TV talk show. When it was time for my segment, I offered to show the host and audience a selection of kite types. First I explained that not all kites are shaped like the Diamond Eddy.

Then I took out a winged box kite of silver Mylar (see Detail 1 in Illus. 197).

Just as I began to describe the kite, the bright overhead studio lights hit the mirrorlike finish on the Mylar. The intense flash caused camera number one to go down with a burned-out mechanical retina. As Murphy's Law would have it, cameras two and three failed for reasons unknown to this guest. The excited producer ran up to me and confiscated the Mylar kite, promising to return it after the show. Dead air

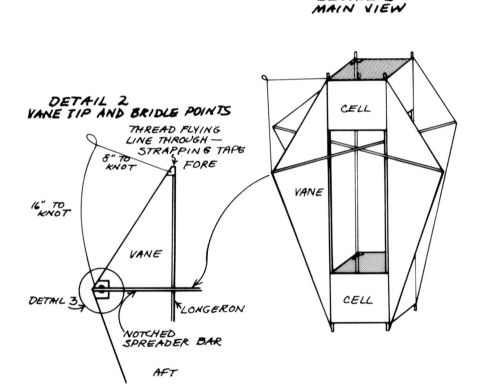

DETAIL 1
MAIN VIEW

CELL

VANE

CELL

DETAIL 2
VANE TIP AND BRIDLE POINTS

THREAD FLYING
LINE THROUGH
STRAPPING TAPE
FORE

8" TO
KNOT

16" TO
KNOT

VANE

DETAIL 3

NOTCHED
SPREADER BAR

LONGERON

AFT

DETAIL 3

TRIM
EXCESS

1"

¼" HOLE

NOTCHED ¼"
SPREADER SPAR

REINFORCE ALL FOUR
VANE WING TIPS
WITH STRAPPING TAPE.

Illus. 197. Details 1–3.

time for nearly two minutes! Compared to this minor disaster, the remainder of my demonstration was uneventful.

At the kite festival the next morning, the sky was blue, the clouds were high, and there was a terrific turnout. The Mylar kite that had stopped the show flew high and bright over the sandy beach all day.

Materials

To make this kite you need:
- 40″ × 48″ sail material: 3 mil. Mylar, Tyvek, kraft paper, or designer shopping bags with art already on them (see the color illustration on page L—this winged box kite is made from a Bloomingdale's department store shopping bag);
- six ¼″ × 48″ dowels cut to size—for four longerons and two spreader spars;
- ½″ Scotch Magic and 1″ strapping tape; and
- 20 lb.–test line—for bridle and flying line.

Details

The following details are shown in Illus. 197.

- (Detail 1.) Main view.
- (Detail 2.) The vane with bridle points.
- (Detail 3.) The reinforced vane tip and the notched spreader spar.

Flight Data: Wind range: 5–20 mph
Line: 20 lb. test
AE: ±65°

Construction

Note: Use ½″ Scotch Magic or other strong transparent tape. Apply strapping tape only where specified.

Cutting, Taping, and Assembly:
1. Place the cell template on the sail material and cut both pieces at same time for symmetry. Mark the longeron positions. See Illus. 198.
2. Position the vane template over four layers of sail material to cut symmetrical vanes (Illus. 199).
3. Cut four ¼″ × 36″ dowels.
4. Tape the longerons to the cells along the marks as shown in Illus. 200. Allow the longerons to overlap the cells by ¾″ on both ends.
5. Join the free edges of the cells with tape; reinforce with tape on the underside of the seam, as well (Illus. 201).
6. Tape one vane to each longeron. All vanes must be aligned with fore and aft points in the same direction. The tape goes from one side of the vane, over the dowel, and back onto the other side of the vane. Strapping tape, fore and aft, secures the vane. See Illus. 202.

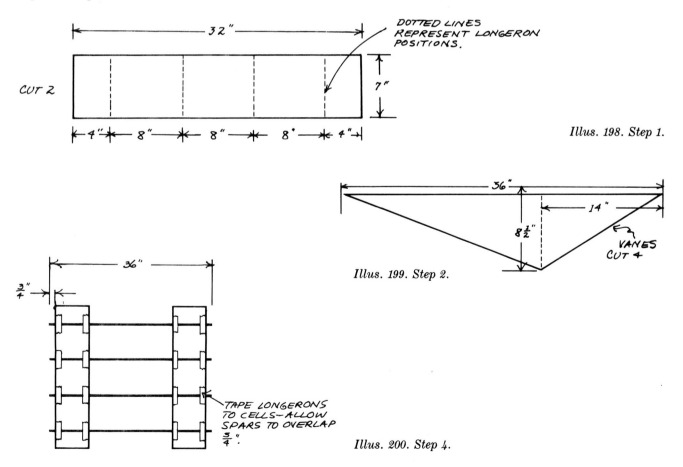

Illus. 198. Step 1.

Illus. 199. Step 2.

Illus. 200. Step 4.

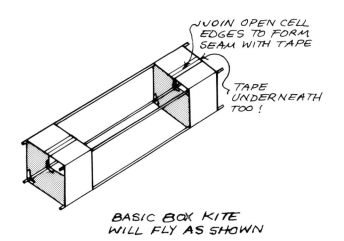

JOIN OPEN CELL
EDGES TO FORM
SEAM WITH TAPE

TAPE
UNDERNEATH
TOO!

BASIC BOX KITE
WILL FLY AS SHOWN

Illus. 201. Step 5.

7. Cut two spreader spars at ¼″ × ±27″; make a ± ½″ notch on all ends and in the same direction. (See Detail 3 in Illus. 197.) When the notches are fitted inside the vane-tip holes, the spreaders must keep the cells open and taut.
8. Use a needle to thread the bridle line through the strapping tape as shown in Detail 2 of Illus. 197.

Instructions for a Mini-Version

To make a mini-version of this kite, divide all dimensions in half, and use ⅛″ dowel, .5 mil. Mylar, button carpet thread for the bridle, and 12 lb.–test flying line. Allow the longerons to overlap the cells by ¾″, as shown.

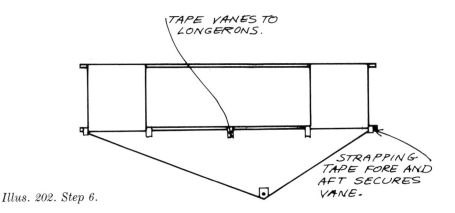

TAPE VANES TO
LONGERONS.

STRAPPING
TAPE FORE AND
AFT SECURES
VANE.

Illus. 202. Step 6.

33
The Delta Box Kite

Design: Courtesy of Alex Dunton

Fast Climber

The climb rate of Alex Dunton's delta box variation (see Detail 6 in Illus. 206) leaves one with a crick in the neck. For six years running, Dunton's kite eclipsed all comers in the altitude-sprint competition held at the Wright Kite Festival in Kill Devil Hill, North Carolina. In this competition, the kite hauling out the most line in 30 seconds wins. As kite justice would have it, Dunton was bettered in the seventh year by two competitors flying replicas (made with

Dunton's help) of—you guessed it—Dunton's own creation.

Dunton's kite is a modified version of Hod Taylor's Delta-Conyne winged triangular box kite (in Illus. 203). Taylor began building kites at 72, and because of his failing eyesight, made some large Delta-Conynes with wing spans of up to 34 feet. Without any venting, a kite this size would pull like an elephant. So, the central cutout on the back of Taylor's design makes sense.

Dunton's delta-box version, however, is much

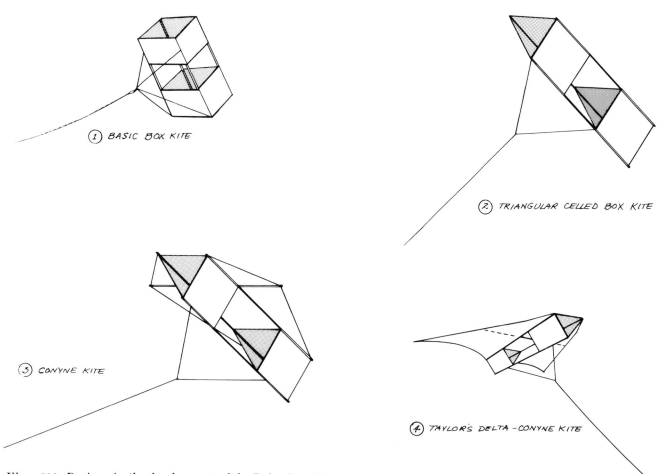

① BASIC BOX KITE

② TRIANGULAR CELLED BOX KITE

③ CONYNE KITE

④ TAYLOR'S DELTA-CONYNE KITE

Illus. 203. Designs in the development of the Delta Box Kite.

smaller and ventless. The uncut middle-rear section of the box cell actually improves lift and soaring ability, especially in low winds.

Materials

To make this kite you need:
- sail: Tyvek Type 14 at 31″ × 84″ (about 2 square yards),
- longeron dowels: two at ³⁄₁₆″ × 31″ and one at ³⁄₁₆″ × 26″,
- wing-spar dowels: two at ³⁄₁₆″ × 31″,
- spreader-bar dowel: ¼″ × 36″ and then cut to fit, and
- three small steel or split key rings

Details

Most of these details are shown in Illus. 204; the exceptions are specifically noted.

- (Detail 1.) Main view.
- (Detail 2.) Forming the triangular box cell, and

joining the front wing section to the back in one step.
- (Detail 3.) Spreader bar. Sew the steel ring onto the wing sleeve—note options A and B in Illus. 205.
- (Detail 4.) Trimming a leaner.
- (Detail 5.) Aft in-flight view.
- (Detail 6 in Illus. 206.) In flight. Bridle: fore leg— 10″; aft leg—16″ to the tow ring.

Flight Data: Wind range: 5–20 mph
Line: 50 lb. test
AE: ±60°

Construction

As you go through these steps, refer to the details.

Cutting:
Note: Only two pieces of sail material are required: one piece for the main part of the kite, which includes the wings and the back of the cell—and the narrow front piece that completes the triangular cell when fitted on the kite face. Dunton prefers using Tyvek Type 14 for this kite.
1. Make pattern templates or mark dimensions directly onto the Tyvek. Allow ½″ for the three lon-

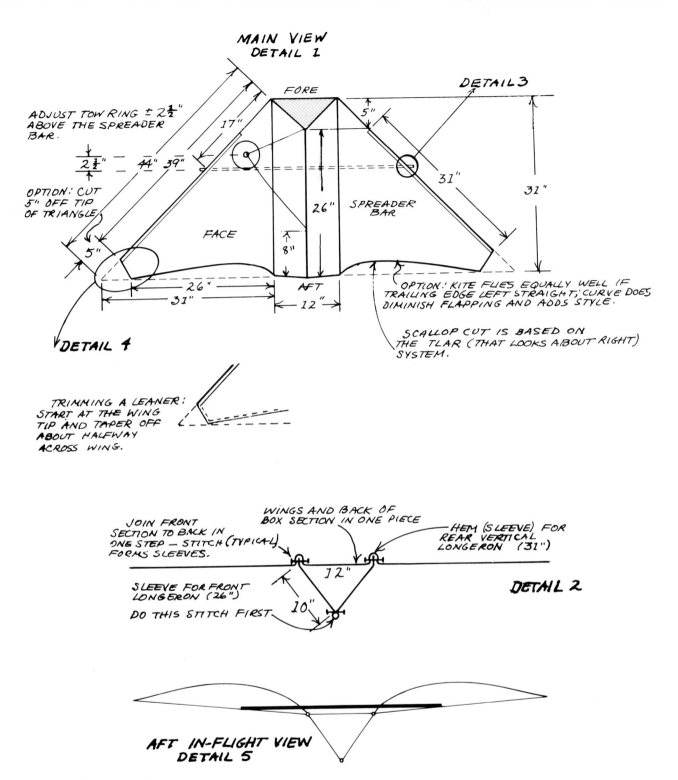

MAIN VIEW
DETAIL 1

FORE

DETAIL 3

ADJUST TOW RING ± 2½"
ABOVE THE SPREADER
BAR.

17"

5"

2½" 44" 39"

31"

OPTION: CUT
5" OFF TIP
OF TRIANGLE

26"

31"

FACE

SPREADER
BAR

5"

8"

DETAIL 4

26"

AFT

31"

12"

OPTION: KITE FLIES EQUALLY WELL IF
TRAILING EDGE LEFT STRAIGHT; CURVE DOES
DIMINISH FLAPPING AND ADDS STYLE.

SCALLOP CUT IS BASED ON
THE TLAR (THAT LOOKS ABOUT RIGHT)
SYSTEM.

TRIMMING A LEANER:
START AT THE WING
TIP AND TAPER OFF
ABOUT HALFWAY
ACROSS WING.

WINGS AND BACK OF
BOX SECTION IN ONE PIECE

JOIN FRONT
SECTION TO BACK IN
ONE STEP — STITCH (TYPICAL)
FORMS SLEEVES.

HEM (SLEEVE) FOR
REAR VERTICAL
LONGERON (31")

12"

SLEEVE FOR FRONT
LONGERON (26")

DETAIL 2

DO THIS STITCH FIRST.

10"

AFT IN-FLIGHT VIEW
DETAIL 5

Illus. 204. Details 1–5.

geron sleeves: two on the back and one along the front of the triangle. Add ±½" to the outside edges of the wings for the wing-spar sleeves. As hot-cutting Tyvek prevents fraying, a hem allowance for the trailing edge is unnecessary. Note: The triangular cell has a 5" cutout-V on the fore section, as shown in Detail 1. This V permits air to channel easily into the core of the kite cell.

For all cutaways, including the wing tips and the curve along the trailing edge, fold the main section in half for symmetry.

Sewing:
2. Form the front longeron sleeve by running a stitch as shown in Detail 2.
3. Sew the front cell to the main section. The two

back longeron sleeves are formed in the one-step process.

Option: Sew the front cell to the main section as shown in the diagram for the Owl Kite (Illus. 207).

4. Fold back the hem allowances for the wing spar sleeves and close by stitching along the length. Tip: Tyvek and white glue work well together. To

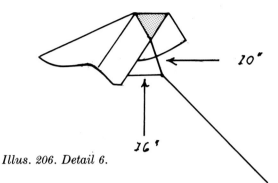

IN FLIGHT

Illus. 206. Detail 6.

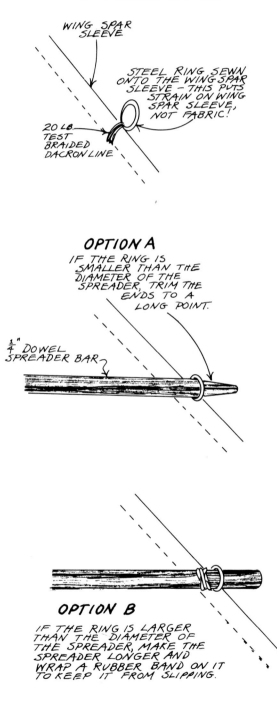

SPREADER BAR DETAIL

WING SPAR SLEEVE

STEEL RING SEWN ONTO THE WING SPAR SLEEVE – THIS PUTS STRAIN ON WING SPAR SLEEVE, NOT FABRIC!

20 LB. TEST BRAIDED DACRON LINE

OPTION A

IF THE RING IS SMALLER THAN THE DIAMETER OF THE SPREADER, TRIM THE ENDS TO A LONG POINT.

$\frac{1}{4}''$ DOWEL SPREADER BAR

OPTION B

IF THE RING IS LARGER THAN THE DIAMETER OF THE SPREADER, MAKE THE SPREADER LONGER AND WRAP A RUBBER BAND ON IT TO KEEP IT FROM SLIPPING.

Illus. 205. Detail 3—exploded view and options.

simplify the sewing, first keep the edge of the sleeve in place with a small amount of white glue along the hem length. (Don't glue the entire hem against the sail.) Then close off (glue or sew) the bottom of the longeron sleeves and wing sleeves.

Assembly:

5. Insert the dowels in the sleeves; the 26″ longeron fits in the front sleeve of the triangular cell. Close off (glue or sew) the top of the longeron sleeves. The wing sleeves may be left open on top.

6. Sew rings onto the wing spar sleeves around the spar as shown. This method, developed by Dr. Phil Modjeski, places stress on the dowel instead of the sail material. Depending upon the ring's diameter, use option A or B for a taut spread across the wing.

7. Cut a length of 50 lb.–test line for the two-legged bridle at the points indicated. Use the dimensions given, though they aren't critical *as long as the tow point is correct.* Sew the bridle line through the Tyvek and around the longeron for a secure hold. Attach a steel or split key ring to the bridle with a lark's head hitch.

8. To set the tow point, lay the kite with its back to the floor and the spreader in place. Pull the ring to either side (see Detail 1) until the bridle is taut. Measure the distance from the tow point to the spreader. Start with the ring about 2″ to 2½″ above the spreader line. This position is usually correct.

Leaners

Dunton doesn't hem or finish the trailing edge of his deltas and delta derivatives until the kite has been test-flown. If the kite leans to the left or right, trim off a small strip on the side it leans towards. Start at the tip and taper the cut halfway across as shown in Detail 4. Before trimming for lean, establish the optimum tow-point setting.

If your kite is unstable, lower the ring towards the trailing edge slightly and try again. When you've located the optimum tow point, or fulcrum, mark the position with a black soft-tip pen for reference, future adjustments, and experiments. Note: Raise or lower the tow point for different wind conditions. Strong winds and humidity deform dowels for a kite that may ultimately favor one side or the other. Sometimes reversing the spreader and both wing spars solves the problem.

Owl Kite Variation

To make this delta-box variation, refer to Illus. 207. The following tips should be helpful:

- Use the dimensions for Dunton's Delta Box, remembering to make allowances for all hems and sleeves.
- The fore section of cell A is in line with the leading edge of the back section (B).
- Plan ahead; sew all reinforcements in place before piecing the kite together.
- Finish the trailing edge with ¼" double-fold bias tape or a ¼" double-fold hem.

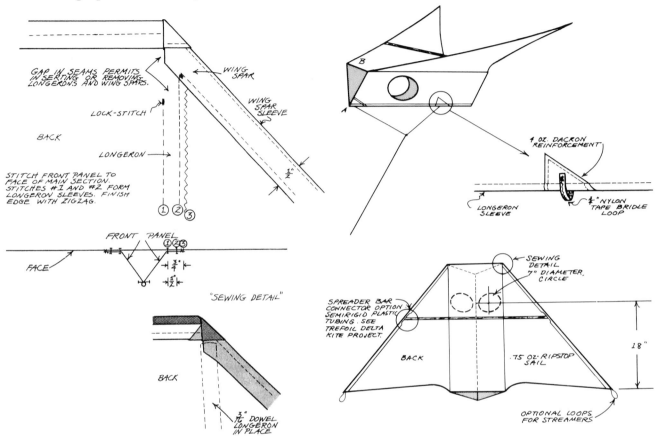

Illus. 207. Owl Kite variation.

34
The Tri-D Box Kite

Design: Courtesy of Peter Lynn

An Air of Minimalism

"I came to the Tri-D Box design from a minimalist approach to structure," says New Zealander Peter Lynn. "I was, at that stage (1977), very Bauhausian and conducted an intensive search for efficient three-dimensional kites."

A school of art and architecture founded in Germany in 1919, the Bauhaus focused on functional craftsmanship characterized by severely economic, geometric design and a respect for materials. Lynn's Bauhaus influence can be seen in the pure and simple double-winged Tri-D Box design—in its uniformity of equilateral triangles and economical use of materials (see Illus. 208).

I was curious as to why Lynn placed a pattern on his purely Bauhausian kite form. It turned out that the curved pattern on the fabric (see the color illustration on page M) was an inherent part of the total concept. The *koru* is a stylized fern frond that symbolizes new life among the Polynesian people. Originally carved onto the prow boards of ancient migratory canoes, it now has come to represent a state of optimism for all New Zealanders.

Though the Tri-D Box Kite can be successfully scaled to larger dimensions, this design is lightweight and offers a combined set of virtues: It soars in light breezes like a delta, while maintaining the stability of a box kite in heavier wind.

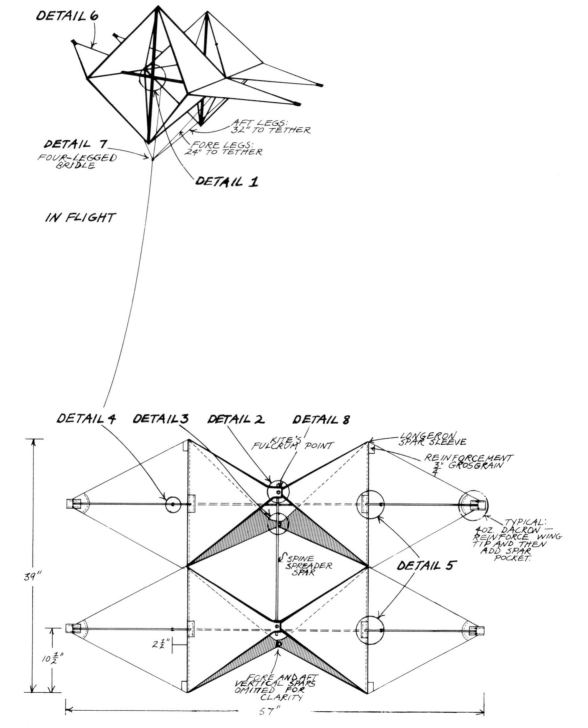

Illus. 208. Details.

139

Materials

For this kite you need:

- 3 yards × 41″ of .75 oz. ripstop,
- ¼″ I.D. semirigid tubing,
- ⁵⁄₁₆″ I.D. semirigid tubing,
- ³⁄₁₆″ clear plastic tubing,
- ¼″ and ³⁄₈″ grommets,
- 10 feet of 50 lb.–test braided-Dacron line—for bridle,
- fibreglass rods:

  - two ¼″ × 28½″—for fore-wing spars,
  - two ³⁄₁₆″ × 28½″—for aft-wing spars,
  - two ³⁄₁₆″ × 28″—for vertical spars,
  - two ³⁄₁₆″ × 40″—for longerons,
  - one ³⁄₁₆″ × 24″—for spine spreader spar,

- reinforcement materials (1.5 oz. ripstop, .4 oz. Dacron, or grosgrain ribbon),
- 1″ nylon webbing for pockets, and
- ¾″ split key ring for bridle.

Materials for Alternative Construction

For kites employing nylon loops or a reinforced crack-and-peel hole system, you need:

- ¼″ nylon loop material,
- spars: ³⁄₈″ hardwood dowel or E 40 epoxy tubing (Note: Either can be substituted for fibreglass rod in the main design),
- arrow nocks and inserts, and
- crack-and-peel ripstop nylon.

Details

The following details are shown in Illus. 208. The first three details are also highlighted in separate illustrations.

- (Detail 1.) Fore and aft connector system: horizontal spar, vertical spar, semirigid tubing, and poly-

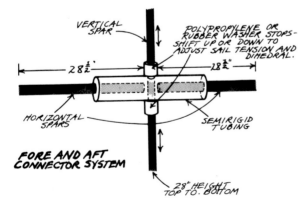

Illus. 209. Detail 1—exploded view.

propylene or rubber washer stops—shift up or down to adjust the sail tension and dihedral. (Also see Illus. 209.)

- (Detail 2.) Bottom connect point. The bottom of the vertical spar is secured in the semirigid tubing that interlocks with the horizontal spine spar spreader bar. (Also see Illus. 210.)

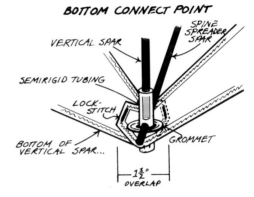

Illus. 210. Detail 2—exploded view.

- (Detail 3.) Top connect point. The top of the vertical spar passes through the grommet. Slide the semirigid-tubing up-or-down spar to adjust tension. (Also see Illus. 211.)

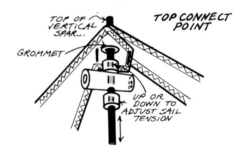

Illus. 211. Detail 3—exploded view.

- (Detail 4.) Thread the bridle loops through the sail with a large-size needle at the position shown.
- (Detail 5.) The fore and aft horizontal wing spars pass through sail-reinforcement holes and bridle loops.
- (Detail 6.) The fabric should be taut at all points. A dihedral angle with the wing tips slightly above the horizontal will improve stability.
- (Detail 7.) Four-legged bridle connects at the key ring with an adjustable lark's head hitch. Fore legs—24″ to tether; aft legs—32″ to tether.
- Option: You may connect the tether directly to the fulcrum on kites under 6′ in height.

Flight Data: Wind range: 4–20 mph
Line: 100 lb. test.
AE: ± 70°
Wear gloves

Construction

Hot-cutting:

1. Hot-cut six rhomboid shapes (equilateral parallelograms with oblique angles), measuring 20½" in height × 36½" in width, out of ripstop nylon. Place the template along the fold edge of the material for a symmetrical cut. Keep the bias in mind when planning the layout, especially when combining colors. (Refer to "Working with Ripstop Nylon.") See Illus. 212.

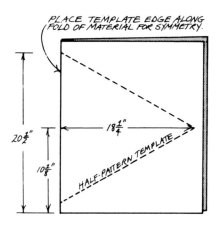

Illus. 212. Step 1.

2. Hot-cut four 1" × 2¾" wing pockets from nylon webbing.

Sewing:

3. Stitch a ¼" hem along the perimeter of each piece (Illus. 213). Note: Panels in the #2 position are the wings and require tip reinforcements for pockets later. Stitch the reinforcements in place prior to hemming.

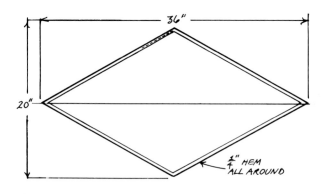

Illus. 213. Step 3.

Option 1: Instead of using pockets and grommets as retainers for wings and vertical spars, an arrow-nock-and-loop system is a useful alternative. Sew ¼" loops at all three tips of each triangle. (See Illus. 214.)

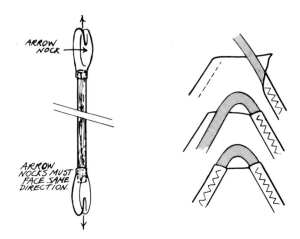

Illus. 214. Step 3—Option 1.

Option 2: Another approach is to hot-cut all triangles. Thus, no hemming is needed. Reinforce wing tips with crack-and-peel ripstop. Use a hot cutter with a conical-shaped tip to melt the holes in the wing tips. Notched dowels must be cut to the exact size to stretch the kite open. (See Illus. 215.)

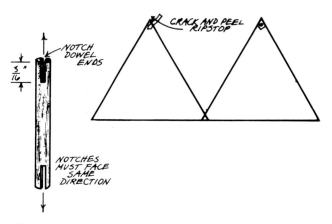

Illus. 215. Step 3—Option 2.

Hot cutting:

4. Stack and align three parallelograms, one on top of the other. Hot-cut all three in half to form two sets of three 20" equilateral triangles welded along the unhemmed base. Note: Prior to cutting, sew a 2" × 4" reinforcement strip on the inside center of the #1 piece as shown in Illus. 216. Repeat these steps with the remaining three parallelograms for a total of four sets of three triangles.

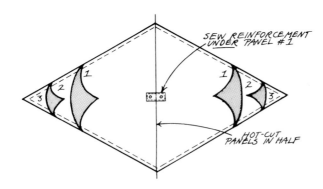

Illus. 216. Step 4.

Sewing:

7. Unfold the triangles along the middle so that panel #1 meets panel #3 as shown in Illus. 218. Form the longeron sleeve by stitching a ½" seam along the length of the kite. Leave a break in the seam near one end to insert the horizontal spar. Reinforce both fore and aft ends of the pocket sleeve with ¾" grosgrain ribbon or other suitable material. Sew nylon-webbing pockets onto the wing tips. The pocket opening is on the same side as the reinforcement patch for the wing-spar pass-through hole.

8. Join the right and left halves of the kite at the top and bottom points with a 1½" overlap at the tips. Secure with a backstitch in both places as shown in Detail 2 in Illus. 210 and Detail 3 in Illus. 211.

Hot Cutting:

9. Use a conical-shaped hot-cutter tip to melt holes slightly smaller than the ¼" grommet at the top and the ⅜" grommet at the bottom of the fore and aft vertical spar supports. (See Details 2 and 3.)

10. Melt holes large enough at the reinforced pass-through point for the wing spars. Be careful not to burn holes in the other sails.

Assembly:

11. Cut plastic tubing as follows: semirigid tubing—two 1½" lengths of ⁵⁄₁₆" and four 1½" lengths of ¼"; clear plastic tubing—six ¼" lengths of ³⁄₁₆".

5. See Illus. 217. Align the fore and aft sections of the first set with an overlap of approximately 1" at the connection point.

   Note: You must first (Detail A) open and separate the welded edges about an inch on both segments where they meet. Then (Detail B) align, hot-tack, and (Detail C) stitch panel-tip #1 with #1 of the other set, wing panel #2 with #2 of the other set, and #3 with #3 of the other set.

6. Hot-cut ¼" in from the edge; then edge-stitch along the entire length. (This procedure is also shown in Illus. 217.) Repeat these steps for the second set. Both sets must be of equal length.

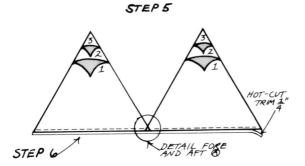
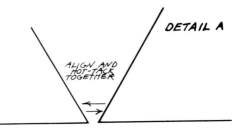
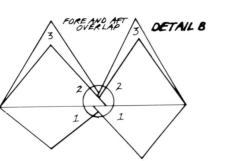
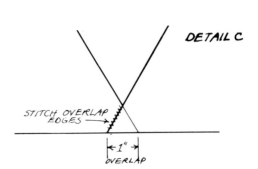

Illus. 217. Step 5, and Details A, B, and C, and Step 6.

142

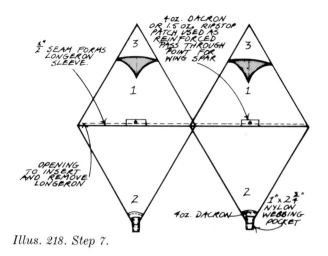

Illus. 218. Step 7.

12. Lay the sails on a flat surface with the wing spar holes and bridle lines facing you. Insert the longerons into the sleeve openings and push them inside for a snug fit. Place the wing spars through the reinforcement holes and bridle loops of the fore section. Position one vertical spreader through the top grommet hole and insert the wing spars. Secure the bottom vertical spar by

flexing it into the tube retainer of the spine spreader spar. Repeat for the aft section.

Square Variation

This kite can be built with squares instead of equilateral triangles. To do so, the kite is scaled to the desired size by utilizing the dimension of one side of the square. The height, width, total sail area, and length of spars required can be conveniently related to this one measurement.

With B representing a side of the square, the formula[1] is as follows: height = $2.8284 \times B$, width = $2.4142 \times B$, total sail surface = $6 \times B^2$, and total length of spars needed = $12.486 \times B$. Rounding off to the nearest whole number provides a good indication of how much material is required.

A square measuring 13″ on a side, for example, breaks down as follows: height = 37″, width = 31″, total sail surface = 7 sq. ft. and total length of spars needed = 162″.

[1]Alex G. Voss, "Peter Lynn Box Formula," *Kite Lines*, Spring 1985, pg. 8.

35
The Kaleidakite

Design: Courtesy of Joel Scholz

A Stacked Tri-D Kite

Joel Scholz, a Texas-based kite builder, was experimenting with Peter Lynn's Tri-D Box Kite variations (see Chapter 34) when he came across Japanese kite-builder Eiji Ohashi's expandable box kites of cypress wood and *shoji* paper. Scholz saw an intriguing relationship and put it into action. Incorporating a Western approach in terms of construction and materials, the resulting 45 square foot Kaleidakite, in essence, is a stacked Tri-D kite.

Although box kites are known as stable fliers, the Kaleidakite possesses an added dimension: In winds over 15 mph, it can be maneuvered as a stunt kite

with dual-line control. Single or dual line, this kite has an unusual flying angle and a geometric look in the air that make a stunning statement. See Illus. 221 and 222 for two views of the kite; see the insert on page H for the kite in color.

Materials

To make this kite you need:

- 3 yards of .75 oz. ripstop of each color (see the color illustration on page H),
- 1.5 oz. ripstop scraps or 4 oz. Dacron—for wing-tip reinforcements,

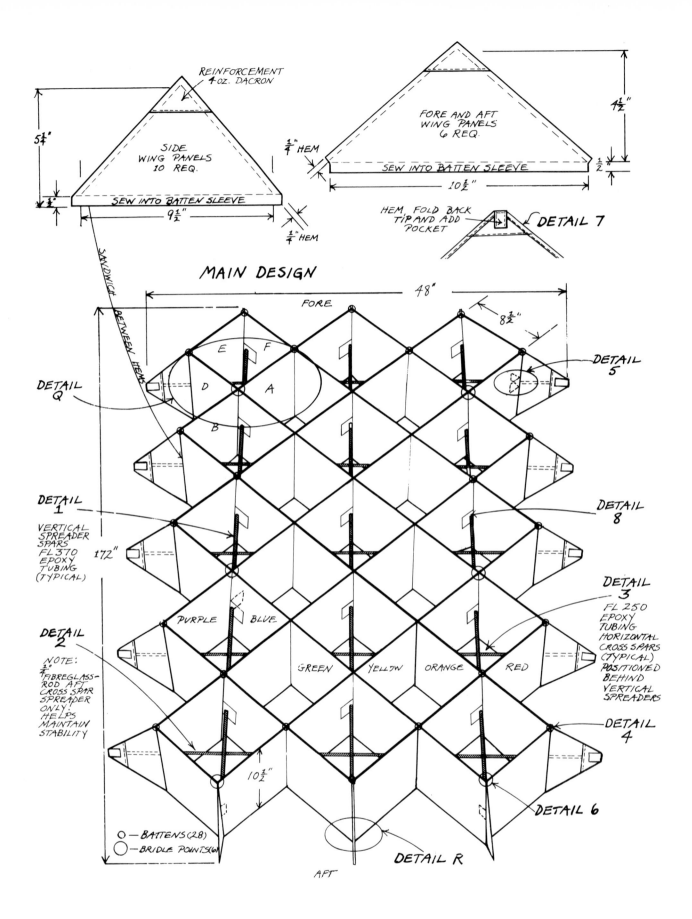

REINFORCEMENT
4 OZ. DACRON

SIDE
WING PANELS
10 REQ.

5¼"

¼"

SEW INTO BATTEN SLEEVE

9½"

¼" HEM

¼" HEM

FORE AND AFT
WING PANELS
6 REQ.

4½"

SEW INTO BATTEN SLEEVE

10½"

½"

HEM FOLD BACK
TIP AND ADD
POCKET

DETAIL 7

MAIN DESIGN

48"

FORE

8½"

E F

D A

B

SANDWICH BETWEEN ITEMS

DETAIL Q

DETAIL 5

DETAIL 1

VERTICAL
SPREADER
SPARS
FL 370
EPOXY
TUBING
(TYPICAL)

172"

DETAIL 8

DETAIL 3

FL 250
EPOXY
TUBING
HORIZONTAL
CROSS SPARS
(TYPICAL)
POSITIONED
BEHIND
VERTICAL
SPREADERS

PURPLE BLUE

GREEN YELLOW ORANGE RED

DETAIL 2

NOTE:
¼"
FIBREGLASS-
ROD AFT
CROSS SPAR
SPREADER
ONLY!
HELPS
MAINTAIN
STABILITY

DETAIL 4

10½"

DETAIL 6

○ — BATTENS (28)
◯ — BRIDLE POINTS (6)

DETAIL R

AFT

Illus. 219. Main design and details.

144

- 1 yard of 1″ grosgrain ribbon or nylon webbing,
- 1 yard of ½″ grosgrain ribbon or nylon webbing,
- 10 sections of FL 250 × 32½″ epoxy tubing plus ferrules,
- six sections of FL 370 × 32½″ epoxy tubing plus ferrules,
- ¼″ × 48″ fibreglass rod,
- six ⁹⁄₁₆″ split key rings—for bridle attachment points, two ¾″ split key rings—for bridle tow points,
- vinyl end caps,
- 100 lb.–test braided Dacron—for bridle lines, and
- seven ³⁄₃₂″ × 48″ fibreglass rods—cut into twenty-eight 10½″ battens.

Details

Refer to Illus. 219 for most of these details; other illustrations are specifically noted.

- (Detail 1.) Vertical spreader bar: FL 250 epoxy tubing (typical).
- (Detail 2.) ¼″ fibreglass rod: aft cross-spar spreader only. Helps maintain stability.
- (Detail 3.) Note: With the kite face in front of you, FL 250 epoxy-tubing horizontal cross-spar spreaders are inserted *behind* the vertical FL 370 epoxy-tubing spars.
- (Detail 4.) The dots indicate the placement of the ³⁄₃₂″ × 10½″ fibreglass-rod battens.
- (Detail 5.) The circled areas indicate bridle-line attachment points—⁹⁄₁₆″ split key rings are looped through batten-sleeve reinforcements. (See the exploded view in Illus. 220.)

- (Detail 6.) The middle vertical spar is longer to allow for tension adjustment. (See Illus. 226.)
- (Detail 7.) Wing-spar pocket and reinforcement material.
- (Detail 8.) All holes are reinforced for spars.
- (Detail 9 in Illus. 221.) Side view and approximate angle of flight.

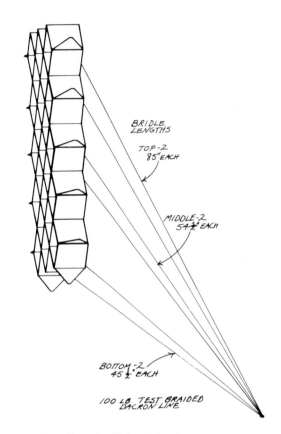

Illus. 221. Detail 9—in flight, side view.

- (Detail 10 in Illus. 222.) Top view. Six-legged bridle: top line = 85″, middle line = 54½″, bottom line =

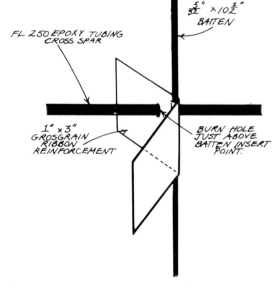

Illus. 220. Detail 5—exploded view.

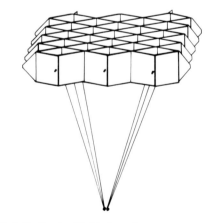

Illus. 222. Detail 10—in flight, top view.

145

45½". Use 100 lb.–test braided Dacron. Join both the bridle and the ¾" split rings for single-line flying. Option: Connect rings to dual lines for stunt-kite maneuverability.

Flight Data: Wind range: 8–18 mph
Line: 100 lb. test—single line
Line: 200 lb. test—dual line
AE: ±65°
Wear gloves

Construction

Hot-cutting:
1. Cut six body panels from .75 oz. ripstop: two (A) 93" × 11" red and purple, and four (B) 90½" × 11"

blue, green, yellow, and orange. Refer to Illus. 223 for dimensions.
2. Hot-cut six fore and aft wing panels: two each of blue, yellow, and orange. Hot-cut 10 side-wing panels: five each of red and purple.
3. All areas in fabric that have spars passing through should be reinforced. Cut reinforcement strips—28 (1" × 3") internal battens; 10 (½" × 2") internal non-batten sleeves; 46 (½" × 2") external (face and back); and six (½" × 3") bridle points. Cut 10 side wing-spar pockets (¾" × 2") and six fore and aft wing-spar pockets (1" × 2").

Sewing:
4. Hem each body panel ¼" on each side for a 10 ½"-deep piece (Illus. 223).

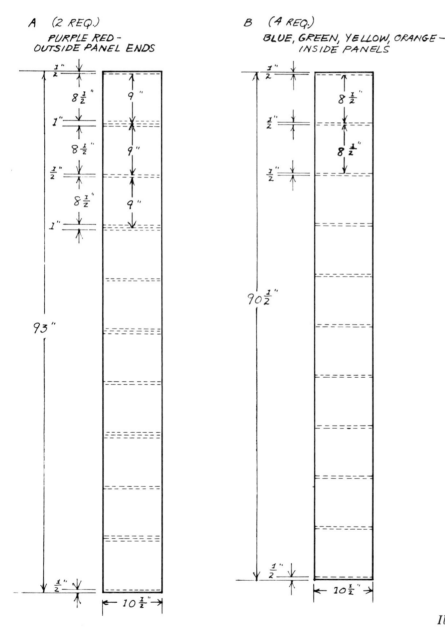

A (2 REQ.)
PURPLE RED –
OUTSIDE PANEL ENDS

B (4 REQ.)
BLUE, GREEN, YELLOW, ORANGE –
INSIDE PANELS

Illus. 223. Dimensions for panels.

5. Align body panels "A" and "B" on a flat surface with their hem fold *facing down*. Seam lines: Mark the connecting stitch lines equally along the panels as shown in Illus. 223.

6. Sew internal reinforcement strips in position at all spar intersection points. Use Illus. 219 for reference.

7. Wings: Hem each wing panel on two sides only; the ½″ edge is sandwiched between the batten sleeves as shown in Illus. 219. Remember to position the reinforcement material inside the wing hem-fold line prior to stitching. Form wing-spar pockets by folding 1″ × 2″ strips of grosgrain ribbon.

Making the cells:

Note: The cells are made by constructing three separate units: (1) purple and blue, (2) green and yellow, and (3) orange and red. Units 1 and 3 are attached to 2.

8. Begin with the purple panel. Remember to maintain uniformity by keeping the hemmed edges facing outward. Insert the wing panels into the side batten folds and then stitch along the marked lines to form the sleeves. Repeat these steps for the red panel.

9. Form unit 1 by aligning the top of the purple panel with the top edge of the blue panel. Insert the blue top wing into the fold and stitch it in place to form the sleeve. Using the positions marked in Step 5, line up the common points where purple meets blue to form the batten pockets.

To complete the bottom cell of unit 1, turn the edges of the purple and blue panels inside out, insert the bottom wing, and stitch to form the batten sleeve; then turn the cell right side out. Finish units 2 and 3 in the same manner.

Continue the process by stitching the green panel to the yellow for unit 2 and the orange to the red for unit 3.

Connect unit 2 to unit 1 along the common seam points and stitch. Repeat for units 3 and 2.

Hot cutting:

10. Use a conical-shaped tip to melt holes in the reinforcement strips to allow the spars to pass through (see Detail Q in Illus. 224). Make a hole in the bottom-middle-wing panel to tie the knotted line (see Detail R in Illus. 225).

Hobby saw:

11. The battens should be a uniform 10½″—the depth of the cells. Because the battens must keep the cells taut, it is important for all 28 fibreglass-rod (³⁄₃₂″ diameter) battens to be cut to fit the cell depth exactly. The overall batten length should include the vinyl end caps.

Sewing:

12. Insert the battens into the sleeve positions and

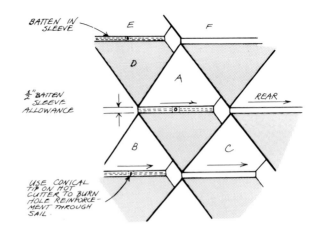

Illus. 224. Detail Q—exploded view.

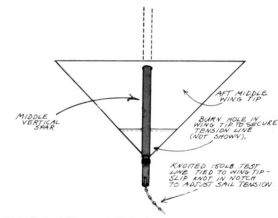

Illus. 225. Detail R—exploded view.

secure them with folded ½″ × 2″ reinforcement strips in both front and back. Stitch the six (½″ × 3″) folded strips at the bridle positions, leaving an opening in the loop edge for the split key rings to pass through.

Hobby saw:

Suggestion: Before cutting epoxy tubing, make prototype spars out of less-expensive wooden dowels to determine exact lengths; then test-fly. Once you're satisfied with the fit, cut the epoxy tubing to size. Include end caps in the overall dimensions.

13. Refer to Illus. 226. For prototype spars, use ¼″ hardwood dowels for the three vertical spars. Two of the spars should be 66¾″ long, and the middle spar should be 68½″ long. Note: the middle vertical spar is notched at the bottom and longer than the others to allow for tension adjustment with the knotted line. Since dowels come in standard 48″ lengths, connect two sections to form the vertical spars with a 3″ external rigid plastic-tubing ferrule.

Use ³⁄₁₆″ × 48″ dowels for the remaining horizontal spars. To help maintain stability, insert a ¼″ dowel for the bottom horizontal spar. A trimmed kite means the sail material is drum tight.

Permanent spars:

- vertical spars—FL 370 epoxy tubing,
- horizontal spars—FL 250 epoxy tubing, and
- aft horizontal spar—¼″ fibreglass rod.

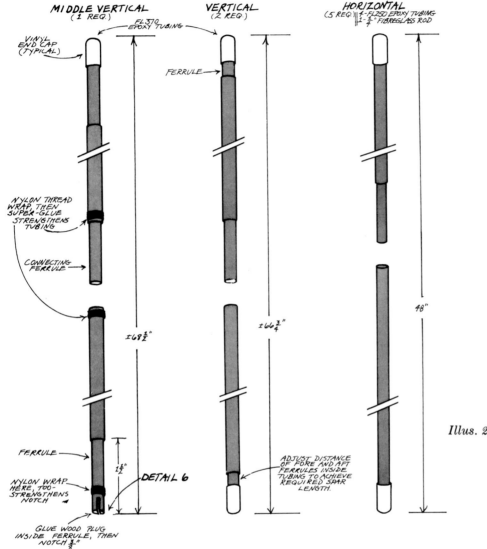

Illus. 226. Spars (including Detail 6).

36
The Gusset Delta

With a Tunnel to Deflect the Wind

It's easy to get so preoccupied that you forget to smell the roses—that you forget to fly a kite. I had been working furiously on the manuscript for this book when I suddenly realized that it had been too long since I had actually flown a kite. So, I rode to a nearby flying field, devoid of human beings, took out one of Jerry Sinotte's Gusset Deltas, and set it free against a crisp blue sky that just makes you feel good to be alive. As I watched the Gusset's characteristic smooth rise upwards, I was struck with the moment—a moment in time I would have missed had I remained fixed on my manuscript and on time itself. As the sun burst through the kite's orange-and-black radiating pattern, I had a sense of eternity at the end of my flying line.

* * *

Instead of channeling air the same as a Zephyr Delta, the Gusset (shown in Detail 11, and in color on page O) has a tunnel shape that deflects the airstream along the continuous curve of its trailing edge. A gusset is a triangular piece of fabric inserted into a garment to improve its fit; this kite has a gusset wedge that improves its structure (see Detail 6).

Materials

To make this kite you need:

- 4 sq. yards of ripstop overall—for sail (color scheme will determine actual yardage of each piece);
- 4 oz. Dacron—for reinforcement and wing-spar sleeve material;
- two sections of 4″ × 5/16″ I.D. nylon-reinforced plastic tubing;
- vinyl end caps and aluminum inserts;
- 3/32″ elastic cord;

- all spars: .317″ O.D. (.266″ I.D.) with .261″ O.D. ferrules:
  - wing spars: 48″,
  - spine: ±46—should fit tight, and
  - spreader bar: 30″ ferrule to ferrule;
- 9/16″ split key ring—for tow point; and
- 100 lb.–test braided Dacron—for bridle.

Details

See Illus. 227 for Details 1, 5, and 6; Illus. 228 for Details 2, 3, 4, and 7; Illus. 229 for Detail 8; Illus. 230 for Detail 10; and Illus. 231 for Detail 11.

- (Detail 1.) Kite half-design view.
- (Detail 2.) Open kite, back view. The base of the gusset measures 5″ at the trailing edge.
- (Detail 3.) Spine insert point on fore, or nose, section, back view.
- (Detail 4.) Wing-spar sleeve tip.
- (Detail 5.) Fore section, half view, showing stitching arrangement.
- (Detail 6.) Gusset wedge.
- (Detail 7.) Spreader bar—reinforced nylon-tubing

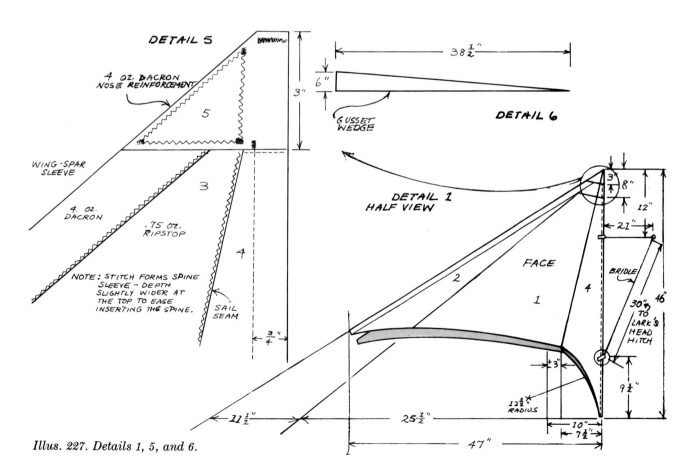

Illus. 227. Details 1, 5, and 6.

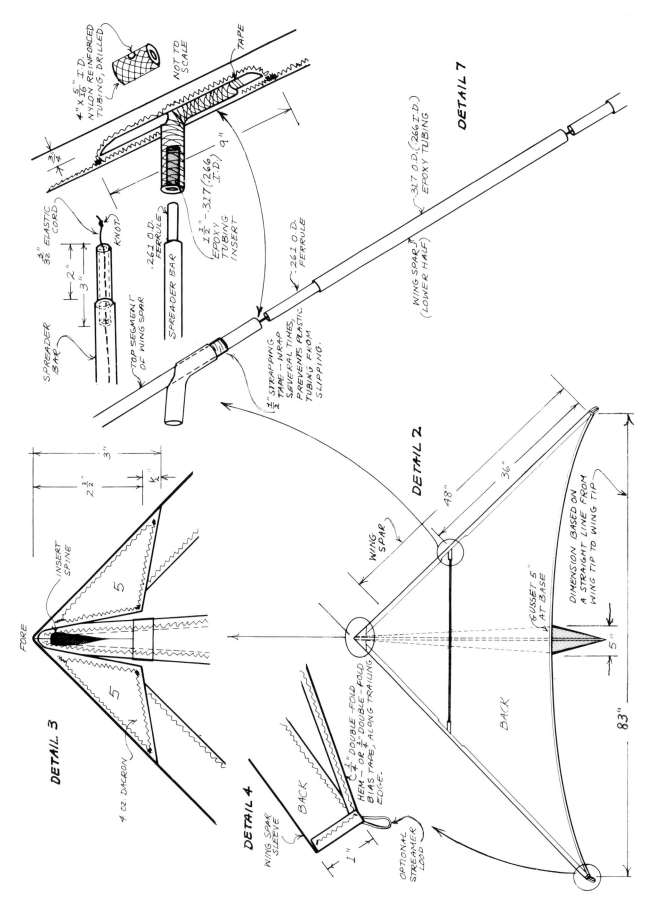

DETAIL 7

4" × 5/16" I.D. NYLON REINFORCED TUBING, DRILLED

NOT TO SCALE

TAPE

3/4"

3/32" ELASTIC CORD

KNOT

3"

2"

.261 O.D. FERRULE

SPREADER BAR

TOP SEGMENT OF WING SPAR

SPREADER BAR

1 1/2"-.317 (.266 I.D.) EPOXY TUBING INSERT

.261 O.D. FERRULE

9"

.317 O.D. (.266 I.D.) EPOXY TUBING

WING SPAR (LOWER HALF)

1/2" STRAPPING TAPE—WRAP SEVERAL TIMES, PREVENTS PLASTIC TUBING FROM SLIPPING.

DETAIL 2

WING SPAR

48"

36"

GUSSET 5" AT BASE

DIMENSION BASED ON A STRAIGHT LINE FROM WING TIP TO WING TIP

5"

BACK

83"

DETAIL 3

FORE

INSERT SPINE

5

5

4 OZ. DACRON

DETAIL 4

WING SPAR SLEEVE

BACK

BACK

1/4" DOUBLE-FOLD HEM — OR 1/2" DOUBLE-FOLD BIAS TAPE, ALONG TRAILING EDGE.

1"

OPTIONAL STREAMER LOOP

Illus. 228. Details 2, 3, 4, and 7.

3"

2 1/2"

1/2"

150

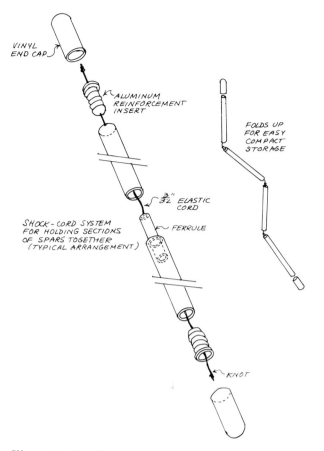

VINYL
END CAP

ALUMINUM
REINFORCEMENT
INSERT

FOLDS UP
FOR EASY
COMPACT
STORAGE

SHOCK-CORD SYSTEM
FOR HOLDING SECTIONS
OF SPARS TOGETHER
(TYPICAL ARRANGEMENT)

$\frac{3}{32}$" ELASTIC
CORD

FERRULE

KNOT

Illus. 229. Detail 8.

connector with epoxy-tubing insert—and wing spar.

- (Detail 8.) Spar shock-cord system, typical arrangement.
- (Detail 9.) Aft bridge loop sewn over spine sleeve.
- (Detail 10.) Open kite, face view.
- (Detail 11.) In flight, with streamers.

Flight Data: Wind range: 4–17 mph
Line: 75 lb. test
AE: ±66°

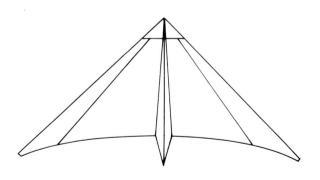

Illus. 230. Detail 10—open-face view.

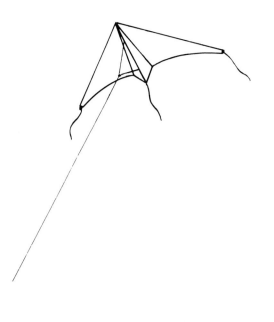

Illus. 231. Detail 11—in flight.

Construction

Note: Since this Gusset Delta is constructed from separate panels (that is, not worked on from the centerline outward for symmetry, as recommended in "The Delta Kite Portfolio"), it requires careful piecing in order to fly true. Tip: Make sure all sections are lying flat on your work surface when you are measuring and positioning—and lying *perfectly* flat when you're sewing.

As you go through these steps, refer to the drawings of the details.

1. Determine your .75 oz. ripstop color scheme, and make allowances for all hot-cut trims and sail seams used throughout—except on wing sleeves. (The sail seam arrangement used on this kite is a straight stitch for seam #1, followed by a zigzag stitch for edge-seam #2. See useful seams in "Reaping What You Sew.") Note: Panel #4 is one piece that has been folded in half and cut to size. Sew panel #1 to #2, and then to #3. Add 4 oz. Dacron wing-spar sleeves to the wing halves. Allow for a spreader bar gap in the sleeves, as shown in Detail 7, *before* adding the sleeves.

2. Use a hot cutter to temporarily baste the right and left sides of panels #1 and #3 to both right and left edges of panel #4.

3. Fold the kite precisely in half. Form the spine sleeve with a stitch along the length, as shown in Detail 5. The 12½" radius arc from the aft tip extends about 3" onto panel #1; the remainder of the trailing edge is a straight cut, though an addi-

tional curve may be added. Remember to add hem allowance if you are not using bias tape along the trailing edge.

4. To add the gusset wedge: First, separate both wing halves from the temporary hot-cut baste. You have made hot-cut trim allowances for this procedure. Again, hot-cut right and left panels #1 and #3 to panel #4, but this time include the edges of the gusset wedge to form a baste for a sail seam.

   Note: *Before* hot-cutting, hem the aft section of the gusset wedge. The narrow fore section of the gusset should be folded back about 3″ from the nose to allow a gap for inserting or removing the spine. See Detail 3. You may wish to extend the wedge (tip of panel #4) by adding a ±2″ piece of 4 oz. Dacron reinforcement that is the depth of the spine sleeve to complete the height of the kite. Once the sail seams are complete, square off the nose with a hot-cutter, stitch across the top, then cut and add Dacron nose reinforcement #5, as shown.

5. Finish the trailing edge and close off the wing-spar sleeves, as shown in Detail 4. Add Dacron reinforcement on the aft end. Though optional, adding streamer loops to the spine aft end and wing tips is recommended for the sheer spectacle of flowing colors.

6. Fold a 1½″ × 3″ strip of Dacron over itself twice for a ½″ × 3″ strip; make two. Then fold them in half and stitch them onto the bridle connect points on the spine.

7. Use overhand-loop knots to attach the bridle, as shown in the half-design view.

8. Instead of cutting or mitre-slicing, drill a hole in the 4″ × ⁵⁄₁₆″ I.D. nylon-reinforced plastic tubing for the wing spar. Insert the epoxy tubing for the spreader, as shown in Detail 7.

9. Cut the wing spars, spine, ferrules, and spreader to the dimensions given. The shock-cord system conveniently contains all the spars. Note: Make the spine using the system shown in Detail 9 without the vinyl end caps.

10. Wing spars: Insert the lower half of the wing spar first; then pull the top section off the ferrule (Detail 7) and insert it in the upper wing sleeve. The other spars fit as shown. Tip: To remove the spine, push from the aft end outward instead of pulling from the top to prevent the spine sections from separating inside the sleeve.

37
The Stone Mountain Kite

Design: Courtesy of Bobby Stanfield

Model of "Tensegrity"

With a sail area of about 40 square feet and a total weight of barely 24 ounces, it's little wonder that this box-delta kite variation was first up and last down at Stone Mountain, Georgia, in 1986, setting a new endurance record there of 25 hours and 17 minutes. (See the Stone Mountain Kite in Illus. 238, and in color on page I.)

A major consideration in designing a kite is the minimum wind necessary to lift it. A kite that will fly well in relation to its size conforms to an acceptable sail load of one ounce per square foot. At nearly half that weight, the Stone Mountain Kite rises upwards in just under a 4-mph breeze. (See the sail-loading formula in the Comparison Chart on page 128 in Chapter 31.) When made of only the lightest material, it develops awesome lift in light air.

Meticulously conceived and crafted by Bobby Stanfield, the Stone Mountain Kite is a model of Spartan efficiency. The lean, open structure clearly illustrates forces pulling and pushing in perfect balance within a closed system so as to maintain the integrity of the structure without it exploding or collapsing. The kite is a model of "tensegrity," a word invented by R. Buckminster Fuller from tensional integrity.

Keep the kite symmetrical and a truly remarkable kite will soon lift from your flying line. Weigh and balance each aluminum protector shaft to maintain optimum balance in flight. Hot-tack or glue sections in place to secure positioning and simplify sewing. Remember Stanfield's credo: Measure twice and cut once.

Materials

To make this kite you need:

- 5 yards red and 10 yards yellow of .5 oz. ripstop—for sail material;
- 1″ strips of 1.5 oz. ripstop—for border and sleeve material;
- eight fishing-guide loops;
- 20 feet of 100 lb.-test braided Dacron—for tension lines and bridle;
- two ¾″ split key rings—for bridle junction and tow point;
- 1⁄16″ ABS plastic sheeting and ¼″ I.D. ABS square tubing, or nylon cable clamps—for wing dihedral connector;
- ¼″ nylon-loop material;
- ¼″ × 48″ dowels connected to make the following lengths:
  - 38¾″ wing spars (two),
  - 62″ jointed for vertical side spars (two),
  - 74″ jointed for spine (one),
  - 19⅝″ wing spreader spars (two) (size may vary slightly depending on type of connector used),
  - 27 1⁄16″ cross spars (three), and
  - 37 3⁄16″ cross spars (three);

- permanent spars: A20 filament-wound epoxy tubing in standard lengths—32½″ (16 tubes);
- crack-and-peel ripstop—to reinforce stress areas (wing-bridle-loop holes) and act as scuff plates where spars rub against sail;
- 5⁄16″ I.D. clear plastic tubing—cut in ¼″ slices as cross-spar retainers (three);
- one .260 aluminum arrow shaft (32½″ standard length)—for protectors, joiners, bottom cross-spar retainers (option: G 50 epoxy tubing at .266 I.D.); and
- .375 × 2′ nylon rod—for end caps.

Details

- (Detail 1 in Illus. 232.) Main view, and (A) dihedral position.
- (Detail 2 in Illus. 233.) Cross-spars, tension-line details, and wing dihedral connection options—fabricated ABS plastic or nylon cable clamps. Tuning kite—adjust vertical and horizontal spars until they are even.
- (Detail 3 in Illus. 234.) Left-aft section of wing "E"; 1″ strip of 1.5 oz. ripstop folded to form finished ¼″ edge binding along leading edges, trailing edges, and keels; wing-sleeve hem formed by folding a 1½″ strip of 1.5 oz. ripstop in half—edge-stitch along the wing to form the spar-sleeve opening; and aft-wing bump detail.
- (Detail 4 in Illus. 235.) Twist nylon end caps until the kite is taut. Nylon end caps are made by drilling

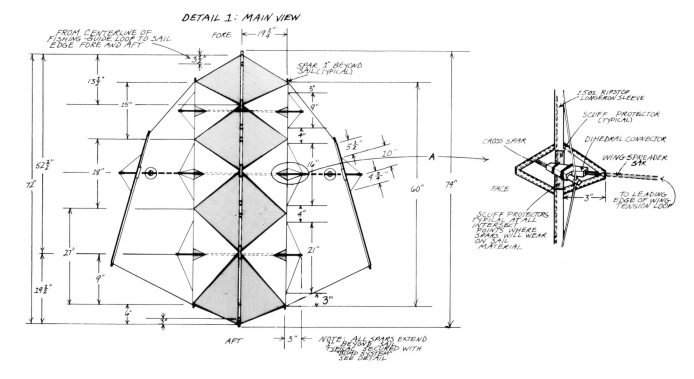

Illus. 232. Main design and (A) dihedral position.

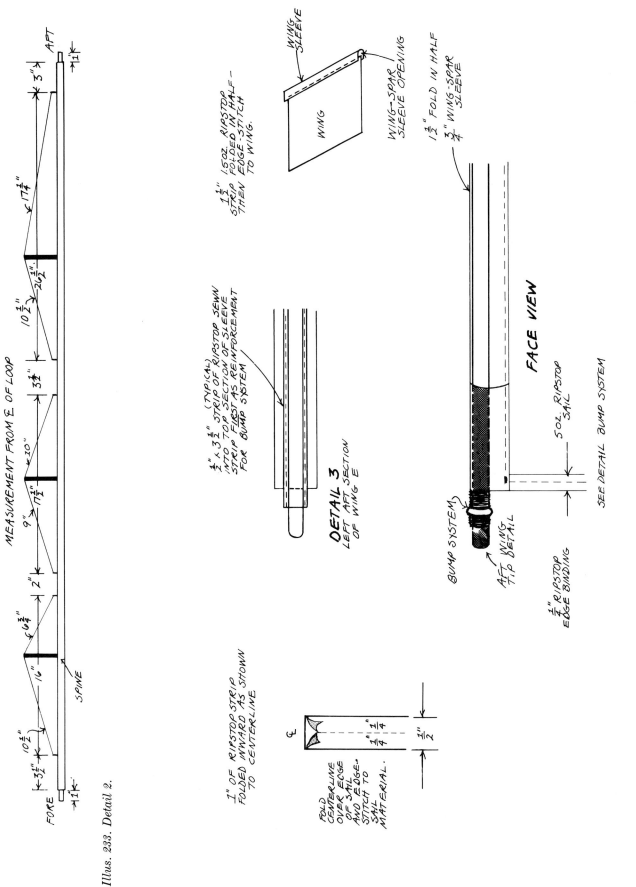

MEASUREMENT FROM ℄ OF LOOP

FORE

$3\frac{1}{2}''$ $10\frac{1}{2}''$ $16''$ $6\frac{1}{4}''$ $2''$ $9''$ $17\frac{1}{2}''$ $10''$ $3\frac{1}{2}''$ $10\frac{1}{2}''$ $26\frac{1}{2}''$ $17\frac{1}{4}''$ $3''$

$1''$

SPINE

$1''$

APT

Illus. 233. Detail 2.

$\frac{1}{4}'' \times 3\frac{1}{2}''$ STRIP OF RIPSTOP SEWN
INTO TOP SECTION OF SLEEVE
STRIP FIRST AS REINFORCEMENT
FOR BUMP SYSTEM

DETAIL 3
LEFT AFT SECTION
OF WING ℄

$1''$ OF RIPSTOP STRIP
FOLDED INWARD AS SHOWN
TO CENTERLINE

℄

$\frac{1}{4}''$ $\frac{1}{4}''$

$\frac{1}{2}''$

FOLD
CENTERLINE
OVER EDGE
OF SAIL
AND EDGE-
STITCH TO
SAIL
MATERIAL.

WING
SLEEVE

WING

$1\frac{1}{2}''$ 1.5 OZ. RIPSTOP
STRIP FOLDED IN HALF
THEN EDGE-STITCH
TO WING.

WING-SPAR
SLEEVE OPENING

$1\frac{1}{2}''$ FOLD IN HALF

$\frac{3}{4}''$ WING-SPAR
SLEEVE

FACE VIEW

BUMP SYSTEM

AFT WING
TIP DETAIL

$\frac{1}{4}''$ RIPSTOP
EDGE BINDING

5 OZ. RIPSTOP
SAIL

SEE DETAIL BUMP SYSTEM

Illus. 234. Detail 3.

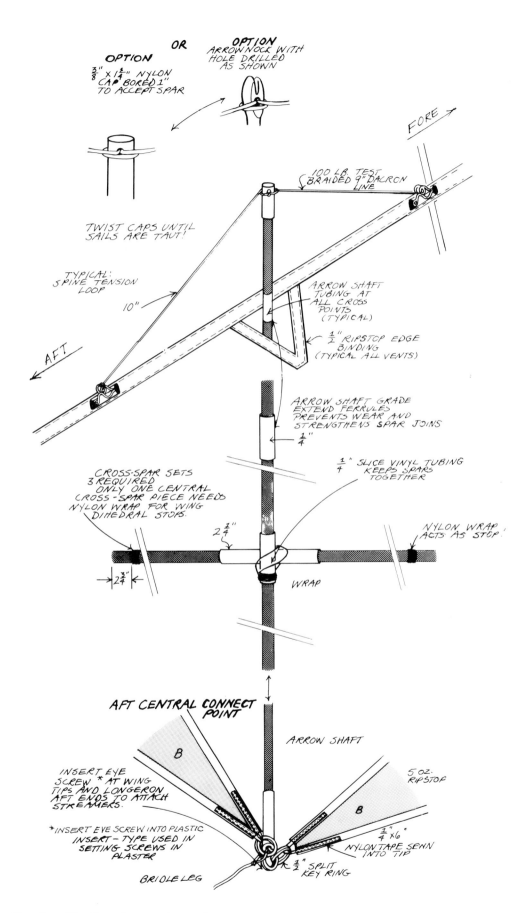

OPTION
OR
OPTION
ARROWNOCK WITH
HOLE DRILLED
AS SHOWN

⅜" X 1½" NYLON
CAP BORED 1"
TO ACCEPT SPAR

FORE

100 LB. TEST
BRAIDED 9"DACRON
LINE

TWIST CAPS UNTIL
SAILS ARE TAUT!

TYPICAL:
SPINE TENSION
LOOP

10"

ARROW SHAFT
TUBING AT
ALL CROSS
POINTS
(TYPICAL)

AFT

½" RIPSTOP EDGE
BINDING
(TYPICAL ALL VENTS)

ARROW SHAFT GRADE
EXTEND FERRULES
PREVENTS WEAR AND
STRENGTHENS SPAR JOINS

¼"

CROSS-SPAR SETS
3 REQUIRED
ONLY ONE CENTRAL
CROSS-SPAR PIECE NEEDS
NYLON WRAP FOR WING
DIHEDRAL STOPS.

¼" SLICE VINYL TUBING
KEEPS SPARS
TOGETHER

NYLON WRAP
ACTS AS STOP.

2¼"

2¾"

WRAP

AFT CENTRAL CONNECT
POINT

ARROW SHAFT

B

INSERT EYE
SCREW * AT WING
TIPS AND LONGERON
AFT ENDS TO ATTACH
STREAMERS.

* INSERT EYE SCREW INTO PLASTIC
INSERT-TYPE USED IN
SETTING SCREWS IN
PLASTER

5 OZ.
RIPSTOP

B

¼" X 6"
NYLON TAPE SEWN
INTO TIP

½" SPLIT
KEY RING

BRIDLE LEG

Illus. 235. Detail 4. (Continued on next page.)

155

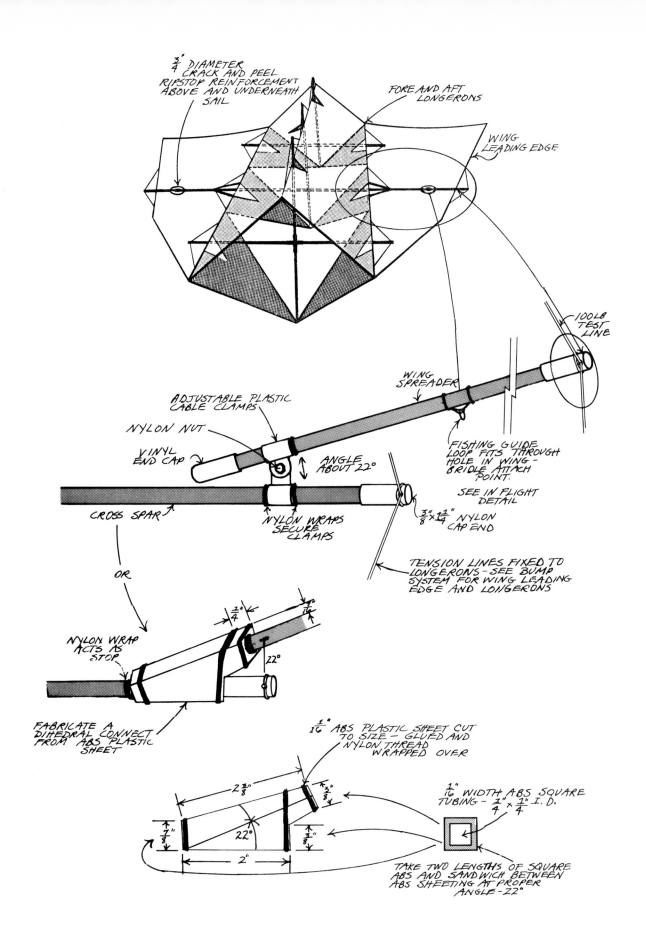

¾" DIAMETER
CRACK AND PEEL
RIPSTOP REINFORCEMENT
ABOVE AND UNDERNEATH
SAIL

FORE AND AFT
LONGERONS

WING
LEADING EDGE

100LB
TEST
LINE

ADJUSTABLE PLASTIC
CABLE CLAMPS

NYLON NUT

VINYL
END CAP

WING
SPREADER

ANGLE
ABOUT 22°

FISHING GUIDE
LOOP FITS THROUGH
HOLE IN WING-
BRIDLE ATTACH
POINT.

SEE IN FLIGHT
DETAIL

CROSS SPAR

NYLON WRAPS
SECURE
CLAMPS

⅜" × 1¼" NYLON
CAP END

OR

TENSION LINES FIXED TO
LONGERONS - SEE BUMP
SYSTEM FOR WING LEADING
EDGE AND LONGERONS

NYLON WRAP
ACTS AS
STOP

¼"

22°

FABRICATE A
DIHEDRAL CONNECT
FROM ABS PLASTIC
SHEET

1/16" ABS PLASTIC SHEET CUT
TO SIZE - GLUED AND
NYLON THREAD WRAPPED OVER

2⅜"

22°

⅞"

2"

1/16" WIDTH ABS SQUARE
TUBING - ¼" × ¼" I.D.

TAKE TWO LENGTHS OF SQUARE
ABS AND SANDWICH BETWEEN
ABS SHEETING AT PROPER
ANGLE - 22°

a ¾" hole in a ⅜" × 1⅛" nylon rod. Drill a ⅛" hole for the line. Option: drilled arrow nock.

- (Detail 5 in Illus. 236.) The longeron sleeve not only serves as the sleeve for the longeron, but also connects upper panels "D" with keels "A," "B," and "C."
- (Detail 6 also in Illus. 236.) Spine. Upper panels "D" are sandwiched and double-stitched between two ½" strips of 1.5 oz. ripstop seam binding. The spine is held in position by tension lines secured to fishing-guide loops on the spine exterior.
- (Detail 7 in Illus. 237.) Typical fore-and-aft-spine and wing-tip ends. (For further details, see Illus. 240.)
- (Detail 8 in Illus. 238.) In flight. Bridle arrange-

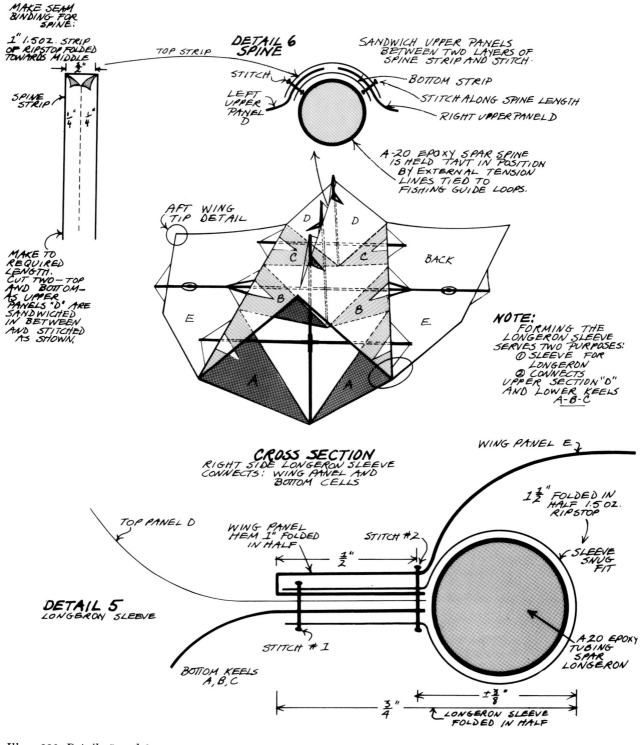

Illus. 236. Details 5 and 6.

157

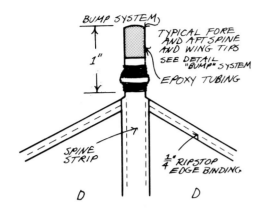

As you go through these steps, refer to the various details.

Hot-cutting:

1. Make templates "A" through "E" to the dimensions shown in Illus. 239. Add a 1″ hem allowance on the long side of wing panels "E." Secure each template over two layers of ripstop. Note: Hot cutting is optional since the perimeter of the material is stabilized with edge binding on all sides.

Sewing:

2. With panels cut to size, sew ¼″ ripstop border material or bias tape on the places marked. The border material may be made from 1″ strips of 1.5 oz. ripstop (see Edge Binding in "Working with Ripstop Nylon" on page 53). Iron along the fold points and centerline for sharp creases. If you're especially adept with your hands, you can forego ironing and simply spray the material with basting glue, fold it between your fingers, position it along the edge, and sew.

3. Stitch ¼″ nylon loops to the bridle points on keel sets "A," "B," and "C" as shown in Detail 2.

   Note: Add ½″ × 3½″ retainer strips of ripstop to form a bump system on the spine, wing sleeves, and vertical spar pockets. See Detail 3.

4. Connect kite-body-panel sets "D" by sandwiching them between layers of two ½″ strips of ripstop; double-stitch as shown in Detail 6.

5. Form wing-spar pockets by folding a 1½″ ripstop strip sleeve in half over the edge of wing panel "E" and then edge-stitch along the length. Next,

Illus. 237. Detail 7.

ment with fore and aft lengths as shown. Cut three sets of 100 lb.–test braided-Dacron bridle lines: 92″, 52″, and 48″ = 30″ fore leg and 18″ aft leg. These measurements are to the tow points or finished knots.

Flight Data: Wind range: 4–25 mph
Line: 120 lb. test
AE: ±70°
Wear gloves

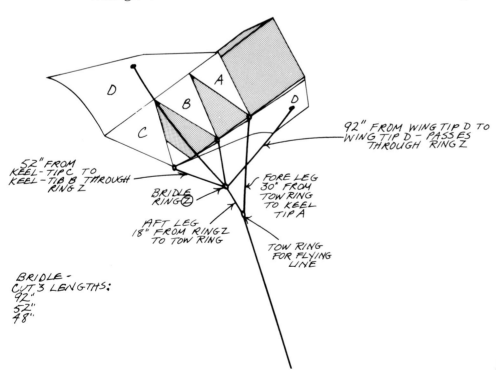

Illus. 238. Detail 8—in flight.

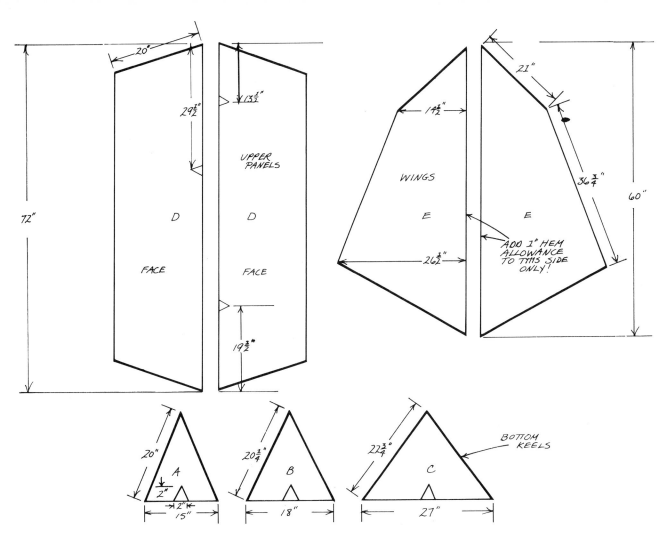

Illus. 239. Templates.

make longeron spar pockets by aligning and sandwiching kite parts "A," "B," "C," and "D" to "E" between the ripstop strip sleeve as shown in Detail 5. Hot-tacking layers of material to the sleeve keeps edges aligned and makes sewing easier.

Assembly:

Note: Aluminum protector shafts (.260) are placed at all spar (A 20–.261 O.D.) cross points as external ferrules over epoxy-tubing joints. (Since not all .260 shafts are precisely the same, check tolerances with calipers for the tightest fit over the epoxy tubing. Use epoxy-tubing external ferrule tubing GL 50M .266 I.D. as an alternate.)

6. Permanently attach vertical and wing spars. Use 2½" metal shafts to secure joints. One drop of super glue at each end of the shaft will hold the tubing in place. A 1" metal shaft protector is sufficient for all other points.

    Note: Do not make cross spars yet.

7. When the permanent spars are cut and pieced together, make stops as follows: Wrap nylon thread around the spar until the thread rises to form a bump that will stop movement along the shaft at that point—approximately 15–20 wraps or more, depending on the thread size. Use a dab of super glue on the thread to begin the wrap and end the wrap. Then saturate the wrap with super glue. Hint: Placing super glue in a solvent syringe improves application accuracy. Practise on scrap first.

    Note: *For stops only*—an alternative to the nylon wrap procedure is to cut ¼" slices of ³⁄₁₆" I.D. clear plastic (polypropylene) tubing. Stretch it over the epoxy shaft and super-glue it in place.

8. Position fishing-guide loops and wrap end connectors tightly and evenly with nylon thread. Fix them in place with dabs of super glue. Inspect a fishing pole for reference.

Hot-cutting:

9. Carefully hot-cut holes along the middle ½" spine strip for the fishing-guide loops to pass through.

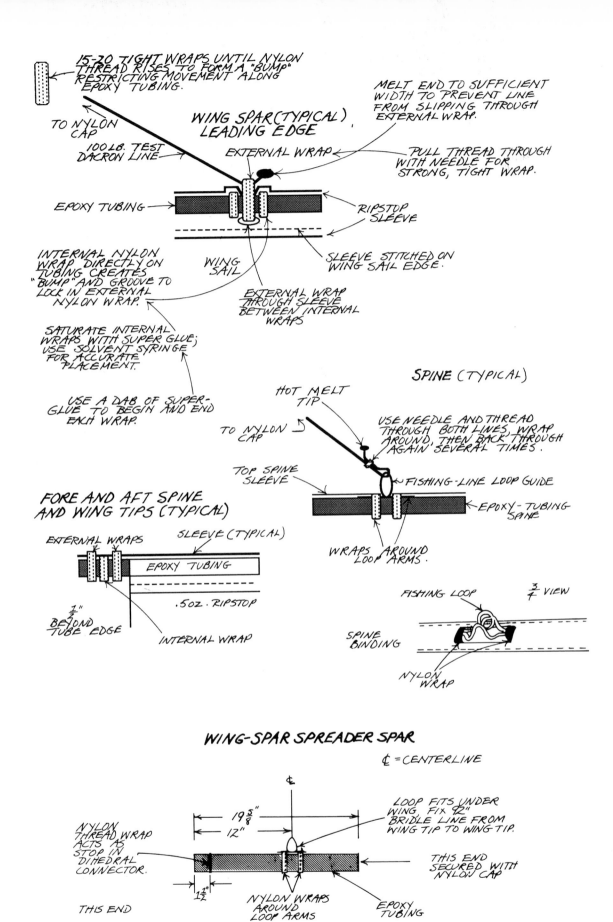

15-20 TIGHT WRAPS UNTIL NYLON THREAD RISES TO FORM A "BUMP" RESTRICTING MOVEMENT ALONG EPOXY TUBING.

MELT END TO SUFFICIENT WIDTH TO PREVENT LINE FROM SLIPPING THROUGH EXTERNAL WRAP.

TO NYLON CAP

100 LB. TEST DACRON LINE

WING SPAR (TYPICAL) LEADING EDGE

EXTERNAL WRAP

PULL THREAD THROUGH WITH NEEDLE FOR STRONG, TIGHT WRAP.

EPOXY TUBING

RIPSTOP SLEEVE

INTERNAL NYLON WRAP DIRECTLY ON TUBING CREATES "BUMP" AND GROOVE TO LOCK IN EXTERNAL NYLON WRAP.

WING SAIL

SLEEVE STITCHED ON WING SAIL EDGE.

EXTERNAL WRAP THROUGH SLEEVE BETWEEN INTERNAL WRAPS

SATURATE INTERNAL WRAPS WITH SUPER GLUE; USE SOLVENT SYRINGE FOR ACCURATE PLACEMENT.

USE A DAB OF SUPER-GLUE TO BEGIN AND END EACH WRAP.

SPINE (TYPICAL)

HOT MELT TIP

USE NEEDLE AND THREAD THROUGH BOTH LINES, WRAP AROUND, THEN BACK, THROUGH AGAIN SEVERAL TIMES.

TO NYLON CAP

TOP SPINE SLEEVE

FISHING-LINE LOOP GUIDE

EPOXY-TUBING SPINE

FORE AND AFT SPINE AND WING TIPS (TYPICAL)

WRAPS AROUND LOOP ARMS.

EXTERNAL WRAPS

SLEEVE (TYPICAL)

EPOXY TUBING

FISHING LOOP

¾ VIEW

SPINE BINDING

.5 OZ. RIPSTOP

½" BEYOND TUBE EDGE

INTERNAL WRAP

NYLON WRAP

WING-SPAR SPREADER SPAR

₵ = CENTERLINE

19⅝"

12"

LOOP FITS UNDER WING, FIX 9'2" BRIDLE LINE FROM WING TIP TO WING TIP.

NYLON THREAD WRAP ACTS AS STOP IN DIHEDRAL CONNECTOR.

THIS END SECURED WITH NYLON CAP

1½"

THIS END

NYLON WRAPS AROUND LOOP ARMS

EPOXY TUBING

Illus. 240. Stanfield's "bump" system—cutaway view.

10. Secure longerons and wing spars, fore and aft, following Stanfield's bump system in Illus. 240. The ripstop should be taut but not distorted.

Sewing:

11. Attach all external tension lines at points marked; all must be evenly spaced on both sides of the kite. Use a needle and nylon thread to secure the line as shown in Illus. 240.

Assembly:

12. Use ¼" dowels for a prototype of the three sets of cross spars. Measure and fit the dowels to size. Temporarily secure them with metal shaft pro-

tectors as required. Since this step is for correct position and a test flight only, use rings cut from ³⁄₁₆" clear plastic tubing held in place with super glue for stops along the shafts and to hold fishing-guide loops on the wing spreader spar.

Trimming the kite: The body should be taut and the wings loose enough to form a dihedral angle in flight. Once you are satisfied that the cross spars fit, use the dimensions of the dowels to cut epoxy tubing and fit with aluminum shafts. Label the cross-spar sets *front, middle,* and *rear* for reference.

38

The Parafoil Kite

Design: Courtesy of Dom Jalbert

Form from the Wind

One of the eight generic kite forms, the parafoil is designed to take full advantage of the aerodynamic principles involved in lifting a rigid wing. This kite is a radical departure in kite design in that it has no rigid members for support and requires only the wind to give it form. The parafoil presented here is adapted from Dom Jalbert's J-10 model (see Illus. 243).

Domina (Dom) C. Jalbert (Illus. 241) had an early fascination with kites and flight, which evolved into an exciting career in aerodynamics and general aviation. In 1964 Jalbert discovered the parafoil, an evolutionary airfoil platform that gained wide acceptance in kiting, parachuting, and other applications.

After landing his Beechcraft airplane at the Boca Raton airport in Florida, he grabbed a yardstick and began taking measurements of the wing's depth and cord. Over the next few weeks, he designed a "ram air" fabric-lifting airfoil—so called because the non-rigid wing maintained its shape through the internal pressure of air in a series of pocket-type cells filled solely by the wind. Though the ram-air airfoil seemed to emerge out of the blue, it was the cumulative result of Jalbert's 25 years of research

with kites, balloons, parachute rigging, and controlling static air-inflated shapes.

Uses for the aerial platform, or parafoil, include oceanographic study, military applications in jam-

Illus. 241. Dom Jalbert. (Photo by Bill Tyrrell.)

ming communications, lifting antennas along the air-defense Distant Early Warning (DEW) lines near the Arctic Circle, aerial remote-control photography in the study of migratory patterns of sea life, sport parachuting—and kite flying for the fun of it.

On June 22, 1987, a red parafoil was flown by the Japan Karakoram Expedition in the Himalayas—from the second-highest peak in the world. The parafoil is ideal for campers and mountaineers since it can be easily folded into a small, lightweight package.

Materials

To make this kite you need:

- 41″ × 8 sq. yards of .75 oz. ripstop,
- ¼″ nylon tape—for bridle and tail loops,
- 30′ of 125 lb.–test line—for bridle lines,
- 12′ of 125 lb.–test line—for tail bridle, and
- (optional) ripstop tail streamers or drogue.

Details

- (Detail 1 in Illus. 242.) Main view.
- (Detail 2 in Illus. 243.) In flight—bridle arrangement.
- (Detail 3 in Illus. 244.) Head-on view of cells.
- (Detail 4 in Illus. 245.) Side rib and keel assembly.

Flight Data: Wind range: 6–20 mph
Line: 150 lb. test
AE: ±70°
Wear gloves

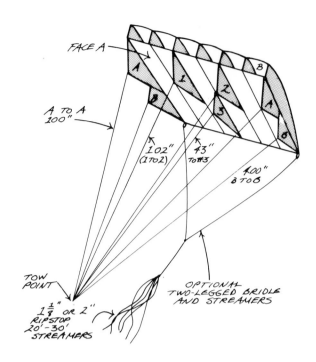

Illus. 243. Detail 2.

Construction

Hot-cutting:
First take a moment to discern the A and B sides of the parafoil's face and canopy for proper marking and sewing.

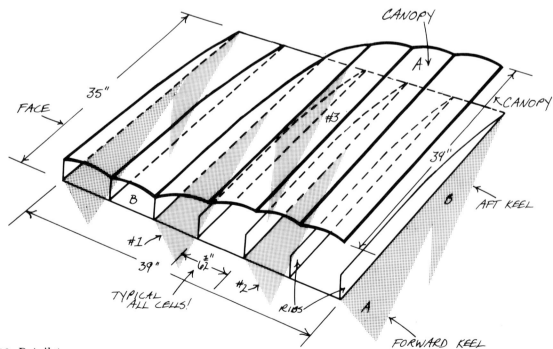

Illus. 242. Detail 1.

162

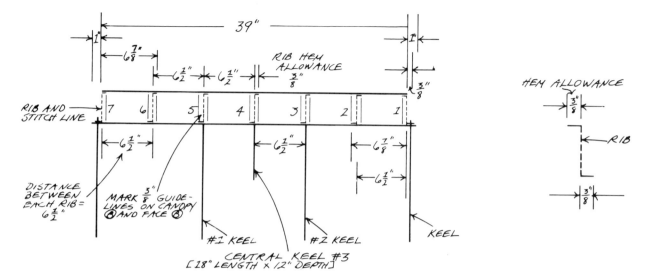

Illus. 244. Detail 3.

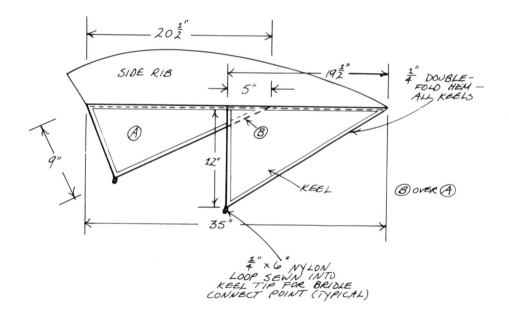

Illus. 245. Detail 4.

1. Make templates for all components: ribs, keels, face, and canopy *to hemmed dimensions.* Allow for a ⅜" hem on the ribs and a ¼" double-fold hem on the keels. The face should be 39" × 35"; cut 41" × 35¾". The canopy should be 39" × 39"; cut 39¾" × 39¾". (Use a square grid to scale or a Flexicurve strip to simplify forming the rib curve.) See Illus. 246 and 247 (Detail 3).

2. Align the templates with the straight of the grain, arranging them to make optimum use of your ripstop yardage. Hot-cut all sections. Position a 2"-vent template over the hole locations on the *internal ribs only*; use a hot cutter with a conical tip to cut out the vents. It is easier to cut out a vent from the inside of a template than cutting around an object, like a plate. Vents in interior ribs maintain equal pressure within all cells for improved lateral balance.

3. Face: Mark rib hem guidelines from the front to the rear along side B. See Illus. 247.

4. Canopy: Mark rib hem guidelines from the front to the rear along side A. See Illus. 248. Note: For more about aligning ribs, see the Sting Ray Kite project.

Sewing:

5. Edge-bind the front and rear sections of both the face and canopy with a ¼" hem.

6. Use a ¼" double-fold hem to complete the edges on all the keels. Sew a 6" × ½" nylon loop in each keel tip for the bridle.

7. Refer to Detail 3 (Illus. 244) for this step. Construct the cells by working from right to left,

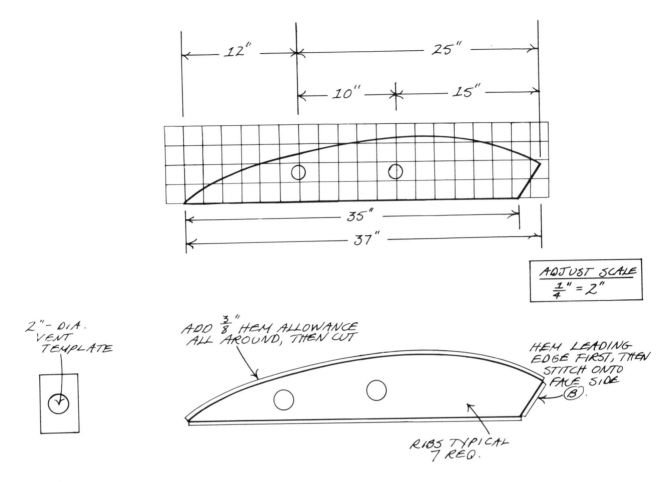

Measurements and labels on the diagram:

12"   25"
10"   15"
35"
37"

ADJUST SCALE
1/4" = 2"

2"- DIA.
VENT
TEMPLATE

ADD 3/8" HEM ALLOWANCE
ALL AROUND, THEN CUT

HEM LEADING
EDGE FIRST, THEN
STITCH ONTO
FACE SIDE
(B).

RIBS TYPICAL
7 REQ.

Illus. 246. Step 1.

beginning with rib 1 and ending with 7. Align the rib hem along the hem guidelines (the broken lines) on the face side (B); next, hot-tack the ribs in position over the stitch (straight) line from the front to the rear. Then sew the ribs to the face along the length.

Note: Hot-tack ribs 3, 4, and 5 with the hemmed straight edge of keels 1, 2, and 3 (the hemmed length of keel #3 is 18″ measured from the rear of the kite, the depth is 12″) along the stitch line at the positions indicated. *Sew together in one run.*

8. Adding the canopy: Sew the ribs from the left to the right on the canopy side (B) along the marked stitch lines. Start by aligning the ⅜″ hem fold of rib 7 with the ⅜″ inside hem on the left side of the canopy. Sew the curve of the rib along the straight of the canopy slowly; inch along for a smooth seam from the front to the rear across the rib radius. Repeat the process for the other ribs.

9. To stitch rib 1 to the inside ⅜″-hem fold line of the canopy, turn the parafoil inside out and sew the seam to complete the cells. Then turn the kite right side out.

10. Stitch the canopy to the face along the rear. Add two ¼″ nylon loops on both ends of the rear to attach an optional two-legged tail bridle for heavier winds.

11. Beginning on either side, align the side hem of keel A over the rib stitch line and then edge-stitch in place. The 5″ overlap of rear keel B goes over A; do not sew the keels together at the overlap. Repeat for the A and B keels on the other side.

Assembly:

12. Fix the bridle shroud lines as follows. Cut four lengths: two 100″—A to A and B to B; 102″—1 to 2; and 43″—keel tip 3. Measurements are from the keel tips to the knot bridle tow point. See Detail 2 (Illus. 243).

13. Tail streamers: Ripstop strips help stabilize the kite in higher winds. Tie 12′ of line to one end of each corner loop to form the two-legged tail bridle; make a loop in the middle and attach about six ripstop streamers (1⅛″ to 2″ wide and from 20′ to 30′ long). While streamers are effective in higher winds, try a stabilizing drogue in moderate conditions.

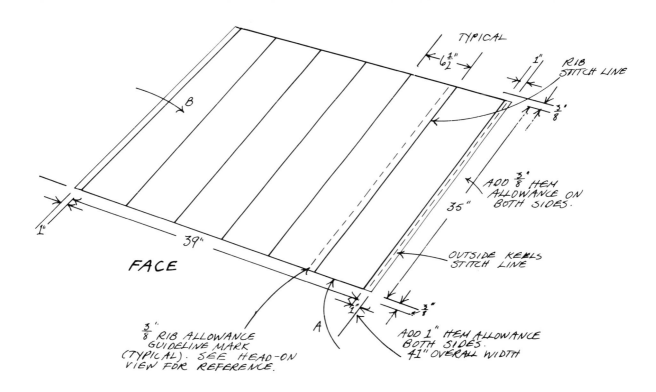

TYPICAL

$6\frac{1}{2}"$

RIB STITCH LINE

$1"$

B

$\frac{3}{8}"$

ADD $\frac{3}{8}"$ HEM ALLOWANCE ON BOTH SIDES.

$35"$

OUTSIDE KEELS STITCH LINE

$1"$

$39"$

FACE

$\frac{3}{8}"$

$\frac{1}{4}"$

ADD 1" HEM ALLOWANCE BOTH SIDES. 41" OVERALL WIDTH

$\frac{3}{8}"$ RIB ALLOWANCE GUIDELINE MARK (TYPICAL). SEE HEAD-ON VIEW FOR REFERENCE.

A

Illus. 247. Step 3.

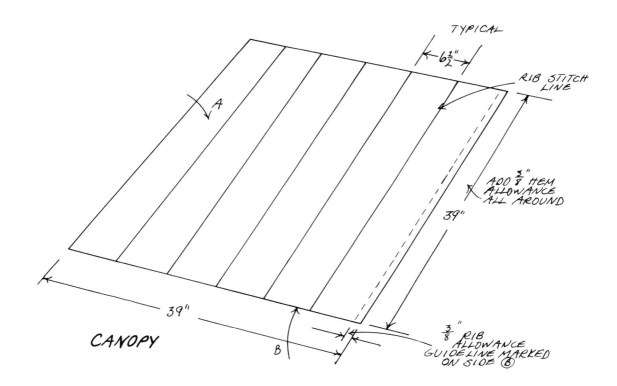

TYPICAL

$6\frac{1}{2}"$

RIB STITCH LINE

A

ADD $\frac{3}{8}"$ HEM ALLOWANCE ALL AROUND

$39"$

$39"$

CANOPY

$\frac{1}{4}"$

B

$\frac{3}{8}"$ RIB ALLOWANCE GUIDELINE MARKED ON SIDE Ⓑ

Illus. 248. Step 4.

39

The Hewitt Flexkite

From Richard Hewitt's Design

Open to Interpretation

The Hewitt Flexkite, shown in Illus. 250, casts an impressive shadow reminiscent of soaring birds and other high-aspect-ratio airfoils, such as hang gliders, sailboards, and a World War II aviation classic—the British Spitfire.

While efficient in the lift department, high-aspect-ratio wing shapes often sacrifice some degree of stability for their efficient lifting capability. (For more about aspect ratio, refer to pages 127–128 in "The Rhomboid Box Kite.") The Flexkite is no exception and unlike an on-board-pilot-controlled aircraft, it must divine its own way at the end of a tether. Despite its stabilizing drogue, the Flexkite has a tendency to overfly its zenith; this means that the kite, after reaching a flight angle of 90° overhead, will often spiral, dive, and then glide earthwards.

True to its high-aspect profile, the compound Flexkite features a high lift/drag (L/D) ratio wing mounted on a sled-kite base. (L/D ratio is discussed on page 18 in "Aerodynamics.") While the kite will never score high for predictability in the air, the basic shape does present aerial artists with an opportunity for self-expression. The Flexkite takes kindly to additions and modifications. Extensions, such as a head, tails, streamers, and elongated wings—all are welcome. The Flexkite variation shown in color on page G (top) has all of these extensions.

Materials

To make this kite you need:

- .75 oz. ripstop—for sail material and drogue;
- 1.5 oz. ripstop—for keels and vertical strips used in piecing wing segments;
- wing-spar sleeve: ¾" double-fold bias tape or strips of nylon taffeta cut on the diagonal to make sewing around curves easier (another option is trimming to size and double-folding wide strips of blanket binding);
- 4 oz. Dacron—for reinforcement material;
- 1" nylon-webbing tape—for leading-edge loop;
- 7' of ½" grosgrain ribbon;
- ¼" double-fold bias tape—for trailing edge;
- 9' of 150 lb.–test line—for two 48" bridle legs to the loop;

- 20' of 50 lb.–test line—for bridle legs and drogue lead lines;
- two ¾" split key rings—for tether point and loop for the drogue lead line;
- two pieces of 40" × 9⁄32" fibreglass rod—for 80" midsection;
- one 9⁄32 I.D. × 3" aluminum ferrule;
- two ¼" × 60" tapered fibreglass rods—for wing tips (fishing-pole blanks or bicycle flag poles) (fit tips with vinyl end caps);
- two ¼" I.D. × 2¼" aluminum ferrules;
- two FL 370 × 43" dowels or one ⅜" dowel—for keel longerons;
- two arrow nocks, adapters, and vinyl end caps for longerons;
- 12" × ½" nylon tape—sewn aftwards on the keel sleeve; and
- 2' of 250 lb.–test line loop—tied to nylon tape on the keel sleeve and slipped over the longeron arrow nock.

Details

See Illus. 249 for Details 1–5, and see Illus. 250 for Detail 6.

- (Detail 1.) Main view.
- (Detail 2.) Double-fold ¾" bias tape or taffeta forms the leading-edge wing spar sleeve.
- (Detail 3.) Wing tip. The fibreglass-rod wing spar tapers towards the wing tips; 4 oz. Dacron reinforcement.
- (Detail 4.) The 12" opening in the sleeve in the middle of the leading edge; 1" nylon tape retainer loop for the wing spar.
- (Detail 5.) Keel detail. See the Sting Ray Kite keel in the next chapter for reference.
- (Detail 6.) In flight. The bridle: 150 lb. test—48" to the lark's head hitch on a ¾" split key ring.

Flight Data: Wind range: 8–20 mph
               Line: 150 lb. test line (minimum)
               AE: ±65°
               Wear gloves

Construction

Note: Here are two different approaches for constructing the sail. You can combine the panels of col-

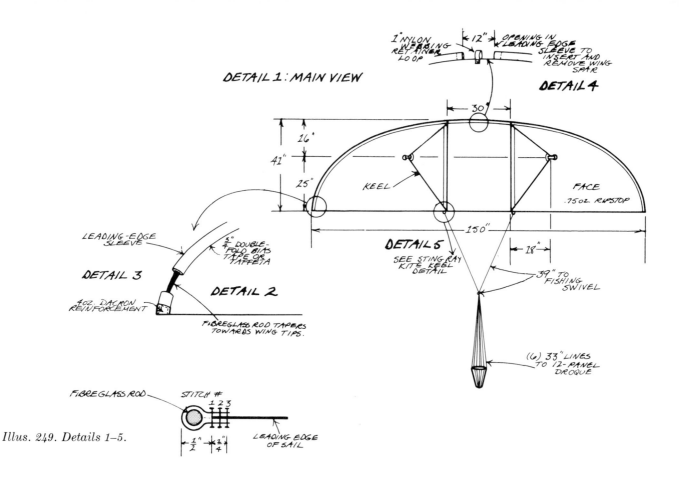

DETAIL 1: MAIN VIEW

1" NYLON WEBBING RETAINER LOOP ← 12" → OPENING IN LEADING EDGE SLEEVE TO INSERT AND REMOVE WING SPAR

DETAIL 4

30"

16"

41"

25"

KEEL

FACE .75oz RIPSTOP

150"

DETAIL 5
SEE STING RAY KITE KEEL DETAIL

18"

39" TO FISHING SWIVEL

LEADING-EDGE SLEEVE

DETAIL 3

¾" DOUBLE-FOLD BIAS TAPE OR TAFFETA

DETAIL 2

4oz. DACRON REINFORCEMENT

FIBREGLASS ROD TAPERS TOWARDS WING TIPS.

(6) 33" LINES TO 12-PANEL DROQUE

FIBREGLASS ROD

STITCH #
1 2 3

½" ¼"

LEADING EDGE OF SAIL

Illus. 249. Details 1–5.

ors with a sail seam to make a bolt of ripstop 41″ × 160″ and then cut the wing using a half-pattern template as in this design. Or, for more precision, you can cut five templates, one for each 15″ sail segment, and piece the wing together. (For this approach, refer to the construction steps in making wings for the

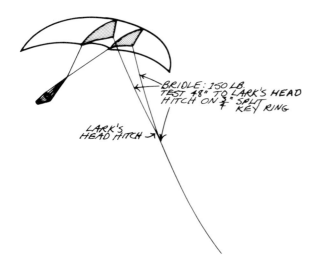

BRIDLE: 150 LB. TEST 48" TO LARK'S HEAD HITCH ON ¼" SPLIT KEY RING

LARK'S HEAD HITCH

Illus. 250. Detail 6—in flight.

Sting Ray Kite in the next chapter and adapt them to the Flexkite.)

Hot-cutting:

1. For this first step, refer to Illus. 251. Kite half-pattern: Make a complete half-pattern wing template by plotting the curve of the wing with the ordinates provided.

    Keel template: Calculate the keel measurements, allowing for the hems and longeron sleeve. Construct and assemble the keels using the same techniques shown for the Sting Ray Kite in the next chapter.

    Plotting an ellipse curve: To construct a precise template or to scale the kite to a desired size, use the convenient percentages shown in the layout formula to establish ordinates of an ellipse curve.

Sewing:

2. Use a sail seam to combine the desired color scheme of the sail. (See the color illustration of the Flexkite on page G for some ideas.)

3. Cut two pieces of ¾″ × 8′ double-fold bias tape. On both strips, turn the end that will accept the wing spar under and stitch it shut along the width. Fold the tape in half. Run the first stitch ½″ in from the fold along the length of the tape to form the wing-spar sleeve. This leaves a ¼″ lip

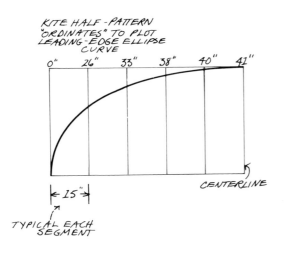

KITE HALF-PATTERN
"ORDINATES" TO PLOT
LEADING-EDGE ELLIPSE
CURVE

CENTERLINE

←15"→

TYPICAL EACH
SEGMENT

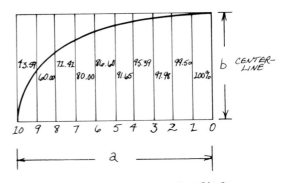

TO PLOT AN ELLIPSE CURVE
OF YOUR OWN DESIGN:

CENTER-
LINE

b

a

① DIVIDE a INTO TEN EQUAL SPACES.
② ORDINATES ARE % OF b.
③ CONNECT POINTS TO FORM
ELLIPSE CURVE.

Illus. 251. Step 1.

that forms a convenient sandwich over the sail leading edge.

Option: Follow the same procedure using 3″ diagonally cut strips of nylon taffeta (available in many colors) to form the ¾″ double-fold leading-edge sleeve. (See Edge Binding in "Working with Ripstop Nylon" on page 53.)

Hot-cutting:

4. Fold the sail fabric in half and align the template edge at the fold line. Hot-cut the sail to the completed dimensions shown in the main view (Detail 1); then add ¼″ double-fold bias tape along the

trailing edge. If you hem the trailing edge, be sure to make an allowance on the sail dimensions for a ¼″ double-fold hem.

Sewing:

5. Stitch the leading-edge sleeve along the ¼″ lip to the sail. (See Illus. 249.) Begin by positioning the sleeve halves (the turned-under ends towards the middle) on the leading edge of the sail 6″ from the middle for a 12′ overall gap. The central gap in the sleeve is for inserting and removing the wing spar. Work from the middle outward. Place the ¼″ lip of the bias tape over the leading

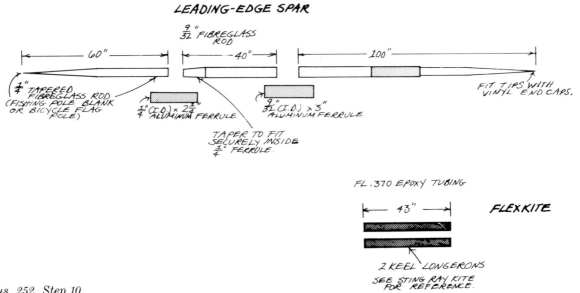

LEADING-EDGE SPAR

Illus. 252. Step 10.

168

edge of the sail and run a second and third double stitch along the wing edge. Then reinforce the wing tips with 4 oz. Dacron.

6. Fold 1″ × 2″ nylon webbing in half and run a stitch ½″ in from the fold to form the wing-spar retainer loop. Reinforce the loop connect area on the sail edge with 4 oz. Dacron. Sandwich the sail between the lip of the nylon webbing and stitch it in position as shown in Illus. 249 (Detail 4).

7. Reinforce the area along the back of the kite where the keel is stitched to the sail with ½″ × 41″ strips of grosgrain ribbon.

Hot-cutting:

8. Hot-cut two keels as indicated in Step 1.

Sewing:

9. The seams that attach the keel to the sail form longeron sleeves, as shown for the Sting Ray Kite. Add nylon-tape loops for a two-legged drogue bridle to the aft points of the longeron sleeves.

Hobby saw:

10. Cut fibreglass wing spars and keel longerons to size as shown in Illus. 252.

Hot-cutting and sewing:

11. Hot-cut 12 panels for the drogue and then assemble. See "Tails and Drogues."

Assembly:

12. Use aluminum ferrules to connect the wing-spar halves first. Insert one half in the leading-edge sleeve and follow with the other half; join them in the middle with the aluminum ferrule. Keel longerons are held in sleeves under tension with the loop, as with the Sting Ray Kite. Attach the drogue lead line to the loop with the fishing swivel. Then add the flying bridle.

40
The Sting Ray Kite

Design: Courtesy of Adrian Conn

The Stitching Zone— Three Days of the Sting Ray

Announcer: You unlock this design with the thread of cotton and polyester. Beyond it is another dimension—a dimension of inches, a dimension of angles, a dimension of seams. You're moving into a realm of ripstop and tubing, of wings and battens. You've just changed bobbins into . . . the stitching zone.

Scene 1: Interior Basement Workshop—Full Moon, Midnight

A thin, intense man works at a feverish pace, precisely cutting different shapes and colors of fabric on a large table. The table is surrounded by piles of neatly stacked templates and other materials and tools of the kite maker's trade.

Announcer (voice-over): Consider, if you will, this man, totally preoccupied with the details at hand. He had descended into his basement to begin working on an idea for a kite; that was three days ago. Now his thoughts spiral in endless loops, and the Sting Ray design conjures up images in his mind of giants flying through primordial oceans. To fully explore this compound variation of sled, parafoil, and delta, he has put all else aside. During this temporary delirium, he has given up his job, spoken to no one, and not eaten. Our builder is driven by a feeling that his idea will work; he is swept away with an inspired vision.

Consider the task of creating something new in the universe; consider the consequences of tampering with nature; consider motivation, that unstoppable compelling force that drives an individual to forego all for a quest of uncertainty. How does our builder feel? Why does he do it? It began as a conventional project. Now it has taken over his life.

Unknown to our builder, he has crossed over into a

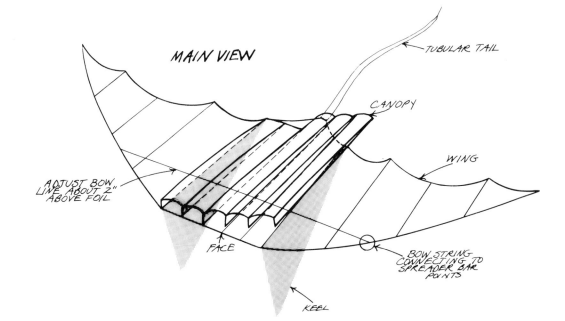

Illus. 253. Detail 1.

domain with no boundaries, with no address, with no escape until the deed is done. Our compulsive builder's arrival is no accident. To enter a place of pure involvement has been his secret wish for a long time. He, like others of faith, are welcome in the Stitching Zone.

* * *

The Sting Ray (shown in Illus. 253, and in color on page F) is a high-aspect-ratio delta stabilized by a central parafoil and tubular tail. It won first prize in the compound kite class at the 1984 Smithsonian Kite Festival in Washington, D.C.

Materials

Note: The color scheme of your Sting Ray will dictate how much ripstop nylon is required for each section (see the Sting Ray in color on page F). However, to establish some idea of how much fabric is necessary, the following square-yardage measurements are based on using one color.

• All ripstop nylon: 30 sq. yards of .75 oz. for wings, 5 sq. yards of .75 oz. for foil, 2 sq. yards of 1.5 oz. for keels, and 2½ sq. yards of .75 oz. for tail—plus strips of 1.5 oz. on wing panels;

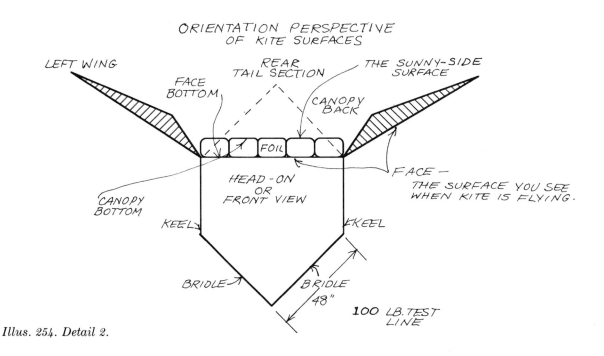

Illus. 254. Detail 2.

- 1 yard of ½″ nylon tape;
- 4 oz. Dacron—for all reinforcements;
- 250 lb.–test line—for longeron loops, pull-out line, and bridle;
- 100 lb.–test line—for bow line;
- two 9/16″ split key rings;
- seven ⅛″ fibreglass-rod battens cut to size and fitted with vinyl end caps on both strips;
- 1″ × 5/16″ I.D. plastic tubing;
- epoxy tubing FL 505, FL 370, and Fl 350;
- two 3″ .294″ ferrules;
- arrow nocks and inserts;
- vinyl end caps;
- two 2⅞″ .300″ aluminum ferrules;
- two 3⅜″ .333″ fibreglass-rod ferrules:
- two 2″ FL 414 epoxy-tubing ferrules;
- two 13/16″ .375″ I.D. brass-tubing ferrules; and
- Velcro hook and loop strips for tail.

Details

- (Detail 1 in Illus. 253.) Main view: parafoil, wing, keel, and bow line.
- (Detail 2 in Illus. 254.) Orientation perspective of kite surfaces.
- (Detail 3 in Illus. 255.) Stitching the keel, wing, and parafoil.

Flight Data: Wind range: 5–15 mph
Line: 150–200 lb. test
AE: ±70°
Wear gloves

Construction

Take some time to comprehend the three basic elements of the Sting Ray—the wings, parafoil, and

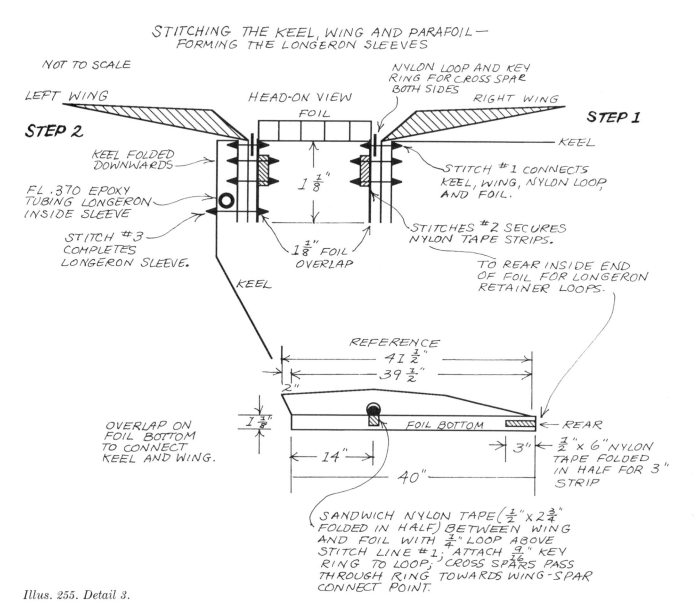

Illus. 255. Detail 3.

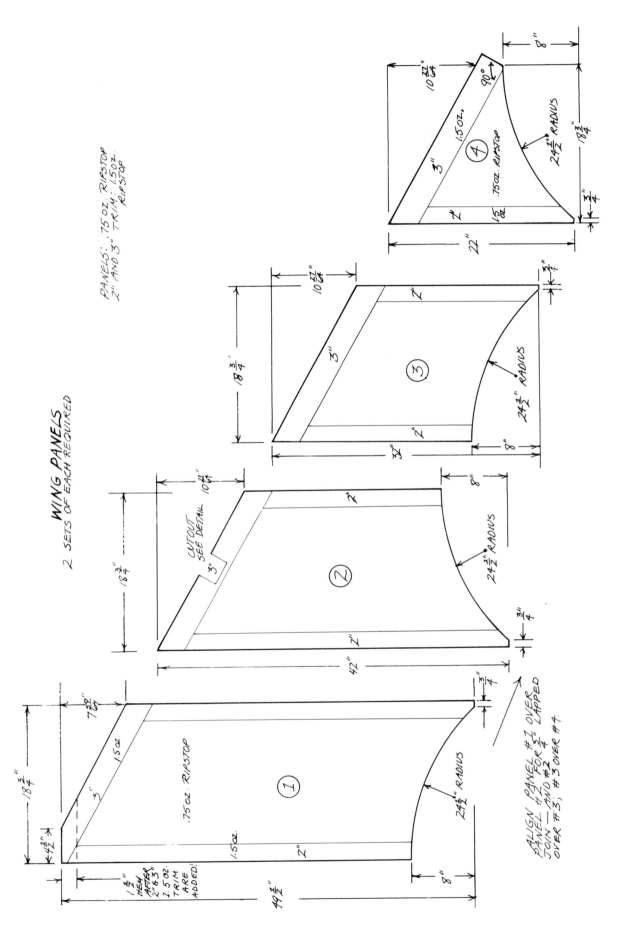

WING PANELS
2 SETS OF EACH REQUIRED

PANELS: .75 OZ. RIPSTOP
2" AND 3" TRIM: 1.5 OZ.
RIPSTOP

CUTOUT
SEE DETAIL

① .75 OZ. RIPSTOP

②

③

④ .75 OZ. RIPSTOP

90°

24½" RADIUS

1.5 OZ.

3"

2"

8"

18¾"

10½" GA

22"

31"

42"

44½"

7½" GA

¾"

4½"

½" HEM AFTER 2" & 3"
1.5 OZ. TRIM ARE ADDED!

ALIGN PANEL #1 OVER
PANEL #2 FOR ¾" LAPPED
JOIN — AND #2 OVER #3, #3
OVER #4.

Illus. 256. Step 1.

keels. Construct this kite in your mind's eye, picturing each step until the initial complexity dissolves into individually understood components. First, complete each section (wings, parafoil, and keels); then connect the wings and keels to the parafoil.

Be sure to make templates for each section of the kite. Hot-tack and hot-cut all sections. (Conn cuts templates from .020 aluminum flat stock.)

Sewing notes: Make all zigzag stitches as close to the edges as possible. The *last* detail of both wings and parafoil is adding the ⅜" bias tape to the trailing edge; add the bias tape to each section *separately*.

1. Cut two sets of each wing panel 1 through 4 to the precise dimensions shown in Illus. 256. All scallops are cut to a 24½" radius.
2. Align a 3" sleeve strip over a 2" strip. Baste the 3" sleeve strip as shown in Illus. 257.

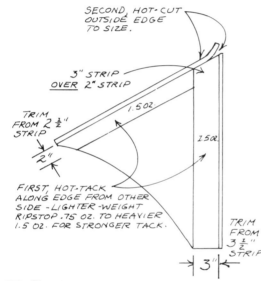

SECOND, HOT-CUT OUTSIDE EDGE TO SIZE.

3" STRIP OVER 2" STRIP

TRIM FROM 2½" STRIP

2"

1.5 OZ.

1.5 OZ.

FIRST, HOT-TACK ALONG EDGE FROM OTHER SIDE - LIGHTER-WEIGHT RIPSTOP .75 OZ. TO HEAVIER 1.5 OZ. FOR STRONGER TACK.

TRIM FROM 3½" STRIP

3"

Illus. 257. Step 2.

3. Note that panel 2 contains a spreader bar cutout. See Illus. 258.
4. See Illus. 259. Connect panels 1 through 4 with a ¾" lapped join seam. Referring to Detail 4, insert two layers (2" × ¾") of 4 oz. Dacron between each lap joint as reinforcements for the fibreglass batten. Tip: Hot-cut both edges of the Dacron strips to form a tube. The Dacron strip is kept in position by stitches on either side and bias tape along the trailing edge.
5. Connect all wing panels and form the wing-spar sleeve. See finished panels 3 and 4 in Illus. 260 as a reference for all panels. Position and stitch a 4 oz. (2" × ¾") spreader-bar scuff plate on the sail back as shown in Step 3 (Illus. 258). Do not close off the batten sleeve when adding the scuff plate.
   Note: Each batten should run the full length of

the wing. Insert the battens last—after the entire kite has been completed.

Parafoil:
6. See Illus. 261. Measure and cut the parafoil bottom and canopy section. Mark the rib stitch and ⅜" rib-hem reference lines, as shown, on the proper side of the fabric. Use a ½" hem along the leading edges of the parafoil's face and canopy.
7. See Illus. 262. Hot-cut the parafoil's ribs. Note the position of the split key ring retainers for the cross-spar spreader bar.
   Note: All stitching is from front to back. Use the head-on view of the parafoil cells in Illus. 261 for reference.
8. Stitch the ribs to the parafoil bottom first; work from right to left (1 through 6). Note: Since you can't effectively stitch the ribs to the rear end point (where the canopy and face converge), fold the aft edge of each rib back about 1" to simplify sewing.
9. Working from left to right, begin by stitching the canopy to rib #6. Sewing the curve to the straight line of the canopy takes patience; Conn sews 1" at a time to achieve a smooth curve. To stitch rib 1 to the inside ⅜" hem fold line of the canopy, turn the parafoil inside out and sew the seam to complete the cells. Then turn the kite right side out.
10. See Illus. 263. Sew the canopy (parafoil back) to the rear of the back of the face. Note the position of the ⅛" fibreglass-rod batten sleeve; sew it on prior to adding the canopy.

Keels:
11. Hot-cut two keels and add 4 oz. Dacron reinforcements, fore and aft, along the longeron sleeve. Note: Mark the stitching guideline on the left keel only; this reference line is necessary for sewing the keel-wing-parafoil from front to back. The sewing reference guideline for the right side (keel-wing-parafoil) is marked on the parafoil face.
    Sew ½" × 5" nylon tape into the hem at the tow points and the front of the keel that extends ½" beyond the leading edge of the kite as shown in Step 12 (Illus. 264).

Wing-parafoil-keel:
   Refer to Detail 3 (Illus. 255).
12. See Illus. 264. The two detailed views of the front-right keel section show the proper stitching, relationship, and arrangement for connecting the wing-parafoil-keel, which also forms the keel longeron sleeves.
13. See Illus. 265. The two detailed views of the rear-right keel section show proper stitching positioning and the keel longeron secured in the sleeve with a 250 lb.–test line loop.

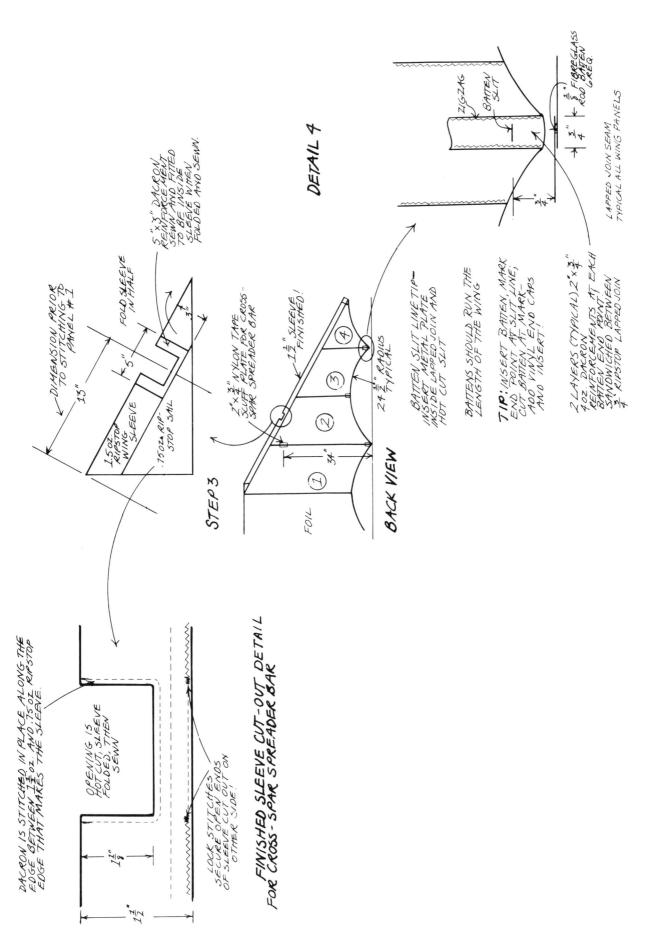

DETAIL 4

ZIG-ZAG

BATTEN SLIT

$\frac{1}{8}$" FIBREGLASS ROD BATTEN 6 REQ.

$\frac{3}{4}$"

$\frac{3}{4}$"

$\frac{1}{2}$"

LAPPED JOIN SEAM TYPICAL ALL WING PANELS

BATTEN SLIT LINE TIP INSERT METAL PLATE INSIDE LAPPED JOIN AND HOT CUT SLIT

BATTENS SHOULD RUN THE LENGTH OF THE WING

TIP: INSERT BATTEN, MARK END POINT AT SLIT LINE, CUT BATTEN AT MARK - ADD VINYL END CAPS AND INSERT!

2 LAYERS (TYPICAL) 2"x $\frac{3}{4}$" 4 OZ. DACRON REINFORCEMENTS AT EACH BATTEN END POINT SANDWICHED BETWEEN $\frac{3}{4}$" RIPSTOP LAPPED JOIN

DACRON REINFORCEMENT SEWN AND FITTED TO BE INSIDE SLEEVE WHEN FOLDED AND SEWN.

5"x3" DACRON

FOLD SLEEVE IN HALF

3"

5"

DIMENSION PRIOR TO STITCHING TO PANEL #1

15"

1.5 OZ. RIPSTOP WING SLEEVE

.75 OZ. RIP-STOP SAIL

2"x $\frac{3}{4}$" NYLON TAPE SLIT PLATE FOR CROSS - SPAR SPREADER BAR

$1\frac{1}{2}$" SLEEVE FINISHED!

STEP 3

FOIL

① ② ③ ④

3$\frac{1}{4}$"

$24\frac{1}{2}$" RADIUS TYPICAL

BACK VIEW

DACRON IS STITCHED IN PLACE ALONG THE EDGE BETWEEN 1.5 OZ. AND .75 OZ. RIPSTOP EDGE THAT MAKES THE SLEEVE.

OPENING IS HOT CUT, SLEEVE FOLDED, THEN SEWN

LOCK STITCHES SECURE OPEN ENDS OF SLEEVE CUT OUT ON OTHER SIDE!

$1\frac{1}{2}$"

$1\frac{1}{2}$"

FINISHED SLEEVE CUT-OUT DETAIL FOR CROSS - SPAR SPREADER BAR

174

Illus. 258. Step 3.

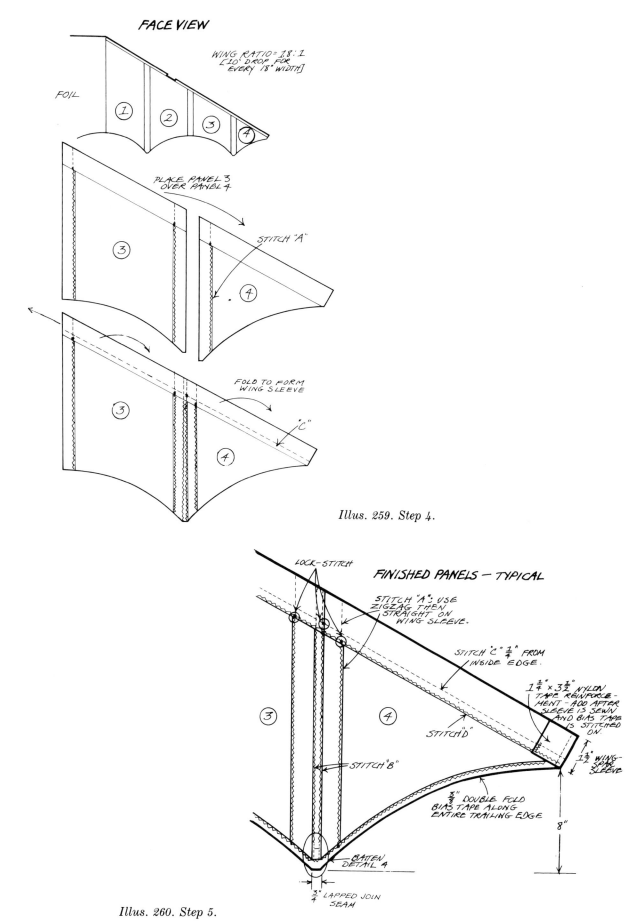

FACE VIEW

WING RATIO = 18:1
[10" DROP FOR EVERY 18" WIDTH]

FOIL

① ② ③ ④

PLACE PANEL 3 OVER PANEL 4

STITCH "A"

③

④

FOLD TO FORM WING SLEEVE

③

"C"

④

Illus. 259. Step 4.

LOCK-STITCH

FINISHED PANELS — TYPICAL

STITCH "A": USE ZIGZAG THEN STRAIGHT ON WING SLEEVE.

STITCH "C" $\frac{1}{4}$" FROM INSIDE EDGE.

③

④

$1\frac{1}{4}$" × $3\frac{1}{2}$" NYLON TAPE REINFORCEMENT - ADD AFTER SLEEVE IS SEWN AND BIAS TAPE IS STITCHED ON.

STITCH "D"

$1\frac{1}{2}$" WING-SPAR SLEEVE

STITCH "B"

$\frac{3}{4}$" DOUBLE FOLD BIAS TAPE ALONG ENTIRE TRAILING EDGE

8"

BATTEN DETAIL 4

$\frac{3}{4}$" LAPPED JOIN SEAM

Illus. 260. Step 5.

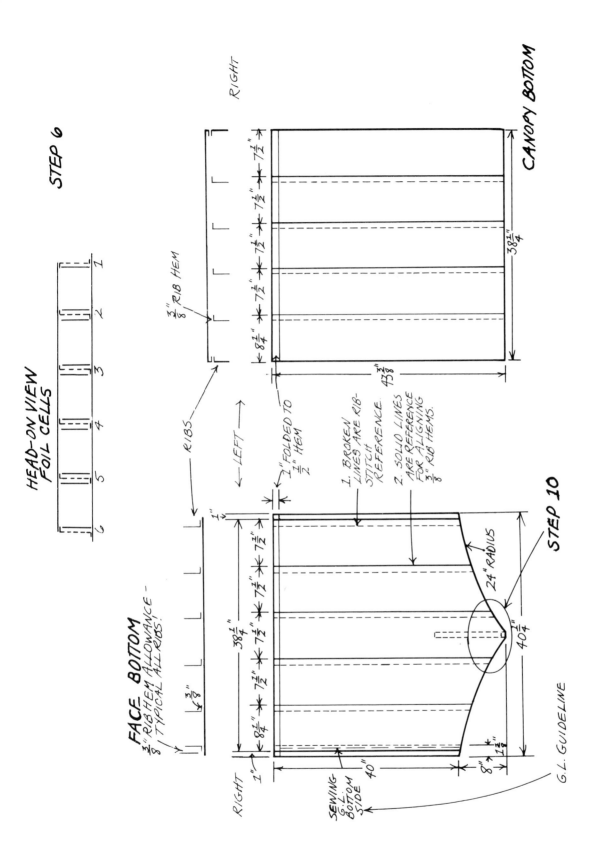

STEP 6

HEAD-ON VIEW
FOIL CELLS

1 2 3 4 5 6

RIGHT

CANOPY BOTTOM

⅜" RIB HEM

RIBS

←LEFT→

1" FOLDED TO ½" HEM

38¼"

43⅜"

8¼" ✳ 7½" ✳ 7½" ✳ 7½" ✳ 7½"

FACE BOTTOM
⅜" RIB HEM ALLOWANCE –
TYPICAL ALL RIBS!

⅜"

1"

38¼"

8¼" ✳ 7½" ✳ 7½" ✳ 7½" ✳ 7½"

RIGHT

1"

SEWING-
G.L. BOTTOM
SIDE

40"

8"

1⅛"

40¼"

24" RADIUS

G.L. GUIDELINE

STEP 10

1. BROKEN LINES ARE RIB-STITCH REFERENCE.

2. SOLID LINES ARE REFERENCE FOR ALIGNING ⅜" RIB HEMS.

176

Illus. 261. Steps 6 and 10.

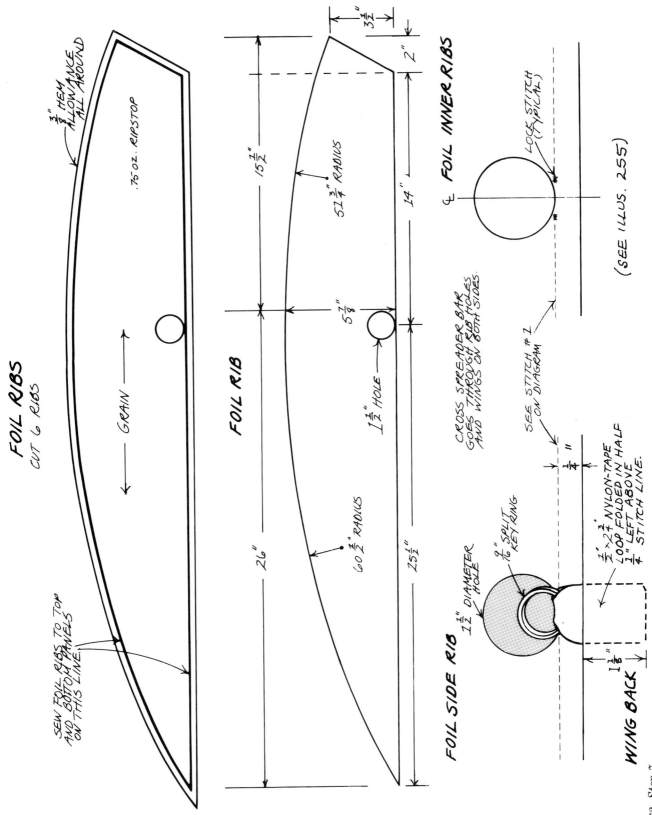

FOIL RIBS

CUT 6 RIBS

¾" HEM ALLOWANCE ALL AROUND

.75 OZ. RIPSTOP

← GRAIN →

SEW FOIL RIBS TO TOP AND BOTTOM PANELS ON THIS LINE.

FOIL RIB

3½"

2"

15½"

51¾" RADIUS

14"

5⅞"

26"

1½" HOLE

60½" RADIUS

25½"

FOIL INNER RIBS

℄

LOCK STITCH (TYPICAL)

(SEE ILLUS. 255)

CROSS SPREADER BAR GOES THROUGH RIB HOLES AND WINGS ON BOTH SIDES.

SEE STITCH #1 ON DIAGRAM

¼"

1"

FOIL SIDE RIB

1½" DIAMETER HOLE

⅞" SPLIT KEY RING

½" × 2¼" NYLON-TAPE LOOP FOLDED IN HALF 1" LEFT ABOVE ¼ STITCH LINE.

1⅛"

WING BACK

Illus. 262. Step 7.

177

CANOPY — FOIL BACK

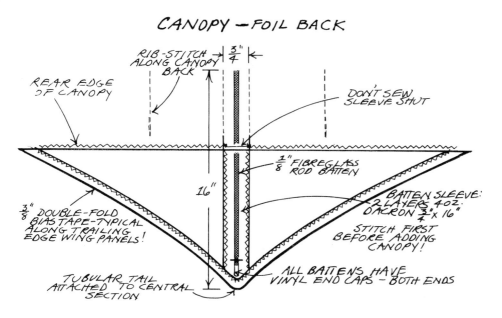

RIB-STITCH ALONG CANOPY BACK

3/4"

DON'T SEW SLEEVE SHUT

REAR EDGE OF CANOPY

1/8" FIBREGLASS ROD BATTEN

16"

3/8" DOUBLE-FOLD BIAS TAPE-TYPICAL ALONG TRAILING EDGE WING PANELS!

BATTEN SLEEVE: 2 LAYERS 4 OZ. DACRON 3/4" x 16" STITCH FIRST BEFORE ADDING CANOPY!

TUBULAR TAIL ATTACHED TO CENTRAL SECTION

ALL BATTENS HAVE VINYL END CAPS — BOTH ENDS

Illus. 263. Step 10.

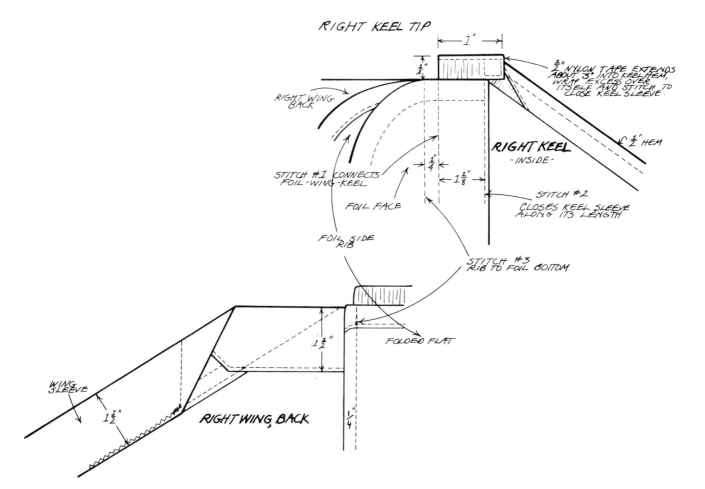

RIGHT KEEL TIP

1"

1/2"

RIGHT WING BACK

1/2" NYLON TAPE EXTENDS ABOUT 3" INTO KEEL HEM, WRAP EXCESS OVER ITSELF AND STITCH TO CLOSE KEEL SLEEVE.

RIGHT KEEL -INSIDE-

1/2" HEM

STITCH #1 CONNECTS FOIL-WING-KEEL

FOIL FACE

1/4"

1 1/8"

STITCH #2 CLOSES KEEL SLEEVE ALONG ITS LENGTH

FOIL SIDE RIB

STITCH #3 RIB TO FOIL BOTTOM

FOLDED FLAT

WING SLEEVE

1 1/2"

1 1/2"

RIGHT WING BACK

1/4"

Illus. 264. Step 12.

178

REAR VIEW, BACK SIDE

RIGHT WING, BACK

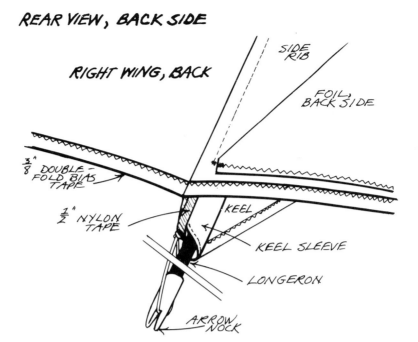

SIDE RIB

FOIL, BACK SIDE

$\frac{3}{8}$" DOUBLE-FOLD BIAS TAPE

$\frac{1}{2}$" NYLON TAPE

KEEL

KEEL SLEEVE

LONGERON

ARROW NOCK

REAR VIEW, FACE SIDE

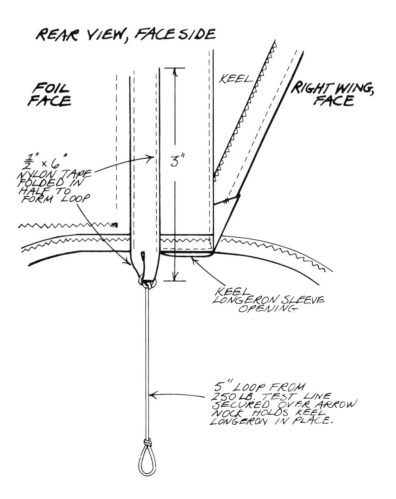

FOIL FACE

KEEL

RIGHT WING, FACE

$\frac{1}{2}$" × 6" NYLON TAPE FOLDED IN HALF TO FORM LOOP

3"

KEEL LONGERON SLEEVE OPENING

5" LOOP FROM 250 LB. TEST LINE SECURED OVER ARROW NOCK HOLDS KEEL LONGERON IN PLACE.

Illus. 265. Step 13.

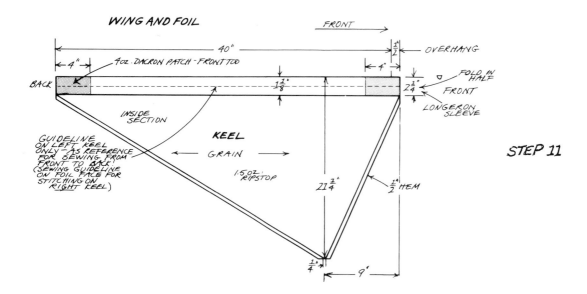

WING AND FOIL

FRONT →

40"

OVERHANG

4"

4oz. DACRON PATCH - FRONT TOO

1½"

1⅛"

4"

2¼"

FOLD IN HALF

FRONT

BACK

LONGERON SLEEVE

INSIDE SECTION

GUIDELINE ON LEFT KEEL ONLY - AS REFERENCE FOR SEWING FROM FRONT TO BACK (SEWING GUIDELINE ON FOIL FACE FOR STITCHING ON RIGHT KEEL)

KEEL

← GRAIN →

1.5 OZ RIPSTOP

21⅞"

½" HEM

¼"

9"

STEP 11

TAIL

FOIL CANOPY

VELCRO TAB KEEPS TAIL FIXED TO REAR END OF FOIL.

STEP 14

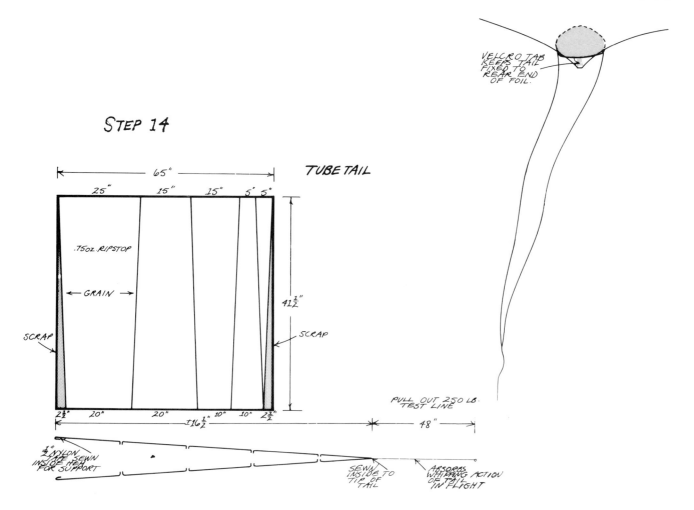

TUBE TAIL

65"

25"   15"   15"   5" 5"

.75 OZ. RIPSTOP

← GRAIN

SCRAP

41½"

SCRAP

2½"   20"   20"   10"   10"   2½"

16½"

48"

PULL OUT 250 LB. TEST LINE

¾" NYLON TAPE SEWN INSIDE HEM FOR SUPPORT

SEWN INSIDE TO TIP OF TAIL

ABSORBS WHIPPING ACTION OF TAIL IN FLIGHT

Illus. 266. Steps 11 and 14.

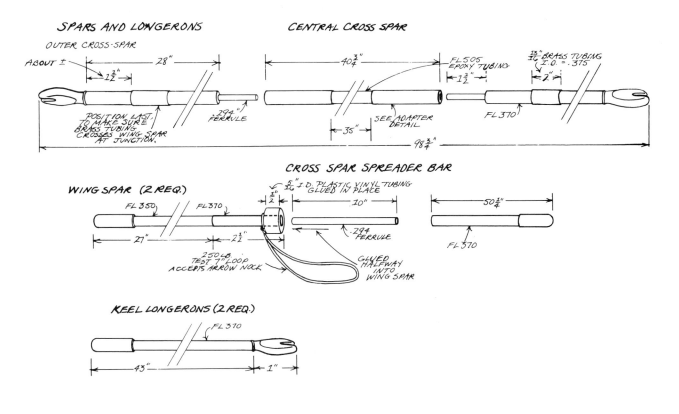

Illus. 267. Step 15.

Tail:

14. See Illus. 266. Cut the tubular tail and stitch as shown. Add a strip of ½″ nylon tape inside the top hem as reinforcement. Sew strips of Velcro, loop to tail top—and Velcro, hook to back center, on the parafoil face as shown. Sew in the 48″ length pull line (which absorbs the whipping action of the tail in flight) with the tube tail inside out; then use the line to pull the tail right side out.

Spreader bar, wing spars, and longerons:

15. Cut spars, ferrules, and aluminum tubing as shown in Illus. 267. To construct the middle cross-spar end adapters, refer to Illus. 268. Note: Determine the precise position for the 2″ brass tubing protector (¹³⁄₁₆″ of .375 I.D.) on the outer cross spars *last*. The brass tubing acts as a scuff plate against the FL 370 wing-spar ferrule. Glue the brass in place and then add an arrow nock.

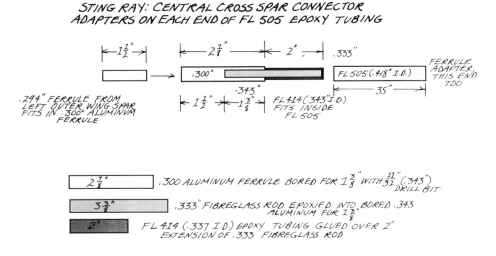

Illus. 268. Adaptors.

41
Coffee Cup Kites

Design: Courtesy of Ron Petralito[1]

Coffee Cup Kites To Go[2]

In the early '80s, architect Ron Petralito began experimenting with polystyrene (plastic foam) coffee cup gliders inside a geodesic dome he had built in the wilds of Wisconsin. During one typically long, isolated winter, Petralito set up an indoor miniature ski jump to scientifically determine the optimum curve for a coffee cup glider. After much trial and error, he discovered that a properly divided, large McDonald's coffee cup generated the most lift.

McDonald's large-size cups are recommended for their aerodynamic superiority; the lip of the cup flares outward, giving the McDonald's cup an edge over other types. Because the cups are standard worldwide, they represent a reliable module and reference to work from. As a result, Petralito developed an airfoil classified as a "slotted Rogallo matrix." This curve, however, is not the only one you can use.

Since developing his original curve, Petralito has improved upon his design with "hi-lift" and "super hi-lift" curves that make lift and performance substantially better. However, as there are no precise reference points on the cup to establish the required symmetrical curvature, a module cannot be provided.

For the technically minded: According to Petralito, using "hi-lift" and "super hi-lift" curves creates two changes. First of all, the cord of the wing cell is lengthened in the critical area of lift. And an effective slot is created between the leading edge of one wing and the trailing edge of another within the matrix of the kite, causing a reduction of turbulence over the top of the trailing wing at high angles of attack. Try altering the curve on the cup and see what you can discover.

Note: If McDonald's large-size coffee cups are unavailable, look for other cups with lips that curve outward. Try cups offered by other fast-food chains. Although, according to Petralito, some efficiency will be lost by not using McDonald's cups, other foam cups will fly well enough.

* * *

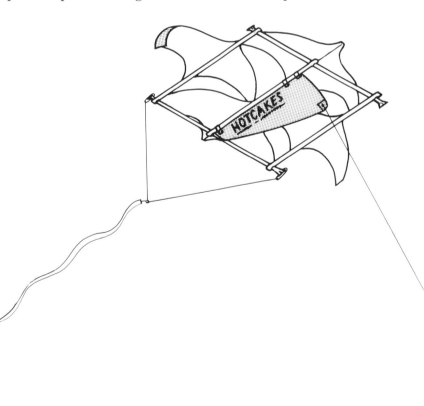

Illus. 269. Detail 1—Short Stack.

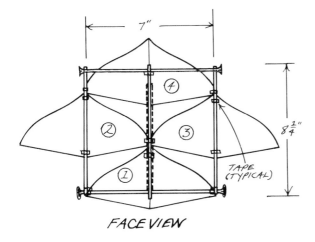

Illus. 270. Detail 2 and Step 11.

Two types of coffee cup kites are presented here—Short Stack, shown in Illus. 269, and the Straw Hotcakes variation, in Illus. 271. Once you understand the basic construction concepts, you'll find that these inexpensive kites can be easy and fun to make.

Short Stack

Materials

To make the Short Stack Kite you need:

• five large McDonald's coffee cups,
• five McDonald's standard 8⅛″ straws,
• one McDonald's Hotcakes plate,
• ½″ Scotch Magic tape,
• ¾″ Scotch Strapping tape,
• three small brass safety pins,
• a sharp pencil,
• an emery board,
• a ballpoint pen—for marking cups,
• a hobby-knife razor,
• lightweight twine—for tail bridle, and
• 9′ to 18′ of Mylar or ripstop streamers—for tail.

Details

• (Detail 1 in Illus. 269.) Short Stack Kite in flight. Four wing cells. Mylar or ripstop tail streamers: 9′ to 18′—more wind, longer tail. (Budget streamers: Tape perforated-edge strips from computer paper to required lengths; if you print a long document, you'll have strips already stuck together.)
• (Detail 2 in Illus. 270.) Face view—four wing cells taped to the straw frame.
• (Detail 3 in Illus. 271.) Straw Hotcakes Kite in flight. Nine wing cells. Mylar or ripstop tail streamers: 12′ to 40′—more wind, longer tail.
• (Detail 4 in Illus. 272.) Face view—nine wing cells taped to the straw frame.
• (Detail 5 in Illus. 273.) Splicing straws.
• (Detail 6 in Illus. 274.) Wing detail.

Flight Data: Wind range: 8–20 mph
Line: 12 lb. test
AE: ±55°

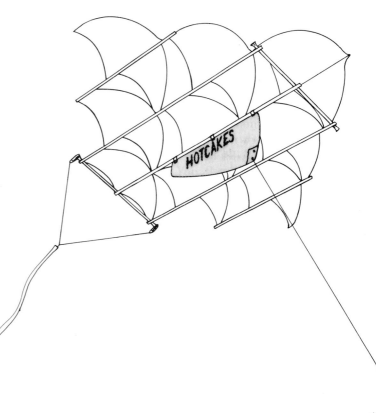

Illus. 271. Detail 3—Straw Hotcakes variation.

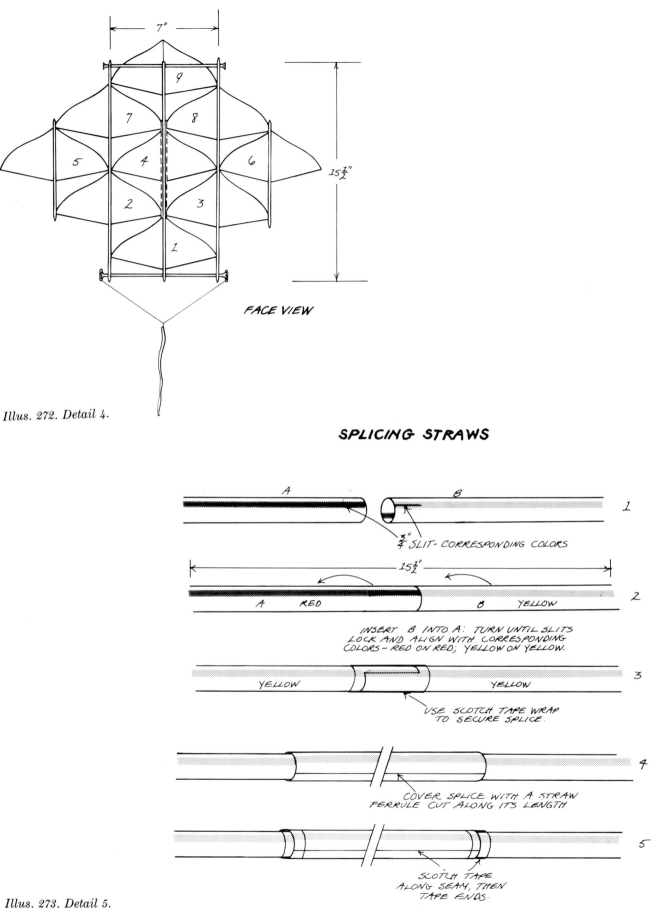

FACE VIEW

$15\frac{1}{2}''$

7"

Illus. 272. Detail 4.

SPLICING STRAWS

A   B   1

$\frac{3}{4}''$ SLIT- CORRESPONDING COLORS

$15\frac{1}{2}''$

A   RED   B   YELLOW   2

INSERT B INTO A: TURN UNTIL SLITS
LOCK AND ALIGN WITH CORRESPONDING
COLORS - RED ON RED; YELLOW ON YELLOW.

YELLOW   YELLOW   3

USE SCOTCH TAPE WRAP
TO SECURE SPLICE.

4

COVER SPLICE WITH A STRAW
FERRULE CUT ALONG ITS LENGTH

5

SCOTCH TAPE
ALONG SEAM, THEN
TAPE ENDS.

Illus. 273. Detail 5.

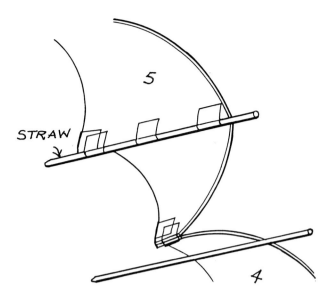

STRAW

5

4

Illus. 274. Detail 6.

Construction

Cutting, taping, and assembly

Making the wing-cell pattern template:

Note: The way the cups are bisected to form the wing curve is crucial and based upon a specific formula. Making just any cut in the cup won't do. Use a ballpoint pen to trace all lines.

1. To bisect a cup, create a visual reference line with a soft-tip pen on a ruled page, such as a page from a steno pad with a page dividing line. Draw horizontal line A–B through the light vertical central line as shown in Illus. 275. Next, carefully poke a ⅛″ hole in the middle of the cup's bottom.

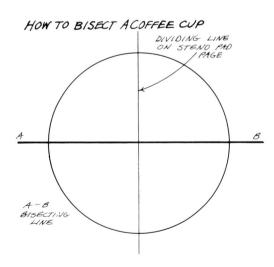

HOW TO BISECT A COFFEE CUP

DIVIDING LINE ON STENO PAD PAGE

A   B

A–B BISECTING LINE

Illus. 275. Step 1.

2. See Illus. 276. Place the lip of the cup over line A–B and use the ⅛″ hole to sight the cross-hair center. Draw a circle around the lip. While still sighting line A–B through the hole, position the cup so that the top and bottom of the shadow lines divide the Golden Arches logo on both sides. Use a flexible straightedge, like a business envelope, as a guide in connecting the top and bottom marks to form the bisecting lines.

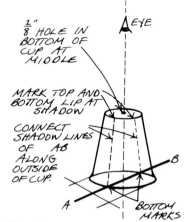

⅛″ HOLE IN BOTTOM OF CUP AT MIDDLE

EYE

MARK TOP AND BOTTOM LIP AT SHADOW

CONNECT SHADOW LINES OF AB ALONG OUTSIDE OF CUP.

B

A

BOTTOM MARKS

Illus. 276. Step 2.

3. See Illus. 277. Place a dot on the lip of the cup on one side of a bisecting line; on the opposite side, place a dot 3½″ up from the lip along the bisecting line directly below the middle of the Golden Arches. Connect the two dots with a line, using the envelope as a flexible straightedge. You must hold the envelope firmly against the cup surface while drawing the symmetrical connecting lines. The bisecting lines represent the shortest distance between the two points.

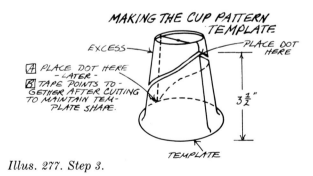

MAKING THE CUP PATTERN TEMPLATE

EXCESS

PLACE DOT HERE

A PLACE DOT HERE - LATER -
B TAPE POINTS TO- GETHER AFTER CUTTING TO MAINTAIN TEM- PLATE SHAPE.

3½″

TEMPLATE

Illus. 277. Step 3.

Work and cut carefully. Insert the point of a hobby knife through the cup at the dot located 3½″ from the lip and cut around to the lower dot on the other side. As you work, you'll end up cutting through the lip; tape the points together to maintain the template shape. Remove the excess; the lower half is the completed template.

4. See Illus. 278. Slip the template over another coffee cup (already bisected following the procedures in Steps 1 and 2) and align them so that the bisecting lines on both the template and cup divide the Golden Arches logo. This method provides a uniform look, with the logo being hidden in the fold of each completed wing cell. Trace the two diagonal lines of the template pattern onto the cup. Remove the template.

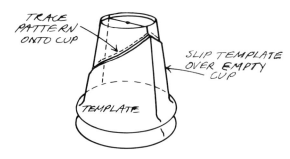

Illus. 278. Step 4.

5. See Illus. 279. Cut the wing cell as follows: Slice the cup along bisecting line A–B; then cover this seam with Scotch double-stick tape. The tape keeps the cup together for the remaining cuts and will hold the wing halves together to form the wing cell later. Cut along the diagonal V-shaped lines to point C on the other side. Discard the bottom excess. Cut through the remaining bisecting-line section C–D.

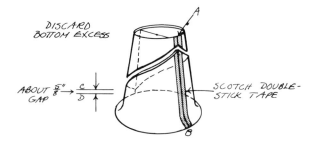

Illus. 279. Step 5.

6. See Illus. 280. Carefully bend and squeeze the wing halves together along the spine lined with double-stick tape to form a conical-shaped wing.

Completed wing cell: The wing is balanced if the spine and both wing tips touch evenly when

placed on a flat surface. Secure the fore and aft sections of the spine with a small piece of Scotch Magic tape.

Tip: Use an emery board to lightly burnish and smooth the leading edges off the wing.

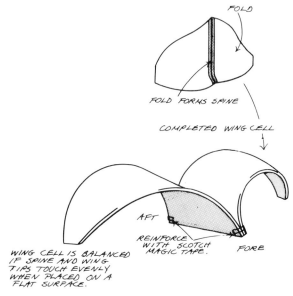

Illus. 280. Step 6.

7. Using the template, assemble three more wing cells.

Making the framework:

8. Remove five straws from their wrappers; use new straws since tape doesn't stick as well to used straws. The straws must be perfectly round; don't use any with creases or bends. Flatten each end of the three straws and tape them as shown in Illus. 281. Make a hole in each end with a sharp paper punch, leaving about 1/8" extra on each end.

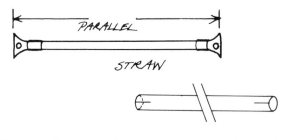

Illus. 281. Steps 8. and 9.

Enlarge all holes with a standard sharpened pencil; support the surrounding straw wall while pushing and twisting until the pencil goes completely through the hole. Be careful not to bend the straw in the process.

9. Take the remaining two straws and cut about a 3/16" slit at each end. Then fold the ends into cone shapes.

186

10. The frame: Insert the cone-ended straws through the holes in the other three straws. Flatten all ends and secure them with tape. All slits should face the same direction, as shown in Illus. 282.

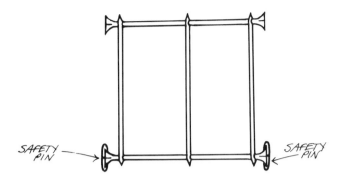

Illus. 282. Step 10.

11. Attach the wing cells with Scotch Magic tape in the sequence shown in Detail 2 (Illus. 270). Begin by positioning cell #1 so that the wing tips are as far aft on the straw frame as possible.

Making the keel:
12. Cut along the lines on the Hotcakes platter to form the keel, as shown in Illus. 283.

Illus. 283. Step 12.

13. See Illus. 284. Reinforce the tip with strapping tape and punch a hole ¼″ from the tip for the tether point.

Illus. 284. Step 13.

14. See Illus. 285. Position the keel on the middle straw of the frame slightly forward of the aft hole; then attach it with strapping tape. Leave a ¹⁄₁₆″ gap between the keel and the straw so that you can fold the kite sideways for storage.

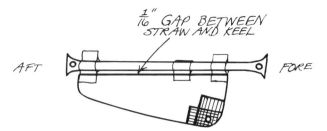

Illus. 285. Step 14.

Making the tail:
15. Refer back to Detail 1 (Illus. 269). Cut a 20″ length of lightweight twine and attach each end in the eyes of two safety pins. Locate the middle of the twine and tie a loop; attach the third safety pin to this loop. Secure the end safety pins to the aft ends of the straws. Add tails (Mylar or ripstop streamers) of different lengths to stabilize the kite in varying wind conditions.

Straw Hotcakes Variation
Materials

To make the Straw Hotcakes variation you need:

- 13 McDonald's standard 8⅛″ straws:
- six straws—spliced to make three 15½″ vertical spars,
- three straws—cut along the length for ferrules over vertical spars,
- two straws—for fore and aft horizontal spars,
- two straws—for outside wing spars;
- three small brass safety pins; and
- 12′ to 40′ Mylar or ripstop streamers—for tail.

Construction

Note: Apply the construction techniques used for Short Stack.

1. Make nine wing cells.
2. See Detail 5 (Illus. 273). Splicing straws: Slit and tape the straws to form three vertical spars. Then secure each spliced spar with a straw ferrule cut along its length.
3. Pass standard straws, fore and aft, through the holes punched in the ends of the vertical spars.
4. Attach the wing cells to the frame in the sequence shown in Detail 4 (Illus. 272). Use standard straws for outside wing cells 5 and 6.
5. Position and attach the Hotcakes keel as indicated with strapping tape.
6. Add tail streamers and fly!

Making a Pencil Glider

You can also make a glider using one wing cell (see Illus. 280) and an unsharpened faceted pencil with a full eraser.

Wing placement: Balance the pencil on a ruler or knife edge to locate the center of gravity; then mark the position. Mark a point 1½″ from the nose (the fore end) on the wing-cell spine. Align the marks on the wing cell and pencil. Position the wing cell on the facet or flat side of the pencil. Lightly tape the nose and tail because wing placement is approximate. If the glider doesn't fly true, move the wing cell forward or backward in small increments; then tape it securely when you're satisfied.

Launch: Hold the pencil between your thumb and forefinger, with the nose slightly elevated, and push forward on a horizontal plane. Don't throw forcefully.

For a slingshot glider, cut a 45° notch halfway through the pencil just behind the eraser ferrule, and hook a rubber band in the notch and hold the tail. Aim high and launch, being careful not to hit your thumb—or anything else.

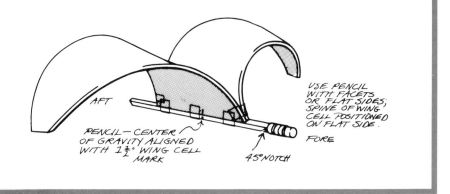

AFT

PENCIL — CENTER
OF GRAVITY ALIGNED
WITH 1¾″ WING CELL
MARK

45° NOTCH

USE PENCIL
WITH FACETS
OR FLAT SIDES;
SPINE OF WING
CELL POSITIONED
ON FLAT SIDE.

FORE

[2]Ron's innovative coffee cup kites first appeared in *Kite Lines*, Spring 1985.

42
Miniature Kites

Eddy, Delta, and Optical Confusion—Courtesy of Charlie Sotich[1]
Modified Japanese Wanwan—Courtesy of Mark Sandy

Good Things Come in Small Packages

Miniatures of various art forms have been popular for centuries in Japan, China, and Southeast Asia—and kites are no exception. Although I had heard that these diminutive members (less than 12 inches) of the kite family offer a special form of flying, I thought that other than being small, nothing was so special about these tethered gnats. But when I had the opportunity to see and fly some miniature kites myself, this familiar cliché suddenly came to mind—good things do, indeed, come in small packages.

Fran Gramkowski, the owner of the High Fly Kite Company, told me that he had two guests from Germany—Mark Sandy and his friend Werner Siebenberg, president of the Berlin Kitefliers Club—and that I had to see Sandy's collection of miniature kites. So, the next day the two paid me a visit.

I cleared my dining room table to make room for Sandy's large black case, which contained nearly thirty plastic transparent packages of miniature treasures from China and Japan, and many of his own creations. Sandy brought out miniature kite after kite for my appreciation.

One little jewel Sandy had made was a Cody Kite that was about 6″ × 2½″ of black tissue paper and delicately honed bamboo spars. His attention to detail was impressive. And it flew—indoors. The wind created by a hand merely moving the flying line was sufficient to make the tiny Cody soar.

Folk heroes and other traditional symbols were hand-painted on meticulously bridled *edo, Nagasaki hata, rokkaku, wanwan,* and *Suruga* kites. Several 3″ Eddy kites were decorated with whimsical, popular German cartoon characters.

Sandy was self-taught in miniature kite building, having learned by analyzing miniature kites he had bought and experimenting as he went along. Before leaving, he drew up a rough design of a Japanese *wanwan,* which he said was easy to build—even for beginners in miniatures.

* * *

Well, as one thing leads to another, I recalled reading in *Kite Lines* magazine that Charlie Sotich had won first prize at the 1984 International Exposition of Small Kites. A well-respected kite enthusiast, Sotich was a past president of the Chicagoland Sky Liners, an active kite club with an international following based in the windy city. One phone call and several days later, a package from Sotich was in my hands. Inside were his AKA Eddy, Thunderbird Delta, and Optical Confusion miniature kites—as well as tips on how to build them. Incidentally, it was with Optical Confusion, shown in Illus. 286, that Sotich won first prize at the International Exposition. A miniature modified delta, it flew in the widest wind range with the most consistent stability and highest angle.

I flew Sotich's little angels and showed them to everyone who came over to my house. I hope you also enjoy them.

Sotich makes use of high-tech materials requiring special handling. His three rules are: Use the lightest materials available, use no more material than necessary, and keep them light! But experiment with other materials; for instance, you can substitute tissue paper and bamboo for Mylar and boron and get very good results.

Tools

Miniature construction requires good lighting and the following tools (see Illus. 287):

- quality tweezers,
- a double-edge carbon-steel razor or scalpel,
- a solvent syringe (available at hobby shops)—for cutting boron in Method 2,
- a magnifying glass (2–3x)—the free-standing or binocular type worn around the head keeps hands free for working—and
- a small metal straightedge.

Materials

To make a miniature kite you need:

- .0006″ Mylar film—for sail and keel,
- .004″ boron wire[2] for spars (about twice the thickness of a human hair),
- .0015″ monofilament suture-grade nylon used in optical surgery—for flying line,

Illus. 286. Charlie Sotich's Optical Confusion.

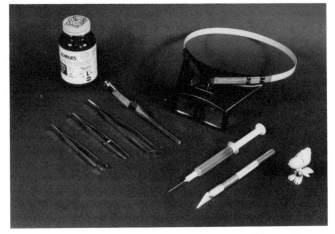

Illus. 287. Basic tools for miniature kites: rubber cement (thinned), tweezers, magnifier, solvent syringe for breaking boron, and sharp hobby knife.

- silk thread—unravelled into fine strands for alternative flying line (several short lengths of unravelled fibre can be joined together to provide the required 3′ to 6′ length),
- 3M Magic Tape—for attaching flying line to tether,
- rubber cement and thinner (five to ten parts thinner to one part rubber cement—experiment to find the right consistency),
- Cyanoacrylate (super glue like Elmer's Wonder Bond Plus),
- Scripto or Sharpie extra-fine permanent markers,
- Scotch drafting tape (no. 230)—for syringe cutting technique,
- ¹⁄₃₂″ × ¹⁄₁₆″ stiff cardboard—for frame (pizza boxes are a good source),
- an expanded polystyrene (plastic foam) meat tray (⅛″ × 2″ × 3″)—for reel, and
- a bamboo skewer (¹⁄₁₆″ × 3″)—for reel handle.

Construction

Tips from Ray Brandes: An adjustable rubber-band clutch used on a two-legged bridle (see Illus. 294) and cat's whiskers. Cats naturally lose a whisker now and then and their owners usually discard them. To the miniature kite builder, however, these thin, strong, and finely tapered whiskers are potential spars for a miniature design. Brandes has a small box full of them.

Tips from W. D. (Red) Braswell: For a stiff sail material that's wafer-thin and light, carefully remove the expanded polystyrene (plastic foam) insulating jacket found on some soft-drink bottles. Its curve makes it especially suitable for miniature rotor and box kites.

Critical to any kite's ability to fly is it's sail-loading ratio. Sail loading refers to how much the kite weighs to the amount of projected area that it must lift. The sail load is the weight divided by the amount of area providing lift. (See the sail loading formula in the chart on page 128.) The Stone Mountain Kite project, for example, is a model of efficiency with 40 square feet of lifting area and a sail loading of about ½ oz. per square foot. To get Sotich's 3″ Eddy to stay aloft in an air current of less than one mph, the sail loading is a scant 0.030 per square foot.

Not only does building miniature kites call for working with different tools and materials, but it also requires learning a few new construction techniques. For instance, boron wire is potentially hazardous and must be handled with great care; so two methods of cutting boron for miniature kite spars are shown Illus. 288 and 289.

Apply the following steps in making Sotich's AKA

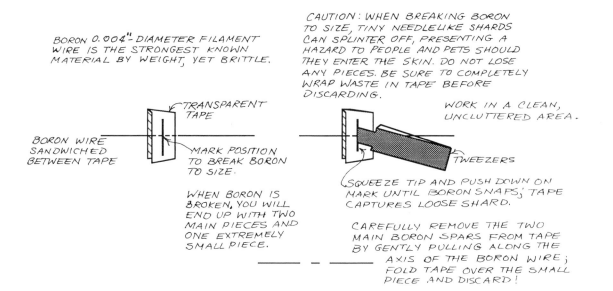

BORON 0.004″-DIAMETER FILAMENT WIRE IS THE STRONGEST KNOWN MATERIAL BY WEIGHT, YET BRITTLE.

TRANSPARENT TAPE

BORON WIRE SANDWICHED BETWEEN TAPE

MARK POSITION TO BREAK BORON TO SIZE.

WHEN BORON IS BROKEN, YOU WILL END UP WITH TWO MAIN PIECES AND ONE EXTREMELY SMALL PIECE.

CAUTION: WHEN BREAKING BORON TO SIZE, TINY NEEDLELIKE SHARDS CAN SPLINTER OFF, PRESENTING A HAZARD TO PEOPLE AND PETS SHOULD THEY ENTER THE SKIN. DO NOT LOSE ANY PIECES. BE SURE TO COMPLETELY WRAP WASTE IN TAPE BEFORE DISCARDING.

WORK IN A CLEAN, UNCLUTTERED AREA.

TWEEZERS

SQUEEZE TIP AND PUSH DOWN ON MARK UNTIL BORON SNAPS; TAPE CAPTURES LOOSE SHARD.

CAREFULLY REMOVE THE TWO MAIN BORON SPARS FROM TAPE BY GENTLY PULLING ALONG THE AXIS OF THE BORON WIRE; FOLD TAPE OVER THE SMALL PIECE AND DISCARD!

Illus. 288. Cutting boron—Method 1.

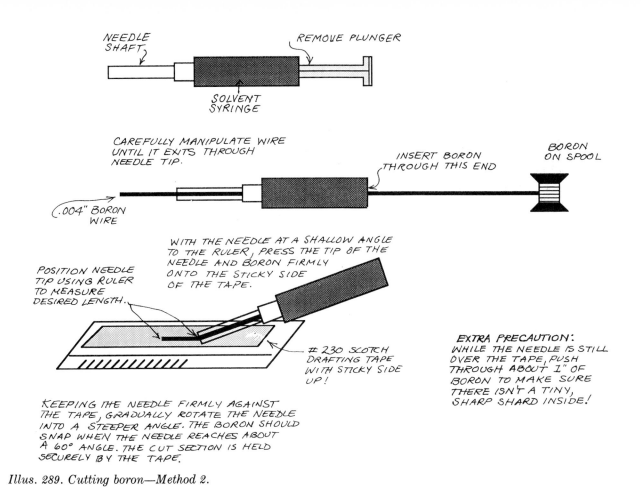

NEEDLE SHAFT

REMOVE PLUNGER

SOLVENT SYRINGE

CAREFULLY MANIPULATE WIRE UNTIL IT EXITS THROUGH NEEDLE TIP.

INSERT BORON THROUGH THIS END

BORON ON SPOOL

.004" BORON WIRE

WITH THE NEEDLE AT A SHALLOW ANGLE TO THE RULER, PRESS THE TIP OF THE NEEDLE AND BORON FIRMLY ONTO THE STICKY SIDE OF THE TAPE.

POSITION NEEDLE TIP USING RULER TO MEASURE DESIRED LENGTH.

#230 SCOTCH DRAFTING TAPE WITH STICKY SIDE UP!

EXTRA PRECAUTION: WHILE THE NEEDLE IS STILL OVER THE TAPE, PUSH THROUGH ABOUT 1" OF BORON TO MAKE SURE THERE ISN'T A TINY, SHARP SHARD INSIDE!

KEEPING THE NEEDLE FIRMLY AGAINST THE TAPE, GRADUALLY ROTATE THE NEEDLE INTO A STEEPER ANGLE. THE BORON SHOULD SNAP WHEN THE NEEDLE REACHES ABOUT A 60° ANGLE. THE CUT SECTION IS HELD SECURELY BY THE TAPE.

Illus. 289. Cutting boron—Method 2.

Eddy, Thunderbird Delta, and Optical Confusion kites (see Illus. 290, 291, and 292), as well as other two-dimensional kites.

Note: Sandy's modified Japanese *wanwan*, shown in Illus. 294, is a straightforward design requiring tissue paper and finely tapered spars of bamboo. Sandy recommends using *Gampi*, a lightweight brand of tissue paper, but other tissue paper will do. After splitting bamboo into thin workable slivers with a pocket knife, use a scalpel and fine sandpaper

to trim and balance the spars. Bamboo can be cut quite narrow while remaining flexible and without losing its stiffness. Nylon monofilament bristle can also be used for spar material. Experiment to find the right stiffness for your diminutive design. (See the Spar Material Chart at a Glance on pages 40–41.)

See Illus. 295 for Steps 1–6; Illus. 296 for Steps 7–11; Illus. 297 for Steps 9A, 10A, and 11A; Illus. 298 for Step 12; Illus. 299 for Step 13; Illus. 300 for Step 14; and Illus. 301 for Step 17.

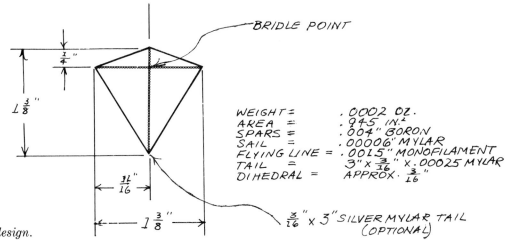

BRIDLE POINT

WEIGHT = .0002 OZ.
AREA = .945 IN.²
SPARS = .004" BORON
SAIL = .00006" MYLAR
FLYING LINE = .0015" MONOFILAMENT
TAIL = 3" x 3/16" x .00025 MYLAR
DIHEDRAL = APPROX. 3/16"

3/16" X 3" SILVER MYLAR TAIL (OPTIONAL)

Illus. 290. AKA Eddy—design.

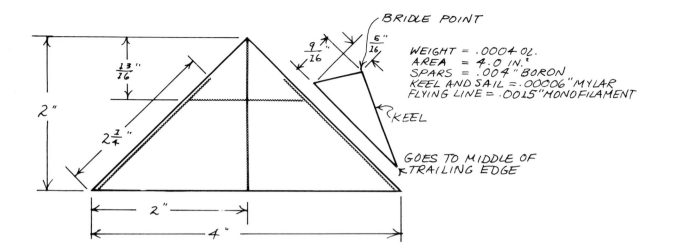

Illus. 291. Thunderbird Delta—design.

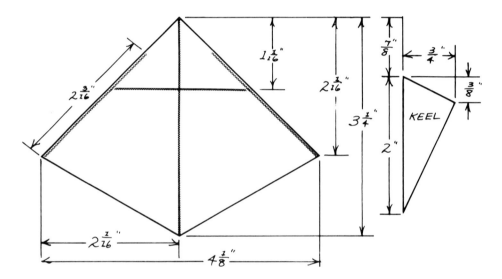

WEIGHT : .0005 OZ.
AREA : 6.7 IN.²
SPARS : .004" BORON
SAIL : .00006" MYLAR
FLYING LINE : .0015" MONOFILAMENT

SAIL LOADING, OUNCES/SQ. FT : .0011
FLYING SPEED : 0.6 MPH

Illus. 292. Optical Confusion—design.

MINIATURE KITE SPECIFICATIONS			
EDDY	DELTA	OPTICAL CONFUSION	
$1\frac{3}{8}$"	4"	$4\frac{1}{8}$"	WING SPAN
$1\frac{3}{8}$"	2"	$3\frac{3}{4}$"	LENGTH
.95	4.00	6.7	SURFACE AREA, SQ IN.
0.0002	0.0004	.0005	WEIGHT, OUNCES
0.030	0.0144	0.0011	SAIL LOADING OZ./SQ. FT.
1.21	0.72	0.6	FLYING SPEED MPH

Illus. 293. Eddy, Delta, and Optical Confusion specifications.

Above: Tri-D Box (pages 138–143).
Right: Fluted Sled (pages 121–125).

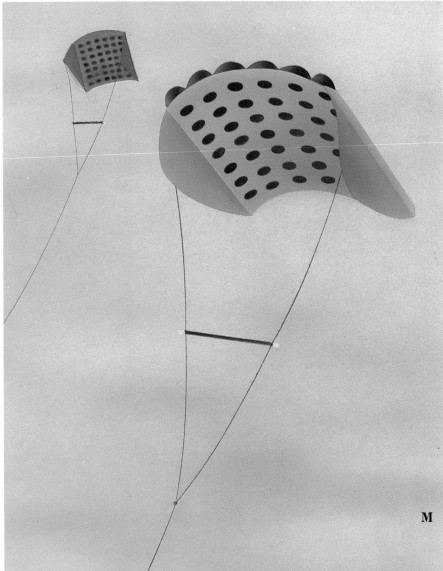

M

Roller (pages 210–215).

N

Top: Gusset Delta (pages 148–152). Bottom: Zephyr Delta (pages 240–242).

Left: Brandes Flare (pages 118–121). Bottom: Trefoil Delta (pages 243–246).

P

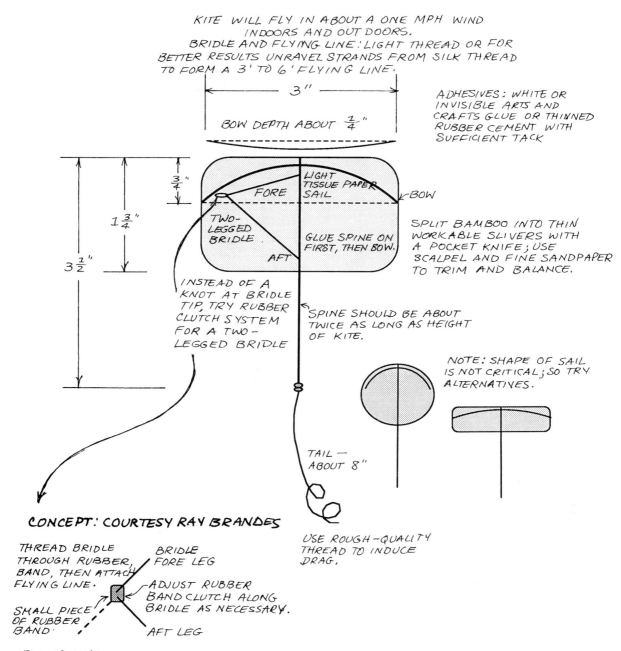

KITE WILL FLY IN ABOUT A ONE MPH WIND
INDOORS AND OUTDOORS.
BRIDLE AND FLYING LINE: LIGHT THREAD OR FOR
BETTER RESULTS UNRAVEL STRANDS FROM SILK THREAD
TO FORM A 3' TO 6' FLYING LINE.

3"

BOW DEPTH ABOUT 1/4"

ADHESIVES: WHITE OR
INVISIBLE ARTS AND
CRAFTS GLUE OR THINNED
RUBBER CEMENT WITH
SUFFICIENT TACK

3/4"

1 3/4"

3 1/2"

LIGHT
TISSUE PAPER
SAIL

FORE

BOW

TWO-
LEGGED
BRIDLE

GLUE SPINE ON
FIRST, THEN BOW.

AFT

SPLIT BAMBOO INTO THIN
WORKABLE SLIVERS WITH
A POCKET KNIFE; USE
SCALPEL AND FINE SANDPAPER
TO TRIM AND BALANCE.

INSTEAD OF A
KNOT AT BRIDLE
TIP, TRY RUBBER
CLUTCH SYSTEM
FOR A TWO-
LEGGED BRIDLE

SPINE SHOULD BE ABOUT
TWICE AS LONG AS HEIGHT
OF KITE.

NOTE: SHAPE OF SAIL
IS NOT CRITICAL; SO TRY
ALTERNATIVES.

TAIL —
ABOUT 8"

CONCEPT: COURTESY RAY BRANDES

USE ROUGH-QUALITY
THREAD TO INDUCE
DRAG.

THREAD BRIDLE
THROUGH RUBBER,
BAND, THEN ATTACH
FLYING LINE.

BRIDLE
FORE LEG

ADJUST RUBBER
BAND CLUTCH ALONG
BRIDLE AS NECESSARY.

SMALL PIECE
OF RUBBER
BAND.

AFT LEG

FLYING LINE

Illus. 294. Modified Japanese Wanwan design.

1. Use a sharp pencil to draw the full-size kite design and spar locations on a piece of white paper.
2. Make a frame that will fit over the design. Take a thin piece (about 1/16") of stiff cardboard and cut out an opening with a 1/4" clearance all around the kite design as shown.
3. Cut a section of Mylar film slightly larger than the opening in the frame.
4. Put small dabs of full-strength rubber cement around the inside edge of the frame opening.
5. Lay the Mylar film over the opening and position it lightly over the cement. Remove any wrinkles

by lifting and shifting edges one at a time. Tack them down again under slight tension.
6. Place the frame over the design with the Mylar film facing you. Use a small ruler and a permanent ink marker to trace the kite outline and keel onto the Mylar. Let the tracing marks extend beyond the completed kite for reference.
7. Position the Mylar over a prepared color-scheme pattern and decorate the Mylar kite sail with a permanent ink marker. Practise coloring on excess Mylar before working on the sail.
8. Turn the cardboard frame over and center the

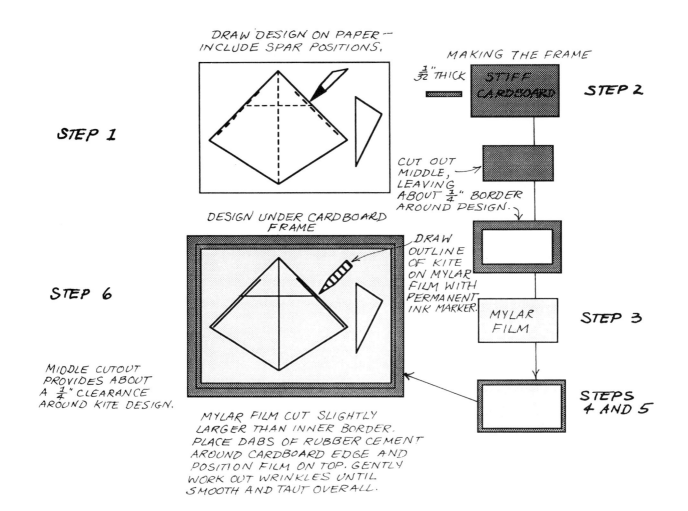

STEP 1

DRAW DESIGN ON PAPER —
INCLUDE SPAR POSITIONS.

MAKING THE FRAME

1/32" THICK   STIFF CARDBOARD   STEP 2

CUT OUT MIDDLE, LEAVING ABOUT 1/4" BORDER AROUND DESIGN.

DRAW OUTLINE OF KITE ON MYLAR FILM WITH PERMANENT INK MARKER.

MYLAR FILM   STEP 3

STEPS 4 AND 5

STEP 6

DESIGN UNDER CARDBOARD FRAME

MIDDLE CUTOUT PROVIDES ABOUT A 1/4" CLEARANCE AROUND KITE DESIGN.

MYLAR FILM CUT SLIGHTLY LARGER THAN INNER BORDER. PLACE DABS OF RUBBER CEMENT AROUND CARDBOARD EDGE AND POSITION FILM ON TOP. GENTLY WORK OUT WRINKLES UNTIL SMOOTH AND TAUT OVERALL.

Illus. 295. Steps 1–6.

outline of the sail over the design. Place the spars on this side since rubber cement dissolves inks. Apply thinned rubber cement (from five to 10 parts thinner to one part rubber cement) to the spars. Use tweezers to accurately manipulate the spars in place. Glue the spars to the Mylar sail.

9. Position and attach the keel with the thinned rubber cement as indicated on the main design.
10. Use a 1/16" square balsa strip to manipulate the keel onto the kite face, as shown in Step 10A.
11. With the spars facing you, carefully cut out the sail using a *sharp* modified carbon-steel razor or

STEP 7

WITH MYLAR FILM FACING YOU, POSITION OUTLINE OF KITE OVER A COLOR-SCHEME PATTERN OF YOUR CHOICE AND DECORATE FILM.

STEP 8

TURN FRAME OVER SO THAT FILM IS NOW TOUCHING AND CENTERED OVER DESIGN. CEMENT SPARS IN PLACE; SEE CROSS SPAR DETAIL.

STEP 9

USE SHARP HOBBY KNIFE, SCALPEL, OR RAZOR TO CUT OUT KEEL FIRST.

SEE RAZOR DETAIL — STEP 9A.

STEP 10

CEMENT KEEL TO SAIL ALONG SPINE ON KITE FACE AS SHOWN IN DESIGN; SEE STEP 10A.

STEP 11

CUT OUT SAIL FOR COMPLETED KITE; SEE STEP 11A.

Illus. 296. Steps 7–11.

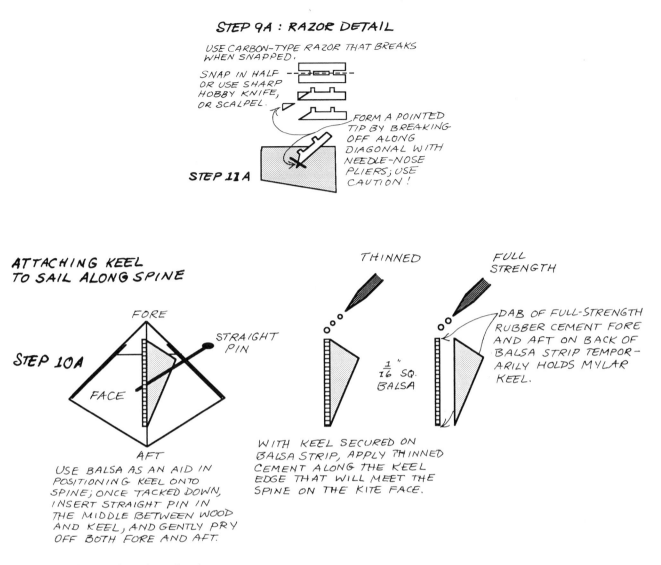

STEP 9A : RAZOR DETAIL

USE CARBON-TYPE RAZOR THAT BREAKS
WHEN SNAPPED.

SNAP IN HALF
OR USE SHARP
HOBBY KNIFE,
OR SCALPEL.

FORM A POINTED
TIP BY BREAKING
OFF ALONG
DIAGONAL WITH
NEEDLE-NOSE
PLIERS; USE
CAUTION!

STEP 11A

ATTACHING KEEL
TO SAIL ALONG SPINE

FORE

STRAIGHT
PIN

STEP 10A

FACE

AFT

USE BALSA AS AN AID IN
POSITIONING KEEL ONTO
SPINE; ONCE TACKED DOWN,
INSERT STRAIGHT PIN IN
THE MIDDLE BETWEEN WOOD
AND KEEL, AND GENTLY PRY
OFF BOTH FORE AND AFT.

THINNED

FULL
STRENGTH

1/16" SQ.
BALSA

DAB OF FULL-STRENGTH
RUBBER CEMENT FORE
AND AFT ON BACK OF
BALSA STRIP TEMPOR-
ARILY HOLDS MYLAR
KEEL.

WITH KEEL SECURED ON
BALSA STRIP, APPLY THINNED
CEMENT ALONG THE KEEL
EDGE THAT WILL MEET THE
SPINE ON THE KITE FACE.

Illus. 297. Steps 9A, 10A, and 11A.

scalpel guided by a small straightedge. Avoid using a dull razor edge that will snag and tear Mylar. (See Step 11A.)

12. For deltas, such as Optical Confusion, the cross spar should extend over the wing spars, allowing the sail to develop the necessary dihedral angle for flight. Cut the cross spar beyond the leading wing edge (between $\frac{1}{64}$″ and $\frac{1}{32}$″ depending on how accurately you measure) as shown.

Options: Rubber-cement the cross spar *only* where it meets the wing spar on the leading edge. For a more secure bond, rubber-cement the cross spar along the entire length across the back of the kite. Both methods work. Try each and evaluate performance differences.

13. If the kite requires a fixed dihedral angle as in the Eddy, join the two cross-spar pieces in a hinge where they meet at the spine. Prop up one edge of the sail. With a toothpick tip, place a small amount of baking soda over the join area to help the super glue cure evenly and quickly. Apply a drop of super glue at the intersection. A drop of glue from the applicator tip is too much. Instead, use the tip of a straight pin to pick up a small drop for placement. Repeat several times if necessary. Breathing (humidity) on the glue join also hastens curing.

14. Tie a simple overhand knot at the end of the flying line and another knot about $\frac{3}{32}$″ down. Stick a piece of 3M Magic Tape (about $\frac{1}{16}$″ × $\frac{3}{16}$″) across the line next to the top knot as shown. Use tweezers to place the tape and line at the tether point. Use minimum pressure on the tape since this step is for correct position only.

15. Test-fly the kite on about two feet of line. Get a feel for how little wind speed (under one mph) is necessary by walking slowly forward until the kite rises. The kite will fly if you simply move the flying line with your hand back and forth in a gentle steady manner, but it takes some practice.

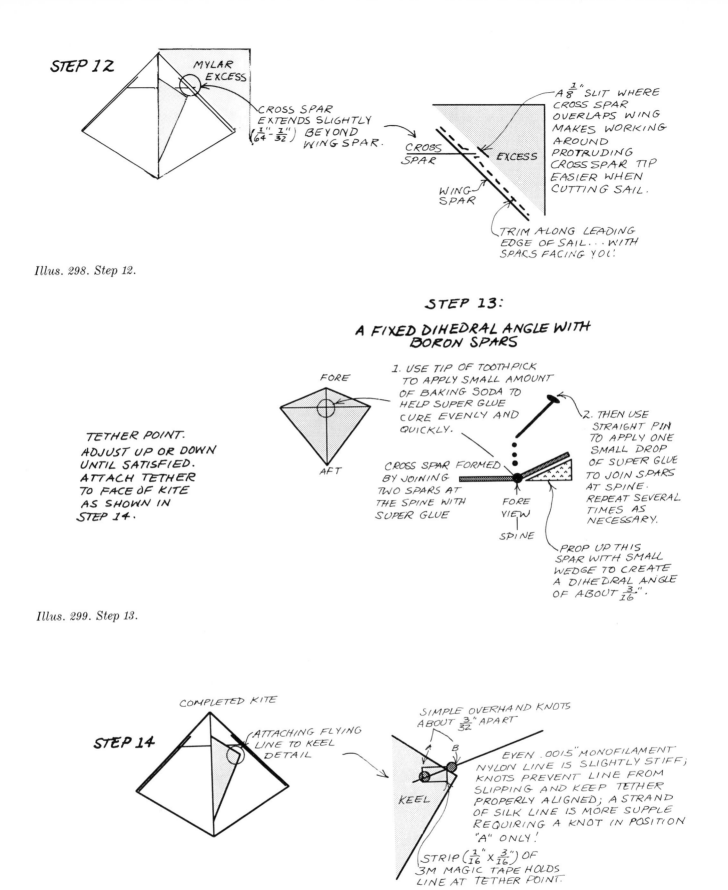

STEP 12

MYLAR EXCESS

CROSS SPAR EXTENDS SLIGHTLY ($\frac{1}{64}" - \frac{1}{32}"$) BEYOND WING SPAR.

CROSS SPAR

WING SPAR

EXCESS

A $\frac{1}{8}"$ SLIT WHERE CROSS SPAR OVERLAPS WING MAKES WORKING AROUND PROTRUDING CROSS SPAR TIP EASIER WHEN CUTTING SAIL.

TRIM ALONG LEADING EDGE OF SAIL... WITH SPARS FACING YOU.

Illus. 298. Step 12.

STEP 13:

A FIXED DIHEDRAL ANGLE WITH BORON SPARS

TETHER POINT. ADJUST UP OR DOWN UNTIL SATISFIED. ATTACH TETHER TO FACE OF KITE AS SHOWN IN STEP 14.

FORE

AFT

1. USE TIP OF TOOTHPICK TO APPLY SMALL AMOUNT OF BAKING SODA TO HELP SUPER GLUE CURE EVENLY AND QUICKLY.

2. THEN USE STRAIGHT PIN TO APPLY ONE SMALL DROP OF SUPER GLUE TO JOIN SPARS AT SPINE. REPEAT SEVERAL TIMES AS NECESSARY.

CROSS SPAR FORMED BY JOINING TWO SPARS AT THE SPINE WITH SUPER GLUE

FORE VIEW

SPINE

PROP UP THIS SPAR WITH SMALL WEDGE TO CREATE A DIHEDRAL ANGLE OF ABOUT $\frac{3}{16}"$.

Illus. 299. Step 13.

COMPLETED KITE

STEP 14

ATTACHING FLYING LINE TO KEEL DETAIL

SIMPLE OVERHAND KNOTS ABOUT $\frac{3}{32}"$ APART

A

B

KEEL

EVEN .0015" MONOFILAMENT NYLON LINE IS SLIGHTLY STIFF; KNOTS PREVENT LINE FROM SLIPPING AND KEEP TETHER PROPERLY ALIGNED; A STRAND OF SILK LINE IS MORE SUPPLE REQUIRING A KNOT IN POSITION "A" ONLY!

STRIP ($\frac{1}{16}" \times \frac{3}{16}"$) OF 3M MAGIC TAPE HOLDS LINE AT TETHER POINT.

Illus. 300. Step 14.

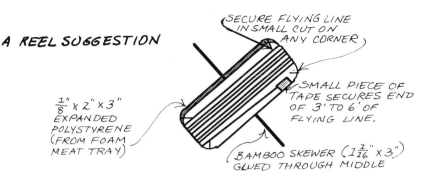

A REEL SUGGESTION

SECURE FLYING LINE
IN SMALL CUT ON
ANY CORNER

$\frac{1}{8}$" x 2" x 3"
EXPANDED
POLYSTYRENE
(FROM FOAM
MEAT TRAY)

SMALL PIECE OF
TAPE SECURES END
OF 3' TO 6' OF
FLYING LINE.

BAMBOO SKEWER ($1\frac{1}{16}$" x 3")
GLUED THROUGH MIDDLE

Illus. 301. Step 17.

If the kite oscillates from one side to the other, lower the tether point. Move the tether point up if the kite dives to one side.

16. Repeat test-flying and adjusting the tether position until the kite flies properly. Tack the tape securely to the line at the tether point.

17. Measure 3 to 6 feet of flying line and wind it onto a reel.

18. Store the kite and reel in a container for protection.

The $2,500,000 Per-Pound Kite

Going once, going twice, sold! A Charlie Sotich 3″ AKA Eddy went for $55 at the American Kitefliers Association auction in 1986. The kite weighed 0.00035 ounces. It would take 2,857 of these kites to weigh one ounce, or 45,712 to weigh one pound. Translated into a dollar-per-pound basis, the kite was worthy of being on Sotheby's auction block at over $2,500,000 per pound.

[1]"How to Make Small (*Really* Small) Kites that Fly" by Charles A. Sotich first appeared in the winter-spring 1987 issue of *Kite Lines* magazine, copyright 1987, Aeolus Press, Inc. Portions of the article are reprinted here with permission.

[2]A good source for Mylar and boron is Model Research Laboratories in Mission Viejo, California.

43
A Rotor Kite

Design: Courtesy of W. D. (Red) Braswell

Rotating Lift from the Wind

The rotor, shown in Illus. 303, is one of the eight generic kite forms. This kinetic kite manifests lift through an autorotating action induced by the motion of the surrounding air currents. With its dynamic surfaces blinking ever faster at the sun, the rotor must be in constant motion to stay aloft. While passive rotors, like windmills and kites, rely solely on available wind for their power, other rotation-lifting surfaces, like airplane and helicopter propellers, are motorized.

The lift principle occurring in a spinning body moving through a fluid or air, as in this case, is known as the *Magnus effect*, after G. Magnus, a mid-nineteenth-century physicist, who observed and recorded the phenomenon. However, nature's use of the Magnus effect predates Magnus's discovery by countless millions of years. Many of us have observed maple seedlings, for example, twirling and gliding earthwards—often catching the winds to travel great distances.

On the official side, while patents for rotor and related gyration-lifting airfoils date back to 1911, interest in rotor kites remains esoteric—though a spinning rotor continues to amaze us.

Materials

To make this kite you need:

- a ±³⁄₁₆″ × 8″ × 12″ expanded polystyrene (foam) meat tray,
- two ±10¼″ foam picnic plates,
- one ³⁄₁₆″ × 48″ dowel—cut to the length of the rotor plus 6″,
- two round head pins,
- a plastic lid from a yogurt cup, coffee can, or margarine tub—for bridle connectors,
- Elmer's Glue-All (white glue),
- 20 lb.–test line—for bridle,
- a hobby knife,
- sandpaper or an emery board,
- wax paper,
- nylon thread,
- super glue like Elmer's Wonderbond Plus, and
- (optional) a Dremel Moto-tool and router.

Details

- (Detail 1 in Illus. 302.) Main view.
- (Detail 2 in Illus. 303.) In flight. 8′ length of 20 lb. test: Connect to plastic bridle points, tie the loop in the exact center, and then attach the tether (flying line) to the loop. (Option: Try flying and maneuvering the rotor from dual lines as with a stunt kite.)

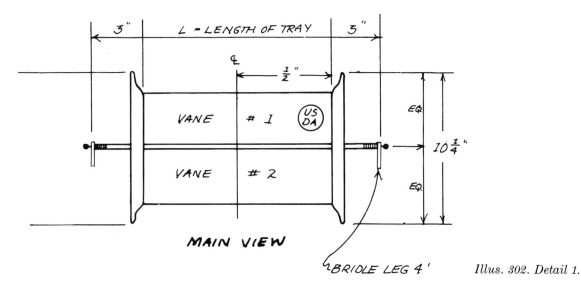

Illus. 302. Detail 1.

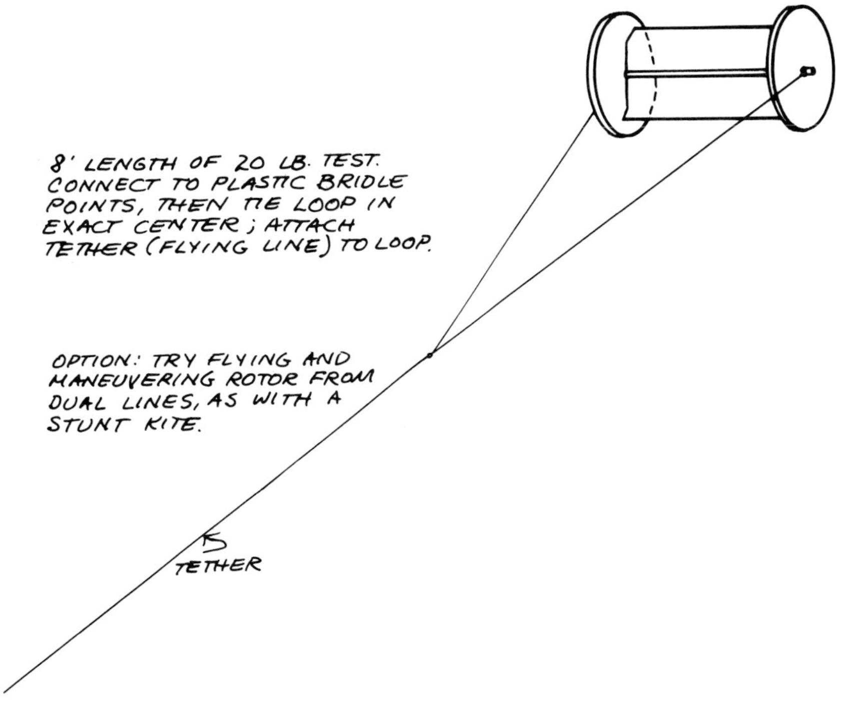

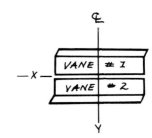

8' LENGTH OF 20 LB. TEST.
CONNECT TO PLASTIC BRIDLE
POINTS, THEN TIE LOOP IN
EXACT CENTER ; ATTACH
TETHER (FLYING LINE) TO LOOP.

OPTION: TRY FLYING AND
MANEUVERING ROTOR FROM
DUAL LINES, AS WITH A
STUNT KITE.

TETHER

Illus. 303. Detail 2—in flight.

Flight Data: Wind range: 8–20 mph
Line: 20 lb. test
AE: ±55°

Construction

Cutting:

1. Use a sharp hobby knife to cut the expanded polystyrene (foam) meat tray. Smooth the rough edges with light sandpaper or an emery board. Trim the edges of the meat tray as shown in Illus. 304. Mark the horizontal centerline *X* and the vertical centerline *Y*. Tip: Use a flexible straightedge, like a business envelope, as guide in marking lines over the tray's curved edges.

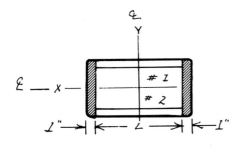

Illus. 304. Step 1.

2. Cut the tray along centerline *X* to form vanes #1 and #2. Reverse the position of vane #2 as shown in Illus. 305.

Ȼ
VANE #1
—X—
VANE #2
Y

Illus. 305. Step 2.

Gluing:

3. See Illus. 306. Cut ³⁄₁₆″ dowel to the length of the vane (L) plus 6″ and mark the middle. Drill a ¼″ pilot hole (pin diameter) in the middle of both ends. Wrap the ends with nylon thread and glue them to prevent splitting.

   Align the centerline of vane #1 with the middle of the dowel and glue in position. Align vane #2 (facing the opposite direction) with vane #1 and glue to form a rotor assembly.

   Option: For a precision join, use a Dremel Mototool with a router attachment to uniformly rout the edges of vanes #1 and #2 that meet at the dowel.

4. See Illus. 307. Place a sheet of wax paper between the rotor assembly and a flat surface to prevent glue from sticking to your work area; make sure the rotors are aligned and flat. Allow to dry overnight.

5. See Illus. 308. Locate the middle of both plates and drill a ³⁄₁₆″ hole in each.

6. See Illus. 309. Sandwich the rotor assembly be-

199

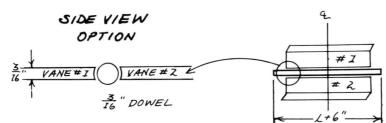

SIDE VIEW
OPTION

$\frac{3}{16}$" VANE #1 ⬤ VANE #2

$\frac{3}{16}$" DOWEL

#1

#2

$L+6$"

DRILL $\frac{1}{4}$" PILOT HOLE IN MIDDLE ON BOTH ENDS.

Illus. 306. Step 3.

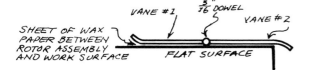

VANE #1 $\frac{3}{16}$" DOWEL   VANE #2

SHEET OF WAX PAPER BETWEEN ROTOR ASSEMBLY AND WORK SURFACE

FLAT SURFACE

Illus. 307. Step 4.

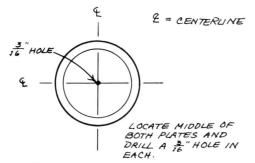

₵ = CENTERLINE

$\frac{3}{16}$" HOLE

LOCATE MIDDLE OF BOTH PLATES AND DRILL A $\frac{3}{16}$" HOLE IN EACH.

Illus. 308. Step 5.

tween the two plates; mark the positions where the rotor meets the plate. Check for gaps and trim the rotor ends for a flush fit. Remove the plates and lightly sand the area where the rotor will be glued.

Glue and sandwich the rotor assembly between the plates. Let it dry overnight.

7. See Illus. 310. Cut two plastic bridle connectors to size (1" × ⅜"). Use a darning needle or other thin, strong, sharp point to make a pin hole. Use a sharp paper punch for both a ⅛" hole and a notch at the tip.

8. See Illus. 311. Take two round head pins and cut both to ½" lengths. Make pin holes large enough to allow free movement of the bridle connector. Place a dab of glue in the holes on the dowel ends. Insert the pins through the bridle-connector pin holes and ⅜" into the dowel ends.

9. To make the bridle knot, fix the bridle line to the connector as shown in Illus. 312.

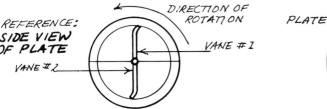

REFERENCE: SIDE VIEW OF PLATE

DIRECTION OF ROTATION

VANE #1

VANE #2

Illus. 309. Step 6.

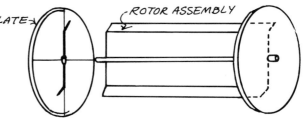

MARK POSITION WHERE ROTOR MEETS PLATE.

ROTOR ASSEMBLY

PLATE →

ROTOR ASSEMBLY SANDWICHED AND GLUED BETWEEN PLATES.

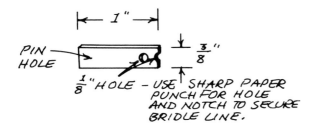

PLASTIC BRIDLE CONNECTOR

1"

PIN HOLE

$\frac{3}{8}$"

$\frac{1}{8}$" HOLE — USE SHARP PAPER PUNCH FOR HOLE AND NOTCH TO SECURE BRIDLE LINE.

Illus. 310. Step 7.

200

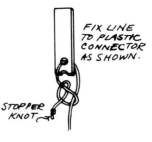

Illus. 311. Step 8.   *Illus. 312. Step 9.*

44
The Parawing Kite

Design by Francis M. Rogallo

The Precursor to the Hang Glider

In 1948 Francis M. Rogallo visualized a device that would combine the aerodynamics of a fixed wing with the flexibility of a parachute and came up with the Parawing. The Parawing, shown in Illus. 315, was patented and then later marketed as a Mylar kite called the Rogallo Flexikite during the 1960s.

Rogallo's early experiments led to the development of the hang glider. A former National Aeronautic and Space Administration (NASA) engineer, Rogallo said he had no way of knowing he was about to start a new sporting activity when he set out to develop a completely portable flexible wing that would conform to the wind. To the father of modern-day hang gliding, the question as to why no one had built a flexible wing before 1948 still remains a mystery.

In addition to the hang glider, the generic delta kite and its many variations—including stunt kites—owe much to Rogallo's wing designs.

Details

• (Detail 1 in Illus. 313.) Main design.
• (Detail 2 in Illus. 314.) Parawing with optional dowel stiffeners.
• (Detail 3 in Illus. 315.) In flight.

Flight Data: Wind range: 7–16 mph
Line: Carpet thread for buttons or light cotton flying line (8–12 lb. test)
AE: ±55°

Construction

Note: This kite will surprise you with its adaptable performance. But you must follow the dimensions given in Detail 1; even minor variations—in a shroud line, for example—will alter the kite's precise balance.

1. Take a 15 sq. in. piece of Mylar (aluminum-coated, 3 mil.) and fold it diagonally. The crease on the face of the sail gives the kite its unique conical shape. Use an iron on a synthetics setting to make a sharp central crease. To prevent the Mylar, a plastic film, from melting, place a piece of paper from a brown bag between the Mylar and the iron. The heat and pressure will help set the crease.
2. Tie the loops in the bridle shroud lines *before* attaching them to the kite sail. This makes it simpler to accurately measure each line to the kite.
3. Use a needle to poke small holes ⅜″ in from the sail perimeter for the bridle connect points and tail bridle. Insert the bridle line through the face of the sail and tie it with a loop so as not to crimp the Mylar, making sure the distance is accurate. For

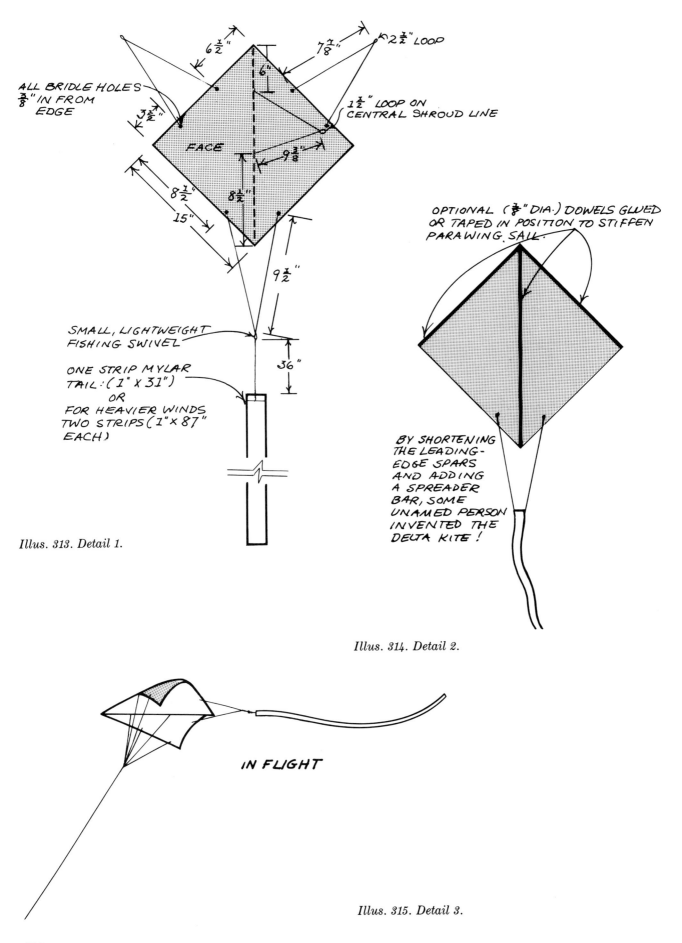

ALL BRIDLE HOLES
⅜" IN FROM
EDGE

6 ½"

7 ⅞"

2 ½" LOOP

6"

3 ½"

FACE

9 ⅜"

1 ½" LOOP ON
CENTRAL SHROUD LINE

8 ½"

8 ½"

15"

9 ½"

SMALL, LIGHTWEIGHT
FISHING SWIVEL

36"

ONE STRIP MYLAR
TAIL: (1" X 31")
OR
FOR HEAVIER WINDS
TWO STRIPS (1" X 87"
EACH)

Illus. 313. Detail 1.

OPTIONAL (⅜" DIA.) DOWELS GLUED
OR TAPED IN POSITION TO STIFFEN
PARAWING SAIL.

BY SHORTENING
THE LEADING-
EDGE SPARS
AND ADDING
A SPREADER
BAR, SOME
UNAMED PERSON
INVENTED THE
DELTA KITE!

Illus. 314. Detail 2.

IN FLIGHT

Illus. 315. Detail 3.

the central shroud, pass each end through the sail, tie them off, and secure them with a piece of tape on the back of the kite.

Optional: Reinforce all bridle holes in the sail with small squares of strapping tape.

4. Add a tail with a small fishing swivel as shown.
5. Attach flying line through the three loops with a slip knot and fly.
6. You can also fly the Parawing as a stunt kite on dual lines. Use a small snap swivel on each line. Attach one to an outside loop and the middle loop; then attach the other to an outside loop and the middle loop, as well. Now your Parawing stunt kite is ready for maneuvers.
7. If you wish to experiment with larger versions or use lighter-weight sail material, glue or tape three ⅛″ dowels on either side and along the crease. During the early 1960s, NASA experimented with stiffeners on full-scale Rogallo kite paraglider re-

covery systems for returning manned vehicles and other payloads from space.

8. Instead of flying the Parawing as a kite, try flying it as a glider. Remove the tail and add a small weight to the place where the three loops converge. Experiment with different weights until you achieve a balance. Tip: Attach a ball of clay to the loops; then add or remove small amounts as necessary. Stand on a chair holding the Parawing glider high overhead, and push it gently forward as you release it. A properly balanced Parawing will glide smoothly across a room.

Option: You won't need bridle lines if you add the dowel stiffeners. Simply fix a small triangular wire harness (connected to the spine and both wing-spar dowels) to hold the clay (the center of gravity) in position under the kite. The modern-day hang glider was, no doubt, invented in a similar manner.

45

The Barn Door Kite

Improved with a Bow

As early as 1885, Alexander McAdie, a researcher following in the footsteps of Benjamin Franklin, used silk-covered barn door–type kites in meteorological experiments at the Blue Hill Observatory in Massachusetts and later for the U.S. Weather Bureau. But unfortunately, McAdie's kites were about as dependable as the weather. As a transport for meteorological devices, the barn door kite was abandoned with the nearly simultaneous introduction of two generic kite forms: the Eddy and the box kites.

The kite presented here (see Illus. 317, and page K for the kite in color) is an improved version of McAdie's barn door kite. The secret of this three-stick kite's superior reliability is its self-stabilizing buoyancy, made possible by its bow, which William Eddy popularized at the end of the nineteenth century with his tailless Eddy Kite (see "The Eddy Kite" on pages 98–102).

Materials

To make this kite you need:

• 40″ × 41″ .75 oz. ripstop, Tyvek, or cotton;
• 40″ × ¼″ twill tape;

• ¼″ grommets;
• 4 oz. Dacron (reinforcement material);
• five "D," or ¾″, split key rings;
• three ¼″ × 48″ hardwood dowels (cut to size) or FL 250 epoxy tubing (with connecting ferrules);
• two guy-line adjusters;
• 4 yards of 50 lb.–test braided-Dacron line—for bridle, bow, and tail bridle;
• 24″ × ¾″ nylon webbing—for pockets;
• 10′ × ¼″ seam edge binding; and
• 20′–30′ × 4″ ripstop or Tyvek—for kite tail.

Details

See Illus. 316 for Details 1–4, Illus. 317 for Detail 5, and Illus. 318 for Detail 6.

• (Detail 1.) Completed kite (back): .75 oz. ripstop sail.
• (Detail 2.) Horizontal spar pocket: guy-line adjuster, bow line, and cross spar.
• (Detail 3.) Diagonal longeron pocket. Loop the bridle line through ¼″ grommets; "D" rings on aft spar pockets for the tail bridle; 4 oz. Dacron reinforcement; stitch ¼″ edge-binding tape over the hem; nylon webbing—¾″ × 4″ folded to form the pocket (typical); stitch the pocket shut.

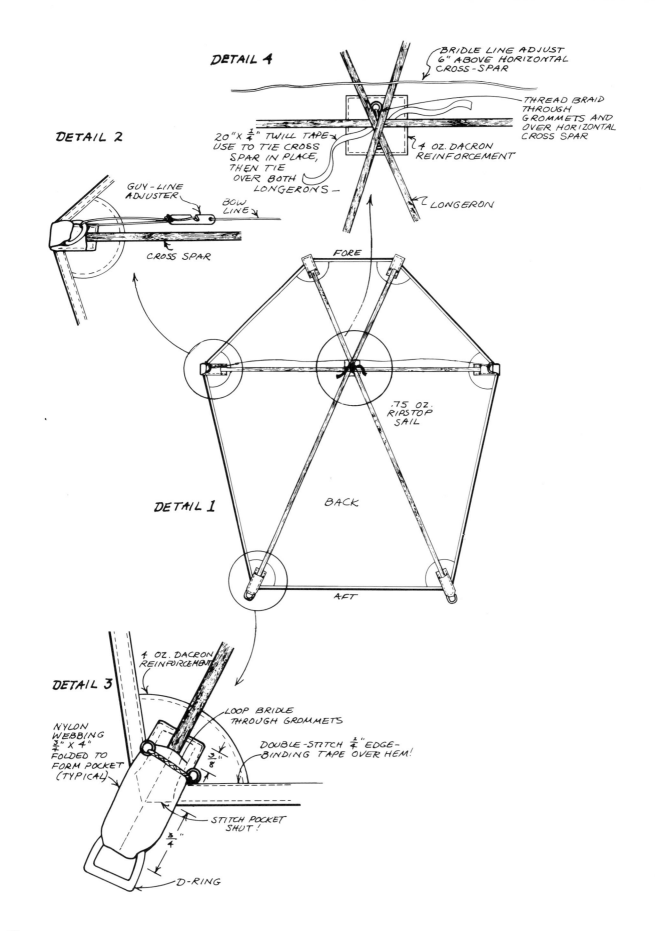

DETAIL 4

BRIDLE LINE ADJUST
6" ABOVE HORIZONTAL
CROSS-SPAR

THREAD BRAID
THROUGH
GROMMETS AND
OVER HORIZONTAL
CROSS SPAR

DETAIL 2

20"X ¼" TWILL TAPE
USE TO TIE CROSS
SPAR IN PLACE,
THEN TIE
OVER BOTH
LONGERONS —

4 OZ. DACRON
REINFORCEMENT

LONGERON

GUY-LINE
ADJUSTER

BOW
LINE

CROSS SPAR

FORE

.75 OZ.
RIPSTOP
SAIL

BACK

DETAIL 1

AFT

DETAIL 3

4 OZ. DACRON
REINFORCEMENT

LOOP BRIDLE
THROUGH GROMMETS

NYLON
WEBBING
¾" X 4"
FOLDED TO
FORM POCKET
(TYPICAL)

⅜"

DOUBLE-STITCH ¼" EDGE-
BINDING TAPE OVER HEM!

STITCH POCKET
SHUT!

¾"

D-RING

Illus. 316. Details 1–4.

- (Detail 4.) Dacron reinforcement patch at the spar junction point; thread the bridle through the grommets and over the horizontal spar. ¼″ × 20″ twill tape ties the horizontal spar in place with an overhand knot. Use a simple bow knot with the remaining twill tape to secure the diagonal longerons.

  Note: All spars are under the bow line. Adjust the bow line to a depth of 6″ above the horizontal spar. A bow depth of 4″ is recommended for light winds. Mark the points on the bow line with a soft-tip pen for reference.
- (Detail 5.) In flight. Five-legged bridle system. Fix the fore lines (36″) and aft lines (42″) to a split ring with a lark's head hitch. The central 32½″ bridle point is taut with the fore and aft lines slightly loose. Even bridle tension occurs during flight.
- (Detail 6.) Three-stick kite variations.

Flight Data: Wind range: 4–15 mph
 Line: 50 lb. test
 AE: ±50°

Construction

Note: Give careful consideration to the placement of the stabilizing-seam edge binding that prevents the kite sail from distorting. For example, if you wish to build the kite with the seam binding on the face of the kite perimeter to complement a design or color scheme, you may dispense with a hem altogether and simply hot-cut the kite to the complete dimensions. If, however, you decide that the seam binding must be on the back of the kite, a hem is recommended, as in the following design.

Hot-cutting:

1. Measure the outline of the kite sail to the dimensions indicated in Illus. 319; this is your fold line for hemming. But remember to add ¼″ beyond the outline for the hem allowance before cutting the sail.
2. Hot-cut seven Dacron-reinforcement patches and six ¾″ × 4″ nylon-webbing strips for the pockets.

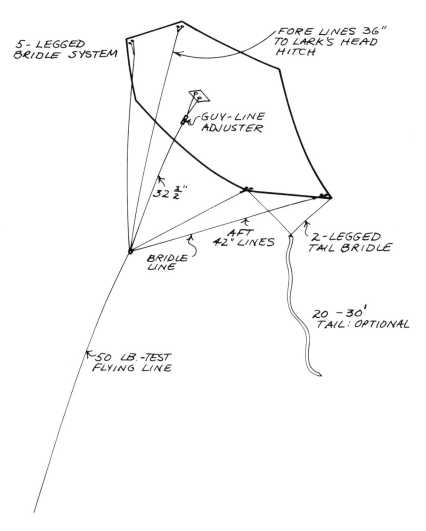

IN FLIGHT

5-LEGGED BRIDLE SYSTEM

FORE LINES 36″ TO LARK'S HEAD HITCH

GUY-LINE ADJUSTER

32½″

AFT 42″ LINES

2-LEGGED TAIL BRIDLE

BRIDLE LINE

20–30′ TAIL: OPTIONAL

50 LB.-TEST FLYING LINE

Illus. 317. Detail 5.

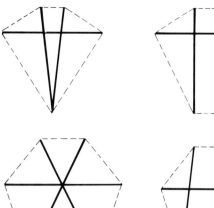

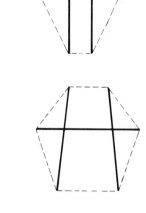

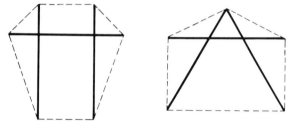

Illus. 318. Detail 6. Three-stick kite variations.

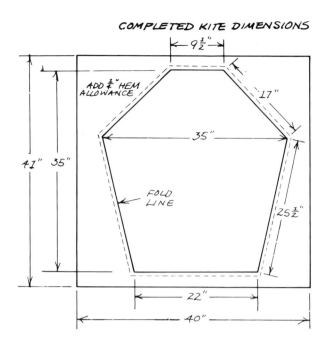

COMPLETED KITE DIMENSIONS

Illus. 319. Step 1.

your hot cutter, melt holes just big enough (about ⅛″) to accept the ¼″ grommets used at the bridle point locations.

7. Cut the horizontal spar and two longerons to fit snugly from pocket to pocket. Round the edges of the ¼″ hardwood dowel to prevent wear on the pockets.

8. Cut the bridle lengths and bow line (40″) from 50 lb.–test braided-Dacron line.

9. To fix the bridle, lay the kite on the floor facing up. Adjust all bridle lines to converge over the junction where the three spars meet. Holding the bridle lines up, use the guy-line adjuster to restrict the central line so that it's slightly shorter than the rest. The slack to the four outside lines will equalize in flight.

10. Rig a bow line between the "D" rings on the horizontal pockets. Mark adjustment points on the line with a soft-tip pen for reference.

Sewing:

3. See Illus. 320. With the sail facing downwards, position the Dacron reinforcements in each corner at the fold line. Sew along the arc side only, lock-stitching the beginning and end. Note: Do this prior to hemming the perimeter of the kite.

4. After hemming the kite, place perimeter binding over the hem and double-stitch as shown in Detail 3 (Illus. 316).

5. Fold, piece, and attach the nylon-webbing pockets to the sail as shown in Detail 3. Sew a 20″ × ¼″ twill-tape strip, positioned vertically, onto the central reinforcement patch (see Detail 4 in Illus. 316).

Assembly:

6. With a pencil soldering iron or a conical tip on

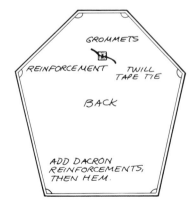

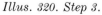

Illus. 320. Step 3.

46
The Triple Yakko Stakk Kite

Design: Courtesy of Martin Lester

Kites in a Train

After English kite maker Martin Lester designed this unusual kite in 1979, he subsequently discovered that its principle had been in use by the Japanese for centuries in the form of a *yakko*, or footman, kite—hence, the name. Unlike its Oriental counterpart, Lester's yakko kite needs no spine and has a self-adjusting dihedral to maintain its balance. His yakko can fly singly or as a stack in a train. See the Japanese yakko kite in Illus. 321; see Lester's Triple Yakko Stakk in Illus. 322 (Detail 4), and in color on page H.

Quick and easy to make, the Yakko Stakk is virtually unbreakable and is an excellent choice for a class or group project. Since the success of a kite train is dependent upon each individually made kite pulling its own weight, a lesson in cooperation is made clear for all concerned.

To get a feel for the fun of flying kites in a train, start with the Triple Stakk as presented here. Adding more kites requires rebridling and beefing up all lines. Lester reports that the longest stack so far and for sheer spectacle is about 200-kites strong.

Materials

To make this kite you need:

- 41″ × 48″ of .75 oz. ripstop—for sail material,
- three ³⁄₃₂″ × 72″ fibreglass rods—cut to size,
- six vinyl end caps—for fibreglass rods,
- nine lightweight fishing swivels,
- 20′ of 50 lb.–test line—for three bridle lines, and
- a ⁹⁄₁₆″ split key ring—for flying-line tow point.

Details

The following details are shown in Illus. 322.

- (Detail 1.) Completed top: aft middle strip, and "ears" that assume a flared-out shape during flight.
- (Detail 2.) Bridle arrangement. Form three bridle lines as shown; the bottom lines join at the lark's head hitch.
- (Detail 3.) Bridle lines: Connect with an overhand knot; use a ⁹⁄₁₆″ split key ring to form an adjustable lark's head hitch.
- (Detail 4.) In flight. In heavier winds, add a stabilizing tail streamer to the aft middle strip.

Flight Data: Wind range 3–25 mph
Line: 50 lb.
AE: ±60°

Illus. 321. The Japanese yakko kite.

Construction

Apply the following instructions for each kite.

Hot-cutting:

1. Hot-cut a piece of ripstop into a rectangle measuring 36″ × 15″. See Illus. 323.
2. Mark the three bridle points (Illus. 323).
3. Take a ¾″ strip of .75 oz. ripstop that is 6″ long and fold it twice onto itself along the length. Run a stitch along the middle and cut it into three ¼″ × 2″ strips—these are the bridle connect tabs.
4. See Illus. 324. Take a sail and overlap its corners ⅜″. Lock-stitch the top corner to the bottom for ¾″. Repeat this sequence for the other side.
5. Starting at the middle bottom (bridle point), double-fold the edge of the sail to form a ⅜″ hem pocket. First sew the vertical seam and then follow the perimeter of the edge to form the pocket as shown in Illus. 325.
6. When you reach the top two bridle points, fold the 2″ strips in half and sew them on as indicated in Illus. 326.
7. Continue to stitch around the edge of the sail, stopping ¾″ short of the middle vertical seam at

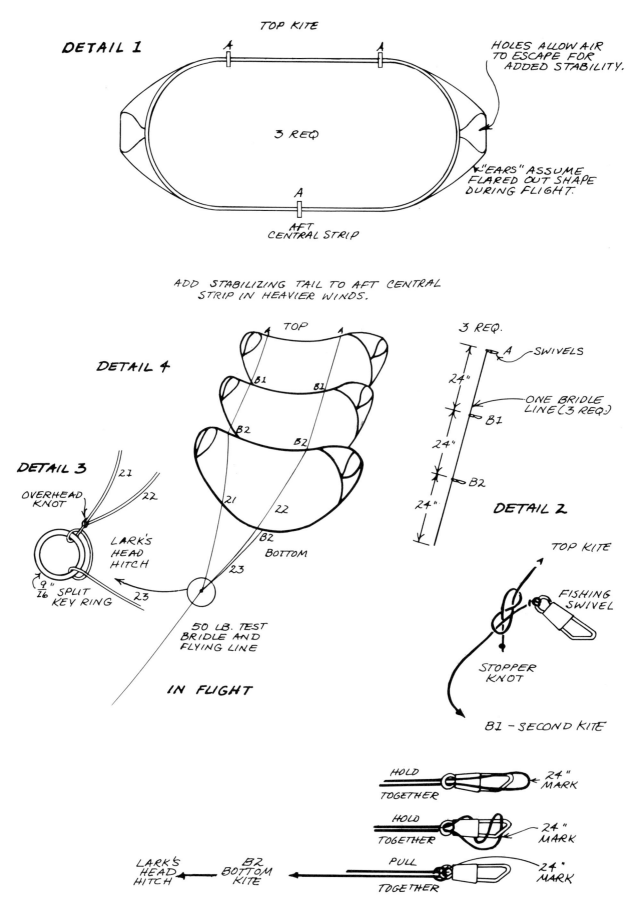

TOP KITE

DETAIL 1

HOLES ALLOW AIR TO ESCAPE FOR ADDED STABILITY.

3 REQ

"EARS" ASSUME FLARED OUT SHAPE DURING FLIGHT.

A

AFT CENTRAL STRIP

ADD STABILIZING TAIL TO AFT CENTRAL STRIP IN HEAVIER WINDS.

DETAIL 4

TOP

B1   B1

B2

B2

21   22

21   22

B2

BOTTOM

23

50 LB. TEST BRIDLE AND FLYING LINE

IN FLIGHT

DETAIL 3

21
22
OVERHEAD KNOT

LARK'S HEAD HITCH

$\frac{9}{16}$" SPLIT KEY RING

23

3 REQ.

A — SWIVELS

24"

ONE BRIDLE LINE (3 REQ.)

B1

24"

B2

24"

DETAIL 2

TOP KITE

FISHING SWIVEL

STOPPER KNOT

B1 — SECOND KITE

HOLD TOGETHER
24" MARK

HOLD TOGETHER
24" MARK

LARK'S HEAD HITCH   B2 BOTTOM KITE   PULL TOGETHER
24" MARK

Illus. 322. Details 1–4.

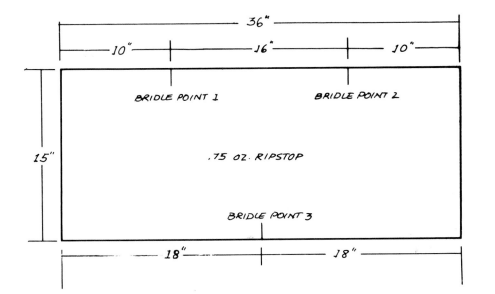

Illus. 323. Steps 1 and 2.

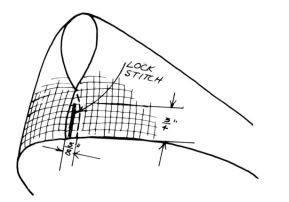

Illus. 324. Step 4.

the bottom where you began. Leave a gap in the hem at this point to insert or remove the fiberglass-rod spar (Illus. 327). Attach the third strip and sew over the top of the vertical seam.

Cutting:

8. Cut a ³⁄₃₂″ fibreglass rod to size, approximately 69″ in length. (Determine the exact length prior to cutting the rod.) Place vinyl caps on both tips. Insert one end into the gap and feed it through the pocket perimeter by alternately pushing the rod and pulling the fabric. Push the remaining end into the pocket opening for a taut fit all around.

9. Use fishing-swivel clips to attach three bridle lines to tabs as shown in Detail 4 (Illus. 322).

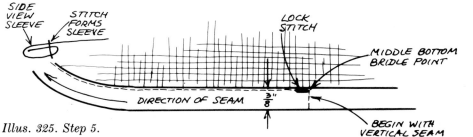

Illus. 325. Step 5.

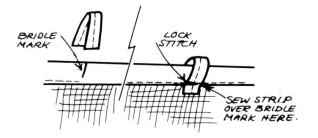

Illus. 326. Step 6.

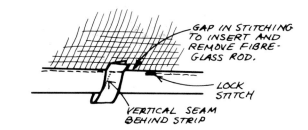

Illus. 327. Step 7.

47
A Roller Kite

After Alick Pearson's Design[1]

The Civilized Floater

Although recognized as a well-behaved light-to-moderate-wind flier, the roller kite is not dependent on ideal conditions. Its self-regulating bridle system compensates for the unexpected by allowing the kite to shed extra wind in severe gusts, which might ordinarily result in a broken line or cause the kite to dive out of control.

Though usually regarded as British, the roller kite is of German origin. During the early part of this century, a *Roloplan* kite was marketed by Steiff, a German toy manufacturer. Because the kite could rise quickly from confined areas like small parks, the Roloplan became popular in densely populated London, where residents began building their own. By the early 1940s, *Roloplan* had become anglicized to *roller*, which is also an affectionate term for a Rolls-Royce.

In London today, as it has been for many years, a favorite patch of green for flying rollers can be found at the Round Pound in Kensington Gardens. A local fraternity of experienced kite fliers known as the Round Pound Fliers maintains that a reliable high angle of flight, stability, and ease of ground launch from a deep-sky reel without losing altitude are the paramount virtues of a good kite. The even-keeled roller meets all of these requirements.

The roller presented here is a version developed by the late Alick Pearson, a former Round Pound flier at Kensington Gardens, who perfected the traditional roller in the early 1970s. Until Pearson simplified the kite, the roller, in its various incarnations, employed cumbersome multilegged bridles—some with both fore and aft rudders. Pearson's elegant improvements include square proportions and a single-loop bridle. For many at the Round Pound, the nose rudder is also conspicuously absent.

Easily launched and pumped up in the lightest of winds on a deep-sky reel, this roller is known for its impressive high angle (65°–80°) of flight. The kite can easily rise thousands of feet in the air on thermals until it's a mere speck against the sky.

To stabilize the sail and defeat ripstop's tendency to stretch, the roller should have its perimeter edge bound. If you use a double-fold hem instead of binding, avoid flying the kite in humid conditions that will eventually distort the ripstop-nylon sail. The kite is shown in Illus. 329 (Detail 6), and in color on page N.

Materials

To make this kite you need:

- 60″ × 41″ .75 oz. ripstop,
- 40″ × ¼″ twill tape,
- 4 oz. Dacron-reinforcement material,
- three 48″ × ⁵⁄₁₆″ hardwood dowels—cut two in half for horizontal spars—leave one full-length for spine,
- vinyl end caps,
- ¼″ grommets,
- 25″ × 1″ nylon webbing—for pockets,
- 6 yards of ½″ edge binding,
- two guy-line adjusters or two-to-four-hole buttons,
- 3 yards of 100 lb.–test braided-Dacron line—for bridle plus fore and aft sail connectors,
- two ⁵⁄₁₆″ I.D. × 4″ aluminum (6061-T grade or better) tubing—for fixed dihedral angle connectors,
- three ⁵⁄₈″ split key rings,
- a heavy-duty rubber band, and
- a ³⁄₁₆″ dowel—batten-cut to size.

Option—for a roller that will fly in heavier winds, use:

- FL 370 epoxy tubing—for spine,
- FL 250 epoxy tubing—for spars, and
- ¼″ I.D. aluminum-tubing connectors.

Details

Details 1–5 are shown in Illus. 328; Details 6 and 7 are shown in Illus. 329.

- (Detail 1.) Main design.
- (Detail 2.) Upper horizontal spar pocket. No stitching across the pocket end.
- (Detail 3.) The lower horizontal spar pocket is sewn in place at an angle to accommodate both the spar and grommet. No stitching across the pocket end.

  The guy-line adjuster maintains proper tension

210

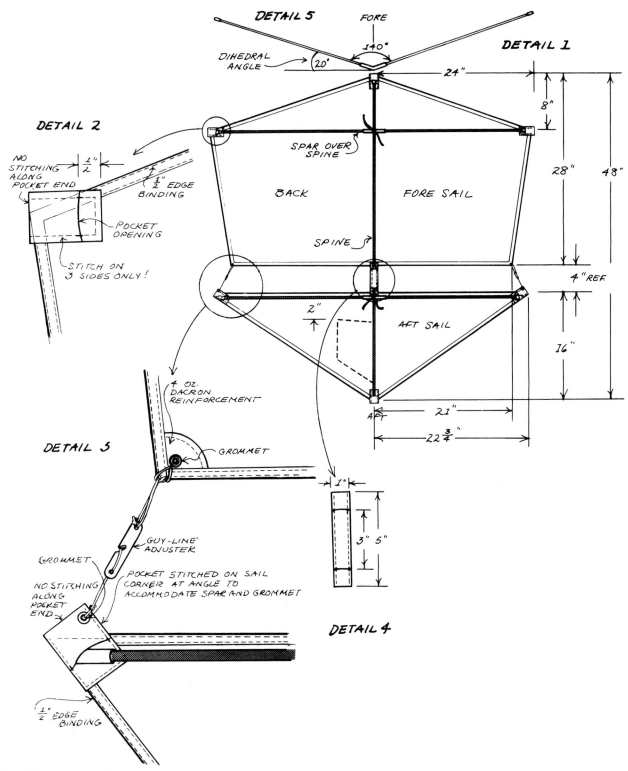

DETAIL 5   FORE

DIHEDRAL ANGLE → 140°

DETAIL 1

20°

24"

8"

DETAIL 2

NO STITCHING ALONG POCKET END

½"

½" EDGE BINDING

SPAR OVER SPINE

POCKET OPENING

BACK   FORE SAIL

28"   48"

STITCH ON 3 SIDES ONLY!

SPINE

4" REF

2"

AFT SAIL

16"

4 OZ. DACRON REINFORCEMENT

DETAIL 3

GROMMET

AFT

21"

22¾"

1"

3"   5"

GUY-LINE ADJUSTER

GROMMET

POCKET STITCHED ON SAIL CORNER AT ANGLE TO ACCOMMODATE SPAR AND GROMMET

DETAIL 4

NO STITCHING ALONG POCKET END

½" EDGE BINDING

Illus. 328. Details 1–5.

and a 4″ distance between the fore and aft sails. Mark the adjustment point on the line for future reference.
- (Detail 4.) Fore and aft sail-sleeve connector.
- (Detail 5.) Fixed dihedral connector with horizontal spars.

- (Detail 6.) In flight.
- (Detail 7.) Self-regulating bridle setup.

Flight Data: Wind range: 3–12 mph
           Line: 75 lb. test
           AE: ±70°

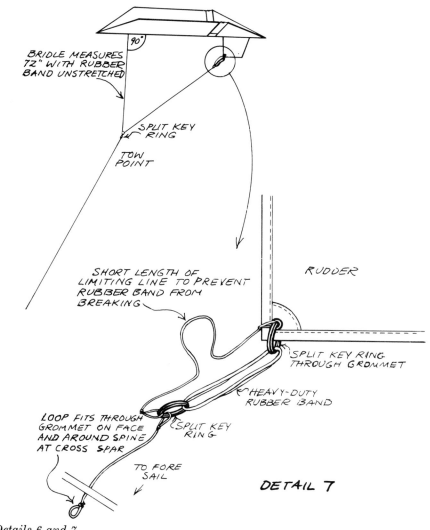

Illus. 329. Details 6 and 7.

Construction

Hot-cutting:

1. Hot-cut five pieces from ripstop yardage as shown in Illus. 330. Add a ½″ hem allowance to all dimensions, except for the rudder batten strip.
2. Hot-cut a Dacron corner reinforcement and glue it in position (use 3M's spray adhesive or a glue stick) on the rudder at the hem fold line as shown in Illus. 331.

Sewing:

3. Referring to Illus. 331, sew the corner reinforcement on the rudder tip along the arc only, lock-stitching the beginning and end. Finish with a ¼″ double-fold hem all around, except for the 10½″ side. Double-stitch the ⅝″ × 15″ strip of ripstop to form a diagonal sleeve. Leave an open space in the stitching to insert the ³⁄₁₆″ rudder batten.

Hot-cutting:

4. Refer to Illus. 331. With a conical tip on the hot cutter, melt a ⅛″ hole in the rudder's bridle connect corner and insert a ¼″ grommet. You can substitute a nylon-tape loop for the grommet.
5. Sandwich the rudder along the 10½″ side between the two aft sail halves with the face sides meeting as shown in Illus. 332. Hot-cutting ¼″ from the edge welds the three pieces together.

Sewing:

6. See Illus. 332. Connect the rudder to the aft sail halves with a stitch ¼″ in from the hot-cut edge. Place the sail face down. Position the rudder off to one side and out of the way before sewing the ¼″ hem flat (a sail seam) with a second stitch along the edge for the length of the aft sail.
7. Referring to Illus. 332, fold the ½″ perimeter hem

212

onto the back on all three sides of the triangular aft sail. Sew a ½″ binding over the hem and stitch twice around. Corners: Fold the sail back ⅜″ and edge-bind over the fold as shown.

Hot-cutting:

8. Pockets: Hot-cut six 2½″ × 1″ strips of nylon webbing.

Sewing:

9. Fold and stitch the pockets to the three corners of the aft sail as shown in the main design (Illus. 328). Use a conical point on the hot cutter to make ⅛″ holes and insert ¼″ grommets in both horizontal spar pockets.

10. Fore sail: With the back of the sail facing you, glue in place and sew the bottom corner Dacron reinforcements at the hem fold line; then turn the ½″ hem towards the back and edge-bind all around. Stitch on three nylon-webbing pockets as shown in Detail 2 (Illus. 328). Reinforce the bridle loop point on the back of the sail with a 1″-square Dacron-reinforcement patch. Use the conical tip to melt three ⅛″ holes for the ¼″ grommets.

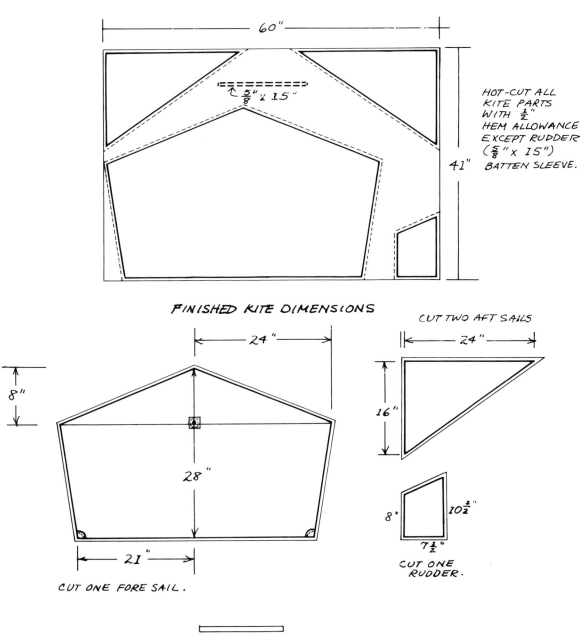

STEP 1

60″

HOT-CUT ALL KITE PARTS WITH ½″ HEM ALLOWANCE EXCEPT RUDDER (⅝″ x 15″) BATTEN SLEEVE.

41″

⅝″ x 15″

FINISHED KITE DIMENSIONS

CUT TWO AFT SAILS

24″

8″

28″

24″

21″

16″

CUT ONE FORE SAIL.

8″   10½″

7½″

CUT ONE RUDDER.

CUT ONE RUDDER BATTEN-SLEEVE STRIP.

Illus. 330. Step 1.

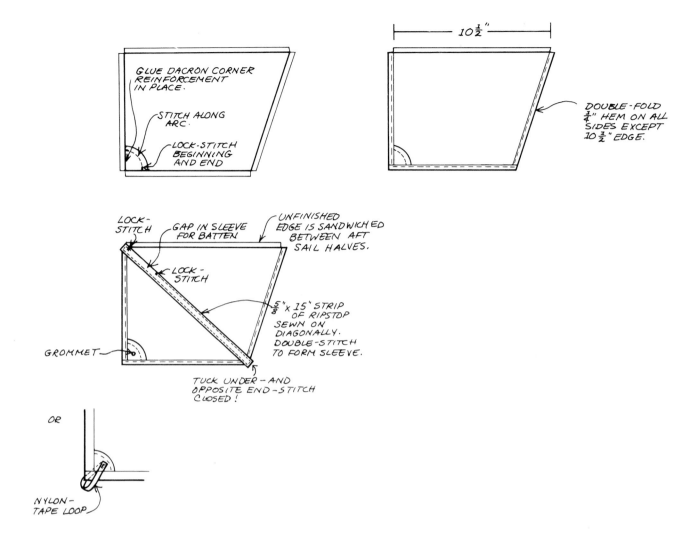

GLUE DACRON CORNER REINFORCEMENT IN PLACE.

STITCH ALONG ARC.

LOCK-STITCH BEGINNING AND END

10½"

DOUBLE-FOLD ¼" HEM ON ALL SIDES EXCEPT 10½" EDGE.

LOCK-STITCH

GAP IN SLEEVE FOR BATTEN

UNFINISHED EDGE IS SANDWICHED BETWEEN AFT SAIL HALVES.

LOCK-STITCH

⅝" X 15" STRIP OF RIPSTOP SEWN ON DIAGONALLY. DOUBLE-STITCH TO FORM SLEEVE.

GROMMET

TUCK UNDER - AND OPPOSITE END - STITCH CLOSED!

OR

NYLON-TAPE LOOP

Illus. 331. Steps 2–4.

11. Form the connecting middle sleeve between the fore and aft sails by stitching a 3″ × 1″ piece of nylon webbing onto the middle of a 5″ × 1″ piece. Position and stitch the sleeve in the middle of the back of the fore sail with the 3″ piece on top. Make sure the distance between the sails is 4″ *before* stitching the sleeve in place on the aft sail.

12. Place a 20″ × ¼″ strip of twill tape vertically on the back of the kite where the spine and horizontal spar intersect. Stitch it in place at the midpoint. Repeat this on the aft section, sewing the twill-tape strip ¾″ down along the centerline.

Assembly:

13. Cut the spine for a tight fit from the top to the bottom pockets. Include vinyl end caps. The spine must pass through the middle sleeve. Use the twill-tape strips on the fore and aft sails and tie the spine in place.

14. Bend both pieces of 4″ aluminum tubing in the middle for a fixed angle of 140°. Tip: With one end of the tube secured along a 180° horizontal work surface, bend the other side 40° up to form the 140° angle.

15. Cut the four horizontal spars to fit tightly from pocket to pocket for the sail to assume the proper camber.

16. Connect the fore and aft sails on each corner with 100 lb.–test line and guy-line adjusters. Make sure that the distance between the sails is a uniform 4″ across.

17. Cut a ³⁄₁₆″ dowel batten to size and insert it into the rudder sleeve opening.

18. Fix the bridle as shown in Details 6 and 7 (Illus. 329). Instead of the bridle breaking or the kite going out of control in gusts, the flexibility of the rubber band allows the kite to alter its flight angle and shed extra wind.

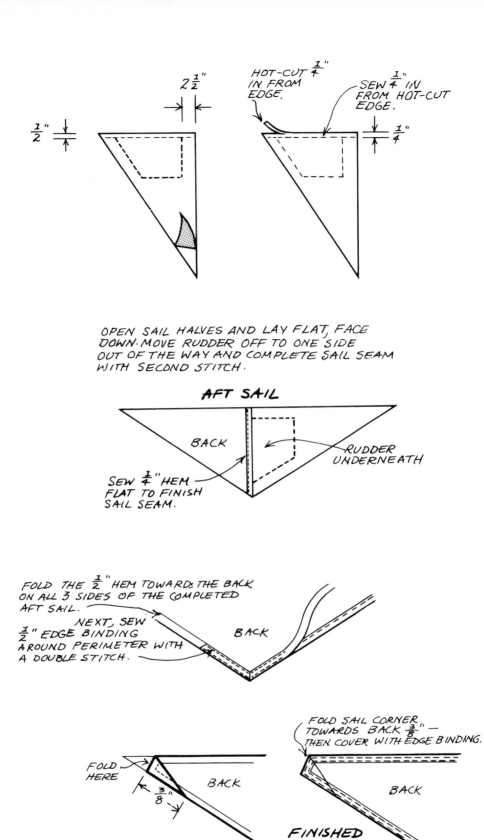

$2\frac{1}{2}''$

$\frac{1}{2}''$

HOT-CUT $\frac{1}{4}''$ IN FROM EDGE.

SEW $\frac{1}{4}''$ IN FROM HOT-CUT EDGE.

$\frac{1}{4}''$

OPEN SAIL HALVES AND LAY FLAT, FACE DOWN. MOVE RUDDER OFF TO ONE SIDE OUT OF THE WAY AND COMPLETE SAIL SEAM WITH SECOND STITCH.

AFT SAIL

BACK

RUDDER UNDERNEATH

SEW $\frac{1}{4}''$ HEM FLAT TO FINISH SAIL SEAM.

FOLD THE $\frac{1}{2}''$ HEM TOWARDS THE BACK ON ALL 3 SIDES OF THE COMPLETED AFT SAIL. NEXT, SEW $\frac{1}{2}''$ EDGE BINDING AROUND PERIMETER WITH A DOUBLE STITCH.

BACK

FOLD SAIL CORNER TOWARDS BACK $\frac{3}{8}''$ — THEN COVER WITH EDGE BINDING.

FOLD HERE

$\frac{3}{8}''$

BACK

BACK

FINISHED CORNER

RUDDER AND AFT SAIL

Illus. 332. Steps 5-7.

The Original Steiff Roloplan

The original Steiff Roloplan from Germany (circa 1930s) had bamboo spars and a porous cotton sail. The sail perimeter was hemmed with a zigzag stitch, and bracing lines kept the structure under even tension.

For those challenged to recreate a bit of kite history, the dimensions for the original Roloplan[2] are shown in the drawing and here are suggested construction materials.

- Sail: cotton or .75 oz. ripstop. All sail cuts are straight; curves on the illustration indicate the shape of the sail under stress during flight.
- Six 35½" spars: two for the spine, two each (four total) for the two sets of cross spars.

Matching cross spars must be equally balanced for strength and flex for best results. Synthetics are generally more uniform than woods.

- Three aluminum ferrules: two bent to form a dihedral angle for cross spars, one to join spine spar halves.
- Spar materials—cross spars: ⁵⁄₁₆" hardwood dowel or FL 250 epoxy tubing; spine: ³⁄₈" hardwood dowel or FL 370 epoxy tubing.
- Bridle line: 100 lb. test.
- Bracing line: 75 lb. test.
- Flying line: 100 lb. test.

To construct this kite, refer to the steps and tips for the roller kite. *Grosse gluck* (good luck).

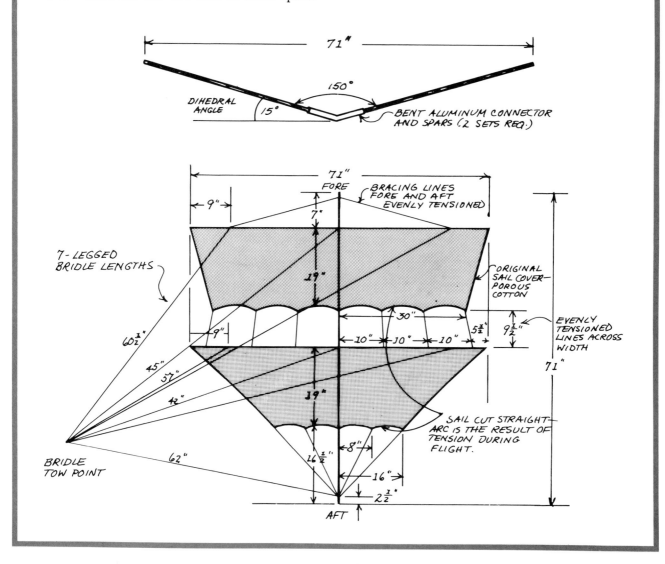

---

[1]With a little help from Dan Leigh and Kevin Shannon.
[2]This rare original was provided by Larry Nuesslein.

48
Origami Bug Kites

Designs: Courtesy of Ed Grauel (Flying Nun, or Chinchbug: Courtesy of William Schaeffer)

Mastering the Crease

Although the ancient Japanese artform of *origami*, or paper folding, discourages cutting and gluing, contemporary *origami* accepts snipping and combining elements. The flexible paper-fold kites presented here are rewarding for their design purity and construction simplicity. These kites make novel gifts that can be mailed to a friend in an envelope.

Use 8½″ × 11″ or 9″ × 12″ lightweight construction paper for most of the kites. Sheets of 20 lb. bond paper will also work. (You can make the Scoopbug from heavier construction paper, and the Tumblebug from yesterday's newspaper.) These flying bugs fare well in winds from 4 to 10 mph. The Chinchbug and Junebug can fly in light winds without a stabilizing tail.

Materials

To make these kites you need:

- 8½″ × 11″ or 9″ × 12″ lightweight construction paper or sheets of 20 lb. bond paper,
- crepe paper cut into ½″ × 10′ streamers,
- cotton or carpet thread—for bridle and flying line,
- gummed loose-leaf reinforcements—for bridle connect points,
- scissors and paper punch,
- stapler (for Chinchbug), and
- white glue or glue stick (for Junebug).

Construction

The following tips pertain to all five origami kites. The construction steps are shown for each individual kite; see Illus. 333–337.

1. Make sharp, even creases.
2. The central concave crease of the kite must face you.
3. Center the overhand knot that forms the bridle loop over the middle crease, making the two bridle legs exactly equal.
4. The bridle line should extend beyond the top of the kite when the bug is lying flat; it should be about 15″ in length.
5. Strengthen the bridle connect points with loose-leaf gummed reinforcements.
6. Connect the tail to the kite with a short length of thread. You can use a ½″ × 10′ piece of crepe paper folded in half and tied in the middle to form a double 5′ tail. Add longer tails for moderate winds.

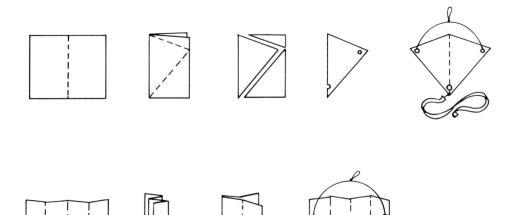

Illus. 333. The Tumblebug.

Illus. 334. The Scoopbug.

217

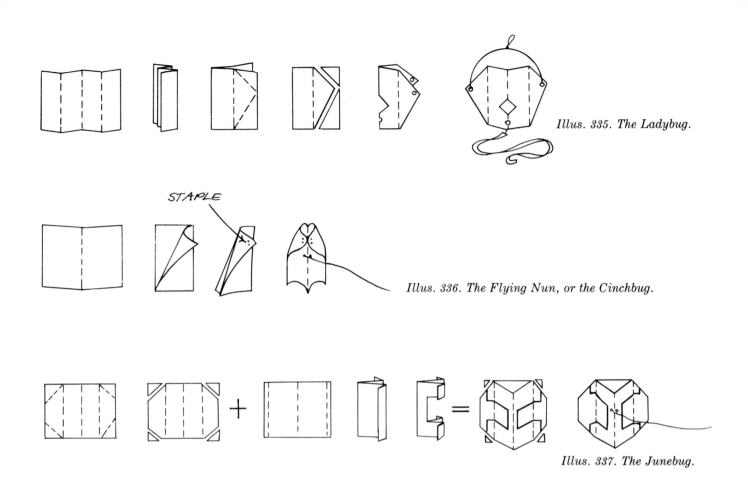

Illus. 335. The Ladybug.

STAPLE

Illus. 336. The Flying Nun, or the Cinchbug.

Illus. 337. The Junebug.

49
Fighter Kites—the Sanjo Rokkaku, Szilagi, and Nagasaki Hata

Flying Tips[1] for Fighter Kites

The fighter kite is maneuverable because it is inherently unstable by design. Controlling a fighter kite requires practice, and having a friend assist you is recommended.

Fly in an open area, free from people. Never try launching your fighter by running with it. Beginners may wish to add a 10-foot crepe paper streamer to stabilize the kite while learning; maneuvers will not be as tight, but control will be easier during this stage. Once you've mastered some skills, the crepe paper tail can be removed.

1. (See Illus. 338.) After attaching your kite line to the bridle with a slip knot, have a friend stand

about 50 feet downwind. Your friend should face you while gently balancing (not grasping) the kite at wing tips B and C with the nose A pointed upwards. Have about 20 feet of kite line off the reel beside you.

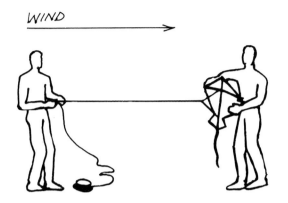

Illus. 338

2. (See Illus. 339.) With a steady 3 to 6 mph wind at your back, pull the line in, hand over hand, to raise the kite in the direction of the nose (A). Maintain tension on the line to keep the kite moving in the direction of the nose. Attempt to get the kite to rise at least 75 to 100 feet in the air; this will give you enough elevation to practise maneuvering the kite.

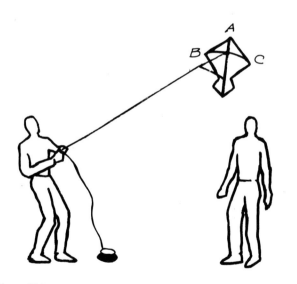

Illus. 339

3. (See Illus. 340.) Once you've practised with a friend and your reaction time in controlling the kite's direction has improved, you can graduate to launching the kite yourself. Again, with the wind to your back, release the kite while maintaining tension on the line.

Illus. 340

4. (See Illus. 341.) The kite may spin and dart from side to side; the idea here is to keep the nose pointed upwards until the kite rises to a maneuvering altitude.

Illus. 341

5. (See Illus. 342.) A quick loosening of the line will cause the kite to become unstable and the nose will

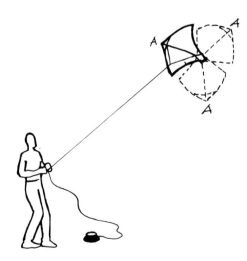

Illus. 342

219

change the direction of flight. When the nose is pointed in the desired direction, placing tension on the line will cause the kite to stabilize and continue in that flight path until slack line is given again. From a safe altitude, try maneuvering right, left, and up—try maneuvering down as you gain confidence.

Note: If at any time the kite feels out of control as it dives towards the ground, don't panic. Pulling harder on the flying line will increase the kite's speed to its doom. Simply dropping the kite line from your hand, however, will stop the potentially destructive power dive.

* * *

To understand the aerodynamics of a fighter kite, see Illus. 343.

The Sanjo Rokkaku Fighter

Building Tips: Courtesy of Kevin Shannon

The Fighting Kites of Shirone

On the West Coast of Japan, 150 miles from Tokyo, lies the small farming community of Shirone. Life there is generally peaceful; but once a year, during the second week of June, after the labor of rice planting is just about over, the tranquility of the village is interrupted by a 250-year-old kite fighting festival.

Opening day is a picturesque fusion of cultures. In contrast to the traditional kite fighting teams parading their colorful arsenals down the crowded narrow

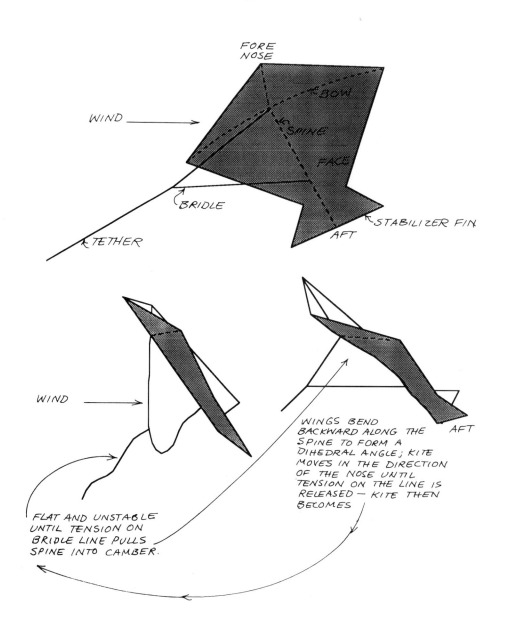

Illus. 343. Aerodynamics of a fighter kite.

streets, there is also the din and hoopla of Western-style marching bands and drum majorettes.

Over the centuries, the kite fighting festival has produced two distinct kite forms: the 22-foot-tall rectangular *o-dako*, and the smaller, typically 8-foot-tall, more maneuverable, hexagon-shaped *rokkaku*. (The *rokkaku* featured in this project is shown in Illus. 346.)

The kite fighting teams consist of at least four to five men for the *rokkaku* and eight to 12 men for the heavier, more cumbersome *o-dako*. Kites remain in their own class: *o-dako* versus *o-dako*, *rokkaku* versus *rokkaku*.

The objective of each team is to skillfully maneuver its kite until it ensnares an opponent's kite. With thousands of spectators looking on, rival teams take their positions on the west and east banks of the Nakanokuchi river. When the winds do come, teams work together in an organized frenzy to loft their sky-bound warriors. Once airborne, the kites are made to dart and swoop overhead.

Inevitably, two kite combatants clash and become mangled and wrapped around each other in an aerial battle over the water. Pulling furiously on their kite's flying line, both teams strain to haul in as much line as possible because every inch of line captured from the opposition means bonus points from the judges.

As a fierce tug of war ensues, flying lines and bridles become hopelessly entangled. The team whose rope breaks first is the loser. But no time is wasted resting on laurels or lamenting a loss. Since each team has numerous kites in its ranks, new *o-dakos* and *rokkakus* are soon launched for yet another skirmish in the sky.

At week's end, if the winds have been favorable, nearly all 1,500 kites built for the festival have been twisted and battered beyond recognition. Beautifully painted kite sails created just days before have been totally destroyed and only the most resilient bamboo frameworks are salvageable from the carnage.

After the festival, life for the villagers soon returns to normal—and stays that way until the following year, when everyone goes a little *tako-kichi* (kite-crazy) and the ritual begins anew.

Materials

To make this kite you need:

- 3 yards × 41″ of .75 oz. ripstop—for sail,
- 40″ × ¼″ twill tape,
- four ¼″ grommets,
- 4 oz. Dacron—for reinforcement material,
- four sections of 32½″ FL 250 epoxy tubing or ⁵⁄₁₆″ hardwood dowel—for horizontal spars,
- two sections of 32½″ FL 370 epoxy tubing or ⅜″ hardwood dowel—for spine,

- interior ferrules (for epoxy tubing) and exterior ferrules (for dowels),
- 24″ × 1″ nylon webbing—for pockets,
- four 1″ split rings,
- ¾″ split ring—for tow ring,
- two guy-line adjusters (two- or four-hole buttons also work),
- 35′ of 150 lb.-test braided-Dacron line—for bridle,
- 12′ of 100 lb.-test braided-Dacron line—for bow lines,
- four wooden beads with holes in middle,
- arrow nock plus arrow nock insert (for epoxy-tubing spine) or arrow nock (for dowel), and
- five vinyl end caps—for horizontal spars and upper part of spine.

Details

See Illus. 344 for Details 1–5 and 7, Illus. 345 for Detail 6, and Illus. 346 for Detail 8.

- (Detail 1.) Main design.
- (Detail 2.) Horizontal spar pockets. Stitch on three sides only; allow a ¼″ space for the split ring to pass through. Lock-stitch the stress points.
- (Detail 3.) Tie the horizontal spars in place using a twill-tape strip. Next, insert the spine over the horizontal spars and under the bow lines; the end of the spine with the arrow nock goes through the aft sleeve and is secured with a wooden bead. With the remaining twill tape, secure the spine against the horizontal spars. Use a bow knot tied diagonally over the spine.
- (Detail 4.) Bridle point (typical). Reinforce with 4-oz. Dacron; then add a ¼″ grommet for the bridle loop that fits around the horizontal spar.
- (Detail 5.) Pull the tension loop until the sail is taut. Secure it by slipping the appropriate wooden bead under the arrow nock. Too much tension will prevent the sail from adopting natural pocketing from wind pressure.
- (Detail 6.) Bow line and pockets.
- (Detail 7.) Use the guy-line adjuster to bow the upper and lower horizontal spars to a depth of 6″ above the spine.
- (Detail 8.) In flight and bridle tow-point position.

Flight Data: Wind range: 4–15 mph
Line: 150 lb. test
AE: ±65°
Wear gloves

Construction

The dimensions of the Sanjo Rokkaku are based on modules, whereby kite builders can conveniently scale the kite to whatever size they choose. Traditionally, the *rokkaku's* proportions (module units) are

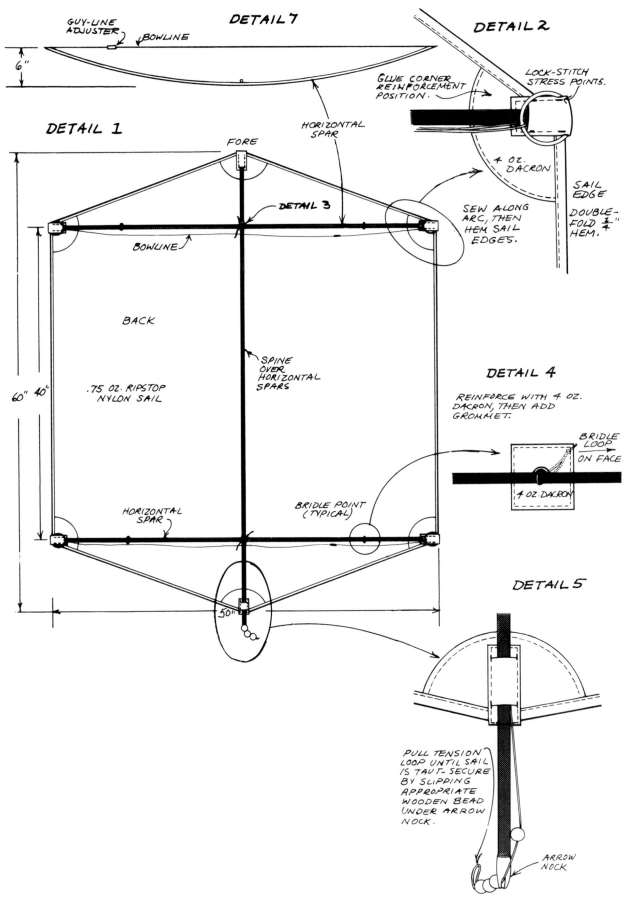

DETAIL 7

GUY-LINE ADJUSTER

BOWLINE

6"

DETAIL 2

GLUE CORNER REINFORCEMENT POSITION.

LOCK-STITCH STRESS POINTS.

4 OZ. DACRON

SAIL EDGE

DOUBLE-FOLD ¼" HEM.

HORIZONTAL SPAR

DETAIL 1

FORE

DETAIL 3

BOWLINE

SEW ALONG ARC, THEN HEM SAIL EDGES.

BACK

.75 OZ. RIPSTOP NYLON SAIL

SPINE OVER HORIZONTAL SPARS

60" 40"

DETAIL 4

REINFORCE WITH 4 OZ. DACRON, THEN ADD GROMMET.

BRIDLE LOOP ON FACE

4 OZ. DACRON

HORIZONTAL SPAR

BRIDLE POINT (TYPICAL)

50"

DETAIL 5

PULL TENSION LOOP UNTIL SAIL IS TAUT. SECURE BY SLIPPING APPROPRIATE WOODEN BEAD UNDER ARROW NOCK.

ARROW NOCK

Illus. 344. The Sanjo Rokkaku—Details 1–5 and 7.

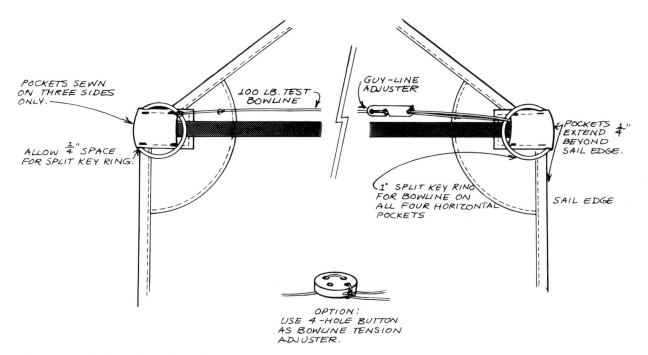

POCKETS SEWN ON THREE SIDES ONLY.

100 LB. TEST BOWLINE

ALLOW ¼" SPACE FOR SPLIT KEY RING.

GUY-LINE ADJUSTER

POCKETS ¼" EXTEND BEYOND SAIL EDGE.

1" SPLIT KEY RING FOR BOWLINE ON ALL FOUR HORIZONTAL POCKETS

SAIL EDGE

OPTION: USE 4-HOLE BUTTON AS BOWLINE TENSION ADJUSTER.

Illus. 345. The Sanjo Rokkaku—Detail 6.

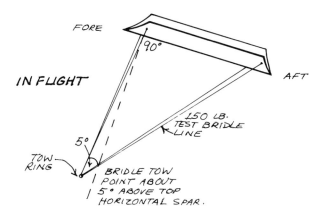

FORE

90°

IN FLIGHT

AFT

150 LB. TEST BRIDLE LINE

5°

TOW RING

BRIDLE TOW POINT ABOUT 5° ABOVE TOP HORIZONTAL SPAR.

Illus. 346. The Sanjo Rokkaku—Detail 8.

4:5:6. The scale chosen for this kite is 10″ for each module unit. Multiply each module unit by 10″ for a *rokkaku* 60″ tall, 50″ wide, and 40″ between the horizontal spars.

As you go through these steps, refer to Illus. 347 and the drawings of the various details.

Hot-cutting:

1. Hot-cut three pieces of ripstop to the dimensions indicated in Illus. 347. A ½″ hem allowance is already included.

2. Lay B and C over A. Align and weld both edges together by hot-cutting ¼″ from the edge.

3. Hot-cut the nylon-webbing pockets as shown in Illus. 347.

Sewing:

4. A sail seam connects B and C to A. Straight-stitch ¼″ from welded edges AB and AC. Open the fabric flat with the back of the sail facing up. Fold ¼″ flap AC towards A and stitch the second row to complete the sail seam. Repeat for the ¼″ flap AB folded towards A. (See "Reaping What You Sew" for sail-seam reference.)

5. After you've completed the sail seams, unfold the material and use a pencil to outline the completed kite's dimensions. This is your fold line for hemming. Add a ½″ hem allowance beyond the outline perimeter *before* cutting out the sail.

Hot cutting:

6. With the sail facedown on the work surface, measure and hot-cut six Dacron reinforcements for each corner of the sail.

Sewing:

7. Position and glue (use 3M's spray adhesive or glue stick) the Dacron reinforcements in each corner at the fold line. Sew along the arc only, lock-stitching the beginning and end. Do this *before* hemming the perimeter of the kite sail.

8. Hem the kite sail. A double-fold finish is preferred because no rough edges will be exposed.

9. Sew nylon-webbing pockets to the sail corners as shown in Detail 2. Attach a 20″ piece of

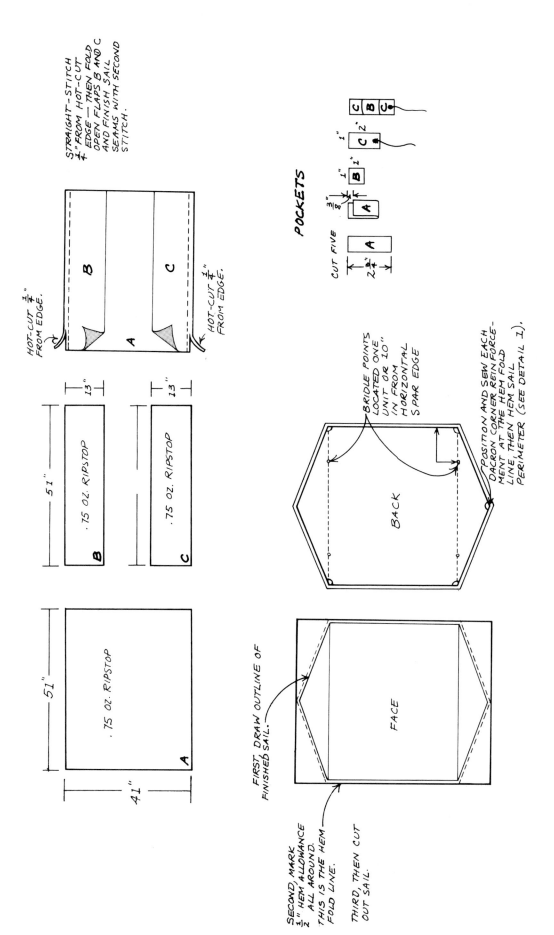

STRAIGHT-STITCH ¼" FROM HOT-CUT EDGE — THEN FOLD OPEN FLAPS B AND C AND FINISH SAIL SEAMS WITH SECOND STITCH.

HOT-CUT ¼" FROM EDGE.

HOT-CUT ¼" FROM EDGE.

B

C

A

51"

.75 OZ. RIPSTOP

B

13"

.75 OZ. RIPSTOP

C

13"

51"

41"

.75 OZ. RIPSTOP

A

POCKETS

C B C

C 2" 1"

B 1" 1"

A 3/8"

CUT FIVE

2 3/4"

A

BRIDLE POINTS LOCATED ONE UNIT OR 10" IN FROM HORIZONTAL SPAR EDGE

BACK

POSITION AND SEW EACH DACRON CORNER REINFORCEMENT AT THE HEM FOLD LINE, THEN FINISH SAIL PERIMETER (SEE DETAIL 1).

FIRST DRAW OUTLINE OF FINISHED SAIL.

FACE

SECOND, MARK ½" HEM ALLOWANCE ALL AROUND. THIS IS THE HEM FOLD LINE.

THIRD, THEN CUT OUT SAIL.

Illus. 347. The Sanjo Rokkaku—sail dimensions.

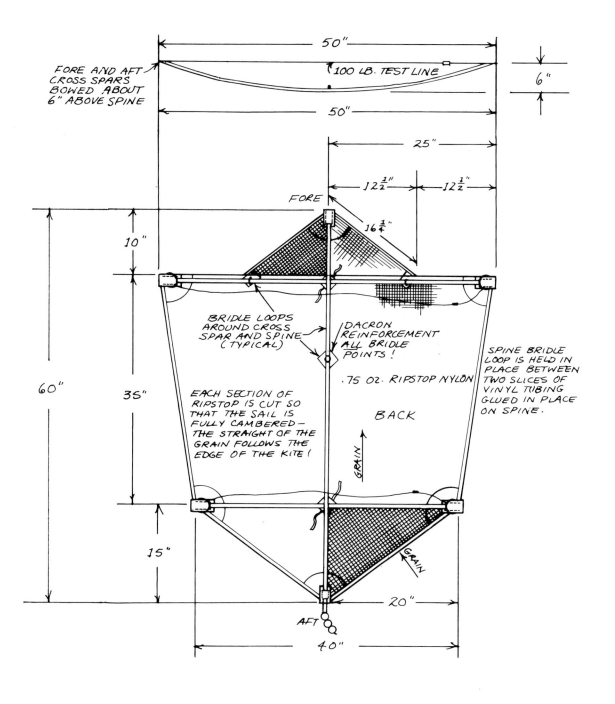

FORE AND AFT
CROSS SPARS
BOWED ABOUT
6" ABOVE SPINE

50"

100 LB. TEST LINE

6"

50"

25"

12½" 12½"

FORE

16¼"

10"

60"

35"

BRIDLE LOOPS
AROUND CROSS
SPAR AND SPINE
(TYPICAL)

DACRON
REINFORCEMENT
ALL BRIDLE
POINTS!

SPINE BRIDLE
LOOP IS HELD IN
PLACE BETWEEN
TWO SLICES OF
VINYL TUBING
GLUED IN PLACE
ON SPINE.

EACH SECTION OF
RIPSTOP IS CUT SO
THAT THE SAIL IS
FULLY CAMBERED —
THE STRAIGHT OF THE
GRAIN FOLLOWS THE
EDGE OF THE KITE!

.75 OZ. RIPSTOP NYLON

BACK

GRAIN

GRAIN

15"

20"

AFT

40"

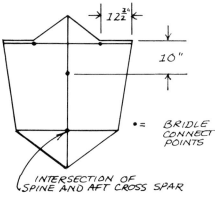

12½"

10"

• = BRIDLE
CONNECT
POINTS

INTERSECTION OF
SPINE AND AFT CROSS SPAR

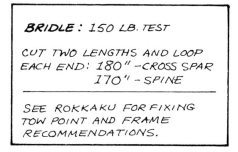

BRIDLE: 150 LB. TEST

CUT TWO LENGTHS AND LOOP
EACH END: 180" – CROSS SPAR
170" – SPINE

SEE ROKKAKU FOR FIXING
TOW POINT AND FRAME
RECOMMENDATIONS.

Illus. 348. Rokkaku variation.

150 lb.–test line to the bottom pocket C using a zigzag stitch.

10. Place a 20″ × ¼″ strip of twill tape vertically on the back of the sail where the spine and upper spar intersect. Stitch it in place at the midpoint. Repeat this for the aft section.

Assembly:

11. The four bridle points are located one module unit (10″) in from each side of both horizontal spar edges. With the front of the kite facing you, use a soldering iron with a conical tip to melt four holes just big enough (about ⅛″) to accept a ¼″ grommet. Note: Reinforce the holes with small squares of Dacron *before* inserting the grommets.

12. Insert 1″ split key rings for the bow lines into each of the four horizontal pockets.

13. Cut and piece the epoxy spine and horizontal spars. The overall lengths include the vinyl end caps. The spine is 65″; the horizontal spars are 50″.

14. Make two bridle lines 180″ each from 150 lb.–test braided-Dacron line. Tie an overhand-loop knot at each end of both lines. Take one bridle line and pass its loops through left fore and aft grommet holes on face side of the sail. Repeat for right side. Next, insert one horizontal spar through both loops and fit the ends into the pockets. Repeat sequence for the remaining horizontal spar.

15. Cut two 6′ lengths of 100 lb.–test braided-Dacron line and rig the bow lines with a guy-line adjuster from ring to ring on the fore and aft horizontal spars.

16. Place the spine over the horizontal spars and under the bow lines. Insert in the fore pocket and secure the arrow nock end in place with an aft tension loop.

17. Adjust the fore and aft bow lines so that each is 6″ above the spine. Mark the correct adjustment points on the line for future reference.

18. With the kite bowed, lay it on the floor facing upwards. Pull both bridle lines together evenly over the middle of the kite; then move the lines forward to a point 5° above the upper horizontal spar. This is the approximate tow point. You may need to make minor adjustments at the flying field.

A Rokkaku Variation

After Lincoln Chang's Design

To make this variation, follow the construction steps for the previous project and refer to Illus. 348. Note: Each section of ripstop is fully cambered; the straight of the grain follows the edge of the kite.

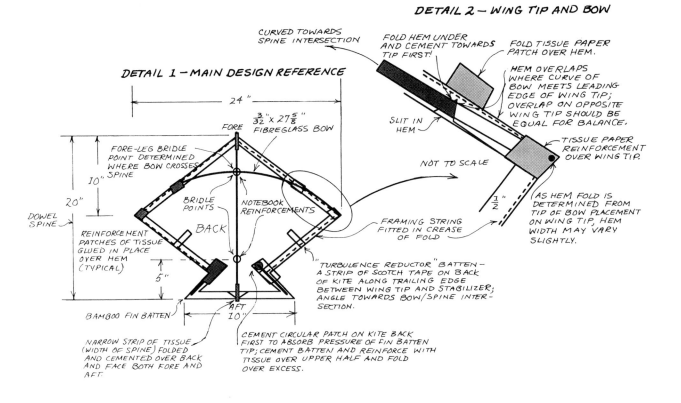

Illus. 349. Details 1 and 2.

226

The Szilagi Fighter

Design: Courtesy of Karl Szilagi

I'll Take Manhattan

It's a cool summer day and all is serene at the Sheep Meadow in New York's Central Park. The sky over the precious patch of open field is partly obscured by the surrounding skyscrapers. Suddenly, a blur of color streaks across the sky from out of nowhere. The aerial intruder nearly grazes the treetops before making a controlled horizontal pass about two feet from the grass. Now, at close range, the striped Madras tissue paper and broad fin stabilizer are clearly distinguishable as a Szilagi Fighter. With its unique profile and fibreglass bow, this fighter (shown in Illus. 350) is an agile, responsive marvel capable of tight turns, straight tracking, and instantaneous response to line control.

Materials

To make this kite you need:

- one sheet of striped Madras tissue paper (20″ × 30″);
- one ³⁄₁₆″ × 20″ dowel—for spine;
- one ³⁄₃₂″ × 27⅝″ fibreglass rod (cut from standard 48″ or 72″ length)—use regular, or extra flex for an even faster kite;
- two flat bamboo battens 4½″ × about the width of a matchstick;
- two loose-leaf notebook reinforcements;
- carpet thread for buttons (cotton-covered polyester); and
- rubber cement.

Details

See Illus. 349 for Details 1 and 2, Illus. 350 for Detail 3, and Illus. 351 for Detail 4.

- (Detail 1.) Main design reference.
- (Detail 2.) Wing tip and bow.
- (Detail 3.) In flight.
- (Detail 4.) Bridle dimensions: The fore leg is 12¾″ to the knot, the aft leg 14¼″ to the knot.

Flight Data: Wind range: 0–12 mph
Line: 12 lb.–test waxed linen or
8 lb.–test cotton line
AE: maneuverable

Construction

1. Make the ⅛″ × ³⁄₁₆″ × 20″ spine by sanding it until it has a flat edge on both sides. See Illus. 352. Leaving slightly more mass (as shown) on the aft end alters the kite's center of gravity. The extra

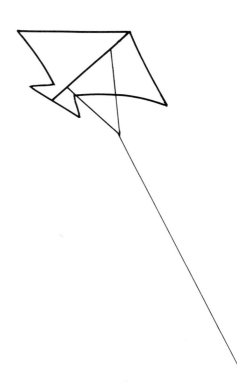

Illus. 350. Detail 3—in flight.

weight on the spine's aft end allows the kite to develop the desired spin when line is slack. Notch the fore end that is used to secure the leading-edge framing string later.

Next, form a slight curve in the spine by gently and carefully flexing it over a flame. The bend should begin 3¾″ down from the notched tip and stop in about the middle of the spine, or 10″ from the fore end.

2. Prepare the ³⁄₃₂″ × 27⅝″ fibreglass bow by notching both ends slightly with a fine-tooth hobby saw. Notched ends must face the same direction. (See Step 12.)

Tip: Before cutting fibreglass rod, measure and mark the length. Position the bow precisely be-

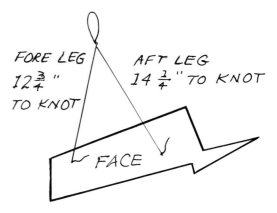

Illus. 351. Detail 4.

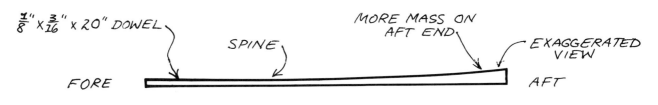

Illus. 352. Step 1.

tween the marks on the wing tips; the bow should intersect 3¾″ down from the top of the spine (see Step 9). If the bow doesn't fit exactly, make some adjustments until it fits and then mark the position. Now, cut the bow to size. The intersection of the bow at the spine can vary to a slight degree; try ⅕ × the spine length—4″ down from the nose of the spine in this case—to note any performance differences. The bow-spine intersect point, however, should not exceed ⅙ × the spine length.

3. See Illus. 353. Fold a piece of 20″ × 30″ tissue paper in half the short way. The kite body and stabilizer fin are cut from one piece of tissue paper.

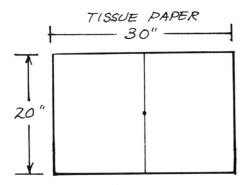

Illus. 353. Step 3.

4. See Illus. 354. Locate the midpoint of 20″ (10″) and make a mark along the fold line. Measure and mark 12½″ outward at a 90° angle from the 10″

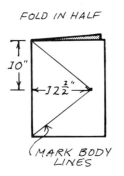

Illus. 354. Step 4.

reference point. Use a straightedge and draw connecting lines from the 12½″ point to the fore and aft tips of the 20″ fold line. When cut and opened up, the wingspan will be 24″ with a ½″ overlap hem all around.

5. See Illus. 355. Measure and mark 5″ up and 5″ out at 90° from the aft point along the fold line. Use a straightedge and connect the reference points with a diagonal line. This forms the stabilizer fin.

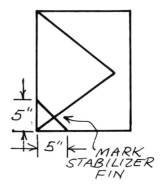

Illus. 355. Step 5.

6. See Illus. 356. With a butter knife and straightedge, score ½″ in from the edge along the pencil outline to form the hem fold. Use a soft-tip pen to mark 12″ from the fold line to the wing tip. Ink should go through both layers of the tissue paper for symmetry.

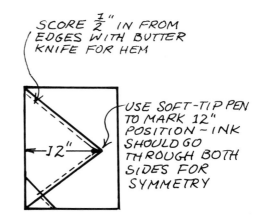

Illus. 356. Step 6.

228

7. See Illus. 357. Keep the tissue paper folded in half for symmetry; then cut along the pencil lines to produce the kite shape.

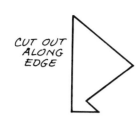

CUT OUT ALONG EDGE

Illus. 357. Step 7.

8. See Illus. 358. Unfold the half-pattern and check to be sure that the score line is ½″ in from the kite perimeter. The bow will fit between the soft-tip pen reference points marked 24″ between the wing tips.

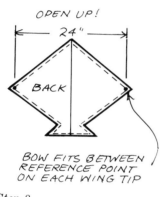

OPEN UP!

24″

BACK

BOW FITS BETWEEN
REFERENCE POINT
ON EACH WING TIP

Illus. 358. Step 8.

9. See the sail cutouts in Illus. 359.

10. See Illus. 360. Cement the spine along the fold line with the notched, narrower end forward. The heated curve in the spine should face the back of the kite. You may add loose-leaf reinforcements to the face of the kite later—or for a more aesthetic look, add them to the back of the kite now. Glue them in position before cementing down the spine. Place one 5″ up from the aft section of the spine and the other at the bow-spine intersection—measured by using the following formula: $\frac{3}{16} \times$ the length of the spine (20″) or 3¾″ from the top of the spine.

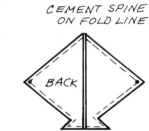

CEMENT SPINE
ON FOLD LINE

BACK

Illus. 360. Step 10.

11. See Illus. 361. Fold hems on the score line along the trailing edges. Take about 5′ of cotton thread and carefully cement the thread (apply some ten-

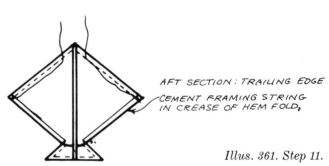

AFT SECTION: TRAILING EDGE
CEMENT FRAMING STRING
IN CREASE OF HEM FOLD;

Illus. 361. Step 11.

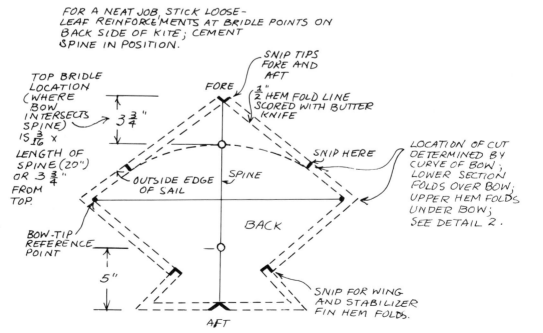

FOR A NEAT JOB, STICK LOOSE-
LEAF REINFORCEMENTS AT BRIDLE POINTS ON
BACK SIDE OF KITE; CEMENT
SPINE IN POSITION.

TOP BRIDLE
LOCATION
(WHERE
BOW
INTERSECTS
SPINE)
IS $\frac{3}{16}$ ×
LENGTH OF
SPINE (20″)
OR 3¾″
FROM
TOP.

3¾″

BOW-TIP
REFERENCE
POINT

5″

OUTSIDE EDGE
OF SAIL

SPINE

BACK

FORE

SNIP TIPS
FORE AND
AFT

½″ HEM FOLD LINE
SCORED WITH BUTTER
KNIFE

SNIP HERE

LOCATION OF CUT
DETERMINED BY
CURVE OF BOW;
LOWER SECTION
FOLDS OVER BOW;
UPPER HEM FOLDS
UNDER BOW;
SEE DETAIL 2.

SNIP FOR WING
AND STABILIZER
FIN HEM FOLDS.

AFT

Illus. 359. Step 9.

sion) into the score line as close to the crease as possible. Use a butter knife or similar tool to push the thread inward.

12. See Illus. 362. Tie a length of string between the notched ends of the fibreglass bow until it assumes the curve it will take on the kite between wing tips. The depth of the strung bow should be ±6″ and the distance from end to end should be 24″.

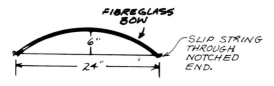

FIBREGLASS BOW

6″

24″

SLIP STRING THROUGH NOTCHED END.

Illus. 362. Step 12.

13. See Illus. 363. Position the bow onto the kite as shown. Slip the trailing-edge framing string upwards into the notches of the strung bow. Cement it in position using a trailing-edge overlap hem at the wing tips. Let dry!

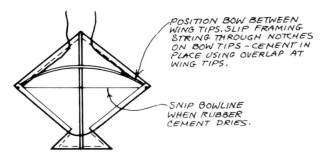

POSITION BOW BETWEEN WING TIPS. SLIP FRAMING STRING THROUGH NOTCHES ON BOW TIPS - CEMENT IN PLACE USING OVERLAP AT WING TIPS.

SNIP BOWLINE WHEN RUBBER CEMENT DRIES.

Illus. 363. Step 13.

14. See Illus. 364. Take both ends of the framing string that passed through the notches on the

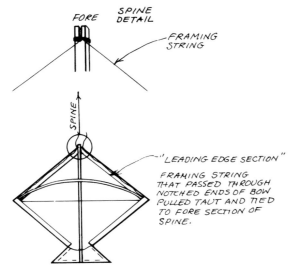

SPINE DETAIL
FORE

FRAMING STRING

SPINE

"LEADING EDGE SECTION"

FRAMING STRING THAT PASSED THROUGH NOTCHED ENDS OF BOW PULLED TAUT AND TIED TO FORE SECTION OF SPINE.

Illus. 364. Step 14.

strung bow, pull them taut along the fold line, and then tie them at the forward notch of the spine.

15. See Illus. 365. Fold the leading-edge hems along the score lines. Cement the framing string as close as possible within the crease. The hem edge should be snipped where the bow curves away from the leading edge. (See Step 9 and the main design view.) Fold and cement the upper part of the leading edge first; then finish by folding the remainder over the bow at the wing tip. The hem fold over the bow must be equal on both sides.

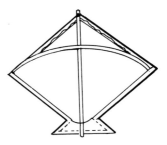

Illus. 365. Step 15.

16. See Illus. 349. Reinforce the wing tips and the fore and aft sections of the spine by cementing small squares of tissue paper in the positions shown in the main design.

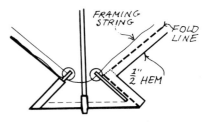

FRAMING STRING

FOLD LINE

½ HEM

Illus. 366. Step 17.

17. See Illus. 366. Snip and fold along the score lines of the stabilizer on both sides. Add circular tissue paper patches for the batten tip. Cement bamboo battens into the crease and fold over the hem.

SNIP OFF REMAINING FRAMING STRING

Illus. 367. Step 18.

Tip: For balanced symmetrical battens, plane both battens together several times on each side, turn them over, and plane the other side; then repeat this procedure until you achieve the desired width. Note: Battens should be thinner (±1/32") towards the spine and slightly heavier (±1/16") as they flare outward.

18. See Illus. 367. Cut two rectangular pieces of tissue paper 1" × 4" and cement them over the bamboo battens on the back of the kite. Fold over the excess and cement as shown. Fold and cement the trailing edge of the stabilizer along the score line.

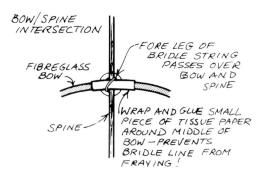

Illus. 368. Step 19.

19. See Illus. 368. To prevent the cotton bridle line from fraying and breaking under stress during flight, wrap and cement a small piece of tissue paper (or tape) around the midsection of the bow.
20. Glue two notebook reinforcements along the spine on the kite back, as shown in Illus. 359.
21. Connect the bridle string with slip knots at the positions shown in Detail 4. The foreleg of the bridle goes around both the spine and bow.

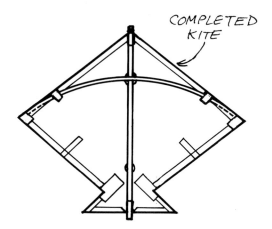

Illus. 369. Completed kite.

The Nagasaki Hata Fighter

Design: Courtesy of Caleb Crowell

A Simplified Version

Like most small Asian fighting kites, the Nagasaki *hata* is basically a square flown diagonally on edge. Its spine and bow are hand-crafted by master Japanese kite makers from high-quality bamboo. Lightweight *washi*, or rice paper, is pieced and glued for the sail, and then decorated in traditional color schemes. As an authentic Nagasaki *hata* fighter kite is difficult to obtain, this design (shown in Illus. 370) is for those who don't mind a variation.

Materials

To make this kite you need:

- two 1/8" × 36" hardwood dowels—wood dowel will warp in humid conditions, so fly in dry weather only for best results (option: in addition to being warp resistant, a 3/32" fibreglass bow will provide uniformly greater flex for a faster kite),
- Scotch transparent and strapping tape,
- rubber cement,
- a 20" × 30" sheet of tissue paper,
- button and carpet thread—for bridle,
- regular sewing thread—for tassels,
- hobby knife,
- scissors,
- ruler or yardstick,
- sewing needle,
- loose-leaf page reinforcements,
- two 4" × ±1/32" fin battens—cut and sanded to size from flat party toothpicks or bamboo slivers, and
- (optional) crepe paper streamers.

Construction

Follow Steps 1–5 using Illus. 370 and 371 for reference. Note: You can enhance this kite by employing some of the techniques for the Szilagi Fighter.

1. Fold, measure, and cut the body of the kite to the dimensions indicated.
2. Cut two rectangles from scrap for the tassels. Fringe the edges as shown.
3. Notch the ends of the bow for the tassel string. Tie on strands of sewing thread and cut them to length.
4. Roll fringed pieces around a scrap of dowel. Tie to wing-tip strings and form tassels. Add optional streamers as shown.
5. Fix the bridle and fly!

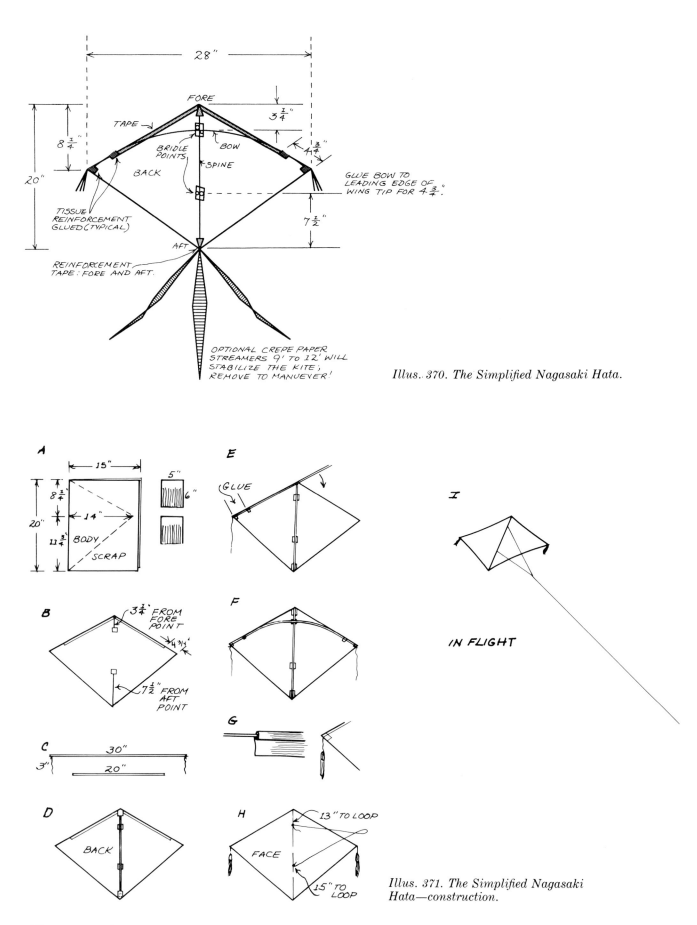

28"

FORE

TAPE

3 1/4"

BRIDLE POINTS

BOW

3/4"

SPINE

8 1/4"

BACK

20"

GLUE BOW TO
LEADING EDGE OF
WING TIP FOR 4 3/4".

TISSUE
REINFORCEMENT
GLUED (TYPICAL)

7 1/2"

AFT

REINFORCEMENT
TAPE: FORE AND AFT.

OPTIONAL CREPE PAPER
STREAMERS 9' TO 12' WILL
STABILIZE THE KITE;
REMOVE TO MANUEVER!

Illus. 370. The Simplified Nagasaki Hata.

A

15"

5"

8 1/4"

6"

20"

14"

11 3/4"

BODY

SCRAP

E

GLUE

I

B

3 1/4" FROM
FORE
POINT

4 3/4"

7 1/2" FROM
AFT
POINT

F

IN FLIGHT

C

30"

3"

20"

G

D

BACK

H

13" TO LOOP

FACE

15" TO
LOOP

Illus. 371. The Simplified Nagasaki
Hata—construction.

¹Tips, courtesy of Grandmaster Kites.

50
The Delta Kite Portfolio

Delta is a symmetrical triangle symbolizing the fourth letter of the Greek alphabet. Delta refers, as well, to the rich, fertile plains, often shaped like a triangle, formed at the mouth of rivers. It's also one of the generic kite forms. To see three variations of the triangular delta kite in color, turn to pages M (bottom) and O.

"The delta design is extremely versatile and there is great scope for individuality, ingenuity, and experimentation," says aeronautical engineer and kite experimenter Dan Leigh, who has been building and refining exquisite delta kites for years. American-born Leigh of Wales generally focuses on light-wind designs. His kites incorporate maximum lift with minimal additional drag. Leigh says his fascination with delta kites has to do with the "lovely way they turn and move in the sky."

For a given design, Leigh opts for a tow point that falls vertically as far towards the rear of the kite as possible while still maintaining reasonable handling. As each design element affects every other element, compromises are made along the way. For example, to design a delta for the highest maximum wind range, light-wind performance (more lift with less drag) is sacrificed. Naturally, the converse is also true. When designing a kite, you need to consider what type of kite you want.

Construction

You can apply Leigh's construction methods that follow to other delta designs featured in this book or designs of your own.

Centerfold:
• To ensure symmetry of the sail, work outward from the centerline on both wing halves at the same time. A single piece of sail material is folded in half with the outline of the kite suitably marked; the centerline is along the fold. To baste sections together for ease of sewing and cutting, Leigh uses a clear glue (a hot tacker achieves the same results) along the inside edge of the spine sleeve. He also glues the trailing edge just outside the finished edge line, which isn't cut until the centerline straight stitch forming the spine sleeve is done.

Spine:
• Having the spine on the underside (face) of the kite achieves two purposes. The spine sleeve provides a strip on which to sew the keel, and the spine can be fitted just tight enough to stretch the stitching

along the centerline so as to assume a slight curve or positive camber.

Spars:
• It is very important to carefully match a pair of wing spars that flex *exactly evenly*. Do this by hand. If the two spars don't flex equally, then the kite will lean or dive to one side in gusts. You could choose extremely stiff spars, but that would contribute to a skittishness, hampering low-level flying, especially on takeoffs and landings. While wood dowel is stiff and light, synthetic spar material like epoxy tubing or fibreglass rod (though heavier) is reliably uniform.

For any given delta design, use a spine that is the same diameter as the wing spar, and a spreader bar that is *one size larger* (use wood equivalent if wing spars are epoxy tubing or fibreglass rod). See Delta Designs, Examples A and B.

Keel:
• The basic keel should be flat when in the air without flapping along the leading edge. A single hem, double-stitched, with a strip of ripstop cut with the grain to reinforce the perimeter will stop any stretch on the bias.

For smaller deltas (60″ wingspan and under), the leading edge of the keel can be in line with the grain and a single stitch along a double-fold hem is adequate.

Experimental keels:
• Experimental keels allow towing-point adjustments that may be convenient for varying wind conditions and necessary for locating the fulcrum on untried and unusual designs. See Illus. 373.

Spreader bar:
• The position of the spreader bar can vary a great deal. For example, a stiff spar spreader can be relatively short and mounted well forward—while a long, more pliable spreader mounted well aft, possibly with flexible wing spars, may also be suitable. A retainer loop threaded around and over the spine helps keep lighter spreader bars from snapping in gusts. (See the detail in Illus. 378.)

If the spreader is too tight, the taut sail will cause the kite to dive, especially in higher winds. One way to gauge the right depth of the spreader bar is to hang the finished kite upside down and measure the gap between the centerline of the sail and the inside edge of the spreader bar. This distance divided by the distance from the kite nose to the spreader-bar attachment point on the wing

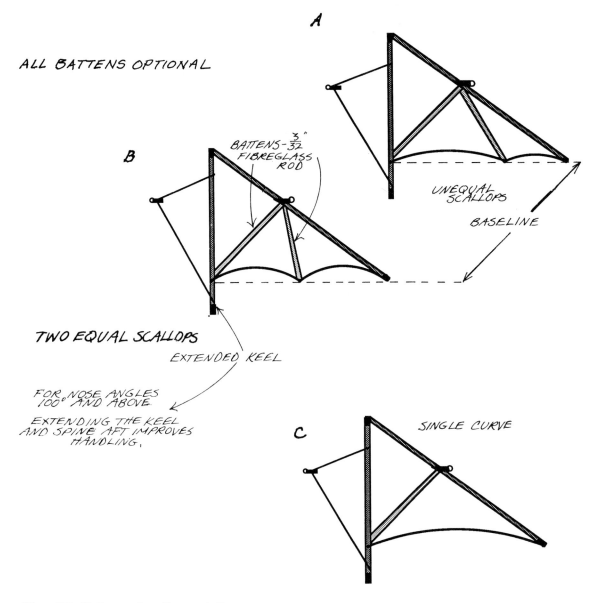

A

ALL BATTENS OPTIONAL

B

BATTENS-$\frac{3}{32}$"
FIBREGLASS
ROD

UNEQUAL
SCALLOPS

BASELINE

TWO EQUAL SCALLOPS

EXTENDED KEEL

FOR NOSE ANGLES
100° AND ABOVE.
EXTENDING THE KEEL
AND SPINE AFT IMPROVES
HANDLING.

C

SINGLE CURVE

Illus. 372. Batten and scallop variations.

leading edge can be expressed as a simple non-dimensional percentage. About 11 percent is average—while on smaller kites flown in higher winds, up to 14 percent or more is considered normal.

Towing point:

• The range shown for a standard delta with an ordinary keel allows for some variations in handling. Small deltas should have the towing point as close to the aft limit as possible.

The issue of placing two grommets at the tow point on the keel tip ostensibly for different wind conditions is questionable. A ½″ variation either way won't make a significant difference in performance. For a standard delta with the tow point, or fulcrum, at 50 percent of the centerline length, a second ring could go on halfway up the front of the keel, at 37½″ of C, as shown in Illus. 373.

Designing your own kite:

• Wing spars are a major consideration. Deltas made with ¼″ × 36″ hardwood-dowel wing spars will be fast and snappy to control; those with ¼″ × 39″ spars will behave over a wider wind range. Spars that are ¼″ × 44″ to 45″ will give maximum light-wind performance without excess flex. Leigh reports successfully using ¼″ × 52″ spars for light-wind deltas.

The extra weight and flex of fibreglass rod and epoxy tubing may indicate a narrower nose angle and spreader bar relatively aftwards.

The basic design relationship will work for wood or synthetic spars. The scale, however, might vary. Fibreglass wing spars may be slightly smaller than equivalent wood spars. See Illus. 374.

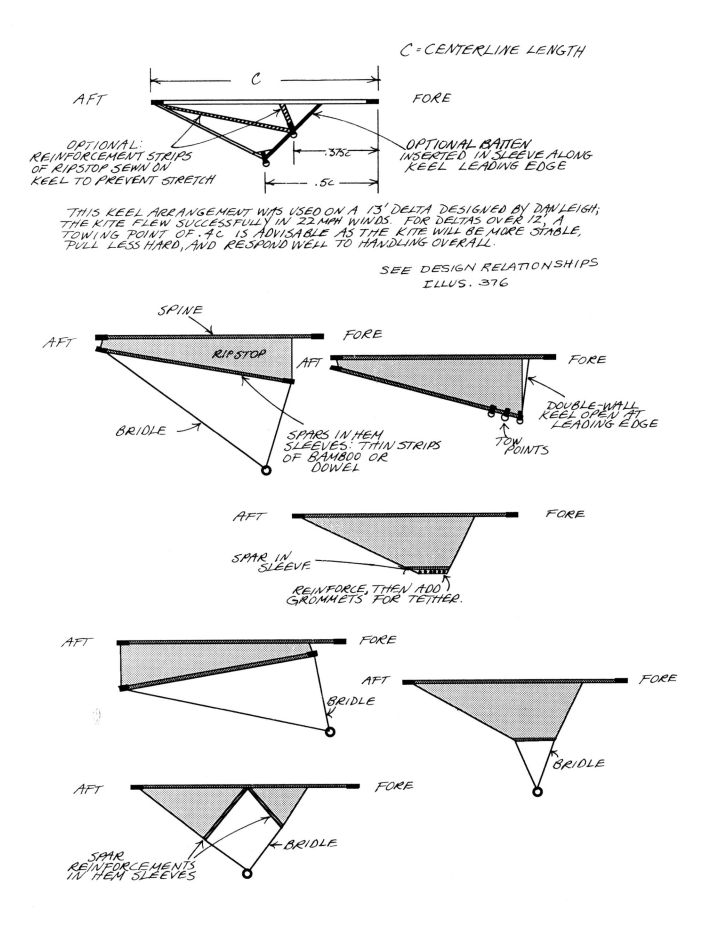

C = CENTERLINE LENGTH

AFT

C

FORE

OPTIONAL:
REINFORCEMENT STRIPS
OF RIPSTOP SEWN ON
KEEL TO PREVENT STRETCH

.375C

.5C

OPTIONAL BATTEN
INSERTED IN SLEEVE ALONG
KEEL LEADING EDGE

THIS KEEL ARRANGEMENT WAS USED ON A 13' DELTA DESIGNED BY DAN LEIGH;
THE KITE FLEW SUCCESSFULLY IN 22 MPH WINDS. FOR DELTAS OVER 12', A
TOWING POINT OF .4C IS ADVISABLE AS THE KITE WILL BE MORE STABLE,
PULL LESS HARD, AND RESPOND WELL TO HANDLING OVERALL.

SEE DESIGN RELATIONSHIPS
ILLUS. 376

SPINE

AFT

RIPSTOP

FORE

AFT

FORE

BRIDLE

SPARS IN HEM
SLEEVES: THIN STRIPS
OF BAMBOO OR
DOWEL

TOW
POINTS

DOUBLE-WALL
KEEL OPEN AT
LEADING EDGE

AFT

FORE

SPAR IN
SLEEVE

REINFORCE, THEN ADD
GROMMETS FOR TETHER.

AFT

FORE

BRIDLE

AFT

FORE

BRIDLE

AFT

FORE

BRIDLE

SPAR
REINFORCEMENTS
IN HEM SLEEVES

Illus. 373. Keels for experimental deltas. Note: All tow points are adjustable.

Smaller deltas:

- Smaller deltas may require additional drag for stability such as a uniform fringe along the trailing edge. Add wing-tip streamers to tiny deltas.

Nose angle:

- Deltas with nose angles of 100° are considered a high-aspect-ratio design that sacrifices some stability for increased lifting efficiency. (For more information on aspect ratio, see pages 127–128 in "The Rhomboid Box Kite.") One solution in counteracting instability on high-aspect-ratio designs is extending the keel beyond the trailing edge. (See Illus. 378.) High-performance hang gliders successfully incorporate this method. The pilot on board acts as the tethered keel to stabilize the fixed wing (a series of battens produce a sophisticated cambered airfoil) at the proper angle. With delta kites that are essentially flat, the spine extending beyond the trailing edge shifts the center of gravity slightly to the rear for a balanced stall; this configuration also allows the deeper stabilizing keel to assume a standard shape.

Battens:

- See Illus. 375. Battens or stiffeners can be used to extend the wing surface. By slightly stretching the outboard part of the wing, a batten prevents the sail from rustling in the wind. The batten and scallop variations in Illus. 372 are based on proven performers. Start with these designs to familiarize yourself with kite performance with and without battens. Flexible fibreglass rods of 3/32" to 1/8" diameter are suitable battens for medium-sized deltas.

A distinction should be made between battens on piloted crafts and those on kites. Battens on kites hold, as opposed to stretching the fabric surface taut as on yacht sails, sailboards, and hang gliders. Whether battens on kites actually improve performance is debatable.

WOOD SPAR DIAMETER	RECOMMENDED WING-SPAR LENGTH	EPOXY TUBING DIAMETER	FIBREGLASS ROD DIAMETER	RECOMMENDED WING-SPAR LENGTH	RECOMMENDED NOSE ANGLE
$\frac{5}{16}$"	54"–60"	.298–.317	.300	50"	98–104°
$\frac{1}{4}$"	36"–48"	.250–.261	.250	41"	90–200°
				34"	90–94°
$\frac{3}{16}$"	27"–36"		.186	25$\frac{1}{2}$"	90°
$\frac{1}{8}$"	17"–24"		.125	17$\frac{1}{2}$"	90°
FOR LARGER DELTAS:					
$\frac{3}{8}$"	60"–82"	.370			90°*
$\frac{1}{2}$"	84"–96"	.505			90°

ON LARGER DELTAS, PLAN ON A NOSE ANGLE OF 90° AND A FORWARD TOW POINT (.40–.42; "B" ON LEGEND) FOR A KITE THAT WILL OPERATE SAFELY IN A WIDE WIND RANGE.

REMEMBER: HIGHER NOSE ANGLE KITES HAVE A CORRESPONDING HIGHER ASPECT RATIO: HIGHER LIFT EFFICIENCY AT THE EXPENSE OF STABILITY.

RECOMMENDATIONS: COURTESY OF DAN LEIGH

Illus. 374. Spar equivalents and recommended nose angles.

* – UP TO 103° ON HIGH-ASPECT RATIO EXTENDED-KEEL DELTAS

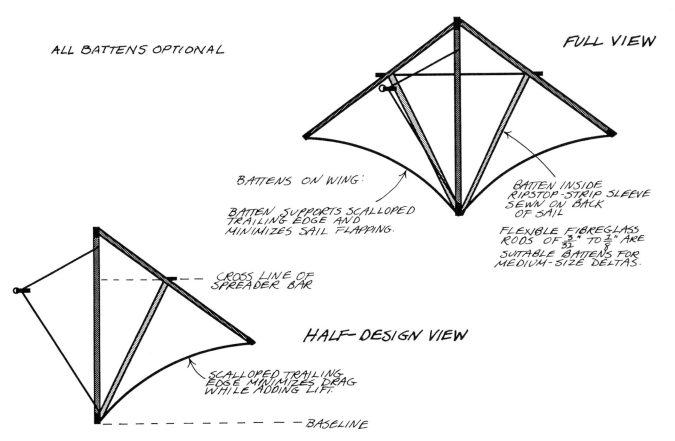

ALL BATTENS OPTIONAL

FULL VIEW

BATTENS ON WING:

BATTEN SUPPORTS SCALLOPED
TRAILING EDGE AND
MINIMIZES SAIL FLAPPING.

BATTEN INSIDE
RIPSTOP-STRIP SLEEVE
SEWN ON BACK
OF SAIL

FLEXIBLE FIBREGLASS
RODS OF $\frac{3}{32}$" TO $\frac{1}{8}$" ARE
SUITABLE BATTENS FOR
MEDIUM-SIZE DELTAS.

CROSS LINE OF
SPREADER BAR

HALF-DESIGN VIEW

SCALLOPED TRAILING
EDGE MINIMIZES DRAG
WHILE ADDING LIFT.

— — — — — — — — — BASELINE

Illus. 375. Single batten and wing scallop.

Delta Designs

Use the following legend to understand Dan Leigh's basic delta design in Illus. 376.

Hc = *height of canopy*
S/2 = *half wing span*
B = *towing point position*
Dk = *depth of fin or keel*
Lk = *length of fin or keel*
Le = *length of leading edge*
Ls = *length of wing spar*
S.B. = *distance from wing tip to spreader-bar attachment point*

Design relationships:
S/2 = 1.0 to 1.15 × Hc (up to ⅓ x with extended keels)
B = 0.4 to 0.5 Hc (0.5 for small kites)
Ls = 0.75 × L.E.
S.B. = 7/9 Ls
Lk = 0.75 Hc
Dk = S/6 or ⅓ (S/2)

Build two deltas based upon the dimensions given in the following examples and compare their perfor-

mance under different flight conditions. Additional designs for delta variations are also in this section (see Illus. 377–379). First-hand experimentation will allow you to discover the benefits and drawbacks of different design relationships. This way you'll have the option of deciding which flight characteristics suit you best.

Example A:
Wing spars = ¼" × 39" hardwood dowel (Ls = 39")
Hc = 35"
S/2 = 40"
B = 17" or 17½"
Lk = 26¼"
Dk = 13⅓"
S.B. = 30⅓"
Sleeves = 1"
Spreader bar = ⁵⁄₁₆" diameter hardwood dowel
Spine = ¼" diameter hardwood dowel
Nose angle = 97.6°

Example B:
Wing spars = ½" × 84" hardwood dowel (Ls = 84")
Hc = 80"
S/2 = 80"
Lk = 60"
Dk = 26"

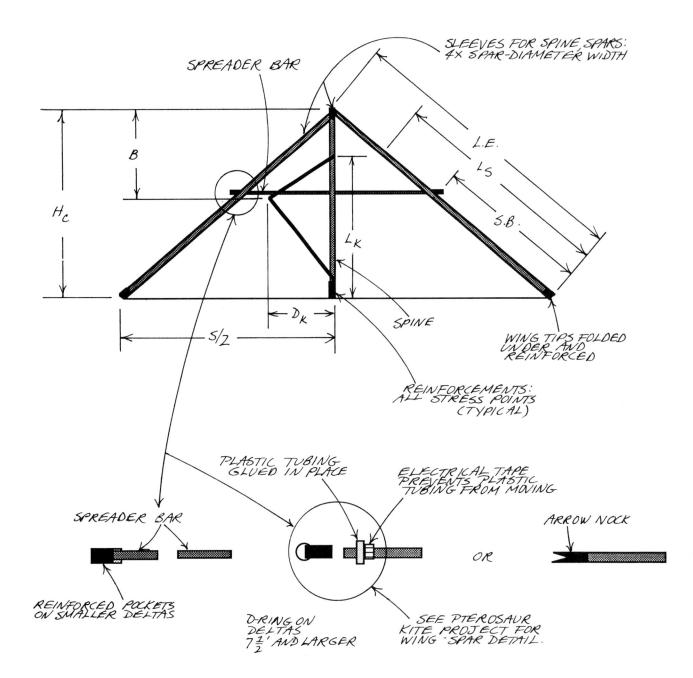

SLEEVES FOR SPINE, SPARS:
4X SPAR-DIAMETER WIDTH

SPREADER BAR

L.E.

L.S.

S.B.

B

H_c

L_K

SPINE

D_K

S/2

WING TIPS FOLDED
UNDER AND
REINFORCED

REINFORCEMENTS:
ALL STRESS POINTS
(TYPICAL)

PLASTIC TUBING
GLUED IN PLACE

ELECTRICAL TAPE
PREVENTS PLASTIC
TUBING FROM MOVING

ARROW NOCK

SPREADER BAR

OR

REINFORCED POCKETS
ON SMALLER DELTAS

D-RING ON
DELTAS
$7\frac{1}{2}'$ AND LARGER

SEE PTEROSAUR
KITE PROJECT FOR
WING-SPAR DETAIL.

Illus. 376. Dan Leigh's basic delta.

S.B. = 65¾"
Sleeves = 2"
Spreader bar = ⅝" diameter hardwood dowel
Spine = ½" diameter hardwood dowel
Nose angle = 90°

Options for B—towing-point placement:
B = 40" (.5 Hc)
B = 36" (.45 Hc)
B = 34" (.425 Hc) (good overall balance point)
B = 32" (.40 Hc)

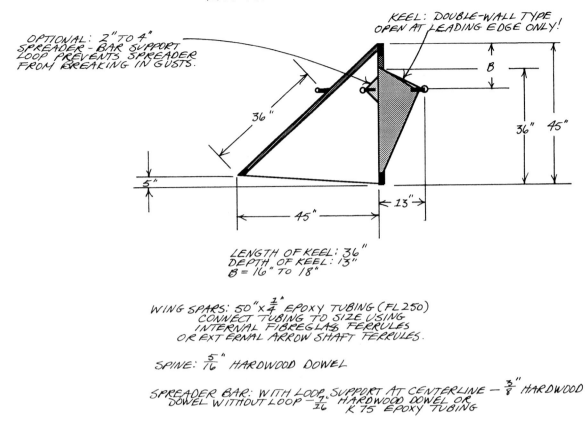

WIND RANGE: 10-18 MPH

OPTIONAL: 2" TO 4" SPREADER-BAR SUPPORT LOOP PREVENTS SPREADER FROM BREAKING IN GUSTS.

KEEL: DOUBLE-WALL TYPE OPEN AT LEADING EDGE ONLY!

B

36"

45"

36"

5"

45"

13"

LENGTH OF KEEL: 36"
DEPTH OF KEEL: 13"
B = 16" TO 18"

WING SPARS: 50" x $\frac{1}{4}$" EPOXY TUBING (FL 250) CONNECT TUBING TO SIZE USING INTERNAL FIBREGLASS FERRULES OR EXTERNAL ARROW SHAFT FERRULES.

SPINE: $\frac{5}{16}$" HARDWOOD DOWEL

SPREADER BAR: WITH LOOP SUPPORT AT CENTERLINE — $\frac{3}{8}$" HARDWOOD DOWEL WITHOUT LOOP — $\frac{7}{16}$" HARDWOOD DOWEL OR K 75 EPOXY TUBING

Illus. 377. Dan Leigh's Double-Wall Keel Delta.

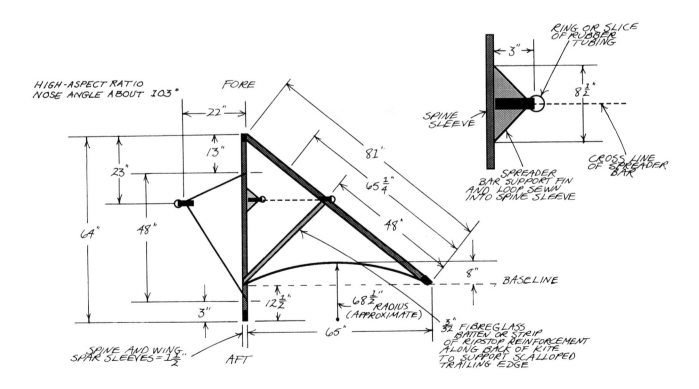

HIGH-ASPECT RATIO
NOSE ANGLE ABOUT 103°

FORE

22"

13"

23"

64"

48"

81"

65 $\frac{1}{4}$"

48"

8"

BASELINE

3"

12 $\frac{1}{2}$"

68 $\frac{1}{2}$" RADIUS (APPROXIMATE)

65"

$\frac{3}{32}$" FIBREGLASS BATTEN OR STRIP OF RIPSTOP REINFORCEMENT ALONG BACK OF KITE TO SUPPORT SCALLOPED TRAILING EDGE

SPINE AND WING SPAR SLEEVES = 1 $\frac{1}{2}$"

AFT

RING OR SLICE OF RUBBER TUBING

3"

8 $\frac{1}{2}$"

SPINE SLEEVE

CROSS LINE OF SPREADER BAR

SPREADER BAR SUPPORT FIN AND LOOP SEWN INTO SPINE SLEEVE

Illus. 378. An extended-keel delta, after Dan Leigh's design.

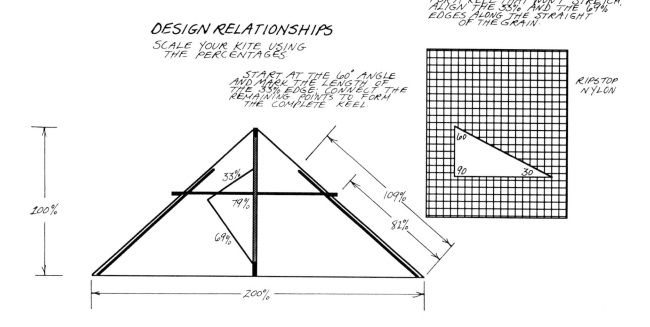

USE A RIGHT
TRIANGLE AS A
GUIDE IN FORMING THE KEEL.

FOR A KEEL THAT WON'T STRETCH,
ALIGN THE 33% AND THE 69%
EDGES ALONG THE STRAIGHT
OF THE GRAIN.

DESIGN RELATIONSHIPS
SCALE YOUR KITE USING
THE PERCENTAGES.

START AT THE 60° ANGLE
AND MARK THE LENGTH OF
THE 33% EDGE; CONNECT THE
REMAINING POINTS TO FORM
THE COMPLETE KEEL.

RIPSTOP
NYLON

33%

79%

69%

100%

109%

81%

200%

Illus. 379. Tony Cyphert's delta.

51
The Zephyr Delta Kite

Design: Courtesy of Ed Grauel

A Light-Wind Gentle Flier

A *zephyr* is a mild breeze as well a fine, light fabric; it's also a modification of the delta kite.

With a standard single flat keel, the delta glides forward whenever the wind pressure decreases; unless there is an updraft or a thermal, the resulting slack in the flying line may cause the kite to loop or dive out of control. In an attempt to reduce or eliminate the forward gliding, Ed Grauel devised a tapered two-sided keel as an air channel, open fore and aft. This addition alleviated most of the problem.

Not one to rest on his laurels, Grauel wondered what would happen if the open-channel keel was closed at the aft end to form a balloon-type keel.

Voilà! The change reduced any remaining tendency for the kite to glide forward. More importantly, the closed aft end produced a light-wind gentle flier—thus the name, Zephyr. See the Zephyr Delta in Illus. 382, and in color on page O (bottom).

Materials

To make this kite you need:

• 2 yards × 41″ of .75 oz. ripstop—for sail and keel (for a contrasting keel, obtain an additional yard of ripstop);

- three ³⁄₁₆″ hardwood dowels: one 33½″ for spine, two 28″ for wing spars;
- ¼″ × 36″ hardwood dowel cut to size—for spreader bar;
- 4 oz. Dacron-reinforcement material;
- ¼″ grommet—for tow point; and
- hardware—for spreader bar.

Details

- (Detail 1 in Illus. 380.) Main design.
- (Detail 2 also in Illus. 380.) Keel.
- (Detail 3 in Illus. 381.) Keel on kite.
- (Detail 4 in Illus. 382.) In flight.

Flight Data: Wind range: 3–21 mph
Line: 50 lb. test
AE: ±55°

Construction

Refer to the details as you go through these steps.

1. Making the sail: Fold a piece of ripstop in half along the centerline; mark all hem and sleeve allowances as well as the keel stitch lines on the kite face. Note: Decide which type of spreader-bar retainer you want and add the required reinforcements and hardware into the design *now.* Refer to the spreader-bar options in both "The Delta Kite Portfolio" and "Construction."

   Hem the wing sleeves first; the 6″ side flaps and trailing edge do not require hemming if hot-cut. Stitch the sleeve as shown. Leave a 1½-inch gap (lock-stitch the beginning and end of the gap in the seam) for inserting or removing the wing spars. Sew the ends shut. Use 4 oz. Dacron reinforcements and lock-stitch the lower wing tip, the fore

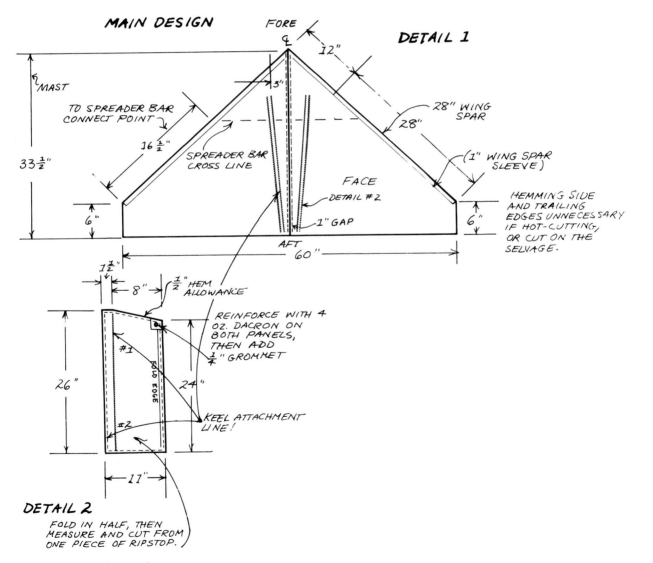

Illus. 380. Details 1 and 2.

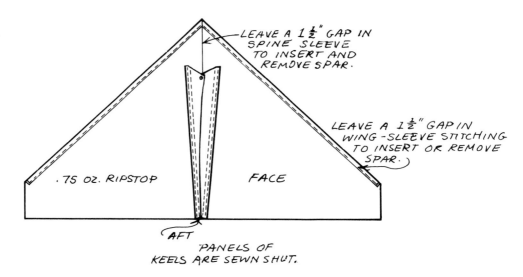

LEAVE A 1½" GAP IN
SPINE SLEEVE
TO INSERT AND
REMOVE SPAR.

LEAVE A 1½" GAP IN
WING-SLEEVE STITCHING
TO INSERT OR REMOVE
SPAR.

.75 OZ. RIPSTOP   FACE

AFT
PANELS OF
KEELS ARE SEWN SHUT.

Illus. 381. Detail 3.

and aft ends of the spine sleeve, and other stress points likely to encounter wear.

2. Making the keel: Fold a piece of ripstop in half and follow the basic instructions in Step 1. Use a ¼" double-fold hem all around, and reinforce the area to receive the tow grommet with 4 oz. Dacron. Run a stitch ½" in from the fold line along the keel length. The finished keel width measures 8" from stitch #1 to the leading-edge stitch along the fold line.

3. Fold the sail in half (the back sides together) along the centerline and run a stitch ½" in from the middle to form the spine sleeve. Hot-tacking along the middle sleeve stitch line aids sewing.

4. Align the keel placement lines. Hot-tack the keel attachment lines #1 to the sail and stitch in place. Repeat for keel attachment lines #2.

5. Insert the wing dowels and spine, and fit the spreader bar to keep the kite flat—but not too taut; the kite sail should be able to pocket naturally in the wind.

6. Attach the flying line and enjoy!

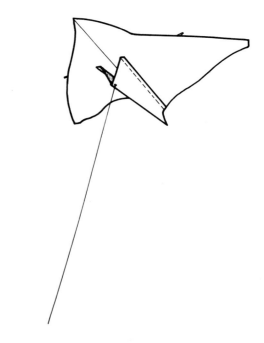

Illus. 382. Detail 4—in flight.

52
The Trefoil Delta Kite

Design: Courtesy of Helen Bushell

A Hydrodynamic Spin-Off

Helen Bushell is a galvanizing force behind the Australian Kite Association with an admitted antipathy towards ventral keels on kites. The problem with conventional deltas, according to Bushell, is that the extended ventral keel throws the kite off course by presenting a curved leading edge to the headwind. The central mast, or spine, support for the spreader bar also holds the sail flat, preventing the kite from conforming to the air flow.

Building on the experimental work of others, Bushell spent over 20 years utilizing her understanding of nautical design principles before patenting the Australian Evolution Trefoil in the mid 1970s. *Trefoil* describes the innovative physical properties of the kite: Two wings are stitched together along a line parallel to a mast that has been placed forward *within* the keel. This configuration produces three working foils (trefoil) joined in the middle along an aerodynamic curve.

By repositioning the mast within the keel, the need for a central support was eliminated, allowing the kite to divide the wind more efficiently without distorting the integrity of the sail. Because the kite had a tendency to overfly and bow at the newly formed mast, Bushell ingeniously corrected the problem by sewing a curve into the wing along the length of the keel.

Bushell reports that the concept for the kite was perhaps an unexpected spin-off from the time she spent at the Chelsea Yacht Club in Australia during the 1960s when winning the America's Cup was everyone's foremost passion. The kite was born in "an atmosphere buzzing with hydrodynamics," says Bushell, and sketches of hull and sail designs.

* * *

Though some kite makers have reported varying degrees of success in building Bushell's Trefoil Delta, mine have all flown well—and here's the reason why. While all deltas rely on a fixed tow point (the keel tip on standard types), the Trefoil Delta is a trifle more sensitive to the *precise placement of the fulcrum* along the mast. But if you cut, sew, and position the fulcrum accurately, you will be rewarded with a lively and capable flier. (See the Trefoil Delta in Illus. 389, and in color on page P.)

With dowels for support during the summer, the Trefoil Delta is light enough to hover overhead in the still air of a thermal. But with a quick change to epoxy spars, it can weather rougher going all year round. The cut of the sail calls for orienting the straight of the weave along the unsupported trailing aft edge—a technique used in sail making to minimize stretch and distortion while getting the most power from minimal wind conditions.

Materials

To make this kite you need:

- 2 yards of .75 oz. ripstop;
- ¼" metal grommets;
- 4 oz. Dacron or 1.5 oz. ripstop—for reinforcement material;
- four 36" × ¼" hardwood dowels—for mast, spreader bar, and wing spars—when light-wind flying and thermal soaring (Helen Bushell uses Australian mountain ash for the mast and spars, since it's light, stiff, and stronger than what's available in Europe or the United States) (option: for a Trefoil that will endure heavier winds, substitute A20 [.260 O.D.] epoxy tubing for dowels);
- two ⁹⁄₁₆" split rings; and
- ³⁄₁₆" semirigid plastic tubing—for wing-spar connectors.

An alternate method for making the wing spreader bar involves using two rubber grommets or washers that fit tightly over ¼" dowel, and four slices of polypropylene tubing.

Details

For Details 1–5, see Illus. 383. For Details 4a, 6, and 7, see Illus. 384. Other illustrations are specifically noted.

- (Detail 1.) Kite half-pattern.
- (Detail 2.) Camber line. Plot and connect the reference points for depth; stitch the wings together to form an aerodynamic curve.
- (Detail 3.) 5" gap in stitching along the sleeve for inserting or removing the mast. Fore and aft ends:

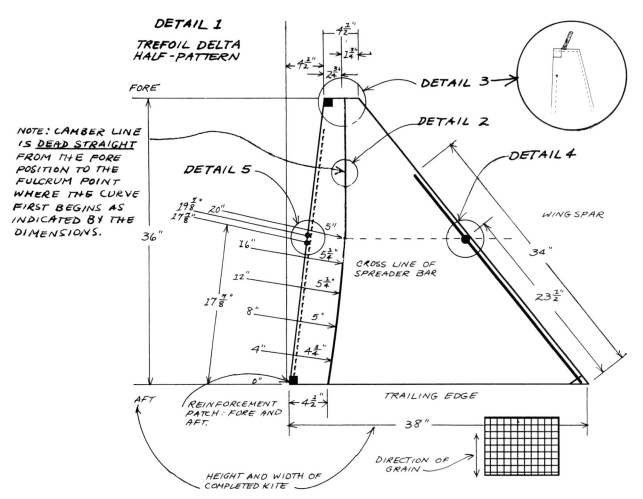

DETAIL 1

TREFOIL DELTA HALF-PATTERN

FORE

NOTE: CAMBER LINE IS <u>DEAD STRAIGHT</u> FROM THE FORE POSITION TO THE FULCRUM POINT WHERE THE CURVE FIRST BEGINS AS INDICATED BY THE DIMENSIONS.

DETAIL 3

DETAIL 2

DETAIL 4

WING SPAR

DETAIL 5

$4\frac{1}{2}$"
$4\frac{1}{2}$"
$1\frac{3}{4}$"
$2\frac{3}{4}$"

$29\frac{7}{8}$" 20"
$17\frac{7}{8}$"
16"
12"
8"
4"

5"
$5\frac{1}{4}$"
$5\frac{1}{4}$"
5"
$4\frac{3}{4}$"

36"

$17\frac{7}{8}$"

34"

$23\frac{1}{2}$"

CROSS LINE OF SPREADER BAR

AFT

REINFORCEMENT PATCH: FORE AND AFT.

$4\frac{1}{2}$"

0"

TRAILING EDGE

38"

DIRECTION OF GRAIN

HEIGHT AND WIDTH OF COMPLETED KITE

Illus. 383. Details 1–5.

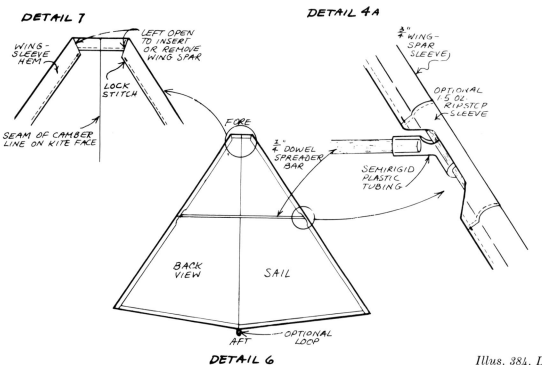

DETAIL 7

WING-SLEEVE HEM

LEFT OPEN TO INSERT OR REMOVE WING SPAR

LOCK STITCH

SEAM OF CAMBER LINE ON KITE FACE

DETAIL 4a

$\frac{3}{4}$" WING-SPAR SLEEVE)

OPTIONAL 1.5 OZ. RIPSTOP SLEEVE

$\frac{1}{4}$" DOWEL SPREADER BAR

SEMIRIGID PLASTIC TUBING

FORE

BACK VIEW

SAIL

AFT

OPTIONAL LOOP

DETAIL 6

Illus. 384. Details 4a, 6, and 7.

stitch reinforcements on two sides only; do not close off the mast spar sleeve.

- (Detail 4a.) ¾" wing-spar sleeve; ³⁄₁₆" I.D. semirigid plastic-tubing spreader-bar connector; ¼" dowel spreader; optional 1.5 oz. ripstop reinforcement inside the sleeve.
- (Detail 4b in Illus. 385.) Alternate method: key ring through the wing-spar sleeve; each end of the spreader bar has a rubber grommet or washer sandwiched between the two slices of tight-fitting polypropylene tubing; the inside slice checks grommet movement; remove the outside slice and position the end through the key ring; replacing the outside slice locks the spreader bar in place.

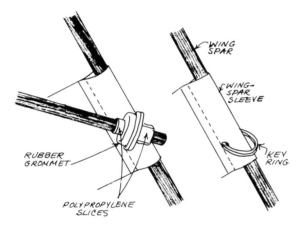

Illus. 385. Detail 4b.

- (Detail 5a in Illus. 386.) Tow points. Reinforce the sail material before inserting the grommets.

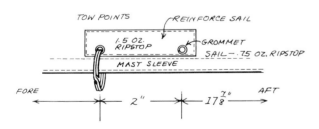

Illus. 386. Detail 5a.

- (Detail 5b in Illus. 387.) Alternate method: the key ring directly through the fabric over the mast, as with the wing spar.

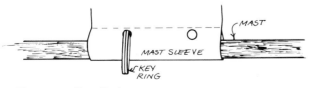

Illus. 387. Detail 5b.

Attach a single-line tether to the fulcrum, the precise balance point of the kite. Lower the position for light winds; raise it for breezier conditions.

- (Detail 6.) Sail, back view. The spreader bar should fit loosely between the sail spar connectors. There is an optional loop for attaching a stabilizing tail or spinner in heavier winds.
- (Detail 7.) Fore section, back view. The wing-sleeve hem—left open to insert or remove the wing spar; the seam of the camber line on the face of the kite.
- (Detail 8 in Illus. 388.) Flight configurations. Trefoil—three working foils joined in the middle along an aerodynamic curve; head-on elevation—wing spars, and mast positioned forward within the keel; end elevation; side elevation—fore and aft; and in–flight view—side elevation.
- (Detail 9 in Illus. 389.) In flight.

Flight Data: Wind range: 2–12 mph
Line: 50 lb. test
AE ±70°

Construction

Refer to the details as you go through these steps.

Hot-cutting:

1. Make a half-pattern template of the kite and allow for the following: Add 1" to the height for the ½" hems, fore and aft; and add 2" to the width for the ¾" wing sleeves, the ½" mast sleeve, plus ½" to cover the ¼" hot-cut trim and the ¼" sail seam—for a sail measuring 37" in height × 40" in width as shown. The *finished* hemmed half-pattern is 36" × 38".

   Fold the ripstop in half with the glossier sides (the kite's face) meeting inward. Position the template so that the straight of the weave is aligned with the trailing edge. Begin with a rough cut *several inches larger* than the 37" height × 40".

Sewing:

2. Connect the rough-cut sail halves with a sail seam along the length of the mast. Open the sail halves and fold them in the opposite direction along the stitch line. After making sure that the sail is perfectly flat, use a pencil and straightedge to draw a parallel line ½" from the seam.

Hot-cutting:

3. Hot-tack the two wing halves along the pencil guideline.
4. Align the trailing edge of the template with the grain and hot-cut the rest of the sail to the overall dimensions of 37" × 40".

Sewing:

5. Open the sail halves and hem (turned towards the back) the fore and aft ends. Finish the fore end as shown in Detail 7. Next, fold the sail in half again and sew along the pencil guideline to form the

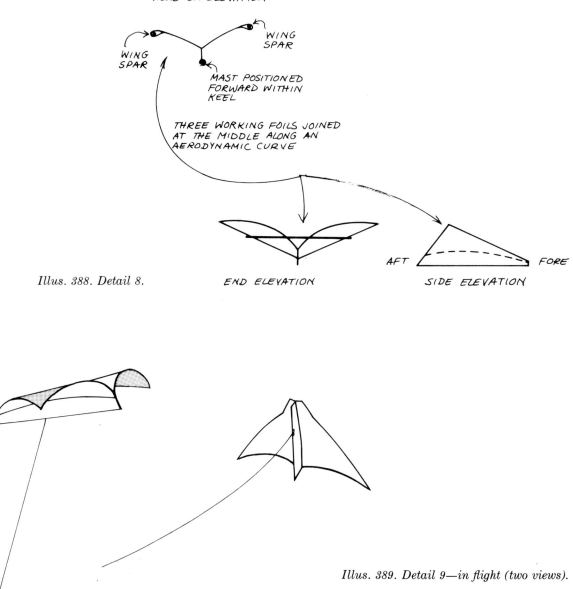

Illus. 388. Detail 8.

Illus. 389. Detail 9—in flight (two views).

mast sleeve; sew over the hot-tack marks for a neat job. Allow about a 5″ gap in the stitching at the fore end for inserting or removing the mast spar. Add reinforcement to strengthen the tow point and the fore and aft ends.

6. Reinforce the spreader-bar points inside the wing sleeve before forming the ¾″ wing-sleeve hem. Lock-stitch the top and close the bottom of the wing sleeves by sewing over the folded wing tip.

7. Measure, mark, and connect the points, establishing the depth of the kite's camber line. Tip: Use a Flexicurve strip or a french curve as a guide for a smooth line. With the kite folded in half, hot-tack the wings together along the camber line. Carefully stitch over the hot-tack

marks along the camber line to form the aerodynamic curve.

Hot-cutting:

8. Use a pencil soldering iron to melt two holes just big enough to accept ¼″ grommets at the tow points. Insert the grommets. Alternate method: Burn a small hole directly through the ripstop near the edge as shown and insert the key ring; use a crochet needle to poke a hole in cotton fabrics.

Assembly:

9. Attach the split rings at the tow points.

10. Cut the mast, wing spars, spreader bar, and semirigid plastic tubing to size and assemble.

53
The Trefoil Dragon Kite

Design: Courtesy of Helen Bushell

A Serpent in the Sky

Up high and dominating the sky like some medieval flying serpent, Helen Bushell's Trefoil Dragon Kite, with its long undulating tail, can be spotted for miles around.

When the Trefoil Dragon is being launched, its animated head often darts, bucks, and swoops defiantly from side to side until it rises above the ground wind turbulence. Once the tail has caught the force of the wind, flaring out to its full length, the kite will begin to fly more peacefully—for the moment, that is. Keep an eye on this good-natured rascal. It has been known to abruptly start a perilous dive from 1,000 feet up in the sky. But don't panic—if you let out line quickly, the dragon will right itself in midair. As a rule, keep about 200 feet of reserve line on your reel for situations just like this—which can occur with any kite. (See the Trefoil Dragon in Detail 1 of Illus. 390, and in color on page E.)

A Launch tip: With the wind at your back, you should have the end of the tail on the ground nearest you and the head farthest away. This method allows the kite to rise in a stable, dignified fashion.

Materials

To make this kite you need:

- 3 yards of .75 oz. ripstop,
- 3′ × ⁵⁄₁₆″ dowel—for mast,
- two 25″ × ¼″ dowels—for wing spars,
- ±22″ × ¼″ dowel—for spreader bar (cut to fit so that sails are taut),
- 11″ × ¼″ dowel—for tail banner,
- 4 oz. Dacron or 1.5 oz. ripstop—for reinforcement material,
- ¼″ nylon-ribbon tape or 100 lb.–test Dacron line—for tether loops,
- 1″ nylon-ribbon tape—for reinforcements (cut to size),
- ¾″ split ring—to attach to nylon-loop tow point,
- ³⁄₁₆″ semirigid plastic tubing—for wing-spar connectors,
- ³⁄₁₆″ polypropylene slices—for tail banner dowel, and
- vinyl end caps.

Option: For a kite that will be less prone to broken dowels, substitute A20 epoxy tubing for all spars and E40 epoxy tubing for the mast.

Details

See Illus. 390 for Details 1–6; the illustrations for the other details are specifically noted.

- (Detail 1.) In flight. The head of the kite is wedge-shaped like a speedboat that is longer than it is wide. To achieve more speed, the kite, like the boat, must sacrifice stability in the form of width. The boat has a rudder to maintain directional control; the kite has a stabilizing tail.
- (Detail 2.) The 30′ gradually tapered tail. The top of the tail is supported by a dowel contained in a snug sleeve banner-style. A ripstop loop (1″ × 80″) absorbs whipping action and prevents the tail from knotting.
- (Detail 3.) Attach the tail with a fishing swivel to the kite's rear nylon loop.
- (Detail 4.) Nylon-ribbon tape reinforces the wing tips and holds the 36″ ripstop streamers.
- (Detail 5.) Vinyl end caps. Tie the line around a ¼″ dowel. Make it secure by gluing a slice of tight-fitting polyethylene tubing over the line. A ¼″ hem prevents twisting, especially on tails over 12′.
- (Detail 6.) Spreader-bar connector. See the Trefoil Delta Kite project in the previous chapter for options.
- (Detail 7 in Illus. 391.) Plot and stitch along the curve to produce the camber, or aerodynamic curve.
- (Detail 8 in Illus. 391 and 392.) Completed half-pattern.
- (Detail 9 in Illus. 391 and 392.) The backward camber at the nose creates a fast forward lift. The long, flat tail is slow and acts to balance the extremes. Insert a ⁵⁄₁₆″ mast through the opening between the reinforcement and the camber line. Reinforcements are fore and aft; keep the mast sleeve open by stitching the reinforcement on the outside edges only!
- (Detail 10 in Illus. 391 and 392.) Tether points. Reinforce prior to stitching the camber line. Add nylon-tape loops for the tether attachment. Tow positions:

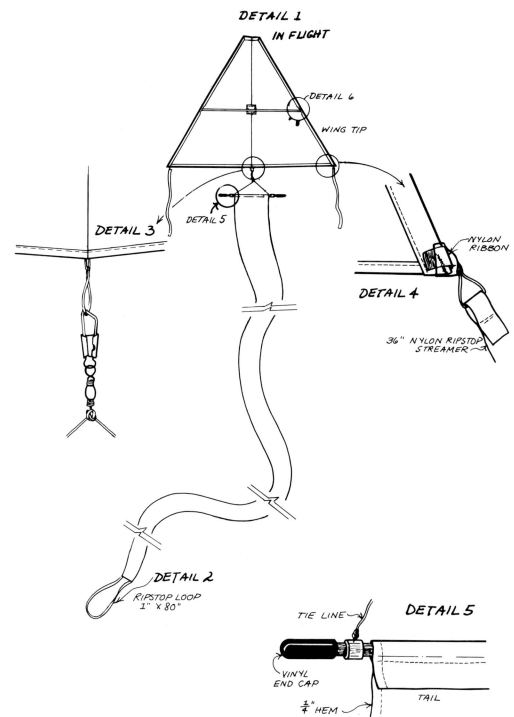

DETAIL 1
IN FLIGHT

DETAIL 6
WING TIP

DETAIL 3

DETAIL 5

NYLON
RIBBON

DETAIL 4

36" NYLON RIPSTOP
STREAMER

DETAIL 2
RIPSTOP LOOP
1" X 80"

TIE LINE

DETAIL 5

VINYL
END CAP

¼" HEM

TAIL

Illus. 390. Details 1–6.

lower loop for low winds; higher loop for higher winds.

• (Detail 10b in Illus. 392.) Option: Use a hot-cutter tip to burn a hole through the fabric at the tether points. Tie 12″ of 100 lb.–test line into a circle; pull it through the hole, around the mast, and back through itself to form a loop for your tether.

Flight Data: Wind range: 6–18 mph
Line: 100 lb. test

AE: ±50°
Wear gloves

Construction

As you go through the following steps, refer to the various details. Note: To make the Trefoil Dragon's head, refer to the instructions for the Trefoil Delta Kite on pages 243–246.

DETAIL 8

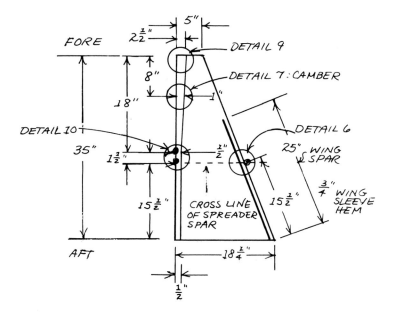

Illus. 391. Detail 8 (also Details 6, 7, 9, and 10).

Hot-cutting:

1. You can cut the kite from one piece of .75 oz. ripstop as shown in Illus. 393. Align the half-pattern head template so that the cambered edge is on the fold of the fabric. Mark the fore and aft end positions on the material for reference. Hot-cut along the vertical where the material overlaps onto itself for a rough rectangular cut. Use the remainder for the tail.

2. With the half-pattern for reference (Illus. 393),

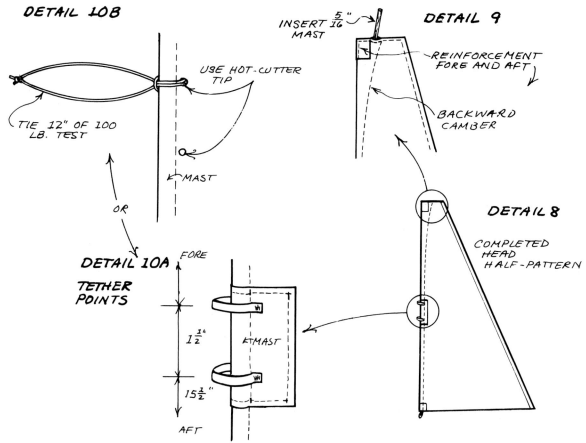

Illus. 392. Details 8, 9, 10a, and 10b.

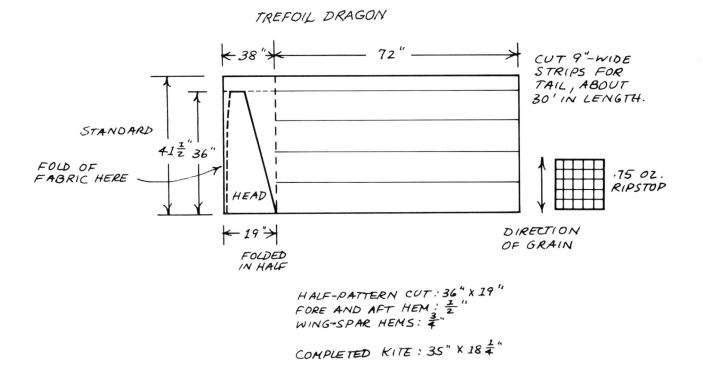

TREFOIL DRAGON

38" 72"

CUT 9"-WIDE
STRIPS FOR
TAIL, ABOUT
30' IN LENGTH.

STANDARD

$41\frac{1}{2}$" 36"

FOLD OF
FABRIC HERE

HEAD

.75 OZ.
RIPSTOP

19"

FOLDED
IN HALF

DIRECTION
OF GRAIN

HALF-PATTERN CUT: 36" X 19"
FORE AND AFT HEM: $\frac{1}{2}$"
WING-SPAR HEMS: $\frac{3}{4}$"

COMPLETED KITE: 35" X $18\frac{1}{4}$"

Illus. 393. Steps 1 and 2.

form the overall head shape by hot-cutting from the fore to the aft along the diagonal.

Sewing:

3. Hem the fore and aft ends. Add an optional wing sleeve and tether reinforcements (refer to the Trefoil Delta).

Assembly:

4. Plot the camber with a pencil and hot-tack along the curve.

5. Complete the head. Don't forget to add a loop for the tail to the aft end. Use a strip of nylon-ribbon tape or 100 lb.–test line.

Hot-cutting:

6. Cut the remaining ripstop into a 9"-wide tail about

30' long that tapers towards the tip. Once the tail is pieced together and *prior to hemming,* you can make a fully tapered tail with the straight of the grain along the outside edges (see "Tails and Drogues"). Another method: Take the last 6' section and cut it to a taper of 3½" at the end.

Sewing:

7. After connecting sections of the tail with a sail seam, use a ¼" hem along each side. Stitch a snug sleeve for the dowel batten and secure it in place with vinyl end caps.

Assembly:

8. Cut the mast, wing spars, spreader bar, and plastic tubing as required and assemble.

54

The Pterosaur Kite

Design: Courtesy of George Peters

A Stylized Prehistoric Creature

Vivid color schemes and meticulous piece work are the hallmark of George Peters's Kites. Here is his stylized interpretation of a prehistoric creature that soared the skies over Europe, Asia, and North America about 80 million years ago. (See the Pterosaur Kite in Illus. 394, and in color on page G.) Favoring light steady winds, the Pterosaur shifts about in the currents and appears almost lifelike against the sky. In near-still air, this high-aspect-ratio design descends in a forward graceful glide, with its belly skimming the earth until touchdown.

Building the Pterosaur requires precise cutting, piecing, and sewing. Familiarize yourself with the instructions until the construction details are clear. Since the Pterosaur is composed of segments, focus on one section at a time. Having all the pieces come together in a magnificent kite at the end is a reward well worth your time and effort.

Materials

Note: If you can't locate exact-size spars, go with the nearest available size. For example, to determine the decimal equivalent of a ⅜″ spar, divide 3 by 8 to get .375″. The nearest-size epoxy-tubing spar would be FL 370. Refer to the Spar Material Chart at a Glance on pages 40–41.

To make this kite you need:
- ripstop: 1.5 oz. of black and purple—and .75 oz. of black, brown, orange, green, and yellow;
- 4 oz. Dacron-reinforcement material, in red and black;
- ¼″ double-fold bias tape;
- ⅜″, ¾″, and 1½″ grosgrain nylon;
- ⅝″ and 1″ nylon webbing;
- ⅜″ I.D. vinyl tubing;
- 1½″- or 2″-wide electrical tape, with smooth finish;
- 1″ metal or nylon ring, D ring, and grommets;
- 8″ × ⅝″ I.D. high-grade aluminum or steel tubing;
- two ½″ (or ⁷⁄₁₆″) × 68⅜″ dowels—jointed for wing spars;

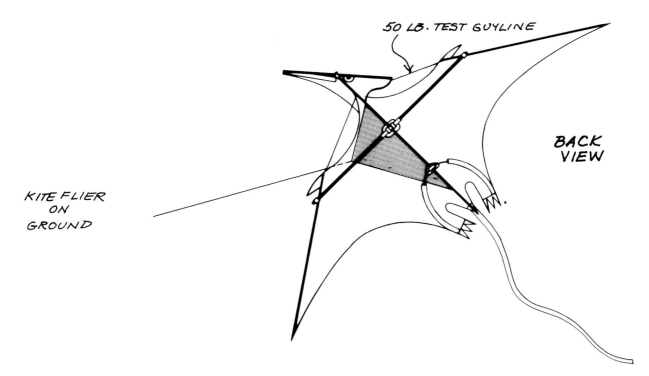

Illus. 394. Pterosaur—in flight.

- brass tubing (two 4″ × ½″ or 7/16″ I.D.)—for wing-spar connectors;
- ⅜″ (or FL 370) × 87″ epoxy tubing—(jointed) for central spar (place vinyl end cap on aft tail end, and glue it halfway inside the tubing at the opposite end for easy insertion in tube connector on the nose);
- ⅜″ (or FL 370) × 40″ epoxy tubing—jointed for nose;
- fibreglass ferrules plus vinyl end caps—for central, nose, and leg spars;
- two 3/32″ × 12″ fibreglass rods—for claw spars;
- two ⅛″ × 33″ fibreglass rods—for leg spars; and

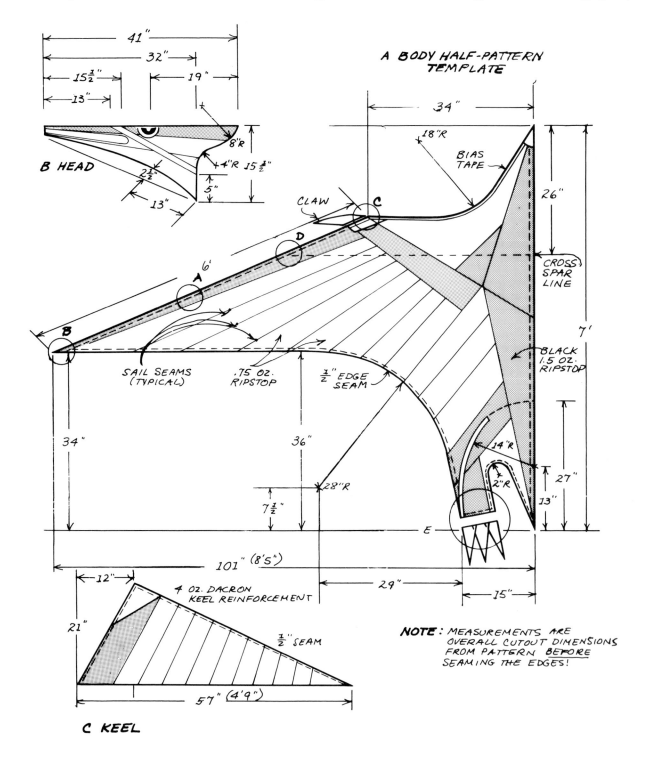

Illus. 395. Head, body, and keel drawn to scale. See Chapter 13 for making a full-size template.

• two ⅝″ (or FL 581) × 46½″ sections of epoxy tubing—for cross spars (to strengthen tube ends, fit with wood dowel plugs as shown—trim dowel if diameter is too large; if too loose, place one or two wraps of smooth electrical tape around plug for a secure fit inside tubing).

Patterns

The following patterns are drawn to scale and are shown in Illus. 395:

• body (half-pattern),
• head, and
• keel.

Details

See Illus. 396 for the following details.

• (Detail A.) Wing sleeve.
• (Detail B.) Wing-tip reinforcement.
• (Detail C.) Upper-wing-sleeve reinforcement.

Flight Data: Wind range: 5–15 mph
             Line: 150–200 lb. test
             AE: ±70°
             Wear gloves

Construction

When broken down, this kite is a series of triangles with radius cuts to form curves. Make templates for sections A (body half-pattern), B (head), and C (keel). Dimensions already include seam allowances. (See Illus. 395.)

A flat cutting surface that is large enough to accommodate the kite's half-pattern templates is necessary.

Though all indicated spar sizes are correct for the kite, cut epoxy tubing, dowels, and fibreglass rods to *fit your kite*, because even the most precise sewing can produce a kite with slightly different dimensions. For example, although the wing-spar dimensions given are 68⅜″, measure the completed wing-sleeve-pocket length on your kite for a snug fit.

Option: Appliquèing sections of black ripstop onto a lighter-shade fabric will expedite the process of forming the wings-and-body shape. However, this shortcut is a trade-off because the beauty of the sun filtering through the piece work will be lost.

Making the Two Wing Halves

Hot-cutting:
Start by making templates of wing half-pattern seg-

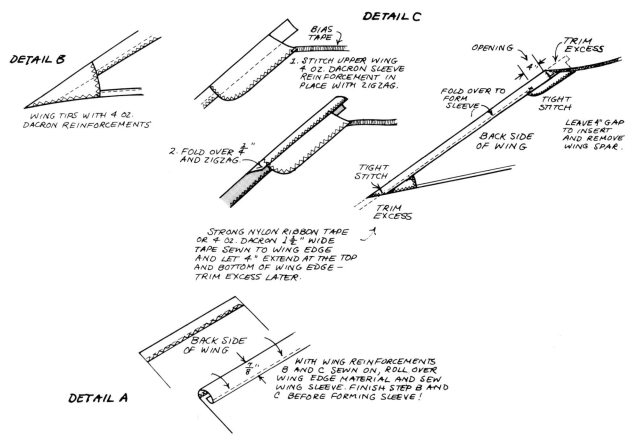

Illus. 396. Sewing the wing sleeve—Details A, B, and C.

ments A through G, as shown in Illus. 397. An overhead projector simplifies the process of making templates by enlarging patterns to full size; the square-and-grid method also works (see "Templates"). Each template should be the size of the finished segment after seaming and hemming. Use a Teflon wheel guide (or other means) to measure and mark allowances around each template for hot-cutting the trim (typically ¼″ added to the hem allowance) and the seams for piecing the segments.

Measure and hot-cut the strips in sections A, C, D, and F. The seam edges contained *within* a section must be cut to fit now, while the overall outside perimeter of each segment must contain extra material for matching, positioning, and cutting later. The Pterosaur's armpit area (H) is the focal point where sections B, C, E, F, and G must converge and align properly.

1. To make matching sets of strips, lay one piece of ripstop over the other end and cut two pieces at the same time. Maintain a balanced bias by having the direction of the grain flow towards the leading edges on both sides. The straight of the weave is less prone to stretching than the diagonal. (See "Working with Ripstop Nylon.")
2. Cut vertical strips by adding ½″ to the width for the ¼″ hot-cutting trim and the ¼″ sail-seam allowance. Hot cutting welds strips together and keeps fabric aligned for sewing. Add several inches to all strip edges that border other sections—section A to B, AB to C, and so on—for aligning and cutting. Add several inches all

around single-piece sections B, E, and G for matching later.

Sewing:
3. A sail seam is used on all the wing parts. Seams fan radially outward from the middle of the kite on both wing halves. The smooth edge of the seam is on the face of the kite. Begin by assembling segments that form sections A through G; individual parts B, E, and G do not require stitching at this point.

Position templates over completed segments A through G. Before cutting, manipulate the segments to confirm that all parts are in correct relation and proportion to one another. Be generous when cutting; it's easier to remove excess material than to add fabric to a segment cut too small.

Hot-cutting:
4. For symmetry, place templates over two sets of rough-cut sections A through G.

Sewing:
5. Connect the body and wing in the following order: A and B to C to D and E. Sew F and G together. Sections B, E, F, and G must converge at armpit H for proper body alignment. Repeat for the other wing half.

Hot-cutting:
6. With the upper part (F and G) and the lower part facing upwards, fold the upper part over the lower and align at intersection H. Hot-cut and weld the top half to the bottom.

Sewing:
7. Stitch the sections together and then open the material for a rough-cut wing half. Repeat for the other wing.

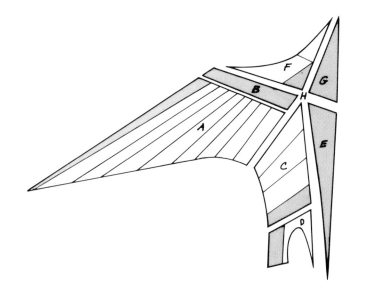
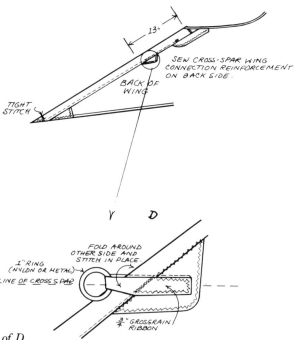

Illus. 397. Wing half-pattern (segments A–G), and exploded view of D.

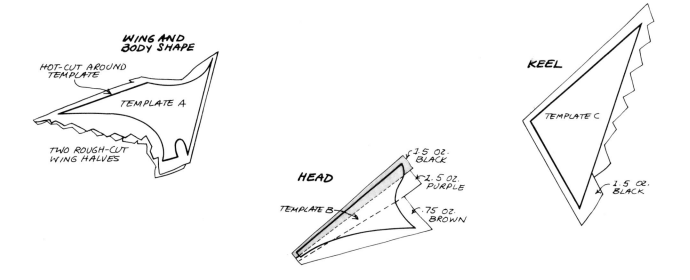

Illus. 398. Templates—body, head, and keel.

Hot-cutting:

8. See Illus. 398. Place half-pattern template "A" over both wings (folded with face sides meeting) and align along the vertical center for proper positioning. Check for symmetry and trim as shown.

Cutting and sewing:

9. Referring to Illus. 395, assemble the head and keel. Cut, sew, and trim the fabric. Use templates "B" and "C" for the head and keel. Hot-cut all Dacron reinforcements, claws, and feet (see Illus. 399 and 400).

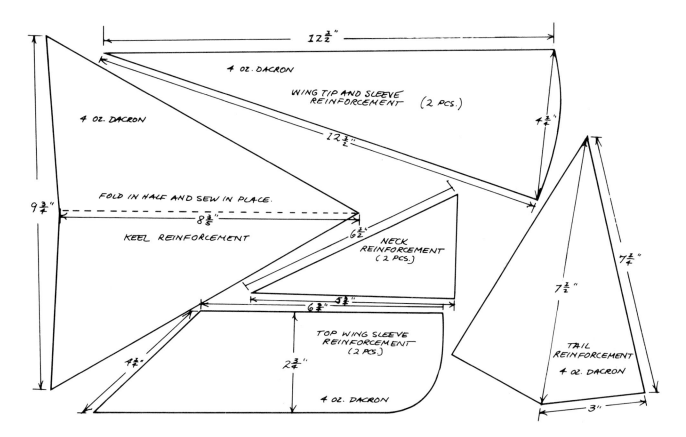

Illus. 399. Reinforcement patterns.

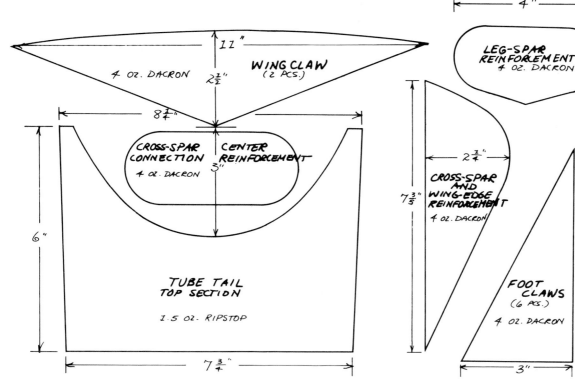

Illus. 400. Reinforcement patterns.

Making the Main Body and Parts

Sewing:

Note: For useful kite seams, refer to "Reaping What You Sew."

10. Sew the wing sleeves as shown in Illus. 396 (Details A, B, and C).
11. Sew on cross-spar wing reinforcements and connectors. Be sure that the rings are in line with the cross spar. See Illus. 397.
12. Wing claws: Follow the assembly instructions in Illus. 401.
13. Complete the head (1 in Illus. 402) and keel (2 in Illus. 403). Connect the keel to the head with a zigzag stitch (3 in Illus. 404).
14. With the keel and head sewn together, align both wings and stitch together along the center. See Illus. 405 (4).
15. Reinforce the tail tip with 4 oz. Dacron and sew

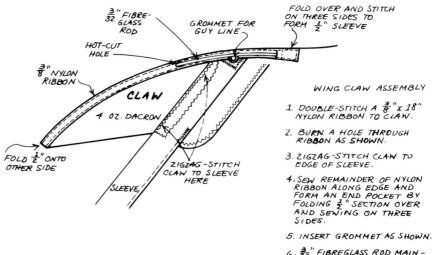

Illus. 401. Wing claw.

HEAD AND EYE

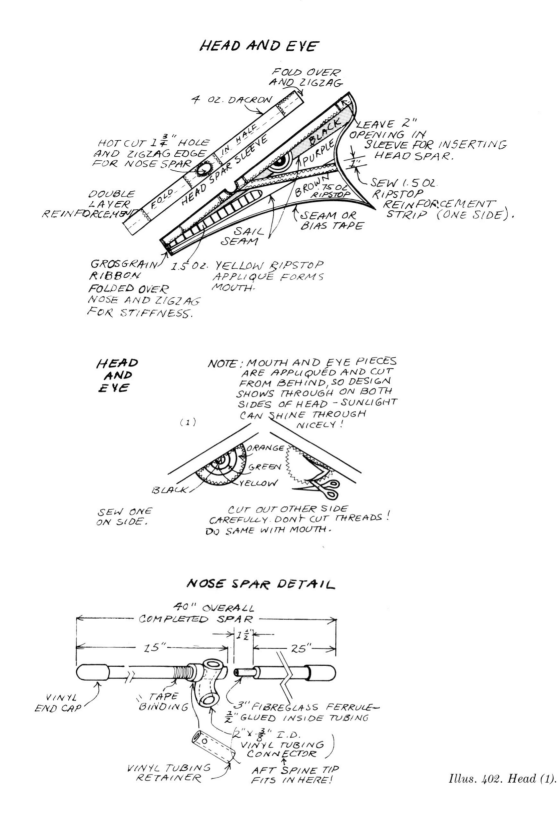

FOLD OVER AND ZIGZAG

4 OZ. DACRON

FOLD IN HALF

HOT CUT 1¾" HOLE AND ZIGZAG EDGE FOR NOSE SPAR

HEAD SPAR SLEEVE

BLACK

PURPLE

LEAVE 2" OPENING IN SLEEVE FOR INSERTING HEAD SPAR.

1"

DOUBLE LAYER REINFORCEMENT

FOLD

BROWN .75 OZ RIPSTOP

SEW 1.5 OZ. RIPSTOP REINFORCEMENT STRIP (ONE SIDE).

SAIL SEAM

SEAM OR BIAS TAPE

GROSGRAIN RIBBON FOLDED OVER NOSE AND ZIGZAG FOR STIFFNESS.

1.5 OZ. YELLOW RIPSTOP APPLIQUE FORMS MOUTH.

HEAD AND EYE

(1)

NOTE: MOUTH AND EYE PIECES ARE APPLIQUED AND CUT FROM BEHIND, SO DESIGN SHOWS THROUGH ON BOTH SIDES OF HEAD — SUNLIGHT CAN SHINE THROUGH NICELY!

ORANGE
GREEN
BLACK
YELLOW

SEW ONE ON SIDE.

CUT OUT OTHER SIDE CAREFULLY. DON'T CUT THREADS! DO SAME WITH MOUTH.

NOSE SPAR DETAIL

40" OVERALL COMPLETED SPAR

15"

1½"

25"

VINYL END CAP

TAPE BINDING

3" FIBREGLASS FERRULE ½" GLUED INSIDE TUBING

2" x ⅜" I.D. VINYL TUBING CONNECTOR

VINYL TUBING RETAINER

AFT SPINE TIP FITS IN HERE!

Illus. 402. Head (1).

---

on the nylon-webbing retainer for the central spar. See Illus. 406 (5).

16. See Illus. 406 (6). Fold the wings upwards and stitch as shown to form the central spar sleeve.

17. Sew the Velcro strip (loop half) to the back of the tail. See Illus. 406 (7).

18. Make foot claws as shown in Illus. 407 and zigzag-stitch in place. Sew on leg spar sleeves (about 20″

long each); then add 4 oz. Dacron reinforcements (E 8).

19. Position and sew cross-spar (10 in Illus. 408) and leg-spar (E 9 in Illus. 407) retainer pockets in place on the back of the kite. Note: Be careful not to sew into the keel on the other side.

20. Tail: See 11 in Illus. 409. Use a sail seam through-out. Add bias tape to the top 1.5 oz. section. Sew

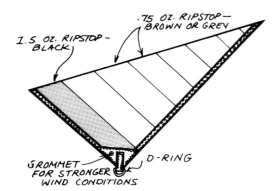

1.5 OZ. RIPSTOP – BLACK

.75 OZ. RIPSTOP – BROWN OR GREY

GROMMET FOR STRONGER WIND CONDITIONS

D-RING

Illus. 403. Keel (2).

the top section onto the .75 oz. tail. Stitch along the entire length to make the tube. Sew the Velcro strip (hook half) in place. Turn inside out.

Finishing steps:

21. The cross-spar connector: See 12 in Illus. 410. Bend an 8″ piece of aluminum or steel tubing into a 155° angle.

22. Use fishing-swivel clips to attach the guy lines (50 lb. test) from the neck to both grommets, located on each wing claw. The lines should be taut enough to support the wings when hanging vertically without distorting the sail. See Illus. 394.

ALIGN WITH MIDDLE OF HEAD REINFORCEMENT STRIP.

ZIGZAG KEEL AND HEAD TOGETHER

Illus. 404. Head and keel connected (3).

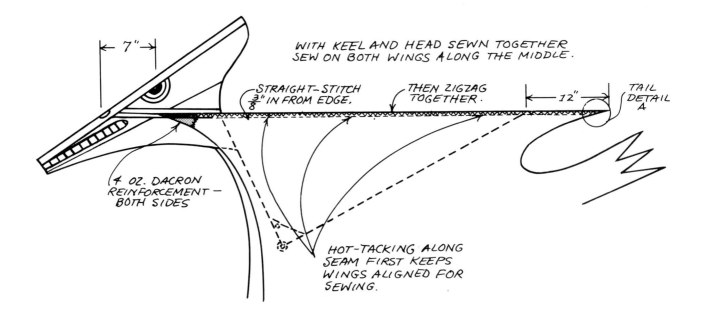

7″

WITH KEEL AND HEAD SEWN TOGETHER SEW ON BOTH WINGS ALONG THE MIDDLE.

STRAIGHT-STITCH 3/8″ IN FROM EDGE.

THEN ZIGZAG TOGETHER.

12″

TAIL DETAIL A

4 OZ. DACRON REINFORCEMENT – BOTH SIDES

HOT-TACKING ALONG SEAM FIRST KEEPS WINGS ALIGNED FOR SEWING.

Illus. 405. Sewing on the wings (4).

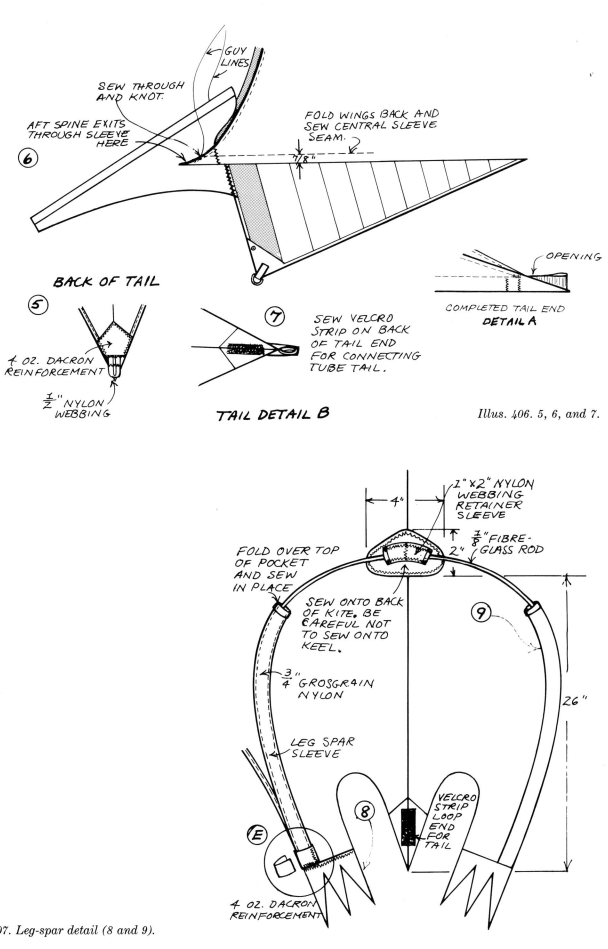

GUY LINES

SEW THROUGH AND KNOT.

AFT SPINE EXITS THROUGH SLEEVE HERE

⑥

FOLD WINGS BACK AND SEW CENTRAL SLEEVE SEAM.

7/8"

BACK OF TAIL

⑤

4 OZ. DACRON REINFORCEMENT

1/2" NYLON WEBBING

⑦

SEW VELCRO STRIP ON BACK OF TAIL END FOR CONNECTING TUBE TAIL.

TAIL DETAIL B

OPENING

COMPLETED TAIL END
DETAIL A

Illus. 406. 5, 6, and 7.

1" X 2" NYLON WEBBING RETAINER SLEEVE

4"

7/8" FIBRE-GLASS ROD

2"

FOLD OVER TOP OF POCKET AND SEW IN PLACE

SEW ONTO BACK OF KITE. BE CAREFUL NOT TO SEW ONTO KEEL.

⑨

3/4" GROSGRAIN NYLON

26"

LEG SPAR SLEEVE

VELCRO STRIP LOOP END FOR TAIL

Ⓔ

⑧

4 OZ. DACRON REINFORCEMENT

Illus. 407. Leg-spar detail (8 and 9).

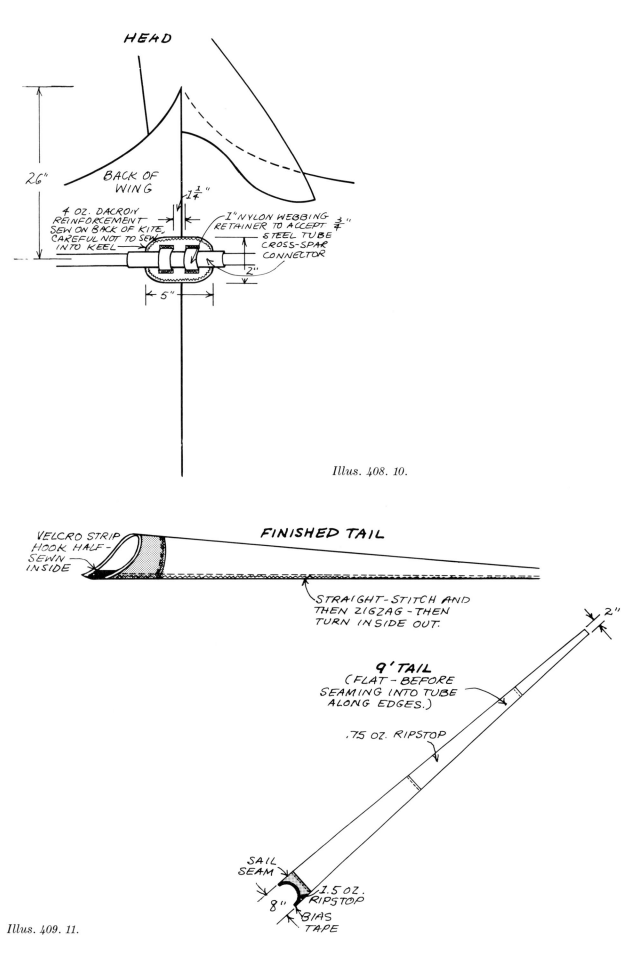

HEAD

26"

BACK OF WING

4 OZ. DACRON REINFORCEMENT SEW ON BACK OF KITE, CAREFUL NOT TO SEW INTO KEEL

1¼"

1" NYLON WEBBING RETAINER TO ACCEPT STEEL TUBE CROSS-SPAR CONNECTOR

¾"

2"

5"

Illus. 408. 10.

FINISHED TAIL

VELCRO STRIP HOOK HALF- SEWN INSIDE

STRAIGHT-STITCH AND THEN ZIGZAG - THEN TURN INSIDE OUT.

2"

9' TAIL
(FLAT - BEFORE SEAMING INTO TUBE ALONG EDGES.)

.75 OZ. RIPSTOP

SAIL SEAM

8"

1.5 OZ. RIPSTOP

BIAS TAPE

Illus. 409. 11.

260

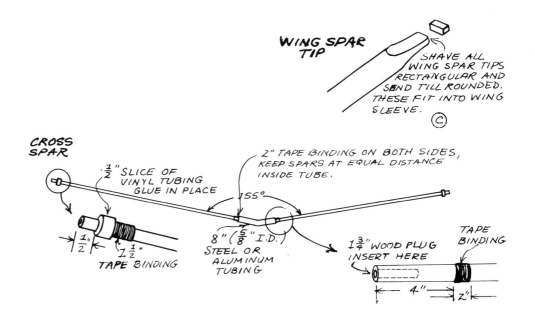

WING SPAR TIP

SHAVE ALL WING SPAR TIPS RECTANGULAR AND SAND TILL ROUNDED. THESE FIT INTO WING SLEEVE. (C)

CROSS SPAR

·1/2" SLICE OF VINYL TUBING GLUE IN PLACE

2" TAPE BINDING ON BOTH SIDES, KEEP SPARS AT EQUAL DISTANCE INSIDE TUBE.

155°

1/2"   1 1/2"

TAPE BINDING

8" (5/8" I.D.) STEEL OR ALUMINUM TUBING

1 3/4" WOOD PLUG INSERT HERE

TAPE BINDING

4"   2"

Illus. 410. 12.

55

The Turbo Stunt Kite

After Lee Sedgwick's Design

Power Flying

"People have gone skiing uphill," maintains Lee Sedgwick, "being pulled by stunt kites. That's real power flying—harnessing the wind with your stack."

Well known for his graceful stunt-kite flying to music, Sedgwick won first place in the Individual Ballet Open class at the Second Annual East Coast Stunt Kite Championships in Wildwood, New Jersey, in 1987. Dog-staking his dual flying line in the ground enabled him to move around directly under his own kite. Seemingly in defiance of physics, the kite hovered demurely just overhead, where he could touch it while still controlling its movements. Sedgwick made it appear as if everything he was doing on the field was effortless. At the end of his performance, the audience cheered wildly and for a long time. Sedgwick flies with a Walkman cassette player. He says, "The music goes inside and out through the kite."

A solid 2-hour stunt-kite-flying session is a good workout: Pulling, shifting, bending, swaying, jump-ing, leaning, running, and moving to the rhythm of the beat are all part of perfecting maneuvers and having fun. Sedgwick spends from 100 to 150 hours choreographing his kite movements to a particular piece of music.

Once you have your stunt kite, the next major consideration is choosing your flying line. Though Kevlar flying line is still an excellent choice for stunt flying, Sedgwick is impressed with Spectra line, particularly the 135 lb.–test variety (see Flying Line Chart at a Glance on page 43). He says Spectra hardly shows wear, even under the extra strain during his dog-stake routines. Since it won't cut through itself the way Kevlar does, he merely ties a plain knot and burns the end to act as a stopper so that the knot won't slip through itself—since Spectra is slippery. Though not critical, an option for a strong loop is to use a no-knot system (see pages 47–49 in "Getting to Know the Ropes"). Sedgwick cautions that although Spectra is stronger than Kevlar, it's also easily cut by Kevlar should their paths cross.

Depending on the type of flying and wind condi-

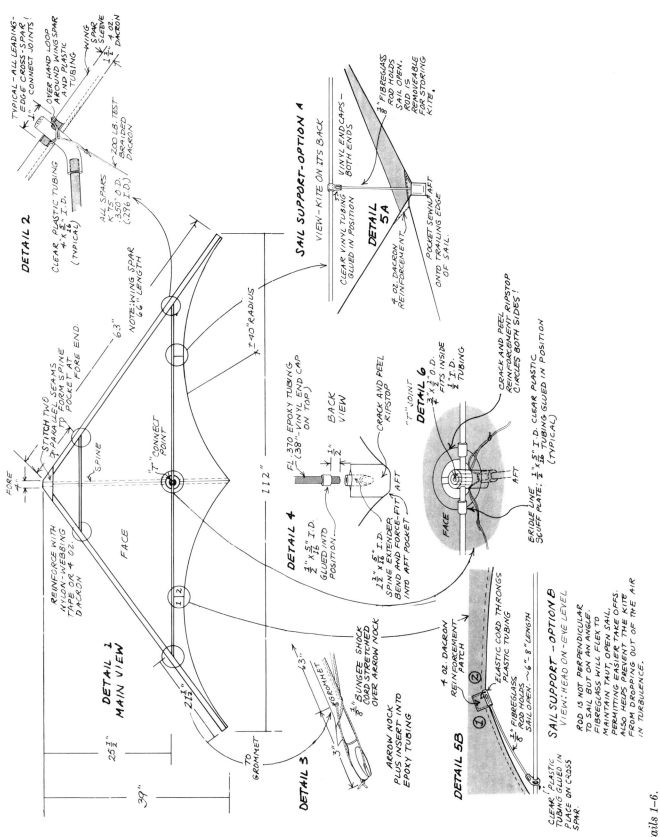

Illus. 411. Details 1–6.

tions, Sedgwick has equipment to meet the need: different sets of handles, and line strengths and lengths. He uses 105 ft. for a single kite, 150 ft. for a stack, and 150 to 200 ft. for ice flying. Naturally, line strength is critical. Lee recommends 135 lb. for a single kite, 200 lb. for power flying in moderately strong winds, and 300 lb. for power flying in stronger winds and stack flying. A safe rule is to employ a no-knot system for all power flying or any conditions where the kite is going to pull you.

"One of the better discoveries I've made is quad-line flying," says Sedgwick, referring to flying a stunt kite from four lines instead of two. He uses Spectra 200 lb. test for the two lines attached to the top bridle and the two attached to the bottom bridle; the result is more control. Sedgwick is flying his five-stack with quad lines in Illus. 412; note how the four-line arrangement wraps behind his arms.

See the Turbo Stunt Kite in Illus. 415, and in color on page J. For more about stunt-kite flying—including flying tips and safety rules—refer back to Chapter 20.

Illus. 412. Lee Sedgwick with quad lines (photo: Pete Hubbell).

Materials

To make this kite you need:

- 4 square yards of .75 oz. ripstop—for sail;
- 4 oz. Dacron—for sleeves and reinforcements;
- crack-and-peel ripstop—for reinforcements;
- ⁵⁄₁₆″ I.D. clear plastic tubing;
- ⅛″ elastic cord;
- ¼″ grommets;
- 1″ nylon webbing—for sail-support pockets (A);
- ⅛″ I.D. clear plastic tubing—for sail supports (B);
- arrow nocks, inserts, and vinyl end caps;
- 350″ O.D. (.296″ I.D.) with .291″ O.D. ferrules—for all spars:

  - spine—FL .370″ × 39″, and
  - cross spars—16″ (upper) and ± 99″ (lower);

- 200 lb.–test braided Dacron—for bridle;
- swivel ball-bearing fishing hooks (200 lb. test)—for bridle setup with Option A;
- ½″ O.D. clear plastic tubing; and
- ½″ I.D. clear plastic tubing.

Details

See Details 1–6 in Illus. 411; the illustrations for the other details are specifically noted.

- (Detail 1.) Main view.
- (Detail 2.) Typical cross-spar connect point.
- (Detail 3.) Wing tip held under tension with elastic cord.
- (Detail 4.) Spine—aft position, back view.
- (Detail 5A.) The ⅛″ fibreglass-rod sail-support spars keep the sail open and help takeoffs; the supports also prevent the kite from dropping out of the air in turbulence. The fibreglass rod is cut to size and runs perpendicular from the lower cross spar to the pocket sewn onto the trailing edge. The rods are removable.

  Sail-support option (Detail 5B): The sail support is angled and secured to the sail inside a clear plastic tubing retainer with an elastic cord.
- (Detail 6.) T-joint, face view.
- (Detail 7 in Illus. 413.) T-joint, back view.
- (Detail 8 in Illus. 414.) T-joint, drilled.
- (Detail 9 in Illus. 415.) In flight. 150 Spectra dual line—200′ each line.
- (Detail 10A in Illus. 416.) Bridle a: basic connect with fishing swivel. Bridle b (option): No metal swivels are required since rigging is entirely self-contained within line knots and loops; measurements given are from the end of one connect point to another.
- (Detail 10B in Illus. 417.) Quad-line bridle setup.

Flight Data: Wind range: 7–25 mph
Line: 135 to 200 lb. test: Spectra
AE: Maneuverable
Dual-line hand grips required

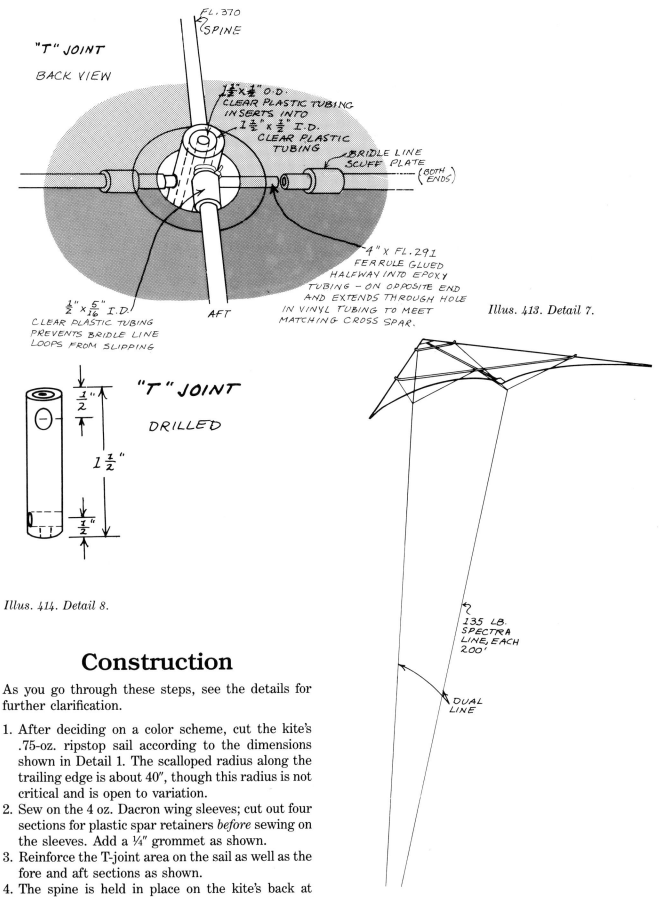

"T" JOINT

BACK VIEW

FL.370
SPINE

1⅛" x ¾" O.D.
CLEAR PLASTIC TUBING
INSERTS INTO
1½" x ½" I.D.
CLEAR PLASTIC
TUBING

BRIDLE LINE
SCUFF PLATE
(BOTH ENDS)

½" x 5/16" I.D.
CLEAR PLASTIC TUBING
PREVENTS BRIDLE LINE
LOOPS FROM SLIPPING

AFT

4" X FL.291
FERRULE GLUED
HALFWAY INTO EPOXY
TUBING — ON OPPOSITE END
AND EXTENDS THROUGH HOLE
IN VINYL TUBING TO MEET
MATCHING CROSS SPAR.

Illus. 413. Detail 7.

"T" JOINT

DRILLED

½"

1½"

½"

Illus. 414. Detail 8.

135 LB.
SPECTRA
LINE, EACH
200'

DUAL
LINE

Illus. 415. Detail 9—in flight.

Construction

As you go through these steps, see the details for
further clarification.

1. After deciding on a color scheme, cut the kite's
   .75-oz. ripstop sail according to the dimensions
   shown in Detail 1. The scalloped radius along the
   trailing edge is about 40″, though this radius is not
   critical and is open to variation.
2. Sew on the 4 oz. Dacron wing sleeves; cut out four
   sections for plastic spar retainers *before* sewing on
   the sleeves. Add a ¼″ grommet as shown.
3. Reinforce the T-joint area on the sail as well as the
   fore and aft sections as shown.
4. The spine is held in place on the kite's back at
   three points: the aft pocket, T connect point, and

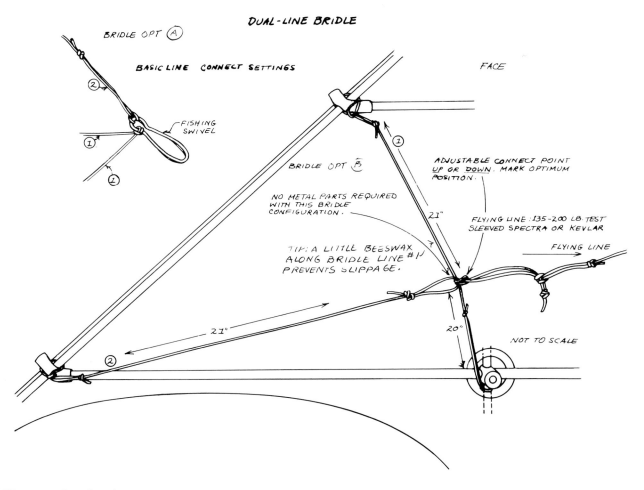

BRIDLE OPT (A)

BASIC LINE CONNECT SETTINGS

FACE

FISHING SWIVEL

BRIDLE OPT (B)

ADJUSTABLE CONNECT POINT UP OR DOWN. MARK OPTIMUM POSITION.

NO METAL PARTS REQUIRED WITH THIS BRIDLE CONFIGURATION.

FLYING LINE : 135-200 LB. TEST SLEEVED SPECTRA OR KEVLAR

21"

TIP: A LITTLE BEESWAX ALONG BRIDLE LINE #1 PREVENTS SLIPPAGE.

FLYING LINE

21"

20"

NOT TO SCALE

Illus. 416. Detail 10A.

parallel seams sewn into the reinforcement at the fore section.

5. Cut and assemble cross spars, ferrules, clear plastic vinyl tubing, and ⅛" fibreglass-rod sail supports using Option A or B. If you choose Option B, a hemostat is useful in pulling the elastic cord through the vinyl tubing. Once through, the elastic is tied off in a loop through the plastic and the 4 oz. reinforcement on the sail. Use vinyl end caps to prevent wear on the top end of the spine, wing spars, and both ends of the sail-support spars.

6. Using ⅛" elastic cord at the wing tips should keep the wing spars under tension without deforming the spar.

7. Attach the bridle lines with overhand loop knots to the points shown.

8. Adjusting the bridle loop: For the kite to fly correctly, the bridle connect points must be equally positioned along line #1. If the kite won't gain altitude, the bridle setting is too low; if the kite doesn't respond quickly, or is sluggish, the bridle is set too low. Once you've located the balance point, or fulcrum, mark the spot on the line with a soft-tip pen for future reference.

Tip: To increase speed, move the bridle connect point upwards; for more pull and tighter turns, adjust the connect point aftwards. Make adjustments in ⅛" to ¼" increments and test-fly the kite before making any further refinements.

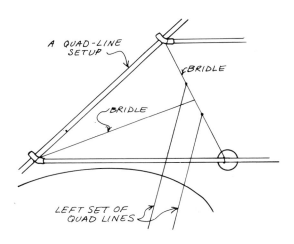

A QUAD-LINE SETUP

BRIDLE

BRIDLE

LEFT SET OF QUAD LINES

Illus. 417. Detail 10B.

56
The Tetrahedron Kite

After Alexander Graham Bell's Design

Inspired by Bell and Fuller

After inventing the telephone, Alexander Graham Bell turned his genius to the quest for manned powered flight. He worked intensely for more than 10 years, continuing his efforts well after the Wright brothers' flight in 1903.

Bell began by building on Lawrence Hargrave's box kite, an invention he called "the high-water mark of progress in the nineteenth century." After experimenting with many kite configurations, including right-angle and obtuse-angle tetrahedrons, Bell eventually hit upon the regular tetrahedron, the shape that inspired this book. A pyramid of four equi-lateral triangles, it had structural strength and relative low weight. Because of the regular tetrahedron's equal sides, the number of cells that can be combined is unlimited (Illus. 418). Only two sides of the four-faceted tetrahedron cell required a sail (Bell used silk) to create a dihedral lifting surface. The concept grew—one cell, two cells, four cells, and up.

On December 6, 1907, Bell launched his 208 lb. Cygnet—a manned 3,393-tetrahedron-celled kite—over Baddeck Bay, Nova Scotia. With a lieutenant from the U.S. Army on board, the large compound kite, outfitted with flotation devices, was pulled over the bay by a steamer. The Cygnet reached an altitude of 168 feet and flew for some 7 minutes. Following a

Illus. 418. Alexander Graham Bell with his wife, Mabel, inside a tetrahedron framework. (Photo from the Library of Congress.)

Illus. 419. R. Buckminster Fuller, model maker of the universe. (Photo courtesy of the R. Buckminster Fuller Institute.)

smooth descent, the kite landed on the water; but when the flying line to the steamer was not released in time, the Cygnet was dragged through the bay and destroyed. Fortunately, the lieutenant survived with only a dunking.

Bell later built Cygnet II, a modified version of the original kite that was capable of housing an engine and a pilot. But the engine in the kite was unable to produce sufficient thrust to lift the new Cygnet, Bell's swan song in aviation.

* * *

I wanted to present the Tetrahedron Kite (shown in Illus. 422) in a way that would illustrate the elegant force of nature called *synergy* by R. Buckminster Fuller[1]. According to Fuller (shown in Illus. 419) the tetrahedron is the basic structural unit of the universe and all structures are synergetic—meaning that the interaction of their different parts has a total effect that is greater than the sum of their effects taken independently. (For more about Fuller and his ideas, refer back to the Preface of this book.)

I had been dabbling with design concepts that were adequate but somehow missed the mark when I had the good fortune of discovering Tensegritoy, an ingenious kit of elastic cords and wooden struts designed for constructing geometric structures based on Fuller's work. Held together in perfect balance under tension and compression, these structures show the invisible forces that Fuller coined *tensegrity*—a contraction of *tensional integrity*.

Later, with various kite parts and the Tensegritoy model lying strewn before me on the kitchen table, I had a sudden inspiration. I picked up two wooden beads and threaded them with a piece of line, knotting each end, and then began pulling on the beads to tense the line. I thought, tetrahedrons, geodesic domes, all structures in the universe for that matter, are tensegrity structures held together in omnidirectional coherency just like the beads and line in my hand. In a flash, the internal line-and-bead suspension system for the Tetrahedron Kite became clear to me, and I put the entire project together in a matter of minutes.[2]

Materials

To make this kite you need:

- 2 yards of .75 oz. ripstop—for sails,
- ¼″ × 96″ nylon tape—for sail loops,
- 4 oz. Dacron—for reinforcement material,
- sixteen .250 × 32½″ standard-length epoxy-tubing spars cut to size,
- four ³⁄₃₂″ × 72″ fibreglass rods cut to size (eight)—for spreader spars,
- ¼″ I.D. × 10″ brass tubing cut to size—for spreader end caps,
- 24″ of ¼″ I.D. clear plastic tubing,
- ⅜″ × 48″ nylon rod—for universal joint fittings,
- 24″ 150 lb.–test line—for tension loop,
- 24″ 100 lb.–test line—for tension loop,
- eight ½″-diameter wooden beads with holes,
- 16 self-locking nylon cable ties,
- 16 nylon bolts and wing nuts to fit ⅜″ hole in universal nylon-spar joint,
- four ⁹⁄₁₆″ split key rings,
- four yards of 100 lb.–test line—for bridle lines, and
- four 4-hole buttons—for line-tension adjustment system.

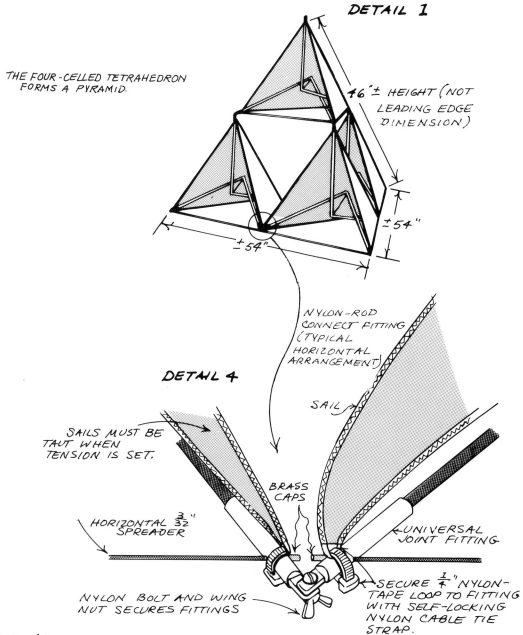

THE FOUR-CELLED TETRAHEDRON FORMS A PYRAMID.

DETAIL 1

46″± HEIGHT (NOT LEADING EDGE DIMENSION)

±54″

±54″

NYLON-ROD CONNECT FITTING (TYPICAL HORIZONTAL ARRANGEMENT)

DETAIL 4

SAIL

SAILS MUST BE TAUT WHEN TENSION IS SET.

BRASS CAPS

HORIZONTAL ³⁄₃₂″ SPREADER

UNIVERSAL JOINT FITTING

NYLON BOLT AND WING NUT SECURES FITTINGS

SECURE ¼″ NYLON-TAPE LOOP TO FITTING WITH SELF-LOCKING NYLON CABLE TIE STRAP.

Illus. 420. Details 1 and 4.

Details

- (Detail 1 in Illus. 420.) The four-celled tetrahedron forms a pyramid. The height is ±46″; the base 54″ × 54″.
- (Detail 2 in Illus. 421.) One-cell tetrahedron. The horizontal 18″ long spars; the vertical 17½″ short spars; the ³⁄₃₂″ fibreglass horizontal spreader; and the ³⁄₃₂″ vertical spreader spar. With the tension line slack, the spars forming the horizontal triangle can be flipped to collapse the cell flat for storage.
- (Detail 3 in Illus. 421.) The bead, line, and button tension-adjustment system. When tension is set, the internal spar sets come close to forming a right triangle—45°, 45°, 90°.
- (Detail 4 in Illus. 420.) Nylon-rod connect fitting

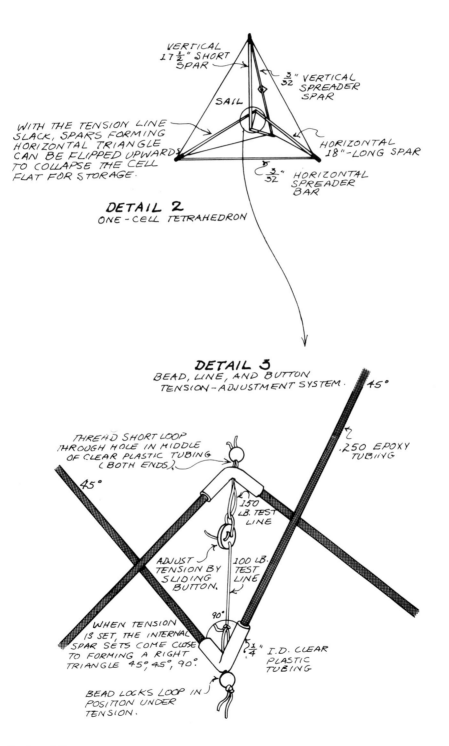

DETAIL 2
ONE-CELL TETRAHEDRON

DETAIL 3
BEAD, LINE, AND BUTTON
TENSION-ADJUSTMENT SYSTEM.

Illus. 421. Details 2 and 3.

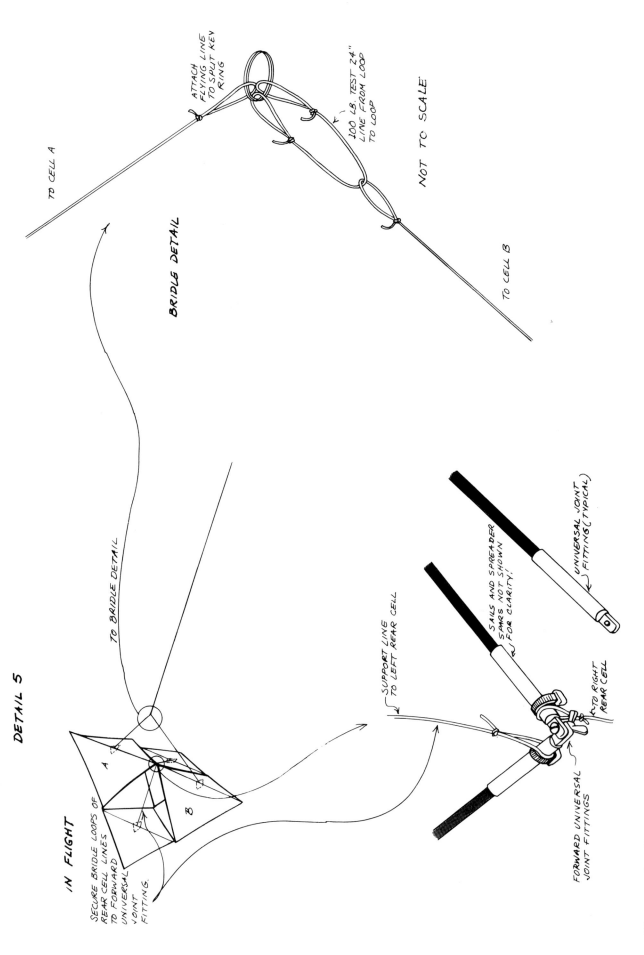

DETAIL 5

IN FLIGHT

SECURE BRIDLE LOOPS OF
REAR CELL LINES
TO FORWARD
UNIVERSAL
JOINT
FITTING.

TO BRIDLE DETAIL

BRIDLE DETAIL

TO CELL A

ATTACH
FLYING LINE
TO SPLIT KEY
RING

100 LB. TEST 24"
LINE FROM LOOP
TO LOOP

NOT TO SCALE

TO CELL B

SUPPORT LINE
TO LEFT REAR CELL

SAILS AND SPREADER
SPARS NOT SHOWN
FOR CLARITY.

UNIVERSAL JOINT
FITTINGS (TYPICAL)

TO RIGHT
REAR CELL

FORWARD UNIVERSAL
JOINT FITTINGS

Illus. 422. Detail 5.

(horizontal typical); secure a ¼″ nylon-tape loop to the fitting with a self-locking nylon-cable tie strap; a nylon bolt and a wing nut secure the fittings.

- (Detail 5 in Illus. 422.) In flight. Bridle arrangement: The flying line is attached to the bridle loops; secure the bridle loops of the rear cell lines to the forward universal joint fittings.

Flight Data: Wind range: 6–24 mph
Line: 100 lb. test
AE: ±45°
Wear gloves

Construction

Sails:

1. Hot-cut four sections to the dimensions shown in Illus. 423 to make four sails. Observe the bias as indicated. Sew A to B, and C to D; then hot-cut both sections along EF. Make allowances for the hot-cut trim and ¼″ hem.
2. See Illus. 424. Sew a 4 oz. Dacron reinforcement in the middle of each sail, and burn a ¼″ hole using a conical tip fitted on a hot cutter.
3. Stitch a ¼″ × 6″ strip of nylon tape to form a short loop in each corner. See "The Tri-D Box Kite" and "The Stone Mountain Kite" for details on sewing nylon tape into the sail tip.

Framework:

4. Cut eight .250 × 17½″ epoxy-tubing spars in short sections; cut eight .250 × 18″ epoxy-tubing spars in long sections.

5. Cut eight 2½″ sections of ¼″ I.D. clear plastic tubing.
6. Drill a ⅛″ hole in the middle of each section of plastic tubing.
7. Cut eight ³⁄₃₂″ × 28″ fibreglass-rod spreader spars.
8. Use a fine-tooth hobby saw to cut sixteen ¼″ × ³⁄₃₂″ I.D. brass-tubing caps.

Universal joint fittings:

9. See Illus. 425. Cut sixteen ⅜″ × 2½″ universal nylon-rod connectors. Make a jig to secure each nylon-rod section and use a drill press to make a hole in one end. Tip: Begin with a small-diameter starter drill bit and work up in size until you achieve the desired diameter—heat builds up quickly and melts nylon. Use a low-speed with short precise cuts. Use a fine-tooth hobby saw to form a rectangular ⅛″ × ½″ slat on the other end and drill a ⅜″ hole as shown.
10. Drill diagonal holes at about a 45° angle in the fittings as shown in Illus. 425. The outside hole should be countersunk slightly larger to allow about half of the brass cap to fit inside the fitting. The angle of each fitting must align properly in two ways: The ³⁄₃₂″ spreader spar must lie flat and taut to form the triangle when the kite cell is assembled and the tension line is set, and the ⅛″-slat extension must face the opposing slat evenly for a secure flat match when secured with the nylon bolt and wing nut. (See Detail 4 in Illus. 420.)

Tip: Before drilling, note the relative position of the diagonal holes in the vertical and horizontal fittings.

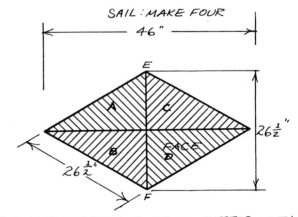

PATTERN: COMPLETED DIMENSIONS

SAIL: MAKE FOUR
46″
E
26½″
26½″
A   C
B   4 oz.
D
F

COMBINE FOUR PIECES OF .75 OZ. RIPSTOP WITH THE STRAIGHT OF THE GRAIN ALONG THE OUTSIDE OR LEADING EDGES. USE A ¼″ DOUBLE-FOLD HEM ON THE LEADING EDGES AND ¼″ SAIL SEAM ON ALL INSIDE HEMS.

THE PATTERN IS BASED ON A RHOMBUS: AN EQUILATERAL PARALLELOGRAM.

Illus. 423. Step 1.

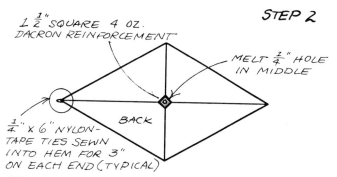

STEP 2

$1\frac{1}{2}''$ SQUARE 4 OZ.
DACRON REINFORCEMENT

MELT $\frac{1}{4}''$ HOLE
IN MIDDLE

BACK

$\frac{1}{4}'' \times 6''$ NYLON-
TAPE TIES SEWN
INTO HEM FOR 3''
ON EACH END (TYPICAL)

FOR NYLON TAPE DETAIL, SEE TRI-D BOX KITE PROJECT,
CONNECTING SAIL TO FRAME OPTIONS.

Illus. 424. Step 2.

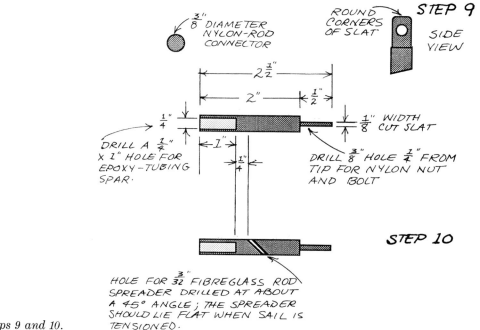

$\frac{3}{8}''$ DIAMETER
NYLON-ROD
CONNECTOR

ROUND
CORNERS
OF SLAT

STEP 9

SIDE
VIEW

$2\frac{1}{2}''$

$2''$

$\frac{1}{2}''$

$\frac{1}{4}''$

$1''$

$\frac{1}{4}''$

$\frac{1}{8}''$ WIDTH
CUT SLAT

DRILL A $\frac{1}{4}''$
$\times 1''$ HOLE FOR
EPOXY-TUBING
SPAR.

DRILL $\frac{3}{8}''$ HOLE $\frac{1}{4}''$ FROM
TIP FOR NYLON NUT
AND BOLT

STEP 10

HOLE FOR $\frac{3}{32}''$ FIBREGLASS ROD
SPREADER DRILLED AT ABOUT
A 45° ANGLE; THE SPREADER
SHOULD LIE FLAT WHEN SAIL IS
TENSIONED.

Illus. 425. Steps 9 and 10.

11. Once you're satisfied that the spreader-spar holes are drilled correctly in relation to the other fittings, insert the ends of the $\frac{3}{32}''$ fibreglass rods through the fittings and use a gel-type super glue to secure the brass caps in place.

The bead-tension system:

12. Using two beads with holes in the center as loop retainers through clear plastic tubing, rig a bow line as shown in Detail 3 (Illus. 421). Repeat for all cells.

Assembly:

13. Secure the nylon-tape loops sewn into the sail tips to the universal fittings with nylon-cable-clamp ties as shown. When tension is applied with the bead bow line, the sail should be taut.

14. Place a $\frac{9}{16}''$ split key ring through the reinforced center of each sail and around the vertical fibreglass-rod spreader spar.

15. The bridle. From 100 lb.–test line, make five 24'' (overall length) bridle lines with a 1'' overhand-loop knot on each end. Attach one bridle line to the split key ring on each cell. The fifth line goes through the loop of the lower cell line and meets the loop of the upper cell to form the bridle as shown in Detail 5 (Illus. 422).

[1] R. Buckminster Fuller was 3 years old when Bell began his flight experiments. Bell's tetrahedron kites and Fuller's geodesic structures are based upon exactly the same principles. Fuller, however, did not learn of Bell's work with the tetrahedron until after he had built the geodesic dome.

[2] I thought my bead-system solution was novel until I came across a tetrahedron kite by Professor Waldof of Worcestershire, England, who, as it turned out, used a similar internal tension/compression system to achieve a favorable strength-to-weight ratio. The idea of passing the spreader bars through the universal joints, and the bridle setup and breakdown for transport feature comes from Professor Waldof's tetrahedron design.

57
Making a Kite Bag

It's a good practice to keep your kite protected when you're not flying. Illus. 426 shows a simple design for making a professional-looking kite bag. Use .75-oz. ripstop nylon for lightweight kites and 1.5-oz. ripstop for heavier loads.

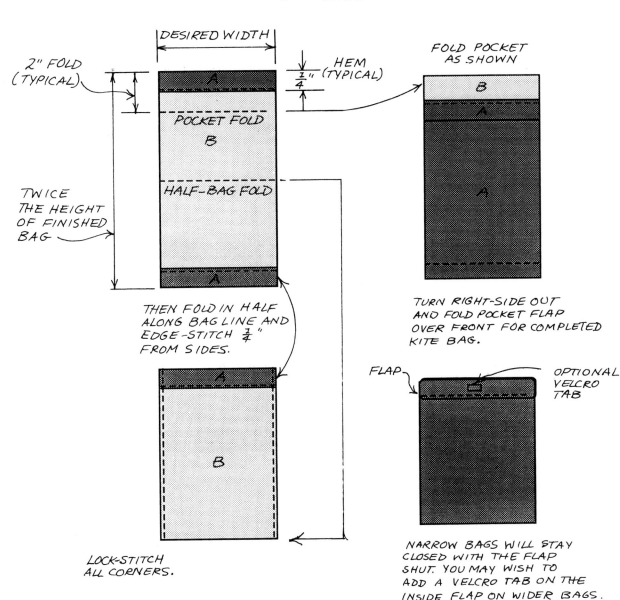

A = OUTSIDE
B = INSIDE

DESIRED WIDTH

2" FOLD (TYPICAL)

HEM (TYPICAL) $\frac{1}{4}$"

FOLD POCKET AS SHOWN

A

POCKET FOLD
B

TWICE THE HEIGHT OF FINISHED BAG

HALF-BAG FOLD

B

A

A

THEN FOLD IN HALF ALONG BAG LINE AND EDGE-STITCH $\frac{1}{4}$" FROM SIDES.

A

B

LOCK-STITCH ALL CORNERS.

TURN RIGHT-SIDE OUT AND FOLD POCKET FLAP OVER FRONT FOR COMPLETED KITE BAG.

FLAP

OPTIONAL VELCRO TAB

NARROW BAGS WILL STAY CLOSED WITH THE FLAP SHUT. YOU MAY WISH TO ADD A VELCRO TAB ON THE INSIDE FLAP ON WIDER BAGS.

Illus. 426. Kite bag design.

APPENDICES

Kite Clubs

Most of these clubs offer kite flies, workshops, and a newsletter on a regular basis.

AUSTRALIA
Australian Kite Association
24 Union Road
Surrey Hills
Melbourne, Victoria
Australia
Newsletter, informations sheets, plans, workshops

BELGIUM
Kite Aerial Photography Worldwide Association
14, Avenue Capitaine Piret
1150 Brussels, Belgium
Magazine and annual event

KAPWA North American Partner:
David Town
112 47th Street
Sea Isle City, New Jersey 08243

CANADA
Alberta Kite Club
Post Office Box 113
Glendon, Alberta
TOZ 1PO
Canada

British Columbia Kitefliers Association
Post Office Box 35653
Vancouver, British Columbia
V6M 4G9
Canada

CHINA
Weifang Kitefliers Association
42 Shengli Street
Weifang City
Shandong Province
People's Republic of China

ENGLAND
Bearly Made It Skydive Squad
48 Laurel Lane
West Drayton, Middlesex
UB7 7TY
England

Blackheath Kite Association
303 Lincoln Road
Enfield, Middlesex
EN1 1SY
England

British Kite Flying Association
Post Office Box 35
Hemel, Hempstead
Hertfordshire, HP2 4SS
England

Kite Society of Great Britain
31 Grange Road
Ilford, Essex
1G1 1EU
England

Midlands Kite Fliers
76 Oxhill Road
Handsworth, Birmingham
B21 9RH
England

Northern Kite Group
41 Ashfield Drive
Clayton Bridge, Manchester
M10 6WJ
England

Wessex Kite Group
16 Brackley Way
Hammonds Green, Toton
Hampshire, SY1 4JY

York Kite Fliers
2 Dewsbury Terrace
York, North Yorkshire
Y01 1HA
England

FRANCE
Association Ephemeres Millenaires
58 rue Jean Bodin
F-49000, Angers
France

Cerf-Volant Club de France
boite postale 186
F-75623, Paris
France

GERMANY (Federal Republic of Germany)
Drachen Club Berlin "Aero-Flott"
Eisenacher Strasse 81
1000 Berlin 62
West Germany

Drachen Club Deutschland
Wandsbeker Chaussee 82
2000 Hamburg 76
West Germany

ITALY
Associazione Italiana Aquilonisti
via Dandolo 19/a
I-00153 Roma
Italy

Club Cervia Volante
via Pinarella 26
I-48015 Cervia
Italy

JAPAN
Japan Kite Association
1-12-10 Nihonbashi
Chuo-ku, Tokyo 103
Japan
The Japanese Kite Museum is also located at the above address.

Shirone Kite Battle Association
Shirone-shi, Sakura-machi
Niigata-ken 950-12
Japan

NETHERLANDS
Nederlands Vlieger Gezelschap
39 Meendaal
6228-GE Maastricht
Netherlands

Vlieger magazine
Redaktieteam
2 Julius Roentgenstraat
2552-KT den Haag
Netherlands

NEW ZEALAND
New Zealand Kitefliers Association
9 Kenef Road
Paremata, Wellington
New Zealand

THAILAND
Kite Association of Thailand
888/88 Ploenchit Road
Mahatun Plaza
Bangkok 10500
Thailand

USA
American Kitefliers Association
1559 Rockville Pike
Rockville, Maryland 20852
Kiting: Journal of the American Kitefliers Association, published six times a year
Annual kiting convention and trade shows
Address membership inquires to:
Robert Price
3839 Dustin Road
Burtonsville, MD 20866

California Kite Group
585 Cannery Row, No. 105
Monterey, CA 93940

Chicagoland Sky Liners Kite Club
Address membership inquires to:
Tom McCune
383 Le Parc Circle
Buffalo Grove, Illinois 60089
Sky Lines, the official newsletter of the Chicago Sky Liners Kite Club, published six times a year

Greater Delaware Valley Kite Society
P.O. Box 888
Newfield, New Jersey 08344
Tight Lines newsletter, published six times a year

Hawaii Kitefliers Association
Post Office Box 612
Pearl City, HI 96782

Maryland Kite Society
8412 Townecrest Court
Gaithersburg, MD 20877

Ohio Society for the Elevation of Kites
1200 Fairhill Road, No. 207
Cleveland, OH 44120

Washington Kitefliers Association
Pacific Science Center
200 Second Avenue, North
Seattle, WA 98109

Kite Events and Festivals

No matter what day of the year, there's a kite festival, exhibit, or international gathering going on somewhere in the world. Here's a brief listing of some long-running and more recently established kite flying events. Dates are subject to confirmation by the sponsoring organization.

February—3 days, the second weekend of the month:
President's Day Kite Fly
on Seaside Beach
Corey Jensen
Windborne Kites
585 Cannery Row #105
Monterey, CA 93940
(408) 373-7422

March—last Saturday of the month:
Smithsonian Kite Festival
on the grounds of the Washington Monument
Public Affairs Office
1100 Jefferson Drive SW
Washington, DC 20560
(202) 357-4090

March—first Saturday of the month:
Jacksonville Kite Tournament
Metropolitan Park
Willey Carley
Recreation Dept.
851 N. Market Street
Jacksonville, FL 32202

March—second Sunday of the month:
Zilker Kite Contest
Zilker Park, Austin, Texas
Sarah Macias
Parks and Recreation
P.O. Box 1088
Austin, TX 78767

March—2 weeks in the middle of the month:
Royal Thai Kite Competition
Pramain Ground, Bangkok
Ron Spaulding
Spaulding and Partners
Thai Kite Heritage Group
412 Rama I Road
Bangkok, 10330
Thailand

March—second weekend of the month:
Oahu Kite Flying Festival
Kapi'olani Park, near Waikiki, Oahu, Hawaii
Tommy Kono
Parks and Recreation

650 S. King Street
Honolulu, HI 96813

March—third Saturday of the month:
Ocean Beach Kite Festival and Parade
Ocean Beach Elementary School, San Diego
Mike Morrow
Recreation Center
4726 Santa Monica Avenue
San Diego, CA 92107

March—last Sunday of the month:
Santa Monica Pier Kite Festival
Santa Monica and Venice Beach, California
Gloria Lugo
Let's Fly a Kite
Fisherman's Village
13755 Fiji Way
Marina del Rey, CA 90291
(213) 822-2561
or
Elaine Mutchnik
The Santa Monica Pier Restoration Group
(213) 458-8900

April—second Saturday of the month:
Carlisle Kite Festival and Rokkaku Challenge
Dickinson College, Carlisle, Pennsylvania
Kevin Shannon
809 Factory Street
Carlisle, PA 17013

April—second Sunday of the month:
April Fool's Kite Fly
Mercer County Park, Trenton, New Jersey
Roger Chewning
The Meadow Mouse
520 N. Pennsylvania Avenue
Morrisville, PA 19067

April—last Sunday of the month:
Kite Fest
Buccleucha Park, New Brunswick, New Jersey
Special Awards for biodegradable/organic kites
Debby Keller
NJ Environmental Federation
46 Bayard Street
New Brunswick, NJ 08901

April—last Saturday of the month:
Maryland Kite Festival
Asbury Methodist Village
Gaithersburg, Maryland
Bill Goodwin
(301) 460-7299
or
Mel Govig
(301) 484-6287

April—last weekend of the month:
Japan Kite Association International Kite Festival
Shimizu City, Shizouku Prefecture, Japan

Masaaki Modegi
Japan Kite Association
1-12-10 Nihonbashi
Chuo-ku, Tokyo 103
Japan

May—first Saturday of the month:
Carmel Kite Festival
Carmel Beach, California

Recreation Department
P.O. Box CC
Carmel, CA 93921
(408) 626-1255

May—first Saturday of the month:
Buck's County Kite Day
Core Creek Park, Langhorne, Pennsylvania

Marci Miller
Parks and Recreation
901 E. Bridgetown Pike
Langhorne, PA 19047

May—last weekend of the month:
East Coast Stunt Kite Championships
on the beach in Wildwood, New Jersey

Pre-registration required
Fran Gramkowski
High Fly Kite Co.
P.O. Box 2146
Haddonfield, NJ 08033

June—five days, beginning the first weekend of the month:
Shirone Giant Kite Festival
Shirone City, Niigata Prefecture, Japan

Kazuo Tamura
Shirone Giant Kite Battle Association
Sakura-machi, Shirone-shi
Niigata-ken 950-12
Japan

June—second Saturday of the month:
Rogallo Kite Festival
Jockey's Ridge State Park,
Nag's Head, North Carolina

John McDowell
Kitty Hawk Kites
P.O. Box 340
Nag's Head, NC 27959
(919) 441-4124

June—second Saturday of the month:
Sky Circus
Grant Park

John Karel
Chicagoland Sky Liners

P.O. Box 3848
Oakbrook, IL 60522

June—third weekend of the month:
International Fokker Kite Festival
Scheveningen Beach, The Hague, Netherlands

Gerard van der Loo
Vlieger Op
Weteringkade 5a
2515-AK Den Haag
Netherlands

June—third Sunday of the month:
Father's Day Kite Festival
Marina Green, San Francisco
Regional West Coast Stunt Kite Championships
Michael McFadden
Kitemakers of San Francisco
590 Chestnut Street
San Francisco, CA 94133
(415) 956-3181
(800) 328-5483

June—six days, beginning the fourth week of the month:
Cervia Volante International Meeting of Kitefliers
Grazia Deledda Free Beach, Cervia, Italy
Claudio Capelli
Club Aquilonisti Cervia Volante
Via Pinarella 26
48015 Cervia (RA)
Italy

June—last Sunday of the month:
Blackheath Summer Kite Festival
Blackheath Common, London

Tony Cartwright
Blackheath Kite Association
78 Dongola Road
London N17 6EE
England

July—7 days, beginning the third weekend of the month:
Black Ships Festival
Brenton Point State Park,
Newport, Rhode Island
Tom Casselman
365 Riverside Street
Portsmouth, RI 02871

August—third week of the month:
Washington State International Kite Festival
on Long Beach
W.S.I.K.F.
P.O. Box 797
Long Beach, WA 98631
(206) 665-5744

September—second weekend of the month:
Bali International Kite Festival
Captain Japa Square, Sanur, Bali
Dinas Pariwisata
Badung Tourist Promotion Board
Jalan Surapati 7
Denpasar 80232
Bali, Indonesia

September—9 days, beginning the second week of the month:
International Kite Competition
Dieppe Beach, Normandy, France
Maryvonne de Casanove
Jean Renoir Cultural Centre
BP 47, 76200 Dieppe
France
35/82-04-43

September—third Sunday of the month:
Family Day Kite Festival
Shoreline Park,
Santa Barbara, California
International Connections
835 Weldon Road
Santa Barbara, CA 93109
(805) 963-2964

September—fourth weekend of the month:
Berlin International Kite Festival
Freizeitpark Marienfelde,
Berlin, West Germany
Michael Steltzer
Vom Winde Verweht
Eisenacher strasse 81
1000 Berlin 62
West Germany
030/784 77 69 /795 47 00

September—fourth weekend of the month:
International Kite Festival
At the D River Wayside,
Lincoln City, Oregon
Steve Lamb
Catch The Wind
266 S.E. Highway 101
Lincoln City, OR 97367

September—fourth weekend of the month:
Sunfest Kite Festival
Beach at 5th Street,
Ocean Beach, Maryland
Bill and Mary Ochse
The Kite Loft
P.O. Box 551
Ocean City, MD 21842

October—second Sunday of the month:
One Sky One World International
Kite Fly for Peace
Events held worldwide
Jane Parker-Ambrose
OSOW—Sky Scraper Kites
P.O. Box 11149
Denver, CO 80211
(303) 433-9518

December—first Sunday of the month:
International Invitational Open
Peanut Butter Cookie Kite Fly and
Bake off
Beach at Seaside, New Jersey
Olan Turner
1628 S. Crescent Blvd.
Yardley, PA 19067

Stunt Kiting

International Stunt Kite Association
P.O. 515
Clute, TX 77531

Organizers of the five largest established stunt kite competitions have formed the ISKA to organize an international circuit to be sanctioned and run under a uniform set of standards. USA competitions are cur-

rently held in California, Hawaii, Michigan, New Jersey, and Texas. Contact the ISKA at the above address for more information.

March—early in the month:
Hawaii Challenge National Stunt Kite Championships
Robert Loera
Kite Fantasy
2863 Kalakaua Avenue
Honolulu, HI 96815

April—middle of the month:
Great Lakes Stunt Kite Championships
Cris Batdorff
Sandcastle
P.O. Box 468
Manistee, MI 49660

April—middle of the month:
Texas Gulf Stunt Kite Challenge
Terry G. Crumpler
Wind Walker Kites
P.O. Box 515
Clute, TX 77531

May—last weekend of the month:
East Coast Stunt Kite Championships

on the beach in Wildwood, New Jersey
Pre-registration required.
Fran Gramkowski
High Fly Kite Co.
P.O. Box 2146
Haddonfield, NJ 08033

September—Labor Day weekend:
National West Coast Stunt Kite Championships
on the Marina Green, San Francisco
Mike McFadden
Kite Caravan
Kitemakers of San Francisco
5739 Christie Avenue
Emeryville, CA 94608

Bibliography

Allen, J. *As You Think*. San Rafael, California: New World Library, 1987. Distributed by The Good Living Catalog, San Rafael, California.

Bakker, R.T. *The Dinosaur Heresies: New Theories Unlocking the Mystery of the Dinosaurs and Their Extinction*. New York: William Morrow and Company, Inc., 1986.

Beard, D.B. *The American Boy's Handy Book: What to do and How to do it*. Boston: David R. Grodine, Publisher, Inc., 1983.

Bridgewater, A. and G. *Easy-To-Make Decorative Kites*. New York: Dover Publications, Inc., 1985.

Budworth, G. *The Knot Book*. New York: Sterling Publishing Co., Inc., 1985.

Bushell, H. *Make Mine Fly*—Volumes 2–6. Victoria, Australia: Australian Kite Association, 1986.

Campbell, J. *The Power of Myth*. New York: Doubleday Books, 1988.

Fuller, R.B. *Synergetics: Explorations in the Geometry of Thinking*. New York: Macmillan Publishing Company, 1982.

Fuller, R.B. *Synergetics 2: Further Explorations in the Geometry of Thinking*. New York: Macmillan Publishing Company, 1983.

Greger, M. *Kites for Everyone*. 1425 Marshall, Richland, Washington, 99352. 1984.

Hart, C. *Kites: an Historical Survey*. Mount Vernon, New York: Paul P. Appel, Publisher, 1982.

Howard, F. *Wilbur and Orville*. New York: Alfred A. Knopf, 1987.

Hunt, L. L. *25 Kites That Fly*. New York: Dover Publications, Inc., 1971.

Jue, D. *Chinese Kites: How to Make and Fly Them*. Vermont & Tokyo: Charles E. Tuttle Company, Inc., 1984.

Macaulay, D. *The Way Things Work*. Boston: Houghton Mifflin Company, 1988.

Pelham, D. *The Penguin Book of Kites*. New York: Viking Penguin, Inc., 1987.

Samuels, M. and N. *Seeing with the Mind's Eye*. New York: Random House Inc., 1987.

Shaw, W. and Ruhen, O. *Lawrence Hargrave: Explorer, Inventor & Aviation Experimenter*. New South Wales, Australia: Cassell Australia Limited, 1977.

Streeter, T. *The Art of the Japanese Kite*. New York & Tokyo: John Weatherhill, Inc., 1985. Distributed by Charles E. Tuttle Company, Inc., Rutland, Vermont.

Kite Lines: Quarterly Journal of the Worldwide Kite Community. Aeolus Press, Inc., P.O. Box 466, 8807 Liberty Road, Randallstown, Maryland 21133-0466.

Acknowledgments

I am grateful to many people for having faith in my vision of this book. Several individuals, however, were a constant source of invaluable information during its preparation—my deepest appreciation to: Fran Gramkowski, of the High Fly Kite Company (in Haddonfield, NJ), for his kite expertise, guidance, and the many kite building materials used to make the projects in this book; Bill Tyrrell, of The Fabric Lady (in Doylestown, PA), for everything I needed to know about ripstop nylon, sewing, and the sail material for the fabric kite projects in the book; Valerie Govig, editor of *Kite Lines Magazine: Quarterly Journal of the Worldwide Kite Community*, for generously furnishing hard-to-find information from her vast treasury of files on kiting; and Caleb Crowell, a friend who not only taught me the secrets of the Indian fighter kite years ago, but did the ultimate sacrifice of a true bibliophile: upon learning of my book project, he immediately loaned me his entire library of kite books.

I would like to give special recognition to: Apple Computer, Inc., Cupertino, CA; Commodore-Amiga, Computer Systems Division, West Chester, PA; DataDesk International, Van Nuys, CA; Dremel Tools, Racine, WI; MacConnection, Marlow, NH; Mirror Technologies, Roseville, MN; Okidata, Mount Laurel, NJ; Singer Sewing Company, Edison, NJ; Viking Acoustical Corporation, Lakeville, MN; WordPerfect Corporation, Orem, UT; Bike Nashbar, Youngstown, OH; and K G Engineering, Inc., Woonsocket, RI.

Also, my thanks to: Almac Plastics Inc., Rahway, NJ (nylon rods and tubing); Arrow Fastener Co., Inc., Saddle Brook, NJ (staplers, rivet tools, glue guns); Balsa USA, Marinette, WI (aircraft spruce, balsa, plywood); Big City Kite Company, Inc., New York, NY (stocks Madras tissue paper for making fighter kites); Black & Decker, Hunt Valley, MD (two-speed reversible drill model 9020 for winding in flying line using Sonntag Reel System); Bland Company, Warren, MI (for trash bags in colors to use for sail material); Boreal Kites, by Gothic Design, St. Thomas, Ontario, Canada (Limited-edition silk screen dyes on ripstop nylon kites by Anne Sloboda and Eric Curtis); Catch the Wind Kites, Lincoln City, OR (carries Adrian Conn's Dragonfly kite); Chartpak, One River Road, Leeds, MA (Cylopak Expandable Interlocking Tube System—ideal for transporting kites); Come Fly a Kite, Santa Barbara, CA (traditional Indian fighter kites and spools); CooperTools—Weller Division, Raleigh, NC (soldering irons and guns); Dritz Corporation, Sewing Notions Division, Spartanburg, SC (extensive line of sewing aids and accessories); Du Pont Company, Wilmington, DE (manufacturers of Tyvek and Mylar); Edmund Scientific Co., Barrington, NJ (Tensegritoy and miniature tools); Flexifoil, Lavallette, NJ (Flexifoil stunt kites); Flying Colors, Boulder, CO (meticulously hand-crafted kites by George Peters); Gayla Industries, Inc., Houston, TX (popular line of plastic kites and Sky Lab Educational, Kite Kit); Grandmaster Kites, Mifflinville, PA (single-line maneuverable kites); Gregor E. McGinnis and Associates, Berkeley, CA (stunt kite reel); International Connections, Santa Barbara, CA (traditional tissue paper and bamboo Indian fighter kites); Into The Wind, Boulder, CO (kites, accessories, plus excellent non-slip heavy-duty leather gloves for kite fliers); Jerryco Catalog, Mail Order Warehouse, Evanston, IL (silk threads and suture material—useful in making miniature kites); Karl Szilagi, % Big City Kite Company, Inc., New York, NY (custom-made Szilagi fighter kites); Kevin Shannon, Carlisle, PA (Rokkaku, Roller, and Bermuda kites—plus limited editions and appliqué kites); K & S Engineering, Chicago, IL (aluminum and brass tubing, tubing cutters, wire, and tools); Leviton Manufacturing Co., Inc., Little Neck, NY (Model 6356 [300W 120V]—slide control dimmer adapted for regulating temperature of soldering iron in heat-sealing plastic); Liddell Aviation, Newfane, NY (quality, hand-crafted, keeled, bowed diamond kites by Jack Liddell); Martin Lester, Bristol, England (three-dimensional kite designs); Micro Plastics, Inc., Flippin, Arkansas (cable clamps, bolts, and nuts); Nasco, Fort Atkinson, WI (craft, art, graphic supplies, and learning materials); One of Jerry's Kites, Ocean Park, WA (Magic and Gusset deltas, plus meticulously sewn kites); Peter Lynn Ltd., Ashburton, New Zealand (Tri-D box kite and other kite designs by Peter Lynn); Plastruct, Inc., City of Industry, CA (solvent syringes—for pinpoint accuracy when gluing and safely breaking boron for miniature kites); Prof. Waldof's Kites, Worchestershire, England (Innovative box and tetrahedron kites, plus a collection of cellular kites by Peter Waldren); Quality Kite Line Reels, Evansville, IN (deep-sky reels); Sailboats of Talbot, Easton, MD (quality reels, with braking control, for light- to heavy-pulling kites); Sky Delight Kites, Austin, TX (Kaleidakite, parrot and bird trains, three-dimensional airplane stunt kites, plus award-winning kite designs by Joel Scholz); Skynasaur, Inc., Louisville, CO (stunt kites and accessories); Squadron Kites, Stratton Air Engineering, Los Alamitos, CA (balsa and Silkspan kite kits); Stanley Tools, Division of The Stanley Works, New Britain, CT (carbide-rod saws for cutting Teflon); Stanton Hobby Shop, Inc., Chicago, IL (kites, windsocks, and accessories); Suspended Elevations, The Gasworks Kite Shoppe, Seattle, WA (hand-crafted, finely detailed kites); Tensegrity Systems Corporation, Tivoli, NY (Tensegritoy—ingenious construction toy based on R. Buckminster Fuller's tensegrity structures); Tethered Flight Limited, Lynnwood, WA (deltas, parafoils, windsocks, and spinners); Top of the Line Kites, San Diego, CA (Hawaiian Team and Spin-Off stunt kites); Velcro USA, Manchester, NH (Velcro fastening systems); Wills Wing, Santa Ana, CA (Skyhawk, Sport 150 and 167, and HP II—award-winning line of production hang-glider designs for both student and experienced recreational soaring pilots); and Jones Optical Company (quality sunglasses for the kite flier).

I wish to also thank the following computer companies and publications for stimulating my creativity, improving my productivity, and helping me sort out the complexities of this project: Abaton Technology Corp., Fremont, CA (Interfax 12/48—innovative modem and FAX device for convenient Macintosh to Macintosh communication); Adobe Systems Incorporated, Mountain View, CA (Adobe Illustrator 88— professional drawing program); Aldus Corporation, Seattle, WA (Aldus PageMaker—top-of-the-line desktop publishing program); Broderbund Software, San Rafael, CA (Geometry and Physics [software for learning]—interactive educational and entertainment programs); Cathay Europa Designs, Kennebunkport, ME (GlobalArt Oriental Images—clip art with an Oriental flair); Channelmark Corporation, Power Up!, San Mateo, CA (HyperTutor— the Interactive HyperTalk Tutorial); Claris Corporation, Mountain View, CA (MacPaint 2.0., MacDraw II, MacWrite 5.0., and FileMaker II—creativity and productivity software for the Macintosh); CompuServe, Columbus, OH (CompuServe—the largest, commercially available on-line information service in the world—and CompuServe Navigator—communication and productivity software program designed specifically for the Macintosh user interface for accessing information from CompuServe); Cricket Software, Malvern, PA (Cricket Paint—a flexible, state-of-the-art monochrome [B/W] painting program with extensive tool palette—and Cricket Draw—a powerful, object-oriented application with sophisticated drawing features); DataViz, Trumbell, CT (MacLink Plus—time-saving file transfer and software translation program between the Macintosh and MS-DOS–based environment); Electronic Arts, San Mateo, CA (DeluxePaint II and Deluxe PhotoLab—color graphics, entertainment, and creativity software); Fifth Generation Systems, Inc., Baton Rouge, LA (Pyro, Powerstation, Suitcase II, and Fastback—utility programs for the Macintosh); Hewlett Packard, Corvallis Division, Corvallis, OR (HP-28S—advanced scientific calculator); Innovative Design Data, Inc., Concord, CA (MacDraft—all-purpose CAD program—and Dreams—midrange, elegant user interface, multi-purpose CAD program); Kensington Microware Ltd., New York, NY (Turbo Mouse—ideal device for controlled accuracy in graphic and design work for the Macintosh); Mediagenic, Menlo Park, CA (Focal Point—HyperCard-based productivity program, featuring a set of desktop tools for getting organized); Microillusions, Granada Hills, CA (Photon Paint and Sky Travel—color graphics, entertainment, and educational software); Mindscape, Inc., Northbrook, IL (GraphicWorks 1.1—professional design software for manipulating graphics and text); M.W. Ruth Co., Cherry Hill, NJ (products for Amiga, Atari ST, and Adam computer systems—software, hardware, and accessories, plus public domain software); Oxxi, Inc., Long Beach, CA (A-Talk III—telecommunications program for the Amiga); Preferred Publishers, Inc., Memphis, TN (Database—full-featured desk-accessory database for organizing text, color images, and graphics—and Vantage—general-purpose desk-accessory turbo text tool and spell checker for word processing, page layout, and databases); Springboard Software, Inc., Minneapolis, MN (Springboard Publisher—desktop publisher, featuring an easy-to-use 3-in-1 integrated program: page layout, word processing, and graphics creation); Software Visions, Inc., Framingham, MA (Microfiche Filer—a flexible, innovative database program for storing text and picture data in an elegant, organized format); Software Ventures Corporation, Berkeley, CA (MicroPhone II—versatile, powerful, telecommunications program for the Macintosh); Symantec Corporation, Cupertino, CA (Symantec Utilities—catastrophe insurance, improved hard-disk utilization for the Macintosh—and MORE II—sophisticated combination outline processor and graphics system to help focus thoughts, organize, and produce effective conclusions); Tecmar, Inc., Cleveland, OH (Tecmar QT Mac 40—convenient, easy-to-use tape backup system for hard disks); The Other Guys, Logan, UT (Reason—series of programs designed to aid writers and editors in editing documents and manuscripts); T/Maker Company, Mountain View, CA (ClickArt Portfolios—graphic images for desktop publishing and presentation programs); 3G Graphics, Kirkland, WA (Images with Impact!—high-resolution [EPS] clip art for use with desktop publishing); Verbatim, Charlotte, NC (DataLife Minidisks, Microdisks, and Tapes—information storage media); Zedcor, Tucson, AZ (DeskPaint and DeskDraw—desk-accessory graphic editor that works with all popular desktop publishing, drawing, and presentation programs for the Macintosh); *AmigaWorld*, Peterborough, NH; and *Macworld*, San Francisco, CA.

In addition, I wish to acknowledge these photography companies for supplying products and services that were helpful in the production of this book: Canon U.S.A., Inc., Lake Success, NY (EOS 650—state-of-the-art 35mm autofocus system camera); Eastman Kodak, Rochester, NY (films and processing); and Polaroid Corporation, Cambridge, MA (Polaroid Spectra System).

METRIC EQUIVALENCY CHART

MM—MILLIMETRES   CM—CENTIMETRES

INCHES TO MILLIMETRES AND CENTIMETRES

INCHES	MM	CM	INCHES	CM	INCHES	CM
⅛	3	0.3	9	22.9	30	76.2
¼	6	0.6	10	25.4	31	78.7
⅜	10	1.0	11	27.9	32	81.3
½	13	1.3	12	30.5	33	83.8
⅝	16	1.6	13	33.0	34	86.4
¾	19	1.9	14	35.6	35	88.9
⅞	22	2.2	15	38.1	36	91.4
1	25	2.5	16	40.6	37	94.0
1¼	32	3.2	17	43.2	38	96.5
1½	38	3.8	18	45.7	39	99.1
1¾	44	4.4	19	48.3	40	101.6
2	51	5.1	20	50.8	41	104.1
2½	64	6.4	21	53.3	42	106.7
3	76	7.6	22	55.9	43	109.2
3½	89	8.9	23	58.4	44	111.8
4	102	10.2	24	61.0	45	114.3
4½	114	11.4	25	63.5	46	116.8
5	127	12.7	26	66.0	47	119.4
6	152	15.2	27	68.6	48	121.9
7	178	17.8	28	71.1	49	124.5
8	203	20.3	29	73.7	50	127.0

YARDS TO METRES

YARDS	METRES	YARDS	METRES	YARDS	METRES	YARDS	METRES	YARDS	METRES
⅛	0.11	2⅛	1.94	4⅛	3.77	6⅛	5.60	8⅛	7.43
¼	0.23	2¼	2.06	4¼	3.89	6¼	5.72	8¼	7.54
⅜	0.34	2⅜	2.17	4⅜	4.00	6⅜	5.83	8⅜	7.66
½	0.46	2½	2.29	4½	4.11	6½	5.94	8½	7.77
⅝	0.57	2⅝	2.40	4⅝	4.23	6⅝	6.06	8⅝	7.89
¾	0.69	2¾	2.51	4¾	4.34	6¾	6.17	8¾	8.00
⅞	0.80	2⅞	2.63	4⅞	4.46	6⅞	6.29	8⅞	8.12
1	0.91	3	2.74	5	4.57	7	6.40	9	8.23
1⅛	1.03	3⅛	2.86	5⅛	4.69	7⅛	6.52	9⅛	8.34
1¼	1.14	3¼	2.97	5¼	4.80	7¼	6.63	9¼	8.46
1⅜	1.26	3⅜	3.09	5⅜	4.91	7⅜	6.74	9⅜	8.57
1½	1.37	3½	3.20	5½	5.03	7½	6.86	9½	8.69
1⅝	1.49	3⅝	3.31	5⅝	5.14	7⅝	6.97	9⅝	8.80
1¾	1.60	3¾	3.43	5¾	5.26	7¾	7.09	9¾	8.92
1⅞	1.71	3⅞	3.54	5⅞	5.37	7⅞	7.20	9⅞	9.03
2	1.83	4	3.66	6	5.49	8	7.32	10	9.14

Index